RELIGIONS, REASONS AND GODS

Traditional theistic proofs are often understood as evidence intended to compel belief in a divinity. John Clayton explores the surprisingly varied applications of such proofs in the work of philosophers and theologians from several periods and traditions, thinkers as varied as Ramanuja, al-Ghazali, Anselm and Jefferson. He shows how the gradual disembedding of theistic proofs from their diverse and local religious contexts is concurrent with the development of natural theologies and atheism as social and intellectual options in early-modern Europe and America. Clayton offers a new reading of the early-modern history of philosophy and theology, arguing that awareness of such history and the local uses of theistic argument offer new ways of managing religious and cultural difference in the public sphere today. He argues for the importance of historically grounded philosophy of religion to the field of religious studies and public debate on religious pluralism and cultural diversity.

PROFESSOR JOHN CLAYTON taught at Lancaster University for 25 years, eventually as Professor of Religious Studies and later as Head of Department. He was Chair of the Department of Religion and Director of the Graduate Division of Religious and Theological Studies, Boston University, from 1997 until his death in 2003. With Ninian Smart, Patrick Sherry and Steven T. Katz he co-edited the three-volume *Nineteenth-Century Religious Thought in the West* (1985, 1988).

ANNE M. BLACKBURN is Associate Professor of South Asia and Buddhist Studies in the Department of Asian Studies, Cornell University.

THOMAS D. CARROLL is a Ph.D. candidate in the Graduate Division of Religious and Theological Studies, Boston University.

RELIGIONS, REASONS AND GODS

Essays in Cross-Cultural Philosophy of Religion

JOHN CLAYTON

PREPARED FOR PUBLICATION BY
ANNE M. BLACKBURN AND THOMAS D. CARROLL

CAMBRIDGE
UNIVERSITY PRESS

CAMBRIDGE UNIVERSITY PRESS
Cambridge, New York, Melbourne, Madrid, Cape Town, Singapore, São Paulo

Cambridge University Press
The Edinburgh Building, Cambridge CB2 2RU, UK

Published in the United States of America by Cambridge University Press, New York

www.cambridge.org
Information on this title: www.cambridge.org/9780521421041

© Cambridge University Press 2006

First published 2006

Printed in the United Kingdom at the University Press, Cambridge

A catalogue record for this publication is available from the British Library

ISBN-13 978-0-521-42104-1 hardback
ISBN-10 0-521-42104-7 hardback

For Anne

Πᾶσα διδασκαλία καὶ πᾶσα μάθησις διανοητικὴ ἐκ προϋπαρχούσης γίνεται γνώσεως.

Aristotle

It is traditions which are the bearers of reason.

Alasdair MacIntyre

Contents

Editorial preface

The proximate point of origin for this volume is John Clayton's 1992 Stanton Lectures, delivered at the University of Cambridge. Clayton had planned to publish his Stanton Lectures soon thereafter with Cambridge University Press. However, that publication was delayed for a variety of reasons. In 1997 he retired from his position as Professor and Head of the Department of Religious Studies at the University of Lancaster to become Professor, Chair of Department, and Director of the Graduate Division of Religious and Theological Studies at Boston University. During the late 1990s Clayton focused primarily on the administrative side of his professional work. By 2000, he had returned in earnest to his Stanton Lectures, deciding that *Religions, Reasons and Gods: Essays in Cross-Cultural Philosophy of Religion* ought to come to publication as a nearly independent typescript rather than as a lightly revised version of the Stanton Lectures. The gods did not smile on Clayton's plans. In the autumn of 2001 he fell seriously ill with a condition requiring exhausting treatment. One year later, he was diagnosed with a second illness, an aggressive cancer that took his life in September 2003.

Clayton recognized that his ambitious plans for the completion of *Religions, Reasons and Gods* would not be realized in this context of ill-health and, accordingly, he revised arrangements for the publication of this volume. With the generous support of editors at Cambridge University Press, he specified a collection of essays (some previously published and some unpublished). These were to articulate the central claims of the Stanton Lectures as well as Clayton's subsequent reflection on the potential contributions of the philosophy of religion to public contexts of increasing religious pluralism, the history of 'the Enlightenment project', and the implications of its history for a reconsideration of the history of philosophy as well as the goals and methods of philosophers of religion. Clayton hoped that Anne M. Blackburn, his partner, would bring *Religions, Reasons and Gods* to publication. Handsome support from

ix

Boston University made possible the involvement of Thomas D. Carroll, a doctoral student with whom Clayton had worked closely prior to his death. Carroll and Blackburn, therefore, have worked together as co-editors of this volume.

Over the course of some months, we explored the materials left behind by Clayton for inclusion in this volume. Previously published essays have been reproduced without further editorial changes, apart from those required to standardize published style or to make current references to Clayton's own work. We have omitted all diacritical marks in transliterated Sanskrit, and have largely followed Clayton's own system of reference notation. Pieces unpublished but evidently complete have likewise received no further substantial editing. One essay crucial to *Religions, Reasons and Gods*, 'The Debate about God in Early-Modern British Philosophy', remained unfinished. Working in the British Library, Carroll drew on Clayton's research notes to retrace investigations made during the year or so before Clayton's death. On this basis, he annotated Clayton's essay and developed an editorial addition and an appendix on natural theology and the design argument in Britain. Clayton had suggested that a paper read in 1996 at a conference on Philosophy of Religion organized by the Commonwealth Institute (London) serve as the final chapter of this volume. Unfortunately, this paper does not remain among Clayton's materials. Despite the good offices of his colleagues, no copy has become available. For that reason, we selected the text of his final Stanton Lecture as the concluding essay in this volume. We have also added a brief introduction to each of the volume's three parts. We have followed Clayton's wishes in the dedication of *Religions, Reasons and Gods*. The essays which follow speak, of course, for themselves, and we do not wish to intrude unduly on readers' encounters with Clayton's work. However, since his essays were written in conversation with several disciplines, and for audiences in rather different cultural contexts, it may be useful to provide some very preliminary points of orientation to this volume.

The essays drawn together here reflect Clayton's preoccupation with matters of cultural and historical *difference* and *location*. It is in one sense no surprise that essays developed in the 1980s and 1990s should evince such concerns, since they were apparent across diverse disciplines in scholarly conversations during that period. Clayton developed these ideas in a distinctive intellectual climate, one characterized by debates about the constitution of and the recognition of 'the Other', the relationships of texts to contexts, the nature and limits of interpretative authority, the history of 'natural' kinds and categories, and so on. The roots of his abiding interest in cultural and historical difference and location are still more complex, however, and significantly autobiographical. Clayton sometimes referred to himself, with both pride and irony, as 'a Texan by birth and conviction'. Texans of Clayton's generation were no strangers to complex configurations of insider–outsider status, and to the experience that a story told one way might be told otherwise in a different context. Clayton's Texas was part of the American Republic yet still oriented in important ways toward an early period of independent (not elephantine) republicanism; it partook of the American West as well as of the American South; it was cross-cut by allegiances oriented toward race and class. And Clayton's Texas was all this at a time of considerable upheaval: the civil-rights movement and American military involvements in Asia. As a young man he moved from this environment to Cambridge, for doctoral studies. In one sense, it was a massive change. Yet, at the same time, his education in Britain assured a formative continuity. It, too, provided a particularly stimulating climate in which to reflect on the intellectual and social processes through which communities are formed, divide and overlap, on the relationships that may obtain between social location and authority, and on the shifting historical contexts within which claims about the prior, and the distant, are made. Emblematic of this period, perhaps, is the position of *The Code of the Laws of Cricket* on Clayton's office bookshelves. At Lancaster and in Boston, *The Code* stood with other 'sacred texts'.

That John Clayton was, in much of his work, inclined to pursue the historically specific character of persons' and communities' involvement with such 'scriptures' owed much to an abiding early interest in nineteenth- and twentieth-century German theology. For many years, even as his scholarly work extended to the study of philosophy and theology in other parts of Europe and Asia, Clayton engaged German theological works that, in a constructive and normative vein, explored the relationships between shifting social and institutional contexts and expressions of religious authority and tradition. Moreover, in doing so, he increasingly entered German academic conversations about the history of theology and philosophy of religion influenced by scholarship in historical sociology and by reflections on the intersection of theology and culture.

In the nineteenth and twentieth centuries, German theologians sought to reconceive Christian theology in the wake of Kant's critique of rational theology. In tracing the history of this reconfiguration of theology, Clayton focused on the development of theologians amidst their cultural and intellectual contexts, consulting correspondence and lectures as well as major theological works. In his scholarship, he sought to reveal the complexity and distinctiveness of theologians, and of their times. The following passage from an essay comparing Tillich and Troeltsch suggests something of Clayton's analytical and historical approach to the study of theology:

At some stages in his development and at specific places in his writings, Tillich reminds one here rather more of Barth and there rather more of Troeltsch. But, all things considered, Tillich was neither simply another spokesman for the newer dialectical theology nor a lingering specimen of the older theological liberalism. He was neither a Barth nor a Troeltsch; he was instead a *Tillich*. But precisely because he was who he was, Tillich stood on the boundary between these two apparently antithetical possibilities. As the situation required, he moved nearer to the one or he moved nearer to the other. He made no final and lasting choice between them. In his life's work, moreover, he sought theologically to mediate between the dialectical theology and theological liberalism. And therein lies not only much of Tillich's historical significance, but also something of his positive significance for the future constructive work of the theologian.[1]

Clayton's conversations with German colleagues shaped the character of his increasingly comparative and historical research programme. So too, of course, did his institutional location in a reasonably new Department of Religious Studies at the University of Lancaster, at a time of growing immigration to Britain, especially from former colonies. To this period date his early efforts to bring central questions from philosophy and the philosophy of religion – about argument and proof, reasons, ends and motives – to bear on texts connected to Buddhism, Hinduism, Judaism and Islam. *Religions, Reasons and Gods* reveals Clayton's interest in drawing together more closely topics and methods in the history of religions and the philosophy of religion. These essays constitute an extended argument in favour of the view that careful investigation of the nature and context of argument may usefully illuminate histories of religious traditions and communities by pointing toward local, group-specific, uses of reason. Clayton's Lancastrian location was one of the conditions of possibility for such an argument, inasmuch as it favoured conversation across the apparent boundaries between philosophers, theologians, anthropologists and historians. Like all British universities,

[1] John Clayton, 'Tillich, Troeltsch and the Dialectical Theology', *Modern Theology*, 4/4 (July 1988), 323–44, 340.

the University of Lancaster was also, especially by Clayton's later years in Britain, an institution profoundly shaped by the character of British higher-education assessment exercises. The administrative strategy followed by Lancaster – which involved, in part, the development of thematic connections across sub-disciplines within religious studies in order to maximize the research and teaching productivity of the faculty – both reflected and shaped the character of Clayton's Stanton Lectures and the ideas developed in this volume. It is not really a surprise that bound RAE (Research Assessment Exercise) volumes, too, stood on Clayton's office bookshelves, less far from books on local rationality than one might initially expect.

The increasing religious diversity that came to characterize Britain and the United States during the latter half of the twentieth century raised the stakes in conversations – scholarly and popular – about relativism and universalism, truth and objectivity, and the possibility of conversation across the boundaries of religions which might be seen as discrete communities of life and language. There are many signs of these debates in *Religions, Reasons and Gods*. Like many philosophical critics during this time, such as Lorraine Code, Richard Rorty and Alasdair MacIntyre, Clayton sought to find a method for philosophy that did not limit it to the foundationalist epistemology increasingly scrutinized by feminist and other philosophers who sought to emphasize the importance of particularity as well as tradition in epistemic agency. Against correspondence theories of truth which, according to some of their critics, characterize truths and the facts they correspond to from a God's-eye view of the world, philosophers such as Rorty and Code emphasized the importance of the contribution made by language, culture and standpoint to the expressions which are subsequently deemed to be true or false. Clayton preferred the notion of 'local rationalities' to general characterizations of rationality *simpliciter*, but he also sought to distinguish his views on the embeddedness of reason within social practices from the attitude toward rationality characterized by some neo-Wittgensteinian philosophers of religion who seem to favour separatism over exchange.

While not always immediately visible, these themes run throughout Clayton's book. They are explicitly present in Part I, which addresses problems of religious diversity and public life. In Chapters 2 and 3, 'Thomas Jefferson and the Study of Religion' and 'Common Ground and Defensible Difference', Clayton attempts to render natural religion less natural as the default discourse of the modern public sphere. This involves historical and programmatic moves. His account of the context for Jeffersonian natural religion emphasizes the reasonably homogeneous Protestant cultural landscape of its origins. This landscape shaped the character of Jefferson's conception of religious discourse fit for public life, and also limited the work required of such a discourse. Clayton juxtaposes Jeffersonian America with late-twentieth-century Britain and America, raising questions about the role of philosophy of religion in an era of greater cultural and religious diversity. Clayton's programmatic work involves recourse to the notion of 'defensible difference', which holds that the tensions of religious and cultural pluralism are best managed by the careful delineation of points of difference as well as attention to areas in which shared ends may be achieved through distinct means, means rooted in distinctive traditions of argument and practice. On Clayton's view, philosophers of religion may play a constructive role in the implementation of the principle of defensible difference. Yet, as the structure of *Religions, Reasons and Gods* reveals, he held that a productive reconsideration of the conceptual frameworks of philosophy of religion required a richer history of the traditions of reasoning and practice out of which the philosophy of religion emerged. Such a historical perspective could help to illuminate the origins of central problems in the philosophy of religion, as well as ways in which such problems reflect more parochial concerns than many contemporary philosophers might initially expect.

Parts II and III of this volume may be seen, in part, as one attempt to provide that historical perspective. Clayton returns explicitly to his vision for the philosophy of religion only at the end of the book, after an extended reconsideration of the histories of philosophy and philosophy of religion as academic disciplines and modes of enquiry. *Religions, Reasons and Gods* is, among other things, a cautionary tale about the subtly powerful workings of anachronism in the origin stories told within academic disciplines. Clayton examines, in treatments of both mediaeval and modern arguments, the conditions of possibility for specific 'thinkable positions', and for the reception of such positions. Such examination serves, on the one hand, his stated aim to illuminate the 'forms of life' within which argument, proof and disproof occurred. In addition, however, through essays developed (to a large extent) diachronically across roughly seven hundred years, he narrates the historical contingency of the practice of philosophy and theology. According to Clayton, the histories of philosophy and philosophy of religion as disciplines are not best told as a streamlined teleology from the vantage point of a present position (whether understood as apogee or nadir). Rather, such histories are to be worked out in tension with the categories and stories which come most naturally to present times and places, and with attention to the extended unintended and unpredictable consequences of ideas and texts in motion – carried by persons within, and across, varied social settings and institutional environments. From this perspective, the pasts of all religious traditions are equally foreign, and Kant is no less a stranger to us than Anselm or Ramanuja.

Chapter 7, 'The Otherness of Anselm', which concludes Part II of this volume, provides a particularly clear window onto Clayton's approach to historical enquiry. Clayton examines the place of theistic proof in Anselm's *Proslogion*. In doing so, he stresses the importance of looking at the *entire text* within which theistic proofs occur, and of attempting to determine the role played by proof as part in relation to text as whole. Moreover, he draws attention to other texts in relation to which the *Proslogion* was written and used by Anselm. Thus, for Clayton, the study of a moment of argument involves the exploration of intra- and inter-textual contexts for such a moment. Why? Because understanding the work accomplished by an instance of rationality requires understanding the rhetorical context (often linked to textual genre) within which such an instance was introduced, as well as the ends (ritual, social, institutional and foundational) it may have been intended to serve. This may be seen as a move to attend to the individual maker of argument both in the foreground and in the background of historical investigation.

On the one hand, Clayton draws our attention to Anselm the person, Anselm the religious, Anselm the maker of meaning. And, on the other, he shows us Anselm as the product of time, place and circumstances. Clayton's Anselm participated in a local understanding of 'reason'. He did not practise heroic, or universal, philosophy. (Indeed, Anselm is for Clayton an important case study through which to meditate upon the relationship between the context of argument and the magnitude of the epistemic achievement claimed for an argument.) In 'The Otherness of Anselm', as in other essays which follow here, we thus see Clayton's persistent movement to evoke now one, now another, pattern of relief in the treatment of arguments, texts, persons and contexts. Clayton was fascinated by the fluidity of visual argument present in Klimt's maximally textured figurative paintings, which can be viewed as an intensification of focus on human physical form and as the effacement of the individual within a pattern. Some of the essays presented in *Religions, Reasons and Gods* – especially those in Part III on debate and early-modern philosophies – bear the marks of this fascination. In these four chapters, Clayton works in part through genealogy to trace the development of the modern in philosophical and religious thought. Rather than finding a singular story of the development of modern Western philosophy, Clayton finds localized enlightenments, with varying qualities. These chapters display again Clayton's earlier emphasis on the distinctiveness and complexity of particular thinkers, yet he also observes here the culturally and historically located conditions for the possibility of argument, highlighting the development of early modernities in France, Germany and Britain. Clayton's narratives draw key intellectual figures in and out of view as formative agents in the constitution of the modern, and of philosophy and philosophy of religion as disciplines.

Ithaca, New York and Boston, Massachusetts, September 2005

Acknowledgments

Time did not allow John Clayton to prepare his acknowledgments for this volume. The Editors hope that Professor Clayton's many friends and colleagues will find herein traces of conversation and disputation, and of his appreciation of their hospitality. In addition to the research funding indicated in his original footnotes to previously published essays, it is appropriate to note support received by John Clayton from Emmanuel College and the University of Cambridge during the preparation of his Stanton Lectures. Clayton was also provided with generous research funds by Boston University beginning in 1997.

The Editors are indebted to the Boston University Department of Religion and the Division of Religious and Theological Studies and to the Boston University Humanities Foundation for supporting completion of this volume after Professor Clayton's untimely death. The financial support offered by the Humanities Foundation enabled Thomas D. Carroll to retrace lines of enquiry indicated by Clayton's research notes and to conduct additional research at the British Library, in order to complete Chapter 10. At Boston University we are particularly grateful to Professor Katherine O'Connor (Director of the Humanities Foundation), Professor Stephen Prothero (Chair of the Department of Religion and Director of the Division of Religious and Theological Studies) and Ms Karen Nardella (Administrator for the Division of Graduate and Theological Studies). We offer thanks to Mr Christian Lammerts for his careful work in formatting Professor Clayton's essays to meet the guidelines of the Press. Dr Kate Brett, Editor at Cambridge University Press, supervised preparation of this volume with a gracious commitment for which we were particularly grateful during the difficult days following John Clayton's death.

In addition, Anne M. Blackburn wishes to acknowledge the research leave and administrative support made possible by her appointment as Yehan Numata Visiting Associate Professor of Buddhist Studies at the

Harvard Divinity School during the spring term of 2005, a period devoted
in part to completion of this volume.

We are grateful for permission to reproduce essays originally published
elsewhere: Chapter 2, 'Thomas Jefferson and the Study of Religion', was
published by Lancaster University in 1992, 35pp.; we wish to thank Mrs
M. E. McClintock, Academic Registrar and series editor of the University
of Lancaster Inaugural Lecture publications for permission to republish
the lecture. Also included in Chapter 2 is an extract from 'Enlightenment,
Pluralism and the Philosophy of Religion', published in *Hermeneutics of
Encounter: Essays in Honour of Gerhard Oberhammer*, ed. F. X. D'Sa and
R. Mesquita, De Nobili Research Library, 1994, pp. 35–59; we are thankful to Professor Dr R. Mesquita and Doz. Dr Utz Podzeit of the De
Nobili Research Library and University of Vienna for permission to
republish this extract. Chapter 3, 'Common Ground and Defensible
Difference', first appeared in *Religion, Politics, and Peace*, ed. Leroy
S. Rouner, University of Notre Dame Press, 1999, pp. 104–27, and we
thank Professor Emeritus Leroy S. Rouner of Boston University for
permission to republish the essay here. Chapter 4, 'Religions, Reasons
and Gods', was initially published in *Religious Studies* 23/1 (1987), 1–17,
while Chapter 6, 'Piety and the Proofs', appeared in *Religious Studies* 25/1
(1990), 19–42; for permission to republish these articles we wish to thank
Professor Peter Byrne of King's College, London. Chapter 5, 'Ramanuja,
Hume and "Comparative Philosophy": Remarks on the *Sribhasya* and
the *Dialogues concerning Natural Religion*', will see first publication in
*Expanding and Merging Horizons: Contributions to South Asian and Cross-
Cultural Studies in Commemoration of Wilhelm Halbfass*, ed. Karin
Preisendanz, to be published by the Austrian Academy of Sciences, Vienna,
2006; we are grateful to Professor Dr Preisendanz of the University of
Vienna for her gracious permission to republish the essay so soon after its
first appearance. Chapter 7, 'The Otherness of Anselm', appeared in *Neue
Zeitschrift für systematische Theologie und Religionsphilosophie* 37/2 (1995),
125–43; we thank Professor Dr Oswald Bayer of the University of Tübingen
for permission to republish the essay in this volume. Chapter 9, 'The
Enlightenment Project and the Debate about God in Early-Modern
German Philosophy', was originally published in *Vernunft, Kontingenz
und Gott: Konstellationen eines offenen Problems*, ed. Ingolf Dalferth
and Philipp Stoellger, (Tübingen: J. C. B. Mohr (Paul Siebeck), 2000),
pp. 171–93; for permission to reproduce this essay, we wish to thank
Professor Dr Ingolf Dalferth of the University of Zurich and Ms Jill
Sopper, Foreign Rights Manager for Mohr Siebeck.

Abbreviations

GS/JA	Moses Mendelssohn, *Gesammelte Schriften.* *Jubiläumsausgabe*
JAOS	*Journal of the American Oriental Society*
KA	*Kants Werke: Akademie-Textausgabe*
KGA	Friedrich Schleiermacher, *Kritische Gesamtausgabe*
Notes Rec. R. Soc. Lond.	*Notes and Records of the Royal Society of London*
OC	*Œuvres complètes* of Rousseau
Op. Om.	*Opera Omnia*
WA	*Weimarer Ausgabe* of Martin Luther
WZKSO	*Wiener Zeitschrift für die Kunde Süd- und Ostasiens*
ZDMG	*Zeitschrift für die Deutsche Morgenländergesellschaft*

CHAPTER I

Claims, contexts and contestability*

Philosophy, a distinguished member of this Society has suggested, is akin to a service industry – and can be likened perhaps to window cleaning.

Through the ages, people as different as Socrates and Luther have noted philosophy's similarity to a variety of service industries, but no one to my knowledge had, prior to Professor Lash, observed its kinship to window cleaning. Neither so noble as Socratic midwifery nor so ancient as the profession to which reason was consigned by Luther, cleaning windows is nonetheless a congenial way to picture the philosopher's trade – assuming, that is, that I have not got the wrong end of the chamois, so to speak.

For I take it that by having likened philosophy to cleaning windows, Professor Lash wanted to make us more attentive to the way that philosophical analysis can sometimes enable us to see more clearly that which has been there – albeit obscurely – in front of our eyes all along. But, whatever his intentions may have been, that is how I would construe the task of philosophical analysis.

Not all philosophers, of course, are content with their lot as window cleaners. Some philosophers insist not only on cleaning the windows, but also on advising their clients where to look. Other philosophers may complain that their customers have the wrong sort of windows or that their windows are ill placed for the best views. And a few may even chide householders for having had the audacity to attempt to clean their own windows, rather than engage the services of a professional philosopher.

Philosophers of religion, like philosophers generally, can be divided in different ways for different purposes. My present ends are sufficiently served if we distinguish broadly between those philosophers, on the one hand, who are inclined to think that religious people would not be able to distinguish sense from nonsense without the assistance of a philosopher

---

* Editors' note: This chapter was prepared as a paper given to the 'D' Society, in Michaelmas 1991.

(preferably of the analytic variety) and those philosophers, on the other hand, who are willing to allow the possibility that they could, even without the external intervention of a philosopher, analytic or otherwise.

Members of the latter group will be inclined to allow the possibility that Bonaventura and possibly even others knew what they meant when they said that God is not a being, but is 'Being Itself'; that the Chandogya Upanisad was not necessarily making a category mistake in asserting that 'Brahman and Atman are one'; and that the Buddhist dialectician Nagasena was not talking through his hat when he told King Milinda that 'rebirth occurs without anything transmigrating' – nor for that matter was the Apostle Paul when he proclaimed that what is sown a physical body will be raised a spiritual body.

Philosophers of the first group, by contrast, would not be inclined in such cases to concede what I would like to call the *presumption of competence*, which is another (and I hope less condescending) way of expressing something of what Donald Davidson has endorsed by commending 'charity' toward the Other. The presumption of competence allows that the basic claims of major religious traditions are likely to be justifiable as 'true' to members of the community concerned. Moreover, where such claims are contested, the communities themselves are competent to deal with issues of what is and what is not acceptable belief or behaviour.

To the presumption of competence, I would add what might be called *the practice of empathy*: namely, the imaginative participation of the observer in the spiritual and cognitive world of the religious tradition under scrutiny.

This is a necessary addition to the presumption of competence because otherwise there is no effective bridge between the observer and the observed, save the culturally imperialist one of accepting as meaningful, etc., only those individual items from the Other's doctrinal scheme that are translatable into one's own cognitive system. Even if every single proposition in one scheme were translated without remainder into one's own system, we might still miss the pattern of the Other's scheme, because what would not thereby be carried over is the network within which the individual propositions were connected with each other and in terms of which their specific location in the scheme is defined.

'Understanding' *in the sense required* is holistic, not atomistic. For 'understanding' in the sense wanted, one requires empathetic participation in the Other's doctrinal scheme.

From the presumption of competence and the practice of empathy, I would generate something that might be called *the maxim of reticence*, which is akin to Husserlian *epochē* except that in my preferred maxim the brackets around judgment are not so firmly closed. (After all, would I be a responsible window cleaner if I failed to tell the customer about necessary repairs, or if I failed to open the window to allow the escape of the occasional trapped fly – to allude to an earlier Cambridge philosopher whose name now dare not be spoken?)

Neither the presumption of competence nor the practice of empathy nor the maxim of reticence in itself precludes the properly philosophical consideration of truth questions, though someone who adopted these guide-lines might be inclined to linger rather a long time over the question *What would it be for such-and-such claim to be true?* and also over the question *What would count as reasons for holding such-and-such claim to be true?* before asking whether such-and-such claim *is* true.[1]

The presumption of competence, the practice of empathy and the maxim of reticence are intended to have the standing merely of what Kant would have called 'counsels of prudence', not that of what he termed 'the categorical imperative'. They are simply recommendations to be followed in order to achieve certain results. They may not conform to everyone's self-definition of philosophy, but they help me clean windows.

The particular window I have set about cleaning in recent years looks out on the roles of rationality in religious contexts. By 'rationality' I mean *giving reasons* for beliefs or practices. In order not to create expectations that are only later disappointed, however, I should make clear that I do not intend here to offer or defend some general theory of rationality, or even a more localized theory of religious rationality. My present aim is more modest. By attending to some of the varied roles of certain arguments within a variety of religious traditions, Eastern and Western, I hope to elucidate something of the range of motives and ends served by 'giving reasons' within religious contexts.

In declaring an interest in the problem of rationality, I am well aware that I am not the first one to have had a go at the precarious panes in that particular window. Since at least the time when I was a student, problems about rationality have been dogging the best minds in wide-flung disciplines within the natural and social sciences. Important contributions to

---

[1] Editors' note: At this juncture, the annotated version apparently prepared for oral presentation contains the following marginal addition: 'Not committed to holding that correspondence theory of truth is adequate in rel[igious] contexts: pragmatic theory may be more appropriate. Not everyone will be happy with this. Not even all pragmatists, some of whom deny that prag[matism] offers a "theory" of truth.'

the clarification of the issues involved have been made by several members of this Society.

Prudence alone would seem sufficient to deter most guest speakers from choosing to raise topics about which the local audience is far more knowledgeable than oneself. But, as I have been forced to concede more than once in my life, prudence was never a Texan's long suit.

Discussion about rationality has tended to focus on issues such as relativism and realism. In the philosophy of religion (at least of the analytic variety) it has been linked more often than not to difficulties concerning the justifiability of basic religious claims, such as the existence of God/s or the veridical nature of at least some religious experiences, etc. These are staple issues for the philosophy of religion, and it is right that they should be regularly canvassed.

Concentrating so much on just the justificatory uses of argument, however, may unwittingly encourage our vision of the religious uses of reason to become constricted, so that we fail to notice much that lies there before our very eyes, and that has lain there all along. As a corrective, I want to suggest a change in the field of focus, so that what has been in sharp focus for a very long time is displaced at least momentarily by some things which have been present only to our peripheral vision. By bringing to the centre of our field of vision features of the scenery which had been pushed to the edges, we may come to see some individual details we have not noticed before, but we may also come to see the whole landscape in a different way. We may even come to see in a new relation those very features, such as the justificatory uses of argument, which were previously the centre of our interests.

I make a simple, even banal, observation: *Religious claims are made and contested in a variety of contexts.*

The observation could be left unsaid were it not for the fact that the philosophy of religion is so often practised in a way that suggests its point had not been taken. No one denies that religious traditions sometimes make claims, or that these claims can be contested, but it is sometimes evidently forgot – *at least methodologically forgot* – that religious claims can be contested in a variety of different contexts. Methodologically forgot because it is so frequently overlooked that what count as 'good reasons' in one set of circumstances may not so count in another. 'Reasons' are always reasons for someone; they become persuasive when they are regarded as 'good reasons' by some audience.

As a way of introducing some distinctions in a rough and ready way, I want to identify three obviously different contexts in which reasons might be given for or against some religious claim: the intra-traditional, the inter-religious and the extra-religious contexts.

Particular claims may be made or contested *within a single tradition.* Let us call this *the intra-traditional context.* What count as 'good reasons' may be predominantly tradition-specific, as would be the mechanism whereby a dispute could be resolved.

Secondly, a claim made within one religious tradition may be contested as a result of a challenge from a second religious tradition. This can be called *the inter-religious context.* Some things that might count as 'good reasons' within an intra-traditional context (citing from authoritative scriptures, for instance) might not count as good reasons in a doctrinal dispute between different religious traditions. Hence the practice of 'giving reasons' would be likely to have different dynamics within inter-religious contexts.

Finally, a religious claim may be contested as a result of a challenge from outside the religious sphere altogether, for example by a 'secular' critic of religion. This I suggest we call *the extra-religious context.* 'Giving reasons' in this context may differ from the intra-traditional context in some of the same ways that it would differ from giving reasons in an inter-religious context. Because of this fact some people, including William Christian, fail to distinguish between reason giving in inter- and extra-religious contexts. But this seems to overlook the way that tacitly religious considerations may affect doctrinal disputes between religious traditions – e.g., both parties would be likely to think that religious issues matter and might both be inclined to accept as reasonable certain features of the world that a more secular mind would question. The presence of such tacit assumptions in discussions across traditions would seem to be sufficient reason to want to distinguish between inter-religious and extra-religious contexts. Even if we are inclined to agree with my colleague John Milbank that some putatively 'secular' mentalities are 'paradoxically unsecular', there would still seem to be practical usefulness in being able to distinguish these two contexts of possible dispute.

For entirely understandable cultural reasons, modern philosophy of religion – not least *British* philosophy of religion – has tended to occupy itself mainly with the last of these possible contexts, to the neglect of the other two.

From this point of view, it is natural that the discussion of rationality in religion should centre on the issue of the justifiability of basic religious claims in a religiously indifferent or intellectually hostile environment. How would the problem of rationality look, however, if we arranged things so that the *intra-* and not the *extra-*religious context were the field of primary interest? Would it then seem equally natural to use the issue of public justifiability as the way into the problem of rationality in religion?

In order to find an answer to that question, I suggest that we change the level of magnification, so to speak, in order to inspect more closely the roles of rationality within religions themselves. I am not recommending that we adopt the intra-traditional perspective as partisans, but that we make it the object of enquiry. Obviously, we can only make a modest beginning here. I shall in this paper do little more than assemble some examples of specific uses of 'reason giving' within religious traditions. I shall use theistic proofs as a test case of such reason giving.

This choice of test case will surely come as no great surprise, since that is the topic I have been researching of late and is the topic of the Stanton Lectures that I shall be giving next year. Even though it cannot come as a surprise, it may still seem at first an odd choice as a test case for *intra-*religious rationality, especially given that the choice is made by someone who has already dropped heavy hints that the issue of the public justifiability of basic religious beliefs may not be the most appropriate point of entry into the question of the roles of rationality in religious contexts.

Surely theistic proofs are justificatory arguments *par excellence*. Are they not inextricably bound up with the attempt from Greek times to the Enlightenment and beyond to find independent and generally compelling reasons for belief in the existence of a Supreme Being, which is not specifically identifiable in detail with the concept of God in any particular religious tradition?

Although theistic arguments have sometimes been put forward for that purpose, not least in post-Enlightenment Europe, it is worth reminding ourselves that most of the theistic proofs that have paraded themselves in front of us in modern times had a kind of pre-history in a less secular and more tradition-specific context. If we look at them within *that* context (or, rather, plurality of contexts), we may see something quite different from their more familiar face. We may find, for instance, that on the whole they seem to have served specifically intra-traditional ends. Although they were sometimes aimed at groups outside the community of faith, we cannot assume from that fact that they were being used in – say – the thirteenth century in much the same way that they were in the seventeenth.

This point could be made by contrasting the place of theistic proofs in the writings of Thomas Aquinas and those of John Locke, each of whom can be regarded for these purposes as representative of their age. They were in fact all along engaged in different projects. For Locke, it is reason which determines what is to count as an authentic revelation, whereas for Thomas it is revelation which determines what is to count as rational. That is to say, if it were to transpire that the teachings of tradition-embodied revelation and the results of rational enquiry into divine things were at variance, Locke would use reason to purge the tradition, whereas Thomas would hold that their variance was sufficient to show that reason had led us astray.

That – it seems to me – is an important difference which has implications for the authority of theistic arguments within religious contexts. For it gives us a criterion for preferring one proof of God over another, a criterion that is expressive of the faith of the community employing proofs apologetically. It may help explain in some cases how Thomas went about drawing up his short list of five ways from amongst the longer list of theistic proofs circulating in mediaeval Europe. It shows how the beliefs of a community can serve as controls on the choice and application of 'rational' arguments. It suggests that 'natural theology' (in some senses of that term) was not itself 'natural' (in at least one sense of that term). Moreover, it suggests that what are regarded as 'good reasons' for the existence of God are reasons that are regarded as good by the community itself.

In an article that I published last year, I suggested that there are some cases in which it seemed that what counted as 'good reasons' were reasons that were regarded as good by the community, *even when they were not regarded as 'good reasons' by the audience outside the community to whom they were addressed.*

If we look closely especially at the uses of theistic argument in religious traditions prior to the Enlightenment, we come to realize that the proofs were not always aimed at individuals and groups outside the community concerned. Frequently, they were from a variety of motives intended for internal use only. For instance, they were used fairly regularly for polemical purposes, in order *to correct defective or deviant beliefs about the nature of God.*

This polemical use of theistic argument was fairly widespread within mediaeval Islamic and Jewish thought. The likes of Saadya Gaon and al-Ghazali, for instance, formulated proofs for the existence of God from the necessary temporality of the creation in order to counter the growing influence of Aristotle's causal proofs within Judaism and Islam. The existence of God was not directly at issue, but proofs for God's existence served as a way of showing an opponent's concept of God to be defective and dangerous to the life of faith. Begin with Aristotle, it was said, and you will end with Strato.

Within text-centred religious traditions, Eastern and Western, theistic arguments have sometimes been used hermeneutically, that is, to assist *with the proper interpretation of sacred texts*. Theistic arguments have been employed in order to clarify the meaning of an obscure text (Ramanuja), in order to reinforce the traditional interpretation of a controversial text (Ghazali) and in order to legitimate a novel interpretation of a given text (Averroes).

Here I offer only one such example, drawn from the writings of Ramanuja, the eleventh-century Vedantan philosophical theologian. Ramanuja did not actually propose any theistic arguments; he was indeed one of their most outspoken opponents within the various Vedantan schools. According to Ramanuja, God is known in his grace through scripture alone, not through inference.

Ramanuja does not reject the validity of inference as such. It was after all one of the six ways of coming to know things that were accepted by Vedantan thinkers of all persuasions. Ramanuja is content to use inference in other matters – including the critique of theistic arguments – but not as a means of showing the existence of God. In his commentary on the Brahma-Sutras, he offers a devastating critique of any possible argument for the existence of God, in the process anticipating by some seven hundred years David Hume's objections to the design argument. What I find more interesting, however, is the use to which that critique is put in Ramanuja's commentary.

The Brahma-Sutras were an attempt to summarize in a systematic way the teachings of the Upanisads, writings which had particular authority for the Vedantic systems. But the Brahma-Sutras, also known as the Vedanta-Sutras, are often cryptic and obscure. They were written in a way that was easily memorized and served mainly as reminders of more elaborate instructions given to those trained in Vedantic thought. Because of their obscurity, however, it was necessary to have commentaries or *bhasyas* in order to guide one through the scriptures. Not just anyone could write such a commentary, but the great teachers did write *bhasyas* on the *sutras*, offering in the process accounts of their distinctive inter-pretations. These commentaries in turn became the basis of schools, and had meta-commentaries written on them by subsequent leaders of the schools. They had, therefore, an importance for the tradition that was in some cases only slightly less than the *sutras* themselves.

Shankara had written a particularly influential *bhasya*, in which he indicated that the third *sutra* could be read in one of two ways and that the first reading is to be favoured:

From its being the source of scriptures [i.e. that Brahman is the cause or author of the Vedas]

From scriptures being the source of its (knowledge) [i.e. only the Vedas can prove to us that Brahman is the cause of the world, etc.].

Shankara favoured the first reading, but Ramanuja favoured the second as the only valid interpretation.

In order to substantiate that interpretation, Ramanuja went through all the sources of knowledge acknowledged by the Vedantic philosophy, eliminating in turn all save one as a possible source of knowledge of divine existence. The point of the procedure, including the repudiation of natural theology, being to give weight to his preferred reading of the third *sutra*. And this, it seems to me, is a fairly clear example of discussion concerning theistic arguments serving hermeneutic ends.

Such a use is far from isolated in the history of religions, but – as already indicated – it is limited, of course, to religious traditions in which sacred texts figure centrally. However, it would be a mistake to assume that the absence of reference to sacred scriptures is itself sufficient to show that a given proof is not being used to fairly specifically religious ends.

The place of theistic proofs in the classical Greek philosophical tradition is sometimes held to be different from their place in religious traditions such as Judaism, Islam and Christianity in virtue of religious considerations being more explicitly associated with the latter than with the former, which is held thereby to represent a purer form of 'rational theology'. It is the case that Jewish, Muslim and Christian writers do sometimes cite sacred texts in association with their theistic arguments and Greek philosophers do not. But it would be wrong to infer from this that specifically religious considerations are absent from the use of theistic proofs within Greek philosophy.

Although other examples come to mind, mainly from Stoic philosophy, Socrates is reported on one occasion to have offered a theistic proof – a version of the design argument – not in order to show that the gods exist, but in order to encourage Aristodemus the dwarf to fulfil his responsibilities to make sacrifices to the gods. The worry expressed to Socrates was not that the Deity might not exist, but that the gods were too exalted to need our sacrifices or to notice whether we make them. Socrates' reply, recorded by Xenophon, is that the Divinity who took such care in the design of the world, down to the smallest detail, would indeed notice whether sacrifices were made.

This last example serves as a bridge to the final and possibly most important group of uses of theistic arguments within intra-traditional contexts: namely, those applications which build up the community, its sense of well being and its solidarity. This group of uses I would call, following a suggestion in a rather different context by Richard Rorty, *edificatory uses of argument*.

Theistic proofs have been used as aids for prayer and devotion (Udayana, Anselm, Cleanthes) and as a basis for meditation (Anselm again, but also Bonaventura). They have also been used as a means of educating followers of a particular religion into its basic beliefs (Ghazali). They have also been used to exhort us to a pious life (Socrates) or simply to express awe and wonder at 'the heavenly stars above and the moral law within'.

All of these – and more – applications of theistic argument were fairly common before the Enlightenment. They show that before the Fall of Modernity, theistic arguments tended to be used to a wide range of ends in addition to the justification of basic religious beliefs to someone who did not already in large measure share those beliefs. They seem to have been used predominantly to enhance the community's sense of solidarity, and when they were aimed outside the community, they were sometimes used in order to reinforce the identity of the community. This seems to suggest that 'giving reasons' served more a practical than a theoretical function. Though this may give us a better understanding of the location of this particular 'reason giving' within the religious past, it may also serve to increase our sense of alienation from 'their' projects.

One main function of these arguments, if not the primary function, would seem to be to enhance the community's sense of solidarity (not quite in Rorty's sense). All of these examples have been taken from the distant past, well away from our own times, defined as they are by the Enlightenment and its aftermath. We might feel comfortable with admitting that they used theistic arguments in that way, to those ends, without feeling it necessary to make connections with our own, more 'enlightened' (in both senses) uses. They were, after all, pre-moderns, and we have moved beyond all that. Their 'otherness' therefore reinforces our own sense of uniqueness and enhances our own sense of superiority by increasing the distance between them and us.

Although I have not used in this talk any modern examples or taken the story into more recent times, I do plan to do so in the Stanton Lectures.

I do want to report, however, that my colleague John Hedley Brooke has in his own research on the British natural theology tradition suggested that the design argument in particular has tended to flourish when it served the social function of mediating between ideologically disparate groups and sects. Its real strength, which enabled it to survive Hume's critique, was less its intellectual force than its adhesive power within an increasingly pluralist society. It served then the practical function of giving a sense of stability and cohesion to a fragmenting society.

But if we come to think that even in modern times the arguments of natural theology survive by their social value of enhancing group solidarity, then the gap between pre-modern and modern functions of argument or 'giving reasons' is greatly reduced. The 'otherness' of the past is harder to sustain, and we are forced through the face of the Other to look at ourselves differently, to reconceive the roles of rationality also in *our* context.

And with that observation we begin to sail toward the very edges of the Objectivist's world into treacherous waters populated by Relativist dragons and American pragmatists. It seems a good point to stop, drop anchor, and decide what to do next: whether to sail further, to turn back to safer seas, or possibly to join Kierkegaard and jump ship altogether.

PART I

Reason and religious pluralism

The introductory chapter, 'Claims, Contexts and Contestability', ends by suggesting that studying the pre-modern history of theistic proofs may support investigation of the selective and collective instrumentality of argument. Clayton indicates a variety of ways in which theistic proofs may function within intra-traditional, as well as inter-traditional, contexts. This discussion reveals his particular interest in the ways in which intra-traditional uses of theistic proofs may enhance 'group solidarity'. Moreover, examining this role of the proofs in pre-modern contexts may render it more easily visible at work in modern contexts.

Such remarks provide a crucial frame for the chapters that follow in Part I. Chapter 2, 'Thomas Jefferson and the Study of Religion', proceeds on several fronts. Against the view that 'natural religion' provides a universal discourse suited to the management of pluralism by virtue of its supra-traditional character, Clayton presents one account of its origins, emphasizing the Protestant Christian character of this 'universal' language of religion. He also notes the limited character of difference required to be managed by such language in Jefferson's day. Jeffersonian America's religious parochialism is juxtaposed with the greater religious pluralism of contemporary Britain and America. Here Clayton argues that the disciplinary language of philosophy of religion retains the parochial character of its origins in natural religion discourse and is thus limited in its capacity to communicate among diverse religious communities. At the same time, however, Clayton refuses to be bound by a neo-Wittgensteinian view that there is no language adequate to the task of communication among religious communities, between language games. This chapter begins to develop two strategies of response to problems of language and religious pluralism. The first involves a comparative, historical and conceptual refinement of the critical vocabulary used within the philosophy of religion.

The second is a matter of practice: the suggestion that debate and the precision of difference may be an effective response to contemporary religious pluralism. Mediaeval Indian philosophical debate provides a model in dialogue with which new modes of contemporary debate and differentiation might be developed. Chapter 3, 'Common Ground and Defensible Difference', develops the account of the practice of debate as the management of pluralism through 'defensible difference' by using human-rights discourse as an exemplary case. This account emphasizes the potential for the accommodation of difference through forms of public reason oriented by legal models, and by close attention to a distinction between the grounds and ends of argument. Chapter 4, 'Religions, Reasons and Gods', is, in part, a return to Wittgenstein, proposing that theistic proofs be examined as moves within religious language games rather than as prior justifications for them. This formulation provides one way to conceptualize the historical study of rationality within religious communities. The discussion of moves within games provides a framing orientation to subsequent chapters that examine in more detail the roles played by theistic proofs in a variety of pre-modern and later contexts, as well as the communities forged or strengthened by theistic argument.

CHAPTER 2

Thomas Jefferson and the study of religion

Thomas Jefferson is not the most likely name to appear in the title of the inaugural lecture of a Professor of Religious Studies in a British university. Not even when the lecture is scheduled so soon after an American presidential campaign, which in its worst excesses resembled so closely the smear tactics pioneered in the campaign of 1800, when the former Southern governor who eventually won was castigated by the Federalists and their supporters as an atheist and moral deviant, who had learned dangerously un-American ways while living abroad, albeit in Paris rather than Oxford.[1] Just as their fundamentalist counterparts today bought newspaper space to warn the nation that a vote for Clinton would be a sin against all that is sacred, so the righteously religious of Yankee New England distributed pamphlets to warn the land against that 'French infidel and atheist' from Virginia who, if elected, would discredit religion, overthrow the church, burn all bibles. After Jefferson's victory, the worried souls of New England actually hid their bibles to save them from impending confiscation.[2]

In placing the name of Thomas Jefferson in the foreground of this inaugural lecture, however, I have both a personal motive and a professional reason.

Toward the end of the eighteenth century, a family of my forebears set sail from the then Lancashire port of Liverpool to the Virginia of Thomas Jefferson. And now, two hundred years later, I am able here to mark that personal if imprecise bicentenary by using their contemporary Jefferson as a focal point for some reflections on the academic study of religion and,

[1] See Charles O. Lerche, 'Jefferson and the Election of 1800: A Case Study in the Political Smear', *William and Mary Quarterly* 5 (1948), 467–91, and Thomas H. Buckley, 'The Political Theology of Thomas Jefferson', in *The Virginia Statute for Religious Freedom: Its Evolution and Consequences in American History*, ed. Merrill D. Peterson and Robert C. Vaughan (Cambridge, 1988), pp. 75ff.
[2] Charles B. Sanford, *The Religious Life of Thomas Jefferson* (Charlottesville, 1984), p. 1.

16

more specifically, on the place of the philosophy of religion within Religious Studies.

For the philosophy of religion as it is typically practised in universities in Britain and America alike is still very largely a construction of that European Enlightenment of which Thomas Jefferson may be looked upon as one of its most representative figures.

It may not seem obvious why one must travel to America in order to find a representative European. In my defence, I appeal to a Frenchman. After his celebrated visit to the United States early in the nineteenth century, Alexis de Tocqueville observed that in *Europe* he had known people who were English or French or German, but only in *America* had he come to know Europeans.[3]

In something of this self-same spirit, it might be said with only the slightest hint of exaggeration that in *Europe* we encounter a French or a German or a Scottish Enlightenment, but only in *America* do we experience the *European* Enlightenment. That suggests we may have greater success in locating a representative of that Enlightenment in America than we would have in Europe, whether we search in Paris or Königsberg or Edinburgh or possibly even Maastricht.

But where to look in America for a representative of the European Enlightenment? Although it may seem to some the natural place to begin, the soil of New England is for our uses stony ground. One distinguished interpreter of British-American colonial history has recently advanced the thesis that the New England colonies were as atypical of the emerging American culture as they had been of the older British order.[4] His findings point us instead toward the once-neglected South, which he claims was paradoxically more typical of both.

Even if Jack Greene's controversial thesis cannot be allowed to stand unchallenged,[5] few would want to quarrel with the more modest claim that Thomas Jefferson of Virginia was one American in whom the mind of the European Enlightenment had received a powerful embodiment.

Thirty years ago this year, President John Kennedy invited to dinner all new Nobel Prize winners from the Western hemisphere. According to a report in the *Washington Post*, the President welcomed his distinguished

---

[3] Alexis de Tocqueville recorded his travel impressions in *De la démocratie en Amérique*, 2 parts (Paris, 1835–40).

[4] Jack P. Greene, *Pursuits of Happiness: The Social Development of Early Modern British Colonies and the Formation of American Culture* (Chapel Hill, 1988).

[5] See John M. Murrin, 'The Irrelevance and Relevance of Colonial New England', *Reviews in American History* 18 (1990), 177–84.

guests on that occasion by calling them 'the most extraordinary collection of talent, of human knowledge, that has ever been gathered together at the White House, with the possible exception of when Thomas Jefferson dined alone'.[6]

Jefferson embodied the ideals of the European Enlightenment both in temperament and in intellectual culture. He was well versed in the classics (insisting, as would any serious student of his day, upon German editions of his Greek and Latin texts[7]) and he was well read in the modern political and philosophical writings emanating mainly from contemporary France and Britain. The scope of Jefferson's interests is exhibited in the titles of the 6,500 books from his personal library that formed the nucleus of the new Library of Congress after the old national public library had been burned by the British in 1814, an act of vandalism that much incensed Jefferson.[8]

Jefferson was also widely travelled and well connected in Europe as a result of the good fortune of having been appointed in succession to Benjamin Franklin as the US Minister to France during the five years preceding the 1789 Revolution, thus enabling him to become acquainted with the main intellectual and political figures of the new order. Despite an unease about compromising the neutrality of his diplomatic status, Jefferson in effect became informal consultant to the National Assembly.[9]

Although he was not (in the circumstances, understandably) over-fond of the British monarch and his ministers, Jefferson was unreserved in his admiration of the British contribution to liberal learning and political theory. Toward the end of his tenure in Paris, he commissioned copies to be made of pictures of Bacon, Newton and Locke, whom he considered to be 'the three greatest men that have ever lived, without any exception'. He insisted that the three busts be painted life-size onto a single canvas in tightly arranged ovals, thus forming them 'into a knot', as he put it, so

[6] *Washington Post* (30 April 1962).
[7] Elizabeth Cometti, ed., *Jefferson's Ideas on a University Library: Letters from the Founder of the University of Virginia to a Boston Bookseller* (Charlottesville, 1950), p. 31. Bernard Bailyn, usually sceptical about the depth of classical learning in eighteenth-century America, praises Jefferson as 'a careful reader of the classics'. *The Ideological Origins of the American Revolution* (Cambridge, MA, 1967), p. 25.
[8] See E. Millicent Sowerby, ed., *Catalogue of the Library of Thomas Jefferson*, 5 vols. (repr. Charlottesville, 1983), and Dumas Malone, *Jefferson and his Time*, VI (Boston, 1981), pp. 169–230.
[9] Howard C. Rice, Jr, *Thomas Jefferson's Paris* (Princeton, 1976), p. 120. For a balanced, critical assessment of the many sides of Jefferson's complex relationship to French culture and politics, see Lawrence S. Kaplan, *Jefferson and France: An Essay on Politics and Political Ideas* (New Haven, 1967).

that they 'may not be confounded at all with the herd of other great men'.[10]

When memory of the War of Independence had begun to fade, but before the War of 1812 had rekindled old animosities, Jefferson hymned the special relationship to which British Prime Ministers now more commonly than American Presidents make appeal: 'Our laws, language, religion, politics and manners are so deeply laid in English foundations, that we shall never cease to consider their history as a part of ours, and to study ours in that as its origin.'[11]

Nor was the Jeffersonian infatuation with the European mind one-sided only. European intellectuals also took admiring notice of Jefferson. While living in Paris, he was asked to assist with the entries on America for the new, expanded French *Encyclopédie méthodique* in which the 'Virginia Statute for Religious Freedom' was printed in full.[12] Later as President, he was sought out by visiting European scholars and scientists. His guests included the Prussian polymath Alexander von Humboldt, whose invitation to dine with Jefferson at the White House in 1804[13] may give us good cause to moderate John Kennedy's claim about the singular quality of White House table-talk when Jefferson ate alone.

However much he embodied the ideals of the Enlightenment, or perhaps *because* he embodied them, Jefferson was sharply critical of European society as he found it on his travels. He was struck by the poverty of peasant life, the harshness of life for women and children, the extent of religious intolerance, not least in German lands. He wrote in his diary, for instance, that in Cologne Protestants were oppressed by the ruling Catholics, and that in Frankfurt the ruling Protestants behaved no better toward the Catholic minority who lived there.[14]

Such experiences only reinforced his already strongly held views on the undesirability of ecclesiastical establishment enforced by law. Falsehood and not truth, he wrote on another occasion, requires the protection of law: 'truth is great and will prevail if left to herself'.[15]

---

[10] Thomas Jefferson to John Trumbull, 15 February 1789.
[11] Thomas Jefferson to William Duane, 12 August 1810.
[12] See Rice, *Jefferson's Paris*, p. 31.
[13] Dumas Malone, *Jefferson and his Time*, III (Boston, 1970), pp. 421–2.
[14] James McGrath Morris and Persephone Weene, eds., *Thomas Jefferson's European Travel Diaries* (Ithaca, 1987), pp. 115, 119.
[15] *The Statute of Virginia for Religious Freedom*, in Peterson and Vaughan, eds., *The Virginia Statute*, p. xviii.

The liberal ideals of the European Enlightenment, to which Jefferson was firmly if inconsistently committed, had (he was certain) a better chance of successful cultivation in the freshly turned soil of America than they had in the hard ground of Europe. 'While we shall see multiplied instances of Europeans going to live in America', he wrote to James Monroe from Paris, 'I will venture to say no man [*sic!*] now living will ever see an instance of an American removing to settle in Europe and continuing there.'[16]

I have alluded to Jefferson's inconsistent commitment to Enlightenment ideals. This is exposed no more damningly than in his ambivalence about slavery. The man who wrote in one of the most eloquent documents of the age about the 'unalienable' human rights of *life, liberty and the pursuit of happiness* and who spoke out against the evils of human enslavement was himself a slave holder. His public and private remarks on this issue were so ambivalent that his authority was later invoked by both sides in the abolition debate in the decades before the American Civil War.[17]

However inconsistent he may have been in other aspects of his social and political thought, even Jefferson's least patient critics generally allow that he maintained by contrast a commendable consistency in his views about the protection due to private choice in the exercise of religion and about the restricted access of religion to public space.[18]

By 'public space' I mean primarily the academy, which is my main interest here, but I readily admit that the phrase calls for more differentiation. We could also speak, for instance, of the market place or political institutions or the communications media as types of public space. Even so, the academy remains the principal object of interest.

Despite the generosity of his critics, I want to suggest that Jefferson's views on religion – or, more accurately, his views on *the study of religion* – are also flawed by an inconsistency. But in this case, the fault lies not so much in the fracture between Jeffersonian practice and Enlightenment ideals (as it was in the case of slavery). This fault runs right through the construction of religion required and entailed by what we have been encouraged of late to call the *Enlightenment project.*

---

[16] Thomas Jefferson to James Monroe, 17 June 1785.

[17] See, e.g., Peterson and Vaughan, *The Virginia Statute*, pp. 162–89, Daniel J. Borstin, *The Lost World of Thomas Jefferson* (New York, 1948), and John C. Miller, *The Wolf by the Ears: Thomas Jefferson and Slavery* (New York, 1980).

[18] See, e.g., Leonard W. Levy, *Jefferson and Civil Liberties: The Darker Side* (Cambridge, MA, 1963).

The 'Enlightenment project' in its most general form is an attempt to identify and to justify without recourse to outside authority or private passion but by the exercise of reason and the limits of experience alone what we can truly know, what we ought rightly to do and what we may reasonably hope. Rationality requires us in our deliberations to achieve neutrality by divesting ourselves of allegiance to any particular standpoint and to achieve universality by abstracting ourselves from all those communities of interest that may limit our perspective. By this means were to be laid foundations on which to build with reasoned confidence.

Of course, this perspective on the 'Enlightenment' enterprise obscures as well as reveals. The Enlightenment was not limited to a single project and was more nearly an experimental laboratory for disparate and often competing projects. Over against the designated project, with its basis in *universal reason*, for instance, we could easily set the opposing 'project' of Johann Gottfried Herder, in whose writings may be found the origins of modern anthropology and the seeds of what we would now be inclined to call cultural relativism.[19]

Even after we have recognized this picture of a unified 'Enlightenment' for the distorted image it is, the idea of an 'Enlightenment project' can nonetheless still usefully guide our reflections. To avoid getting involved in the exegesis of interpreters of that project as different as Habermas and MacIntyre, however, I will invent something that I shall now call *the Jeffersonian project.*

In respect to philosophy of religion, that project can be regarded as the attempt to establish from a tradition-free, confessionally neutral starting-point logically sound and universally compelling reasons to accept the existence of God, the immortality of the soul and the authority of the moral law. Built into the framework of the project is a distinction between 'natural religion', on the one hand, which was claimed to be universal in embrace, rational in character and benign in its consequences to the extent that it was thought to contribute to the stability of the social order and to unify the whole of humankind into what was then called, much too restrictively by our lights, 'the brotherhood of man'. The 'positive' or determinate religions, on the other hand, were said to have no more than local appeal, to be based on irrational authority, to be sustained by priestcraft and to lead to intolerance and division within and between

---

[19] See, e.g., Herder's *Ideen zur Philosophie der Geschichte der Menschheit* (1784–91; repr. Darmstadt, 1966).

nations. In the Jeffersonian enterprise, natural or rational religion is thought fit for public space, whereas the particular sects are privatized.

Jefferson had been the third US President, but he directed that the following be inscribed on his tombstone, 'and not a word more':

> Here was buried Thomas Jefferson,
> Author of the Declaration of American
> Independence [and of] the Statute
> of Virginia for religious freedom,
> and Father of the University of Virginia.

Out of deference to local sensitivities, I shall not dwell on his authorship of the Declaration of American Independence. But I must report the fact that when Jefferson and Adams both died on 4 July 1826, the fiftieth anniversary of the signing of that Declaration, Americans at the time were disposed to take the event as a token of the blessings of providence on both the document and its author.[20]

Nor shall I dwell long on the Virginia Statute for Religious Freedom, important though it is for Americans because it informed the drafting of the First Amendment to the US Constitution. That Amendment declares that 'Congress shall make no law respecting the establishment of religion, or prohibiting the free exercise thereof.'

Martin Marty of the University of Chicago, with a kind of hyperbole that can pass itself off in the American Midwest as understatement, declares that the Virginia Statute is the key moment marking the close of the Age of Constantine and the opening of the modern age.[21] The immediate intent of the Statute was more modest: namely, to effect the disestablishment of the Anglican Church. But its wider effect, through its influence on the First Amendment, has been to erect what Jefferson had called a 'wall of separation' between church and state.[22]

Subsequent judicial interpretation by the American Supreme Court has raised and reinforced that wall, which for Jefferson had been neither

---

[20] See Merrill D. Peterson, *The Jefferson Image in the American Mind* (New York, 1960), pp. 3–14, where reference is made to *A Selection of Eulogies Pronounced in the Several States in Honor of These Illustrious Patriots and Statesmen John Adams and Thomas Jefferson* (Hartford, 1826).

[21] 'The Virginia Statute Two Hundred Years Later', in Peterson and Vaughan, *The Virginia Statute*, p. 2.

[22] The phrase was originally introduced by Jefferson in a communication to a Committee of the Danbury [Connecticut] Baptist Association dated 1 January 1802. He took some care over the wording of his communication, seeking also the advice of Levi Lincoln, the Attorney General of the United States: 'You understand the temper of those in the North, and can weaken it, therefore, to their stomachs: it is at present seasoned to the Southern taste only' [Thomas Jefferson to Levi Lincoln, 1 January 1802].

especially high nor particularly substantial.[23] But it is the Jeffersonian project and not the extended American narrative that demands our attention here. The purpose of Jefferson's relatively more modest wall is to trace the boundary between the 'private realm', on the one side, where sectarian religious practices were protected from interference either by the state or by rival groups and the 'public realm', on the other side, to which access was limited to matters of common consent.

In Jefferson's view, it was not a matter of public interest whether a citizen had this religion or that, or for that matter no religion at all. As he colourfully put it on one occasion, 'it does me no injury for my neighbour to say there are twenty gods, or no god. It neither picks my pocket nor breaks my leg.'[24]

This privatization of religion and separation of personal belief from civic virtue in the Jeffersonian project 'set the tone' (as Richard Rorty puts it) for the American liberal tradition.[25] And so it did, but that is only part of the story; in Thomas Jefferson's vision, but not in that of some who came after him, the privatization of religion and the severance of personal belief from civil rights is complemented by another emphasis. Also important is the Jeffersonian provision for religion's access to public space, on condition that it express 'natural religion', and not partisan, 'sectarian' religious interests.

To tell this side of the story, we turn our attention now to the third accomplishment by which he wished posterity to measure his life: namely, his having founded the University of Virginia.[26]

Jefferson made no provision in the Statutes of the University of Virginia for a professor of divinity. Nor was this simply an oversight. He had made an unsuccessful attempt earlier as Governor to have the faculty of theology closed at the College of William and Mary, his own *alma mater*. He had come to the view that confessional theology was not a proper object of academic study, since it was based on appeals to irrational authority and not grounded in public reason. The chairs of divinity, therefore, should be dispersed to cognate faculties.

[23] See Robert M. Healey, *Jefferson on Religion in Public Education* (New Haven, 1962), and A. E. Dick Howard, 'The Supreme Court and the Serpentine Wall', in Peterson and Vaughan, *The Virginia Statute*, pp. 313ff.

[24] *Notes on the State of Virginia*, query XVII, in *Writings*, ed. Merrill D. Peterson (New York, 1984), p. 285.

[25] 'The Priority of Democracy to Philosophy', in Peterson and Vaughan, *The Virginia Statute*, pp. 257ff.

[26] See Virginia Dabney, *Mr Jefferson's University: A History* (Charlottesville, 1981); Healey, *Jefferson on Religion in Public Education* (New Haven, 1962); and Malone, *Jefferson and his Time*, III, pp. 365ff.

One chair would not readily fit elsewhere. It had been endowed by Robert Boyle for the purpose of instructing Native Americans in the principles of Christianity. Jefferson proposed in effect to subvert it

by maintaining a perpetual mission among the Indian tribes, the object of which, besides instructing them in the principles of Christianity, as the founder requires, should be to collect their traditions, laws, customs, languages, and other circumstances which might lead to a discovery of their relation with one another, or descent from other nations. When these objects are accomplished with one tribe, the missionary might pass on to another.[27]

Having been outmanoeuvred by the clergy on that earlier occasion, however, he made sure on this occasion that the Statutes of the new University contained a clause excluding Divinity. But space was created within the University for consideration of normative religious claims that were fit for the public domain: namely, those claims regarded as being held in common by all religious groups, including

the proofs of the being of a God, the creator, preserver, and supreme ruler of the universe, the author of all the relations of morality, and of the laws and obligations these infer, [which] will be within the province of the professor of ethics; to which adding the developments of these moral obligations, of those in which all sects agree, with a knowledge of the languages, Hebrew, Greek, and Latin, a basis will be formed common to all sects.[28]

Of those items specific to different religious communities, Jefferson wrote on behalf of the Commissioners of the University, it had been determined 'to leave every sect to provide, as they think fittest, the means of further instruction in their own peculiar tenets'.

Although Jefferson had no desire to exclude consideration of normative religious claims as such from the public sphere, he did nonetheless wish to control entry to that sphere by excluding all consideration of what he regarded as sectarian belief, those beliefs expressing a parochial commitment and not grounded in public reason.

This serves to highlight how in modern no less than in pre-modern times a dominant ideology, whether 'secular' or 'ecclesiastical', can through its control of public institutions define the criteria of access to public space and thereby deny entry to non-conforming traditions of enquiry. As regards philosophy of religion, this means the control of what count as reasons in matters religious and in effect what count as 'religion'

[27] *Notes on the State of Virginia*, query XV, in *Writings*, p. 277.
[28] *Report of the Commissioners for the University*, in *Writings*, p. 467.

and 'God'. Jefferson's views on the study of religion, therefore, illustrate the exercise of such control, based on a deep suspicion of tradition-specific or 'sectarian' religious discourse.

The strength of that suspicion is easily shown. On his eightieth birthday in 1823, another former President and fellow Freemason, John Adams, sent Jefferson his salutations in the form of a wish that he might continue in life and health until he become a Calvinist. Which is to say, that he should so continue until that place than which no warmer can be imagined freezes over.

Jefferson accepted the salutations of his former rival graciously and observed that the wish, if fulfilled, would make him immortal, because 'I can never join Calvin in addressing *his* god.'[29] Calvin, he reckoned, was in fact an atheist, believing not in 'the God whom you and I acknowledge and adore, the Creator and benevolent governor of the world; but a daemon of malignant spirit'. Against their clearest intentions, the likes of Calvin in fact encourage atheism by insisting that their God alone is true and that the only reliable knowledge of deity is through Christian revelation, which has local appeal at best and serves only to exclude five-sixths of humanity from reliable knowledge of God's existence and nature.

This, Jefferson insisted, plays into the hands of Diderot, d'Holbach and their ilk by making the foundation of religion a 'local' revelation defended by the church in an incoherent and irrational way, rather than (as Jefferson commended) by affirming the foundation of true religion as being universally available to all in experience of the world and the free exercise of reason.

Writing with innocence of any infection by the scepticism of Hume (whom he knew as an English historian,[30] not as a Scottish philosopher), Jefferson boasted that if we view the universe 'in its parts general or particular',

it is impossible . . . for the human mind not to believe that there is, in all this, design, cause and effect, up to an ultimate cause, a fabricator of all things from matter and motion, their preserver and regulator while permitted to exist in their present forms, and their regenerator into new and other forms.

'Natural religion', so conceived, is presumed to be universally available and to give confidence in the certainty of religious belief, whereas the

---

[29] Thomas Jefferson to John Adams, 11 April 1823.
[30] See Thomas Jefferson to John Norvell, 14 June 1807, and Thomas Jefferson to William Duane, 12 August 1810.

more idiosyncratic claims of particular confessions contribute to the acid of scepticism in matters religious, leading helplessly to materialism and atheism.

Natural religion alone finds a place in public space, because it alone can stand up to 'reason and free enquiry'. The particular religious confessions, if they desire to enter public space, must do so on the same terms: namely, with recourse to reason alone and without support from alleged revelation or some other irrational authority or from cultural privilege through legal establishment.

This was not meant to be punitive.

Jefferson truly believed that rational theology – the universal, tradition-free discourse that had been given privileged access to the public space of the academy – could lay a common foundation in which to ground a public religious discourse capable of expressing a kind of *consensus gentium*.[31]

Even as Jefferson wrote these confident words, however, the foundations of natural theology had already begun to crumble as a result not least of their having been put to the test by that writer whom *we* know more readily as a Scottish philosopher than as an English historian. Rather than providing solid foundation in universal reason or becoming ground of unity between disparate groups, 'natural theology' was itself becoming a matter of dispute within philosophy, almost as divisive as the sectarian creeds themselves. Moreover, recent studies of the period have tried to show that the increasing weight natural theology had been asked to carry itself became a major factor in the rise of modern atheism.[32] Or, as the eighteenth-century freethinker Anthony Collins sniped in a remark aimed at Samuel Clarke, it would never have occurred to anyone to doubt God's existence if theologians had not tried so hard to prove it. This is one way that the Jeffersonian project ended in irony, but there is another.

Jefferson had fully expected this rational religious discourse to extend its domain beyond the academy and to become the religion also of the Republic. It was not only intended to stand above the fray by embodying what the several religious sects had in common; it was also expected simultaneously to undermine the authority of the individual sects by showing them to be irrational. Otherness would eventually be overcome through the totalization of reason.

---

[31] Merrill D. Peterson, *Thomas Jefferson and the New Nation* (New York, 1970), p. 958.
[32] See Michael J. Buckley, *At the Origins of Modern Atheism* (New Haven, 1987), and Alan Charles Kors, *Atheism in France, 1650–1729*, vol. 1: *The Orthodox Sources of Disbelief* (Princeton, 1990).

This would be enabled through the guarantee of religious liberty expressed in the Virginia Statute and, later, the US Constitution. Jefferson seems to have held that in a society where all religious groups had equal protection of the law and, therefore, equal access to the market place, citizens would through the exercise of free choice always choose the sect that is highest in rationality. Market forces would thereby eliminate faulty goods, thus driving rationally defective religions out of business.[33]

It may show how little Jefferson understood the cultural values of a consumer society, if he thought that by allowing all religious sects free access to the public market, market forces would squeeze out faulty goods. But that is not the point I wish to press just here.

The second paradox of Jefferson's public policy in respect to religion arises from the fact that this universal, rational religion which, in contrast to religion's more local expressions, was regarded as fit for the academy is in fact identical to Jefferson's own personal religious preference.[34] That is to say, in the Jeffersonian project, public policy and private commitment finally coincide.

Jefferson was a very private man in all respects, but especially in respect to the expression of his own religious views. As he put it in response to the curious who enquired after his beliefs, his views on religion were between him and his God and concerned no one else: 'Our particular principles of religion are a subject of accountability to our god alone. I enquire after no man's, and trouble none with mine.'[35] They may have concerned no one else, but he confided them nonetheless at great length in correspondence addressed to close friends, becoming less discreet as he became older. Jefferson was born an Anglican and died one, his final words being from the *nunc dimittis*: 'Lord, now lettest thou thy servant depart in peace.'[36] His private beliefs, however, were rather nearer to what we have come to associate in the Church of England today with some Bishops than with lay parliamentarians.

Jefferson has been described, not inaccurately, as a 'demythologized Christian'.[37] Although he believed in God as Creator and providential agent, he rejected the Trinity, all claims to the Divinity of Christ, miracles, prophecies and such. But he did believe in the eternal life of

---

[33] See, e.g., *Writings*, pp. 285f.   [34] See Healey, *Jefferson on Religion*, pp. 114ff., 252f.
[35] Thomas Jefferson to Miles King, 26 September 1814.
[36] See Sanford, *The Religious Life*, p. 3.
[37] Eugene R. Sheridan, 'Introduction', in *Jefferson's Extracts from the Gospels*, ed. Dickinson W. Adams (Princeton, 1983), p. 39.

the self in the presence of God. The mission of Jesus was to restore natural religion, not to found a new sect. And the moral code of Jesus, as well as his teachings about God and the soul, if shorn of the distortions by the gospel editors, conform wholly to natural religion: namely, there is one God, who is all perfect; there is a future state of rewards and punishments; and the sum of religion is to love God and one's neighbour as oneself.[38]

His views on religion were far from original and conformed closely to radical religious writing of his day. Although his opinions in such matters were influenced by the English deists and by the French philosophes,[39] through the writings of his friend Joseph Priestley in particular he came to be persuaded of the truth of Unitarian Christianity,[40] and might well have associated himself with that group had there been such a community in Virginia.[41]

Unitarianism, he was convinced, embodied the truth of Jesus' teachings and, therefore, conformed to natural religion.[42] It would, he fully expected, eventually become the religion of the Republic.

Viewing the bitter Calvinist–Unitarian controversy of New England from the comfortable distance of more worldly Virginia, Jefferson foresaw the irresistible victory of Unitarianism over all Trinitarian forms of Christianity. The Trinity had become a normative Christian belief, he was convinced, not by its being contained in the teachings of Jesus or by the force of reason, but by the 'sword of civil government'. Once religion was divorced from civil authority (as it had been in America), he reasoned, the primitive Unitarian faith of Christianity would as a matter of law-like necessity reassert itself.

He made this claim in 1822 in a private letter, to which he added, 'I confidently expect that the present generation will see Unitarianism become the general religion of the United States.'[43] A similar link between religious liberty and the ascendancy of Unitarian Christianity had been made a few months earlier in another private letter:

[38] Thomas Jefferson to Benjamin Waterhouse, 26 June 1822; Thomas Jefferson to William Baldwin, 19 January 1810. See also Jefferson's 'Syllabus of an Estimate of the Merit of the Doctrines of Jesus Compared with those of Others', in Adams, ed., *Jefferson's Extracts*, pp. 332–6.

[39] See, e.g., the entries in *Jefferson's Literary Commonplace Book*, ed. Douglas L. Wilson (Princeton, 1989).

[40] Concerning Priestley's influence on Jefferson, see Sheridan, 'Introduction', in Adams, ed., *Jefferson's Extracts*, pp. 14ff.

[41] So speculates Sanford, *The Religious Life*, p. 6. See also Thomas Jefferson to Benjamin Waterhouse, 19 July 1822 and 8 January 1825.

[42] Thomas Jefferson to Benjamin Waterhouse, 22 June 1822.

[43] Thomas Jefferson to James Smith, 8 December 1822.

Had the doctrines of Jesus been preached always as purely as they came from his lips, the whole civilised world would now have been Christian. I rejoice that in this blessed country of free enquiry and belief, which has surrendered its creed and conscience to neither kings nor priests, the genuine doctrine of one only God is reviving, and I trust that there is not a *young man* [*sic!*] now living in the U.S. who will not die an Unitarian.[44]

His confident predictions about the future religious preferences of the Republic turn out to be no more reliable than were his equally confident predictions that no American would ever choose to live in Europe! But the accuracy of Jefferson as prophet is not what interests us about his private comments on the future prospects of Unitarianism.

What interests us here is the conformity of Jefferson's private views on Unitarianism and his public policy toward the sort of non-sectarian religious discourse fit for the academy. It becomes clear that the vision of universal, tradition-free natural religion, which is supposed to be above all particularities and attain through reason a kind of objectivity, is in fact none other than a secularized form of Christianity and more narrowly in this case of liberal Protestantism. If large numbers of people both in America and in Europe were persuaded that philosophical theism expressed the universal 'natural religion' it purported to express, rather than being the quasi-Christian construction it was, this may have been because European and American society at the time was religiously so homogeneous, despite its sectarian rivalries.[45]

That was then, but this is now.

Yet many philosophers of religion continue to conduct business in the same terms. They speak, for example, of 'God' as if such were self-evidently a key concept for all religions or as if a generic concept of God were sufficient to cover all cases; they speak of the 'immortality of the soul' as if it were self-evident that all religious people believed they had

---

[44] Thomas Jefferson to Benjamin Waterhouse, 26 June 1822.

[45] Although it has become fashionable to read 'pluralism' (religious and ethnic) back into early American experience, in order to underscore that America has been a pluralist society from the start, it is important not to lose sight of the fact that the kind of religious pluralism that exercised Thomas Jefferson and his contemporaries at the close of the eighteenth century was in fact the pluriformity of Christianity and, more accurately, the proliferation of competing Protestant groups [see Healey, *Jefferson on Religions*, pp. 265f.]. According to the best statistics available, almost 90 per cent of the citizens of the United States circa 1800 who belonged to a religious community identified themselves with some Protestant group. About 10 per cent were Roman Catholics and only 0.5 per cent were Jewish. If we focus more narrowly on the Virginia of Thomas Jefferson, we find only competing Protestant groups represented in any significant numbers. At the turn of the century, there was not one Roman Catholic church within the Commonwealth of Virginia and the nearest Jewish congregations were in Philadelphia to the north and Charleston to the south. See Edwin Scott Gaustad, *Historical Atlas of Religion in America*, 2nd edn (New York, 1976).

souls and that securing their immortality were for them the *summum bonum* of life. There is then in much recent philosophy of religion a tendency to speak of a narrow range of parochial topics that are presumed to be 'universal' religious problems, a preoccupation with rational justifi cation of putatively foundational religious claims and a neglect of more typical uses of argument in religious contexts.

All these things can be said to betray the extent to which modern philosophy of religion continues to be a construction of the European Enlightenment and the extent to which it is anachronistically tied to an older, culturally less pluralistic social circumstance in which the different religious communities actually present were largely varieties of the same religious tradition, sharing a common narrative, even if they were disposed to read it differently.

In such a circumstance, it may be understandable and may even have been responsible for philosophy to try to offer a framework in which matters of religious consensus can be expressed and debated. At its best, the Enlightenment provided for its time a public discourse in which religious claims could be clarified and contested.

But in a time, such as ours, of more radical pluralism, what sort of job is it reasonable for philosophy of religion to try to do? *This* is the question toward which I am wanting us to move. And to make that move, I suggest that we leave the Virginia to which my forebears sailed at the end of the eighteenth century and return to the Britain to which a family of their descendants set sail in the world-eventful year of 1968.

The Britain we found – I almost said *discovered*! – was adjusting (as it still is) to being a more pluralistic society than any previous generation could have imagined. Workers from mainly 'New' Commonwealth countries began arriving after the War. They brought with them, not only their much-needed economic skills, but also their traditions and values. And there came into Britain religious groups not previously represented here on so large a scale, especially Muslims, Hindus and Sikhs.[46]

June and I arrived in Britain only months after the infamous speech given in Birmingham by Enoch Powell that ended with the paragraph beginning with the chilling words, 'Like the Roman, I seem to see "the River Tiber foaming with much blood".'[47] By good fortune, Powell's

---

[46] See *The British: Their Religious Beliefs and Practices 1800–1986*, ed. Terence Thomas (London, 1988).

[47] The text of that and other speeches of Powell from the period were published and analysed in Bill Smithies and Peter Fiddick, *Enoch Powell on Immigration* (London, 1969). For the text of Powell's Birmingham speech, see pp. 35–43.

apocalyptic vision of 1968 has not been realized in *fin-de-siècle* Britain, but events in lands not that far from here should remind us that xenophobia is an evil power that no people can presume to have exorcized.

The 1960s were also a time when main-line Christian churches were in sharp decline in Britain. Theologians, no less than sociologists, were convinced that secularization was inevitable and irreversible. That confidence may have been shaken a little elsewhere,[48] but statistics still record a steady decline in church membership in Britain.[49] By 1970, the percentage of the adult population belonging to a Christian church had dwindled to just over 20 per cent; by 1990, it had declined a further 5 per cent.[50]

For this reason, I would argue, the influx into Britain of people from Asia, Africa and the Caribbean has had a much greater impact on the specifically *religious* profile of British society than it has had on the broader *ethnic* profile.

The combination of new religious groups entering the population and the decline of traditional religious groups within the existing population has generated a religiously more variegated landscape in the United Kingdom. In 1970, for instance, there were sixteen adult Christians for every adult member of a non-Christian religious group in the United Kingdom. By 1990, the ratio had been reduced to four to one. By the end of the decade, it could become a little less than three to one.

Historically, the main non-Christian religious group in Britain has been Judaism. But there are now twice as many Sikhs and Hindus as there are Jews in the UK. And according to the best statistics available to us, it would appear that there are now roughly ten times as many Muslims as there are Jews. Moreover, there are already more Muslims than Methodists in the UK. And by the end of the decade there may be more Muslims than Reformed Christians (which includes the United Reformed Church in England, the Church of Scotland, and the Presbyterians of Wales and Northern Ireland).

---

[48] Compare Phillip Hammond, ed., *The Sacred in a Secular Age* (Berkeley, 1985) with Steve Bruce, ed., *Religion and Modernization* (Oxford, 1992).

[49] See A. H. Halsey, ed., *British Social Trends since 1900*, 2nd edn (Basingstoke, 1988), table 13.13, p. 540. These statistics, gathered by Peter Brierley, may be 'softer' than one might wish, but they are the best available to us at the moment.

[50] See Peter Brierley, ed., *UK Christian Handbook 1989–90* (London, 1988), table 6a, p. 144. Wide variations are shown, however, among the several parts of the United Kingdom: in England, 11 per cent of adults belong to a Christian church; in Wales, 22 per cent; in Scotland, 32 per cent; but in Northern Ireland, 75 per cent. See also table 10, p. 150. For more up-to-date statistics relating to England only and their analysis, see Peter Brierley, *'Christian' England: What the English Church Census Reveals* (London, 1991).

Even if these projections should turn out to be a bit wide of the mark, however, religious pluralism in Britain is already a fact, and its practical effects are only beginning to be felt, not least in discussions about religious education. If I may be allowed to make a strategic point about my own department: it is likely that the kind of Religious Studies pioneered at Lancaster is going to be even more important nationally in the next twenty-five years than it has been in the past twenty-five.

But what demands, if any, does this new circumstance in British society make on the practice of the philosophy of religion? It would be easy enough to protest that the agenda of a discipline should be determined by the requirements of the discipline itself, not by social or political circumstance. In the case of a subject area like Religious Studies, however, pluralism is already an item of agenda in that the diversity of religious traditions is its proper object of study. And what of the philosophy of religion in particular?

I have already suggested that the Enlightenment enterprise, of which modern philosophy of religion is a lingering reminder, ends in a paradox created by its own foundationalist pretensions to speak with a universal and neutral voice, when its tone is more nearly parochial and partisan. I have also suggested that the Enlightenment attempted to deal with pluralism by privatizing particular interests and commitments, so that public space was a realm of consensus. But precisely just such a consensus is what is lacking in a religiously pluralistic context, where the individual traditions share no common narrative structure.

Some would make it the task of philosophy of religion in such a circumstance to set about establishing a new consensus within pluralism, and to do so in much the same liberal spirit as the Jeffersonian project, namely, by denying that differences ultimately matter.

They may seek to do so by claiming that all religions worship or contemplate the same Ultimate Reality, that they represent different paths to the same final goal. The British philosopher John Hick is a forceful advocate of this sort of response to religious pluralism.[51] However attractive it may at first seem, it raises problems similar to those raised in its earlier Enlightenment incarnation.

Religions are not just different ways of worshipping or contemplating the same Ultimate Reality. What is experienced as 'Ultimate' is specific to the tradition concerned. But Hick wants to claim that all religions

---

[51] Hick's philosophically most refined defence of this thesis may be found in his Gifford Lectures, *An Interpretation of Religion: Human Responses to the Transcendent* (London, 1989).

experience in worship or contemplation the same Ultimate Reality, however diverse the doctrinal schemes in which that experience is embedded.
At one level, he allows, Ultimate Reality may be variously experienced
within individual traditions as one or many, personal or impersonal,
simple or complex; but at a deeper level of understanding, he insists, it
must be one and the same Reality, since there is only one Ultimate. But to
claim, as Hick seems to claim, that what all religions experience as
Ultimate must be the same Ultimate Reality is to be guilty of what
logicians call a 'quantifier-shift' fallacy.

To explain what is meant by such a fallacy, I offer this example: from
the claim that everyone loves someone, it does not follow that everyone
loves the same person. If we add to this that everyone experiences the
love of their life as the most wonderful person in the world, it still would
not follow that everyone loves the same person, since regarding one's
beloved as 'the most wonderful person in the world' is itself part of what
it means to be in love. By the same reasoning, from the claim that
everyone is ultimately concerned about something, it does not follow
that everyone is Ultimately concerned about the same thing. Likewise,
from the claim that all religions worship or contemplate what they
conceive and experience as Ultimate Reality, it does not follow that they
worship or contemplate, experience or conceive, the same Reality.

Nor are religions just different paths to a same goal; they are different
paths to different goals. The goal aimed at is as tradition-specific as the
path taken. The goal is constituted as goal by the path chosen. It is the
tradition followed that allows the practitioner to recognize the goal as
goal.

Suppose a devout Buddhist monk, having been guided all his life by the
precepts of the *Visuddhimagga*, finds that upon having reached the final
jhana, he has contrary to all expectation not passed 'beyond nothing
whatever' to dwell in 'the attainment of neither perception nor non-
perception', but has been treated instead to a vision of the love of the
Triune God or of the Muslim heaven with all its physical delights or of
'the celestial city', of which John Hick wrote so fondly in an earlier
incarnation.[52]

Such a vision may be thought to be highly unlikely, if not culturally
impossible. But, for the sake of argument, let us assume that it did occur.
If so, it would not be recognized *by a Theravadin* as the goal. It would

---

[52] See *Faith and Knowledge* (London, 1957), pp. 177ff.

more nearly be taken as a sign that something must have gone badly wrong. 'The Path of Purity' has efficacy if and only if it leads to precisely the goal toward which it is directed, that is, to the goal that is identified as such by Theravada.

The goal for a Theravadin is to find release from the round of existence by achieving liberation in *nibbana*; for a Muslim, to gain entry as a resurrected body into a material heaven with physical rewards and pleasures; for an Advaita Vedantin, to be reabsorbed as self (*atman*) into Brahman. To limit comment to just these examples: the third one entails the return of the spiritual self to the Whole from whence it originated; the second entails the preservation of the self in its physical identity; and the first entails the continuation of no self at all.

These are hardly the same goals. The three possibilities cited do not all entail *selves* in the same sense, do not all engender *transformations* in the same sense, do not all embody *Reality* in the same sense. To practitioners of the three religious traditions used to illustrate difference, these are not incidental differences, differences that might be set aside as a way of winning the consensus required as the cost of admission to public space; it is, rather, just such differences that finally matter to them – and it should be just such differences that interest also the philosopher of religion!

This may seem to lead us in the direction of Wittgensteinian language games, which might be thought to offer a way of preserving just such differences in virtue of recognizing the idiosyncrasy of particular religious traditions. But this is done at the cost of giving up the possibility of the public contestability of their claims. According to at least some versions of this style of philosophy, there can be neither agreement nor disagreement between (say) a 'theist' and an 'atheist' or between people belonging to different religious traditions, since they are not *playing the same game* or even *inhabiting the same world* (to use the long-familiar rhetoric of Wittgensteinian-speak).

Although I do not think that *this* is the way to be taken by philosophy of religion in a religiously pluralistic society, I do not want to belittle the gains of Wittgensteinian philosophy of religion. To my mind, the principal philosophical gain was its having reminded us, on the one hand, that religious language has a wide variety of uses besides making cognitive claims and its having given us new sensitivity, on the other hand, to the importance of context when interpreting even cognitive claims. That is to say, in having shown us that religious claims cannot be isolated from their context and that this context includes the spiritual practices with which they are associated, as well as the doctrinal schemes in which the claims are made, and in terms of which they have the meaning they have.

But much Wittgensteinian philosophy of religion can be viewed in retrospect as having adopted a strategy of retrenchment – that is, one of creating a protected space for religious claims at a time when the dominant religious group in this country felt increasingly beleaguered by the forces of secularization. In effect, this strategy privatized religious discourse by isolating such discourse from *public* contestability. In spite of philosophical gains, it has had the effect of marginalizing religion still further within public space.

Our present circumstance, however, is arguably defined at least as much by steadily increasing religious pluralism as it is by the progress of secularization. And *in such a circumstance,* the withdrawal into self-contained 'language games' has more radical social consequences. If carried out consistently across all distinct religious communities, it would engender a plurality of religious enclaves, immune both from public scrutiny and from engagement with other religious groups. Such a direction would be as impoverishing spiritually as it would be worrying politically.

The otherness of the Other must be protected, by every means, but not at the price of abandoning public contestability of religious claims, whether of a cognitive or of an ethical kind. The consequences of the Wittgensteinian approach, therefore, are almost an inversion of those of the Enlightenment project. The one preserves particularity and difference, but at the expense of public contestability; the other preserves public contestability, but at the expense of particularity and difference. Is it possible to combine public contestability and respect for particularity and difference? Not, I believe, unless we can relocate the place of the Other in the philosophy or religion.

Neither a Jeffersonian project nor a Wittgensteinian 'game' requires the presence of the Other for its undertaking. The first one makes the Other invisible by rising above differences in an effort to occupy neutral ground in which otherness is overcome by Utopian reason, whereas the second makes the Other invisible by self-enclosure behind the walls of its own particularity.

A different kind of model for philosophy, one in which the Other is neither made invisible nor just tolerated, can be found – I believe – in the classical Indian *vada*-tradition of philosophical contest or public debate. And this model, I will try to suggest briefly, may point us in more promising directions than those paths we have been strolling along since at least the European Enlightenment.

I am not, of course, suggesting that India has *solved* (if that is the right word) the 'problem of pluralism'. No one who reads the newspapers could want to claim *that*. We must be careful not to idealize the Indian tradition, either in the manner of that long line of Europeans who have in hopeful expectation turned their eyes eastward at times of cultural pessimism in the West or in the manner of those Hindu thinkers who beginning about a century ago attempted with some success to export neo-Vedantan philosophy to the West as if Vedanta alone had the right to represent the spiritual and intellectual traditions of India.

Although we must take care not to idealize the distant Other, there is no reason why the excesses of past enthusiasms should prevent our accepting help wherever it may be found in an effort to adapt our understanding of the philosophical task to the more pluralistic circumstance in which we now practise our craft. And it must be allowed that India has longer and more sustained experience of religious pluralism than have most lands.

The Indian *vada*-tradition, which stretches back to before the beginning of the Common Era, is rooted in methods of Brahmanic instruction and discussion about the meaning of Vedic ritual texts, but it developed over time into a public forum for contesting the claims of competing viewpoints in religious philosophy.[53] Indeed, one way to tell the tale is to say that the competing philosophical *darsanas* or 'perspectives' were themselves a result of the enhanced precision and discrimination that these debates encouraged, just as individual concepts and doctrines were made more precise in and through public debate.[54]

In any given debate, there were of course a winner and a loser, but in the long run the debates contributed to a sharpening of boundaries between the emerging perspectives. We can say that the philosophical perspectives constructed themselves through debate.

---

[53] Regarding that development, see, *inter alia*, Erich Frauwallner, *Nachgelassene Werke*, 1 (Vienna, 1984); J. C. Heesterman, 'On the Origins of the Nastika', *WZKSO* 12/13 (1968/1969), 171–85; David P. Jackson, ed., *The Entrance Gate for the Wise: Sa-skya Pandita on Indian and Tibetan Traditions of Pramana and Philosophical Debate*, 2 vols. (Vienna, 1987); Bimal Krishna Matilal, *Logic, Language and Reality: An Introduction to Indian Philosophical Studies* (Delhi, 1985); Michael Torsten Much, *Dharmakirtis Vadanyayah*, 2 vols. (Vienna, 1991); Gerhard Oberhammer, 'Ein Beitrag zu den Vada-Traditionen Indiens', *WZKSO* 7 (1963), 63–103; Esther A. Solomon, *Indian Dialectics: Methods of Philosophical Discussion*, 2 vols. (Ahmedabad, 1976–8); Giuseppe Tucci, *Pre-Dinnaga Buddhist Texts on Logic from Chinese Sources* (repr. Madras, 1981); Alex Wayman, 'The Rules of Debate according to Asanga', *JAOS* 78 (1958), 29–40; Michael Witzel, 'The Case of the Shattered Head', *Studien zur Indologie und Iranistik* 13 (1987), 363–415.

[54] See, e.g., George Chemparathy, 'Two Early Buddhist Refutations of the Existence of Isvara as the Creator of the Universe', *WZKSO* 12/13 (1968–9), 85–100.

We have a record of that process, albeit an imperfect and incomplete one, in the form of doxographical treatises written at different times from the point of view of individual *darsanas*, epitomizing the central teachings and standard arguments of their own and opposing schools.[55] They were compiled, it would seem, as primers for those who engaged in debate to ensure that members of their own school had sufficient knowledge of the main claims and arguments of other schools on topics that might arise, so that they could defend their own position effectively against attack and so that they could in turn attack their opponents at what (from their own school's perspective) appeared to be their weakest point.

The preparation of such primers, however, required the different schools to think more systematically about their own positions on the main topics of philosophy and also to think more systematically about their opponents' positions. What emerged was an increasingly well-developed articulation of the various philosophical positions, each carried out from the perspective of a different school.

From this process emerged a clearer conception of the nature of differences between the individual schools that had survived the pressures of debate. Not all had survived having their basic claims publicly contested, and some schools grew gradually together until they finally merged. The eventual result was a determinate set of perspectives acknowledged as worthy opponents in debate.[56] Philosophical contests were thus tradition-*constituting*. By means of public debate, rationality constructed itself.

---

[55] An early, if not the earliest, extant characterization of different philosophical schools in India dates from some time before the fourth century CE: *The Kautiliya Arthasastra*, ed. and trans. by R. P. Kangle (Bombay, 1963). But the earliest known doxography in the proper sense of giving a systematic presentation of determinate philosophical systems would appear to be contained in a Buddhist text composed in the sixth century. [See Olle Qvarnström, *Hindu Philosophy in Buddhist Perspective: The Vedantatattvaviniscaya Chapter of Bhavya's Madhyamakahrdayakarika* (Lund, 1989).] Other important doxographies are Haribhadra's *Saddarsanasamuccaya*, a compact Jaina text from the eighth century; the *Sarvasiddhantasangraha*, a Vedantin text attributed to Sankara, but more likely dating from the eleventh century; the *Mkhas jug*, a thirteenth-century work composed by the great Tibetan Buddhist Sa-Skya Pandita, more commonly called Sa-pan; Madhava's *Sarvadarsanasangraha*, a well-known Vedantin text from the fourteenth century; and Madhusudana-Saravati's *Prasthanabheda*, another Vedantin text originating in all likelihood in the seventeenth century. What we learn about the construction of the Indian philosophical tradition from these doxographies is supplemented also by a number of related philosophical texts containing apologetic accounts of the author's own and polemical accounts of rival philosophical schools. In some ways the most impressive of such works is the massive *Nyayamanjari* by the ninth-century Naiyayika logician Jayanta Bhatta, who – according to his son, Abhinanda – had the gift of the blarney. The English translation of the first volume of the *Nyayamanjari* runs to 914 pages!

[56] Sa-pan makes this point explicitly in his *Mkhas jug*. See *The Entrance Gate for the Wise*, II, pp. 340ff.

But the conduct of public debates was also tradition-*constituted*, in the sense that reasons could be given during a disputation that were reasons for one's own school, even when they were not also reasons for members of the opponent's school. It may help if I give an example to illustrate both the structure of the debate and the way that tradition-specific reasoning could be introduced into an inter-traditional debate.

Buddhists and orthodox Hindus disagreed about the nature of the self.[57] Both believed (as did almost all religious groups in India) in the doctrine of rebirth, but they did not agree about its nature and mechanics. The orthodox Hindus held that the self is eternal substance and that this self is successively reborn, but the Buddhists had a 'bundle-theory' of the self and held that rebirth somehow occurs without anything transmigrating.[58]

The nature of the self, therefore, was a frequent topic of disputation between Hindu and Buddhist logicians. An eleventh-century Hindu logician named Udayana has left us a treatise on the nature of the self which can be read as an epitome of the most successful debating points to be made on behalf of the orthodox Hindu position.[59]

The treatise divides naturally into two main parts, as would a philosophical disputation in India, the one *negative* and the other *positive* in purpose. Negatively, one must undermine the opponent's position; positively, one must offer separate arguments for one's own position. Only if both tasks are successfully completed could one be declared the winner of a philosophical contest.

There were clear conventions about what were allowed to count as reasons in the conduct of each half of the debate. In the negative half, one was required to give a fair statement of the opposing position, the arguments in its favour, and the arguments that can be used against it. In prosecuting this task, one could only use reasons that were acknowledged as reasons for the opponent's *darsana*. Although one could not cite the authoritative scriptures of one's own tradition (unless they were also authoritative for the opponent), one could cite the opponent's scriptures, if it could be shown – for instance – that the opponent's position is

---

[57] For a philosophically rigorous analysis of the issues involved in their disagreement about the self, see Claus Oetke, *'Ich' und das Ich: Analytische Untersuchungen zur buddhistisch-brahmanischen Atmankontroverse* (Stuttgart, 1988).

[58] See, for instance, Nagasena's classic attempt to explain this peculiarly Buddhist doctrine of rebirth to King Milinda in the *Milindapanha*.

[59] Part one of Udayana's *Atmatattvaviveka* has been edited and translated by Chitrarekha V. Kher and Shiv Kumar (Delhi, 1987). For a summary of Udayana's treatise, see Karl H. Potter, ed., *The Encyclopedia of Indian Philosophies*, II (Princeton and Delhi, 1977), pp. 526–57.

inconsistent with those scriptures. Even if one had demolished the opponent's case to the satisfaction of the judge, one could not be declared the outright winner of a debate unless positive proofs were put forward in support of one's own position.

Positive proofs might be based on reasons that were shared with one's opponent – such as an appeal to sense experience or to valid inference.[60] But positive proofs could all the same be based on tradition-specific reasons that were not acknowledged as reasons by one's opponent. Such tradition-specific reasons were not introduced in order to cut off debate or to assert their privileged authority. For they, too, were open to challenge from the outside. Although authoritative within one's own tradition, such grounds were not immune from public contestation.

In making his positive case, Udayana argued that the orthodox doctrine of the self could be proved from sense experience, from inference and from the testimony of Vedic scripture. A Buddhist could have accepted experience and inference as ways of coming to know something and, therefore, as grounds for claiming to know it. There were still sufficient differences between Buddhist and Naiyayika understandings of experience and inference to allow a lively debate within even those limits.[61] But a Buddhist could not in any circumstances have recognized an appeal to the testimony of Vedic scripture as a reason for believing that the self is eternal substance.

So Udayana set about establishing the authority of the Vedas in respect to the doctrine of the self. First, he argued, Vedic teaching about the self is internally consistent. A Buddhist might well have wanted to quibble about the consistency of the *atman* doctrine as it is found in the Vedas. But even if it were allowed that the Vedic teaching about *atman* is consistent, this would not be a reason *for a Buddhist* to accept the doctrine as true. Udayana claimed, secondly, that Vedic scriptures are trustworthy because they have a reliable author. This is one of the conventional reasons in support of any appeal to the authority of verbal testimony in Indian philosophy. But the Buddhists did not accept (or did not typically accept) that verbal testimony could have cognitive authority. They

---

[60] Of the publicly recognized *darsanas* in Indian philosophy, only the Carvaka or 'materialists' denied the validity of inference as a means of knowledge; and among the Carvaka, only some of them denied the reliability of sense experience. As it happens, the only extant text from this particular *darsana* expresses just such scepticism: see Eli Franco, *Perception, Knowledge and Disbelief: A Study of Jayarasi's Scepticism* (Stuttgart, 1987).

[61] See, e.g., the article on *anumanam* or 'inference' in Gerhard Oberhammer, ed., *Terminologie der frühen philosophischen Scholastik in Indien*, 1 (Vienna, 1991), pp. 43–60.

accepted only experience and inference as valid means of knowledge. Udayana added, finally, that the reliable author of the Vedic scriptures is none other than *Isvara*-God, whose existence is demonstrable by rational arguments.[62] But the Buddhists were not theists and did not accept as logically sound any possible argument for the existence of God.

The appeal to Vedic authority, therefore, is unlikely to have impressed any Buddhist opponent. And Udayana cannot realistically have expected by such arguments to convince a Buddhist of the truth of the orthodox position concerning the nature of the self or *atman*. But Udayana might well have expected by laying out so clearly the structure of the Hindu position thereby to give both his fellow Naiyayikas and their Buddhist opponents an understanding of the precise nature and grounds of their difference. By offering his tradition-specific reasons, however, he was not intending to cut off discussion; he was, instead, defining its grounds.

Although this brief account does justice neither to Udayana's treatise nor to the Indian debating tradition as such, it is I hope sufficient to show that a different model is at work here than the one at work in the European Enlightenment, as exhibited in 'the Jeffersonian project'. I would underscore four crucial points of difference between the Jeffersonian model with which we began and the Indian debating model I have just sketched:

1. In the Jeffersonian model, tradition-specific reasons have no place in public rationality. In the Indian model, tradition-specific reasons can have a place in public rationality: admission to public space is gained through contestability, not neutrality.
2. In the Jeffersonian model, universal reason is a 'given' and is just applied to particular cases. In the Indian model, reason constructs itself in and through its operations in public debate.
3. In the Jeffersonian model, the Other is not necessary for public rationality. In the Indian model, the Other is necessary in that it is through engagement that both the Self and the Other construct themselves.
4. In the Jeffersonian model, the end served by rational debate is the achievement of consensus. In the Indian model, the end served by rational debate is the clarification of difference.

---

[62] Each of the theistic proofs used by Udayana derives from a function of Siva within the Nyaya-Vaisesika system that he represented. For an account of the place of theistic argument within Udayana's philosophical strategy, see my 'Piety and the Proofs'. Editors' note: This appears as Chapter 6 of the present volume.

The direction in which this lecture has been leading points to the need for a reorientation of philosophy of religion, away from the pretension of reason's providing a common foundation for religious claims and toward the more modest aim of philosophy's providing a common discourse in which the nature of religious difference can be clarified.

In so doing, however, I obviously do not wish to rule out *a priori* the possibility of uncovering particular areas of convergence between religious traditions. I mean rather that the point of the exercise does not *require* there to be such convergences in order to justify the undertaking. It is not only the reaching of agreement that marks progress in discussion; progress can also be marked by a deeper understanding of the nature of difference.

However impressive its technical achievements, modern philosophy of religion remains rooted in the Enlightenment invention of natural religion and morality, the Enlightenment ideal of context-independent rationality, and the Enlightenment creation of a generic God. When taken together, these three comprise the foundations of 'theism', the religious faith for everyone and no one in particular.

Abstract nouns like 'religion', 'rationality' and 'theism' fit so *naturally* into philosophical discourse, we may be pardoned for forgetting that they are themselves *constructions of modernity* that are required and entailed by 'the Enlightenment project', which – as I have tried to show – ends in irony and paradox.

The project I would propose to put in its place requires a series of displacements in the philosophy of religion: in the place of religion, rationality and God, I would substitute *religions, reasons and Gods.*

Philosophical preoccupation with 'natural religion' would be displaced by interest in the variety of religious traditions in all their particularity.

Philosophical preoccupation with the abstract ideal of context-free rationality would be displaced by an examination of the concrete activity of giving reasons in specific religious contexts. Rationality constructs itself in its operations. In religious traditions, one way to get at the operations of rationality is to look at what count as reasons when their claims are contested. This entails also tracing the ends served by religious argument: the point of an argument is shown by what it is used to do.

Philosophical devotion to the generic God of 'theism' would be displaced by closer attention to the place and nature of gods in religious traditions. Not only do gods come in all shapes and sizes, some with determinate properties and others with no properties at all, but gods also play different roles in different traditions. In some cases, they may play no religiously important role at all. When I speak of 'gods', therefore, I do so in the spirit of the Texas Securities Act, as amended 1975:

If the sense requires it: words in the present tense include the future tense; in the masculine gender include the feminine and neuter gender; in the singular number include the plural number; and in the plural number include the singular number; 'and' may be read 'or' and 'or' may be read 'and'.[63]

In this lecture, I have been looking from a variety of different angles at the importance of context, including the philosopher's own context. Not all things are appropriate to all times; not every project can be undertaken in every circumstance.

Academic projects, like the academic disciplines themselves, are enabled or hindered by the institutional structures in which they are undertaken. *What sort of institutional context is required for the sort of project I have been commending to you in this lecture?*

First, it would need to be an institution that attaches at least as much importance to freedom of conscience in religious matters as that enshrined in the Virginia Statute for Religious Freedom or in its second cousin, twice removed (so to say), namely, Lancaster University's Royal Charter.

Secondly, it would need to be an institution in which the academic study of religion is itself well established as an inter-disciplinary and cross-cultural subject, one in which there are experts in every major religious tradition and in each academic method appropriate to their study, encompassing the social sciences as well as the humanities.

But religious studies cannot be just inward-looking. Nor can philosophy of religion *of the sort envisaged here* be undertaken in ignorance of developments in literary and social theory, gender studies and cultural analysis. It requires then, thirdly, an ambience that enables and nurtures scholarly interaction and co-operative enquiry among interested practitioners of the humanities and social sciences beyond the limits of their own departments, whose boundaries in any case are somewhat arbitrarily drawn.

In short, Vice-Chancellor, it would need to be an institution not unlike the University in which it is my privilege to profess the academic study of religion.

---

[63] Article 581–4(J), *Vernon's Annotated Texas Statutes.* I am grateful to my brother, the Hon. Judge Joe D. Clayton, for having supplied me with a copy of this legislation.

APPENDIX:[64]ENLIGHTENMENT, PLURALISM AND THE PHILOSOPHY OF RELIGION[65]

Public contestability and the construction of reason

Neither a Jeffersonian project nor a Wittgensteinian 'game' requires the presence of the Other for its undertaking. The first one makes the Other invisible by rising above differences in an effort to occupy neutral ground in which otherness is overcome by Utopian reason, whereas the second one makes the Other invisible by self-enclosure behind the walls of its own particularity. A different kind of project for philosophy, one in which the Other is neither made invisible nor just tolerated, is suggested by the classical Indian *vada*-tradition of philosophical contest or public debate.

Can this 'pre-modern' tradition (or, more accurately, confluence of traditions[66]) point us in more promising directions than those paths we have been strolling along in relative comfort since at least the European Enlightenment? When 'read' in a particular way, I believe it can. But we must proceed with caution. I am certainly not wanting to suggest that India has *solved* (if that is the right word) the 'problem of pluralism'. No one who reads the newspapers could want to claim *that*. Nor am I wanting to suggest that indigenously Indian religious traditions are intrinsically more 'tolerant' than are predominantly Western religious traditions. Indeed, using the word 'toleration' in this context is itself problematic.[67] We must be careful not to idealize the Indian tradition,

---

[64] Editors' note: Clayton specified that the second portion of this essay ('Enlightenment, Pluralism and the Philosophy of Religion') be published as an appendix to the lecture entitled 'Thomas Jefferson and the Study of Religion'.

[65] Originally given as lectures at the University of Munich and at the Free University in Amsterdam. It was written during my tenure as a Visiting Fellow at Emmanuel College, Cambridge, and incorporates research undertaken during two extended visits working in Vienna. For their hospitality and helpfulness, I am indebted to Professor Gerhard Oberhammer and his colleagues in the Institute of Indology at the University of Vienna and in the Institut für Kultur- und Geistesgeschichte Asiens at the Austrian Academy of Sciences. I am also grateful to the British Academy for their continued support of the research programme of which this essay forms a part, and to the Master and Fellows of Emmanuel College for their having elected me to the Quatercentenary Visiting Fellowship for the Michaelmas Term 1992.

[66] See Oberhammer, 'Ein Beitrag zu den Vada-Traditionen Indiens', 63–103, and Solomon, *Indian Dialectics*.

[67] Cf. Paul Hacker, 'Religiöse Toleranz und Intoleranz in Hinduismus', *Saeculum* 8 (1957), 167–79, and Albrecht Wezler, 'Zur Proklamation religiös-weltanschaulicher Toleranz bei den indischen Philosophen Jayantabhatta', *Saeculum* 27 (1976), 329–47. See also *Inklusivismus: eine indische Denkform*, ed. Gerhard Oberhammer, Publications of the De Nobili Research Library, Occasional Papers 2 (Vienna, 1983).

whether in the manner of that long line of Europeans who have in hopeful expectation turned their eyes eastward at times of cultural pessimism in the West or in the manner of those Hindu thinkers who beginning more than a century ago attempted to export neo-Vedantin philosophy to the West, as if Vedanta alone had the right to represent the intellectual and spiritual traditions of India.

Although we must take care not to idealize the distant Other, there is no reason why the excesses of past enthusiasms should prevent our seeking resources wherever they may be found in an effort to adapt our understanding of the philosophical task to the more pluralistic circumstance in which we increasingly now practise our craft. And it must be allowed that India has longer and more sustained experience of religious pluralism than have most lands. Indian pandits have for millennia lived permanently with something that has directly confronted philosophers only intermittently in traditionally Christian and Islamic lands. At such times when religious pluralism was a cultural fact in Islamic and Christian societies, a discourse for *inter*-traditional debate did begin to emerge, but its long-term development was cut short by changes in the political situation, resulting in the Other becoming 'invisible' in the public realm. In consequence, both *kalam* and scholasticism developed instead into conservative, *intra*-traditional discourses. The uninterrupted experience of religious difference in Indian cultural history, by contrast, both allowed and required the development of a dialectical tradition enabling participants in the diverse 'perspectives' – *astika* and *nastika* alike – publicly to dispute points of difference.

Indian debating traditions have their origins before the beginning of the Common Era. In Brahmanic circles, *vada* arose out of the question-and-answer methods of instruction in the meaning of Vedic ritual texts or metaphysical puzzles suggested by those texts.[68] There are several examples of this recorded in the Brahmanas and in the early Upanisads.[69] But none is more dramatic than the celebrated account of Gargi in book three of the Brhadaranyaka Upanisad. This remarkable woman not only asked a question beyond what her male interlocutors deemed her entitled to ask, but she found a clever way of raising the question again by appealing to male vanity, thereby finessing an answer even after she had

---

[68] See, e.g., J. C. Heesterman, 'On the Origins of the Nastika', *WZKSO* 12–13 (1968–9), 171–85, and Solomon, *Indian Dialectics*, pp. 21ff.

[69] See, e.g., Walter Ruben, 'Über die Debatten in den alten Upanisads', *ZDMG* 83 (1928), 238–55.

been formally cautioned to desist, a warning that could be ignored in normal circumstances only at the risk of forfeiting one's life.[70]

This, however, was not the only source of *vada*. It may have developed also from ancient Brahmanic methods of resolving legal disputes and from medical practitioners' methods of arriving at an agreed diagnosis or method of treatment.[71] In addition, philosophical dialectic had independent origins outside Brahmanic circles within Jaina and Buddhist groups, each of which had developed its own distinctive procedures and categories which eventually fed into the mainstream tradition of *vada*.[72] The Jaina *agamas* and the Buddhist *pitakas* abound in accounts of controversy within their circles concerning the correctness of rival doctrinal interpretations. Despite the warning ascribed to the Buddha in the Digha Nikaya and elsewhere against engaging in any doctrinal dispute that risks schism, the Buddhist contribution to the debating tradition through such eminent logicians as Vasubandhu, Dignaga and Dharmakirti proved decisive in transforming public philosophical disputes within India into a fairer and more rigorous forum for testing the truth-claims of competing *darsanas* or 'viewpoints'.[73]

Representatives of any philosophical perspective – Brahmanic, Buddhist or even Carvaka – had free access to that forum, providing they were willing to have their school's claims publicly challenged. *Contestability*, not (as in the Jeffersonian project) *neutrality*, was the price of admission to public space in the Indian *vada* tradition.

One way to tell the tale is to say that the several philosophical *darsanas* were themselves outcomes of the enhanced precision and discrimination that these debates encouraged, just as the distinctive doctrines of the individual groups were made more exact through being submitted to public scrutiny.[74] In any given debate, there were of course a winner

---

[70] See, e.g., Michael Witzel, 'The Case of the Shattered Head', *Studien zur Indologie und Iranistik* 13 (1987), 363–415.

[71] See Solomon, *Indian Dialectics*, pp. 71–100.

[72] See *ibid.*, pp. 30–63, as well as Oberhammer's 'Beitrag zu den Vada-Traditionen Indiens' mentioned above.

[73] See, e.g., Alex Wayman, 'The Rules of Debate according to Asanga', *JAOS* 78 (1958), 29–40; Giuseppe Tucci, *Pre-Dinnaga Buddhist Texts on Logic from Chinese Sources* (repr. Madras, 1981); Michael Torsten Much, *Dharmakirtis Vadanyayah*, vol. I: *Text*, Vol. II: *Übersetzung und Anmerkungen* (Österreichische Akademie der Wissenschaften, phil.-hist. Kl. Sb 581. Bd.); Jackson, ed., *The Entrance Gate for the Wise*. See also Bimal Krishna Matilal and R. D. Evans, eds., *Buddhist Logic and Epistemology* (Dordrecht, 1986).

[74] See, e.g, Chemparathy, 'Two Early Buddhist Refutations', Richard P. Hayes, 'Principled Atheism in the Buddhist Scholastic Tradition', *Journal of Indian Philosophy* 16 (1988), 5–28, and Gerhard Oberhammer, 'Zum Problem des Gottesbeweises in der indischen Philosophie', *Numen* 12 (1965), pp. 1–34.

and a loser. And opponents from different *darsanas* engaged in debate in order to defeat their opponents and to establish the superiority of their own perspective. To be defeated in an important debate involved loss of face and, depending on the wager, could have serious consequences. Some schools, most notably Nyaya, had the reputation of being ready to use any means, fair or foul, in order to win in debate.[75] However important winning was to those who engaged in debate, the long-term effect of the debating tradition was to firm up the differences between the emerging *darsanas* by sharpening up the boundaries between them. We might say that the several philosophical perspectives constructed themselves through debate.

We can gain at least some insight into how this occurred by examining the informal listings of *darsanas* scattered in ancient texts and by comparing the more systematic doxographies that were compiled from the point of view of the various *darsanas* as epitomes of the central teachings and standard arguments to be found within their own and rival perspectives. The earliest known list of philosophical schools, possibly dating from as early as the third or second century BCE, names just three: Samkhya, Yoga and Lokayata.[76] Only gradually did there emerge what we have grown used to finding named in modern textbooks of Indian philosophy as the 'classical' six *astika* systems of Nyaya, Vaisesika, Samkhya, Yoga, Mimamsa and Vedanta and the 'traditional' *nastika* systems of the Carvakas (or Lokayatikas), Jainas and Buddhists.[77] Most early Indian doxographies *do* show a marked preference for naming *six* systems, but they draw up different shortlists, according to their own perspectival interests. Why it was thought to be desirable for there to be just *six* to a set remains a mystery which we cannot hope to unravel here. Nor is it the most important issue for our needs: we want to discover how perspectival interests contributed to the way the proposed set, whatever its number,

---

[75] This view, frequently expressed in Buddhist sources, would seem to be confirmed to some extent by the fact that even a respected thinker like Jayanta could condone the use of 'dirty tricks' in order to avoid defeat in debate against skilled dialecticians from other schools whose victory might otherwise confuse and mislead the ignorant or the untrained. Jayanta Bhatta, *Nyayamanjari: The Compendium of Indian Speculative Logic*, trans. Janaki Vallabha Bhattacharyya (Delhi, 1978), pp. 21f.

[76] See the *Kautiliya Arthasastra*, ed. and trans. R. P. Kangle (Bombay, 1963), ch. II, §1, v. 10. But see also Paul Hacker, 'Anviksiki', *WZKSO* 2 (1958), 54–83.

[77] This construction of Indian philosophy became canonical in the West through the widespread influence of such surveys as F. Max Müller's *The Six Systems of Indian Philosophy* (London, 1899). It survives, sometimes with apologies, in standard introductions to Indian philosophy, including Ninian Smart's recently reissued *Doctrine and Argument in Indian Philosophy* (Leiden, 1992 [1st edn, London, 1964]).

was construed. This enquiry is made easier by the survival of a handful of doxographical treatises prepared from the point of view of the several *darsanas*. The oldest extant texts of this sort are Buddhist in origin,[78] but there are also others written from the perspective of the Jainas, Naiyayikas and pre-eminently that of the Vedantins.

Such doxographies were evidently used as primers for those who engaged in debate to ensure that members of their own school had sufficient knowledge of the main claims and arguments of other schools on topics that might arise, so that they could defend their own position effectively against attack and so that they could in turn attack their opponents at what (from their own school's perspective) appeared to be their weakest point. The preparation of such primers required the individual schools to think more systematically about their own positions on the main topics of philosophy and also to think more systematically about their opponents' positions. What eventually emerged was a well-developed statement of the various philosophical positions, each carried out from the perspective of a different school, and organized according to their distinctive doctrinal principles and debating strategies. The effect of this difference in perspective can be illustrated by reference to four representative doxographies, produced from the viewpoint of Nyaya, Jaina, Vedanta and Bauddha or 'Buddhism'.

1. Jayanta's *Nyayamanjari* provides a systematic account of the Nyaya system as it had developed by the tenth century and a polemical refutation of other recognized *darsanas* from a Nyaya standpoint. Jayanta seeks to legitimate Nyaya's place among the branches of Vedic science by showing that Nyaya is the only philosophical system able to establish through argument the authority of the Vedas. But he acknowledges that there are popularly thought to be *sattarki* or six systems of logic: Carvaka, Jaina, Bauddha, Samkhya, Mimamsa and Nyaya-Vaisesika. These I take to correspond to what Jayanta understood by the six *darsanas*. Not of course in the sense that a *darsana* can be reduced to *tarka*, but in the sense that each *darsana* must of necessity make use of logic when it engages in dialectic and debate, as they all did. But Nyaya alone has as its prime responsibility the justification of Vedic authority.

---

[78] Aryadeva's *Satasastra*, a polemical dialogue between a Buddhist and various 'unbelievers', was written some time before the fifth century CE [see Tucci, *Pre-Dinnaga Buddhist Texts on Logic*]. For an account of another early Buddhist doxography from the eighth century, see Olle Qvarnström, *Hindu Philosophy in Buddhist Perspective: The Vedantatattvaviniscaya Chapter of Bhavya's Madhyamakahrdayakarika* (Lund, 1989).

The *sattarki* are divided into two groups of three, according to their acceptance or rejection of the authority of Vedic scripture.[79] The three *avaidika* systems are dismissed out of hand as being unable to defend an authority they do not accept. Of the three *vaidika* systems, he says, neither Samkhya nor Mimamsa has more than the most superficial competence in logic. The Mimamsakas are in any case responsible for another branch of Vedic learning, the interpretation of ritual texts. They should stick to hermeneutics, he says, and leave apologetics to the Naiyayikas. For only they have the requisite skill in dialectic and argument to counter the corrosive effects of ignorance, doubt, error and bad judgment, by mounting an effective defence of the Vedic *sabda* against its enemies, whether the 'wretched' Carvaka or the 'arrogant' Buddhists, and against its inept defenders amongst the Samkhya and the Mimamsaka. Most of the more than nine hundred pages remaining in the first volume of the *Nyayamanjari* are given over to a polemical attack on rival views of logic, language and epistemology. At each turn Jayanta defines and defends the Nyaya position over against the positions adopted by the other five recognized *darsanas*.

2. In contrast to the Naiyayika Jayanta's massive *Nyayamanjari*, the Jaina Haribhadra's compact *Saddarsanasamuccaya* consists of fewer than two hundred lines in Sanskrit.[80] But within those two hundred lines, he manages without once wavering in his tone of fairness and objectivity to give an exact and balanced summary of the *darsanas* as they were viewed by him. As its title suggests, the compendium covers six systems of philosophy. Haribhadra's listing is similar to Jayanta's *sattarki*, except that he omits the Carvaka and treats the Nyaya and Vaisesika as separate schools.[81]

All six *darsanas* in Haribhadra's set, however, are regarded as *astika*, including not surprisingly his own system, the Jaina.[82] In practice, the term *nastika* is always used to designate some 'other' and is never used to

---

[79] See *Nyayamanjari*, pp. 4ff.

[80] Haribhadra, *Sad-Darsana Samuccaya: A Compendium of Six Philosophies*, ed. and trans. Satchidananda Murty, 2nd edn (Delhi, 1986).

[81] *Ibid.*, p. 3. The number six does not seem to be accidental. Having noted there was disagreement as to whether Vaisesika should be viewed separately from Nyaya, he says that if they should be counted together he would add to his list the Carvaka *in order to make up the six*. This seems to suggest that at least by Haribhadra's time a set of *sad-darsanas* was expected, even if there was no consensus as to *which six*. There are exceptions to the rule of six, most notably Madhava's well-known *Sarvadarsanasangraha*, which covers sixteen *darsanas*, thirteen of which would count as *astika* in the Brahmanic scheme.

[82] *Sad-Darsana Samuccaya*, p. 96.

describe the self. From Haribhadra's perspective, only the Carvaka are *nastika*. How does he construe the difference between *astika* and *nastika* systems of philosophy? As a member of an *avaidika* group, he is not likely to adopt the traditional Brahmanic principle of distinguishing *astika* from *nastika* according to their acceptance or repudiation of Vedic authority.[83] He adopts instead doctrinal principles that more nearly serve the interests of the Jainas.

According to Haribhadra, the wise measure difference between philosophical systems by examining their conceptions of divinity (*devata*)[84] and their understandings of the true path of liberation (*moksa*). He differentiates his six *astika* systems from each other by comparing their respective doctrines of divinity and liberation. But neither of these doctrines has any role at all in the Carvaka system, with the result that it falls outside the class of *astika* philosophies. Their being regarded as *nastika*, however, did not in this (or any other case) imply that the Carvaka were being excluded from participating in inter-darsanic debate. The Indian *vada* tradition was never in this sense exclusive. The line dividing *astika* from *nastika* was drawn variously by different *darsanas*, but it was always a distinction made *within* the circle of possible opponents in order to differentiate óne kind of worthy opponent from another, and not a line drawn *around* the circle of worthy opponents in order to exclude dissenting groups from access to public debate.

Nor did their being classed as *nastika* mean that the Carvaka were regarded by the Jaina Haribhadra as being devoid of all truth. The different perspectives developed individual strategies for dealing with the *nastika*. The Jainas (as well as the Advaitins) viewed the sum of *darsanas* as forming a hierarchy of truth. The individual *darsanas* were perceived by Haribhadra as participating partially in the highest truth, which was known fully in the Jaina system alone. As a debating strategy,

---

[83] Yet this criterion is more nearly pragmatic than substantive, since the Brahmanic *astika* did not all take that much heed of the Vedas. 'Même dans les domaines les plus orthodoxes', observed Louis Renou, 'il arrive que la révérence au Veda soit un simple "coup de chapeau", donné en passant à une idole dont on entend ne plus s'encombrer par la suite.' *Etudes védiques et paninéennes, Volume VI: Le destin du Véda dans l'Inde* (Paris, 1960), p. 2.

[84] He does not specify that the divinity must be a Creator God (*isvara*), since that would exclude the Jainas, who were in this sense non-theistic or, to use Zimmer's term, 'transtheistic'. The *devata* for the Jainas, according to Haribhadra, 'is the Master of Jainas, free from attachment and aversion; by whom was killed delusion, the great wrestler, who has absolute knowledge and perception; who is worthy of worship by the masters of Gods and demons; the teacher of things as they actually are; and who attained the highest end by destroying all *karmas* in their entirety'. *Sad-Darsana Samuccaya*, p. 60.

this would allow Haribhadra disarmingly to affirm his opponent's propositions as expressing limited truth, to be taken up and perfected within the Jaina system.

3. This kind of debating strategy is exhibited nowhere more cunningly than in the *Sarvasiddhantasamgraha*, a work traditionally ascribed to Sankara, but now thought to have been produced in the twelfth century by an unknown Advaitin.[85] Like Jayanta, he divides the *darsanas* into *astika* and *nastika*, depending upon whether the authority of the Vedas is affirmed or denied. These two groups are organized into two sets of six.[86]

The twelve systems are then arranged in ascending order, starting with the hapless Carvaka or, as they are here called, Lokayata. As he moves from one system to another, the author alters his perspective (in more than one sense!) and, writing often in the first person, speaks *as if* he were an adherent of whichever system was currently being refereed. He offers no external criticism of any system whilst representing its point of view. After taking up a new perspective, however, he would use that system's tenets to criticize a preceding system's views. So, the Carvakas are criticized from a Jaina perspective, which is then criticized from a Buddhist perspective, and it in turn from a Nyaya-Vaisesika standpoint, etc. By this means, he works his way progressively up the hierarchy of systems until he finally reaches Advaita Vedanta, the system which is supposed to possess all truth in perfect proportion.

Now it might be thought that this 'inclusivist' strategy of the Advaitins (and of the Jainas) is a counter-example to my claim that it is *difference* that is clarified through debate. After all, the Advaitin (and also Jaina) strategy is to claim that whatever portion of truth is found in any other philosophical system is taken up and embraced also by Advaita (or Jaina). But, paradoxically, this is precisely the difference between the Advaita Vedanta (or Jaina) and the 'other' perspectives: the Other has aspects of truth, whereas we alone possess truth in its fullness. And, moreover, one is left with a difficulty of incommensurability between *that* claim as it is made by a Jaina and that *same* claim as it is made by an Advaitin. But, that

---

[85] On the question of the authorship and date of the *Sarvasiddhantasamgraha*, scholars now follow Moriz Winternitz in his *Geschichte der indischen Litteratur*, III (Leipzig, 1922), p. 419. But M. Rangacarya, who translated the text into English (Madras, 1909), accepted the attribution to Sankara.

[86] The *astika* systems are traced back to the six traditional authors of the *sutra* texts in which Vedic authority is accepted; Aksapada (or Gotama), Kanada, Kapila, Jaimini, Vyasa, Patanjali [*Sarvasiddhantasamgraha* 1.23]. He arrives at six *nastika* systems by sub-dividing Buddhists into their four traditional schools and adding these to the Lokayatikas (or Carvakas) and the Jainas [IV.40].

said, it must be allowed that their difference in perspective on this point is something that each would have been willing to have contested publicly by the other or, for that matter, by any learned opponent.

4. From a Buddhist perspective, none of the above ways of construing *darsanas* would have been appropriate. Although different Buddhist pandits have proposed different schemata, I want here to mention only the way they were construed by the thirteenth-century Tibetan monk Sa-skya Pandita in his treatise *Mkhas jug*, part three of which is concerned with philosophical debate.[87] Those learned people worthy of engaging in debate are either Buddhists or adherents of one of five 'non-Buddhist sects': Mimamsa-Vedanta, Samkhya, Nyaya-Vaisesika, Jaina or Carvaka.[88] Although there were also other 'popular' sects in Tibet, they were not in Sa-pan's view 'worthy opponents' because they were not properly trained in epistemology, logic and the art of dialectic. These five recognized sects exhaust the philosophical possibilities outside Buddhism. Anyone who claims not to be speaking from one of *these* positions is either a representative without knowing it or someone without a coherent viewpoint.

In Sa-pan's construction, the consideration that binds together all 'non-Buddhist sectarians', and that also distinguishes them from Buddhists, is their belief in the existence of a 'self' or *atman*. But the 'sectarians' understand the self in two senses: Carvakas believe the self to exist only here and now and to be annihilated at death, whereas the other four sects believe the self to be eternal. The Buddhist no-self doctrine, so claims Sa-pan, enables one to negotiate a middle way through such 'sectarian' differences.

These four pandits, writing from different perspectives, vary not only in their darsanic loyalties, but also in the way they construe the set of *saddarsanas* and in the principles by which they define connections between one *darsana* and another. Jayanta distinguished systems by means of a formal criterion (place of the Vedas) and, amongst the Vaidika, by means of a functional criterion (responsibility for a Vedic science). Haribhadra, by contrast, used more nearly doctrinal criteria for differentiating one *darsana* from another. 'Pseudo-Sankara' ordered the *darsanas* hierarchically according to their approximation to the fullness of truth in Advaita Vedanta. And, finally, Sa-pan construes the difference between

[87] Jackson, ed., *The Entrance Gate for the Wise*, II, pp. 323ff. (s. n. 38).
[88] He actually calls them by the following names, which he then declares to be synonyms for the terms used above: Vaidika, Samkhya, Aulukya, Ksapanaka and Carvaka [II, pp. 344f.]. Buddhists are sub-divided into the four traditional Indian schools (Vaibhasika, Sautrantika, Yogacara, Madhyamaka) and then sub-divided again to arrive finally at *six* Buddhist schools [II, pp. 347f.].

Buddhist and non-Buddhist in terms of the doctrine of the self and arranges the Buddhist schools according to a hierarchy of spiritual attainment.

These four texts are no more than moments in a complex history. But they represent crystallizations of the grounds of difference as perceived from the standpoint of four disparate perspectives.

None of the *darsanas* was left unaffected by this extended process of polemic and debate. But each one was affected differently. At one time independent perspectives, Nyaya and Vaisesika moved toward each other until they finally merged, with the combined *darsana* integrating the logical and dialectical skills of the one with the 'realist' ontological commitments of the other. And the Naiyayikas, once non-theistic, became forceful apologists for what might be called somewhat anachronistically 'rational theism'.[89] At one time subsidiary to Mimamsa, Vedanta came to have a separate existence from what then came to be known as Purva-Mimamsa. And, as Vedanta became conceptually more variegated within and eventually acquired political advantage without, it assumed an increasingly prominent place in tractates displaying the *saddarsanas*.

Not all perspectives survived having their basic claims contested in debate. Although evidently regarded at the time of Kautiliya's *Arthasastra* as equal in standing to Samkhya and Yoga, the Carvaka may have failed to clear the hurdle of public contestability, surviving not in its own right as a living *darsana*, but only as a stereotyped image in the polemical texts of other *darsanas*.[90] Why, then, did it continue to be treated as a possible perspective even after it had ceased to be an active presence within Indian philosophy? Quite simply, I would venture to suggest, because the Carvaka represented a philosophical position that is not otherwise represented amongst the darsanic systems. Only the Carvaka represented materialism in ontology; only they rejected inference as a *pramana*; only they denied the cycle of rebirth and the moral basis of world order. In short, without

---

[89] For an analysis of contrasting spiritualities in non-theistic and theistic Nyaya, see Gerhard Oberhammer, *Wahrheit und Transzendenz. Ein Beitrag zur Spiritualität des Nyaya*, Österreichische Akademie der Wissenschaften, Sb. 424 (Vienna, 1984).

[90] 'Their position is far from being a living philosophical challenge to the authors of later times; it appears rather fossilised in its contents and argumentation. There is no "dialogue" between the materialists and their opponents. The criticism of the ideas of immortality and retribution, which are basic premises of the history of *karma*, is preserved by the tradition; but it is not much more than a relic from the distant past' [Wilhelm Halbfass, *Tradition and Reflection: Explorations in Indian Thought* (Albany, 1991), p. 293]. Even so, the *Tattvopaplavasimha*, apparently the only text written from a 'materialist' perspective to have survived, exhibits a polemical vigour suggesting that its author may well have been a formidable opponent in debate with his contemporaries in the eighth century. Franco, *Perception, Knowledge and Disbelief.*

the Carvaka the construction of philosophical systems would have been left unbalanced and incomplete.

And this gives us perhaps a clue to the way that the set of philosophical *darsanas* achieved its definitive shape. Each recognized *darsana* represents a possible point of view, without which the 'set' would have been incomplete. This explanation is made more plausible by Sa-pan's remarks cited above, to the effect that the traditional Indian *darsanas* exhaust the possibilities philosophically, so that everyone who holds a coherent position holds one of these positions, whether they know it or not. Given his views about the superiority of all Indian philosophical traditions to any Chinese or native Tibetan tradition, one cannot but suspect his motives in drawing a circle around meaningful discourse in so restrictive a way. But his remarks nonetheless offer an intriguing perspective on the construction given the *darsanas* within the Indian tradition. A perspective that may be reinforced if we look at them from another angle.

The sense of symmetry and balance in the set of possible *darsanas* is suggested also in the pattern that emerges in epistemology in respect of the recognized *pramanas* or ways of coming to know that p (or that $\sim p$) which, in turn, become grounds for claiming to know that p or that $\sim p$. It is usual in Indian texts to discuss six possible *pramanas*: namely, perception, inference, testimony, analogy, presumption and non-cognition. 'Non-cognition' here means that if none of the other five *pramanas* obtains in respect to a claim that p, then this is itself an additional reason for concluding that $\sim p$.

If we correlate the six possible *pramanas* with the recognized philosophical systems, a *pramana triangle* (as it might be called) comes into view (see Table 2.1).

Although reality was less tidy than this projection would make us believe, it may still lend some support to the view, fostered by Sa-pan, that the Buddhist and 'sectarian' perspectives collectively possess some kind of coherence, in the sense that between them they cover all of the perceived possibilities in (Indian) philosophy. If there is any merit in this view, then one product of the practice of *vada* could be said to be a determinate set of *darsanas* acknowledged as worthy opponents in debate. Philosophical debate was thus tradition-*constituting*. Through contesting and being contested, so to say, rationality constructed itself.

But the conduct of public debates between *darsanas* was also tradition-*constituted*, and this in at least two senses: first, in the obvious sense that the topic of debate was always a point of difference between competing *darsanas*, and secondly, in the sense that reasons could be given during a

Table 2.1. *Ways of coming to know; reasons for claiming to know*

	Perception	Inference	Verbal testimony	Analogy	Presumption	Non-cognition
Carvaka	X					
Buddhist/Jaina[91]	X	X				
Samkhya-Yoga	X	X	X			
Nyaya-Vaisesika	X	X	X	X		
Mimamsa[92]	X	X	X	X	X	
Advaita-Vedanta[93]	X	X	X	X	X	X

disputation that were reasons for one's own school, even when they were not also reasons for members of the opponent's school. It may help if I give an example to illustrate both the structure of debate and the way that tradition-specific reasoning could be introduced into an inter-darsanic debate.

As already noted, Buddhists and Brahmanic Hindus did not agree about the nature of the self.[94] Both believed in a doctrine of rebirth, but they did not agree about its nature and mechanics. The orthodox Hindus held that the self (*atman*) is eternal substance and that this self is successively reborn, but the Buddhists had a 'bundle-theory' of the self and held that rebirth somehow occurs without anything transmigrating.[95] The nature of the self, therefore, was a frequent topic of disputation between Hindu and Buddhist logicians.

Udayana's treatise on the self, the *Atmatattvaviveka*, can be read as an epitome of the most successful debating points to be made on behalf of the orthodox Hindu position.[96] So successful was his polemic that the

[91] Being *avaidika*, neither Jainas nor Buddhists could have accepted Vedic *sabda* as a valid *pramana*. But Jainas did acknowledge their own scriptures as a valid *pramana*. Buddhists would typically claim to rely on perception and inference alone in debate, insisting that Buddhist scripture had authority only if its reliability could be established by perception or inference. Even so, Buddhists engaged in both 'reason-based' and 'scripture-based' debates. See, e.g., Jackson, ed., *The Entrance Gate for the Wise*, II, pp. 332–40.

[92] Jaimini accepts only perception, inference and verbal testimony; Kumarila accepts all six.

[93] Visistadvaita-Vedanta and Dvaita-Vedanta, however, more typically accept only perception, inference, verbal testimony and *possibly* analogy, but not presumption and non-cognition.

[94] For a philosophically rigorous analysis of the issues involved in their disagreement about the self, see Oetke, '*Ich*' *und das Ich*.

[95] See, e.g., Nagasena's classic attempt to explain this peculiarly Buddhist doctrine of rebirth to King Milinda in the *Milindapanha*.

[96] Section one of the *Atmatattvaviveka* has been edited and translated by Chitrarekha V. Kher and Shiv Kumar (Delhi, 1987). For a summary of the full treatise, see Potter, ed., *Encyclopedia of Indian Philosophies*, II, pp. 526–57.

book became known popularly as the *bauddhadhikkara,* or 'the disgrace of the Buddhists'!

The treatise divides naturally into two main parts, as would a philosophical disputation in India, the one *negative* and the other *positive* in purpose. Negatively, one must undermine the opponent's position; positively, one must offer separate arguments for one's own position. Only if both tasks are successfully completed could one be declared the winner of a philosophical contest. There were clear conventions about what were allowed to count as reasons in the conduct of each half of the debate. In the negative half, one was required to give a fair statement of the opposing position, the arguments in its favour, and the arguments that can be used against it. In prosecuting this task, one could only use reasons that were acknowledged as reasons for the opponent's *darsana.* Although authoritative scriptures of one's own tradition could not be cited in debate unless they were also authoritative for the opponent, the opponent's scriptures could be cited to show – for instance – that the opponent's position is inconsistent with those scriptures. Even if one had demolished the opponent's case to the satisfaction of the judge, one could not be declared the outright winner of a debate unless positive proofs were put forward in support of one's own position.

Positive proofs might be based on reasons that were shared with one's opponent such as an appeal to sense experience or to valid inference. But positive proofs could all the same be based on tradition-specific reasons that were not acknowledged as reasons by one's opponent. Such tradition-specific reasons were not introduced in order to cut off debate or to assert their privileged authority. For they, too, were open to challenge from the outside. Although authoritative within one's own tradition, such grounds were not immune from public contestation.

In making his positive case, Udayana argued that the orthodox doctrine of the self could be proved through perception, inference and Vedic scripture. A Buddhist could have accepted perception and inference as ways of coming to know something and, therefore, as grounds for claiming to know it. Even within those limits, there were still sufficient differences between Buddhist and Naiyayika understandings of perception[97] and inference[98] to sustain a lively debate lasting more than twelve

---

[97] See, e.g., Bimal Krishna Matilal, *Perception: An Essay on Classical Indian Theories of Knowledge* (Oxford, 1986).

[98] See, e.g., the article on *anumanam* or 'inference' in Gerhard Oberhammer, unter Mitarbeit von E. Prets und J. Prandstetter, *Terminologie den frühen philosophischen Scholastik in Indien. Ein*

centuries! But a Buddhist could not in any circumstances have recognized an appeal to the testimony of Vedic scripture as a reason for believing that the self is eternal substance. So Udayana set about establishing the authority of Vedic scripture in respect to the doctrine of the self.

First, he argued, Vedic teaching about the self is internally consistent. The Buddhist might well have wanted to quibble about the consistency of the *atman* doctrine as it is found in the Vedas. But even if it were allowed that the Vedic teaching about *atman* is consistent, this would not be a reason *for a Buddhist* to accept the doctrine as true. Udayana claimed, secondly, that Vedic scriptures are trustworthy because they have a reliable author. This is one of the conventional reasons in support of any appeal to the authority of verbal testimony in Indian philosophy. But the Buddhists did not accept (or did not typically accept) that any verbal testimony could have cognitive authority. They accepted only perception and inference as valid means of knowledge. Udayana added, finally, that the reliable author of Vedic scripture is none other than *Isvara*-God, whose existence is demonstrable by rational arguments.[99] But the Buddhists were not theists and did not accept as philosophically sound any possible argument for the existence of God.

The appeal to Vedic authority, therefore, is unlikely to have impressed any Buddhist opponent. And Udayana cannot realistically have expected by such arguments to convince a Buddhist of the truth of the orthodox position concerning the nature of the self or *atman*. But Udayana might well have expected by laying out so clearly the structure of the Hindu position thereby to give both his fellow Naiyayikas and their Buddhist opponents an understanding of the precise nature and grounds of their difference. In offering his tradition-specific reasons, however, he was not intending to cut off discussion; he was, instead, staking out the grounds of contestation.

Although this brief account does justice neither to Udayana's classic treatise nor to the Indian *vada*-tradition as such, it is, I hope, sufficient to show that a different model is at work here than the one at work in the European Enlightenment, as exhibited in 'the Jeffersonian project'. I would underscore four crucial points of difference between the

---

Begriffswörterbuch zur altindischen Dialektik, Erkenntnislehre und Methodologie, Band 1: A-I, Österreichische Akademie der Wissenschaften, phil.-hist. Kl. 223 Bd. (Vienna, 1991), pp. 43–60.

[99] Each of the theistic proofs used by Udayana derives from a function of Siva within the Nyaya-Vaisesika system which he represented. For an account of the place of theistic argument within Udayana's philosophical strategy, see my article 'Piety and the Proofs'. Editors' note: This appears as Chapter 6 of the present volume.

Enlightenment model with which we began and the Indian debating model with which we conclude:

1. In the Enlightenment model, tradition-specific reasons have no place in public rationality. In the *vada* model, tradition-specific reasons can have a place in public rationality. Admission to public space is gained through contestability, not neutrality.
2. In the Enlightenment model, universal reason is a 'given' and is simply applied to particular cases. In the *vada* model, reason constructs itself in and through its operations in public debate.
3. In the Enlightenment model, the Other is not necessary for public rationality. In the *vada* model, the Other is necessary in that it is through engagement that both the Self and the Other construct themselves.
4. In the Enlightenment model, the end served by rational debate is the achievement of consensus. In the *vada* model, the end served by rational debate is the clarification of difference.

The direction in which this essay has been leading points to the need for a reorientation of philosophy of religion, away from the pretension of philosophy's providing a common foundation for religious claims and toward the more modest aim of philosophy's providing a common discourse in which the nature of religious difference can be clarified. In so doing, however, I obviously do not wish to rule out *a priori* the possibility of uncovering particular areas of convergence between religious traditions. I mean rather to stress that the point of the exercise does not *require* there to be such convergences in order to justify the undertaking. It is not only the reaching of agreement that marks progress in discussion; progress can also be marked by a deeper understanding of the nature of difference.

Seeing the difference is the beginning of understanding.

CHAPTER 3

Common ground and defensible difference*

The vigour with which radically conservative religious movements have gained ground around the world – East and West, North and South – caught the liberal intellectual establishment unprepared. Many consoled themselves at first by insisting that it was a temporary blip and predicted that the corrective forces of secularization would soon reassert themselves and set things back on course in and beyond the West. However, this has not happened. In the mean time, the liberal community has gone on the offensive, warning with uncharacteristic sensationalism against domestic culture wars or global clashes of civilizations if commonality is not maximized. Rawlsians may have soberly realized that citizens of modern democratic societies share less in common than they had once imagined, but they have not abandoned the strategy of seeking out and expanding the possible patches of overlapping consensus that may survive. This typifies the intuitive response of liberalism, both classical and contemporary, to diversity: privatize difference and cultivate common ground as a means of containing the potentially destructive social effects of cultural, especially religious, diversity.

Who indeed could doubt that staking out and tending common ground is the first thing required to overcome difference and to create a common good? Where there are differences of opinion between persons or states or religions, most of us instinctively look to strategies that maximize common ground. The image of common ground evokes public parks and village greens. It is an image full of warmth and reassurance, exuding a sense of community and well being. It is an image that can inspire even the likes of former British Prime Minister John Major to eloquence in homage to village cricket, warm beer, and prim spinsters cycling to Evensong.

---

* Inaugural Lecture as Professor of Religion, Chair of the Department of Religion, and Director of the Graduate Division of Religious and Theological Studies at Boston University.

But the image of common ground has another side, one that has to do with control and power. Access to shared space requires a willingness to conform to rules (usually posted) that regulate hours of access, modes of dress, kinds of activities that are permitted not only by visitors but also by their pets. Such regulations are rarely oppressive, but *are* occasionally idiosyncratic. Access to common ground is never entirely free of regulation; the regulations on display reflect local community standards, and the more nearly one approximates those standards, the less difficulty one will have feeling 'at home' in public space.

Common ground is not always unitive; it can be the cause of conflict. Sometimes the greater the share in common ground, the more destructive the conflict. It might be observed, at the risk of seeming overliteral, that no one has more common ground than do the Palestinians and the Israelis. *What they share in common is in fact the basis of their conflict.* Common ground, in short, does not always contribute to peace. Nor, I would add, does radical difference necessarily give cause to worry about imminent culture wars at home or impending clashes of civilizations on the global scene.

Clarification of defensible difference, not identification of 'common ground', may be what is required to gain the co-operation of disparate religious interests in achieving pragmatically defined goals that enhance human flourishing. This approach would entail a shift from focusing on reasons as grounds to focusing instead on reasons as motives and on reasons as goals; that is to say, focusing less on the *grounds* of argument and more on the *ends* of argument. That, at least, is the possibility I want to put forward. To get there, however, there is groundwork to be done.

The terms *public* and *private* are notoriously slippery – and not just in England, where public schools are private, or just in America, where the private lives of politicians are treated as matters of intense public concern. So upside down have public and private become that more Americans can name women with whom the President has been sexually linked than can name members of his cabinet. One does not have to wait for a Gallup poll to be confident that more Americans could discuss in lurid detail the President's private sexual preferences than could intelligently discuss his public policies. Even apart from this episode, however, it has to be allowed that the conceptual boundaries between *public* and *private* are somewhat indeterminate. The private sphere can be extended to cover everything that is not an official function of government, or it can be restricted to what goes on between consenting adults within their own four walls. The public realm can be conceived narrowly, or it can be

expanded in liberal democracies to include anything open to all qualified members of the public, such as the market place, the academy and
the 'public square'.

For the American conscience, however, it is organized religion's possible involvement in matters political that causes greatest suspicion about
religion's public role. This suspicion is deeply rooted in our origins as a
nation. The Republic and its ideals were forged at a time when the
European liberal thinking that so impressed the likes of Jefferson and
his generation had served up a minimalist idea of civil government.
Citizens were to be left relatively free of interference to pursue their
own vision of the good life, providing that pursuit did not impede the
ability of other citizens to pursue theirs. In respect to organized religion,
this was perceived to have two consequences, both of them embodied
eventually in the first amendment to the US Constitution: it is not the
business of federal government to privilege parochial religious interests by
establishment, but it is the business of government to protect the free
exercise of religion from hindrance, be it initiated by those hostile to
religion, by other religious groups or by some agency of government.

Jefferson spoke of the need for a 'wall of separation' between the state
and the affairs of religion, a phrase over which he took some care. It was,
he admitted, seasoned to Southern tastes, and he feared it might be too
strong for the more delicate digestion of those living in the North.[1] In
retrospect, his intended wall was neither especially high nor particularly
substantial. It was more like the back wall of an English terrace house:
high enough to keep the neighbours' children and pets out of the flower-
beds, but low enough not to exclude light or exchanges of local gossip on
the weekends. For instance, Jefferson did not think all forms of religion
unfit for access to public space; rational religion retained privileged rights
of access to the public arena. However modest his wall may have been, it
has been raised and reinforced by subsequent custom, legislation and
judicial interpretation, until it is now a formidable barrier that effectively
excludes religious access to the public realm. Even though the wall may
have been 'improved' over time, its foundations remain Jeffersonian.
He set the tone of the American liberal tradition by insisting on the
separation of personal belief from civic virtue. In Jefferson's view, it is not
of public concern whether a citizen has this religion or that or no religion
at all.

---

[1] Thomas Jefferson to Levi Lincoln, 1 January 1802.

Religion in the Jeffersonian project was effectively privatized and made subject to market forces, not to state monopoly. Though it is not actually entailed by Jefferson's position, the extended 'wall of separation' threatens to deny private religion access to public space or influence in defining public virtue. The liberal state is fully secular; public reason, secular reason; public virtue, secular virtue. Critics of modernity sometimes point to the privatization of religion as an important aspect of the much-hyped loss of community and fragmentation of cultural values. Accompanying this indictment has gone a call, first from the right and more recently from the left, to reassert religion's right of entry to the public sphere of civic life.

Early architects of classical liberalism anticipated the charge. In a recent article on religion and community in the thought of the Scottish economist Adam Smith, Charles Griswold has examined the initially counter-intuitive argument of *The Wealth of Nations* that incorporating religion into civic life *undermines* community by leading to a variety of public vices, including fanaticism and intolerance, while the privatization of religion *builds up* community by encouraging a variety of liberal virtues, including moderation and tolerance.[2] On this account, diversity of religious interests in a society leads not so much to culture wars as to peace and harmony.

How does it do that?

If the civil government withdraws from the religion business, so to speak, and favours no religious persuasion with establishment, then religion – being based on a combination of volatile and irrational factors – can be predicted to fragment into a large number of independent sects. These sects will then compete vigorously for new members, since their very survival depends upon the moral and financial support of their member-ship. In order to make themselves more attractive to more people, however, the individual sects will tend to moderate their more extreme positions. They will then adopt a less strident and more tolerant attitude toward other groups, an attitude which is highly conducive to commu-nity. Ergo, privatization leads to an enhanced sense of community.

Earlier, I noted the hold that the image of 'common ground' has on our thinking about ways to avoid the destructive effects of religious difference. It would seem *prima facie* that Adam Smith's appeal to the imagery of the market offers an alternative that values diversity positively without

---

[2] Charles L. Griswold, Jr, 'Religion and Community: Adam Smith on the Virtues of Liberty', *Journal of the History of Philosophy* 35/3 (1997), 395–419.

requisite 'common ground'. First impressions may be misleading, however, so it will be necessary to return to this issue. Before doing so, it may prove useful to see how Jefferson used forces at work in the market place to project the future of religious diversity in America.

The privatization of religion, Jefferson insisted, was an advantage both to the state and to true religion. Establishment leads to the corruption of the state and of religion alike. Exclusion of parochial religious interests from the public arena is necessary both for the integrity of the state and for the prosperity of true religion. Privatization advantages the state, he argues in language reminiscent of Smith, because a diversity of 'good enough' religious groups in a society acts to stabilize and to moderate religious excesses. Writing at a time when many states still had legally established churches, Jefferson pointed to the successful experiments in New York and Pennsylvania where, in the absence of legal establishment, religious diversity and public order happily flourished together:

Religion is well supported; of various kinds, indeed, but all good enough; all sufficient to preserve peace and order: or if a sect arises, whose tenets would subvert morals, good sense has fair play, and reasons and laughs it out of doors, without suffering the state to be troubled with it. They do not hang more malefactors than we do. They are not more disturbed with religious dissensions. On the contrary, their harmony is unparalleled, and can be ascribed to nothing but their unbounded tolerance, because there is no other circumstance in which they differ from every nation on earth. They have made the happy discovery, that the way to silence religious disputes, is to take no notice of them.[3]

That last sentence is telling. In it we glimpse how Jefferson's private opinion on the pointlessness of sectarian religious disputes and the irrationality of parochial religious interests colours his recommendations for public policy in respect to religion. Religion is privatized not to allow a hundred flowers to bloom but to subject the diverse religious sects to the corrective forces of the market place that serve to control fanatical excess and also to instil liberal virtues, such as tolerance and 'good sense'. Privatization of sectarian religion effectively allowed Jefferson to institute his private religious preferences as public policy. The forces of the market place, not the forces of state, would be used to maximize rationality in religion.

In a society where all religious groups have equal protection under the law and free access to the market place, citizens can be expected to shop around a bit, but they will eventually settle on the 'best buy', which in

---

[3] Thomas Jefferson, 'Notes on the State of Virginia (1787), Query 17', in *Thomas Jefferson: Writings*, ed. Merrill D. Peterson (New York, 1984), p. 287.

Jefferson's estimate would be the religious option that is highest in rationality. 'Reason and free enquiry are the only effectual agents against error. Give a loose to them, they will support the true religion, by bringing every false one to their tribunal, to the test of their investigation.'[4] Unregulated market forces would eliminate faulty goods, thus driving rationally defective religions into liquidation. Religious diversity, for Jefferson a given, is viewed as an instrument of its own destruction. Irrational parochial interests give way over time to the superior market leadership of rational religion, which emerges not just as market leader, but as unregulated monopoly. And it does so not by the force of legal establishment but by the power of persuasion, in and through the sort of 'free enquiry' idealized in Enlightenment rationality.

This seems rather distant from Adam Smith. For Smith, diversity is not simply tolerated until true religion can eliminate its false competitors; it is actively encouraged. The greater the diversity, the better, on Smith's account. But this is misleading. Encouraging diversity is as strategic for Smith as it is for Jefferson. Both men regarded all sectarian religious groups as fundamentally irrational. The two men differ only in their views of how rational religion overcomes what is patently false and irrational. For Jefferson, it would occur by sects being displaced one by one by rational religion. For Smith, it would occur as gradual modifications to all the sectarian options as part of the overarching process of moderation, until they all finally converge at or near 'pure and rational religion'.

In both accounts of diversity, difference is an embarrassment, a sign of irrationality, to be overcome by the totalization of reason. Otherness may be publicly tolerated, but it is privately held in utter contempt.

Smith and Jefferson judged the religious sects of their acquaintance to be irrational, in part because their style of argument did not conform to the canons of public rationality idealized in what is widely called by supporters and detractors alike the 'Enlightenment project' – a phrase that has all the descriptive credibility of the 'Holy Roman Empire'. Having myself tried elsewhere to define it, I shall resist the temptation to do so again here.[5] For present purposes, it is sufficient to note that in its terms, we are required in all our deliberations to attain neutrality by divesting ourselves of allegiance to any particular standpoint and to achieve universality by abstracting ourselves from all those communities of interest that may limit our perspective. As

---

[4] *Ibid.*, p. 285.
[5] See my Inaugural Lecture as Professor of Religious Studies at the University of Lancaster, 'Thomas Jefferson and the Study of Religion'. Editors' note: This appears as Chapter 2 of the present volume.

sovereign selves we lay sound foundations on which to build with reasoned confidence. This account evokes procedures outlined by Descartes in his *Discourse on Method* and applied in his *Meditations on First Philosophy*.

Descartes is your worst nightmare as a neighbour. No sooner has he bought the house next door than he begins worrying that it may be haunted. Then one day he mutters that roofs have been known to leak and infers from this datum that his roof must be unreliable. The next thing you know, he has the roof off and then begins to dismantle the place floor by floor, room by room, until he has the ground cleared. Not content, he digs on until he hits bedrock. With a worrying air of Gallic self-satisfaction, he then proceeds to lay new foundations and to begin rebuilding his house. You offer to help, but he refuses all assistance.

According to the terms of the Enlightenment project, we must learn to rely on ourselves alone and not on others, present or past, if we are to avoid error. The free use of reason by a sovereign self, unencumbered by all such entanglements, is a sure guide to truth, justice and virtue. It is also sufficient to discover all that is necessary to know about God, immortality of the soul, and the requirements of the moral law.

Rational religion is supposed to be public religion both in the sense of its being open equally to all and in the sense of its being supported by reasons that are reasons for everyone – that is, it is imagined to conform to classical liberal canons of public rationality. Rational religion was not treated as one sect among other sects, but as the ground common to all religious sects, from which they may deviate to varying degrees, the degree of their deviation being a measure of their irrationality. In practice, however, 'rational religion' was little more than the residue that remained after eliminating all the distinguishing doctrines of the diverse Protestant groups that proliferated in parts of Europe and in much of eighteenth-century America. It was able to pass itself off as 'universal' only because of the paucity of knowledge about religious traditions that had no share in the narrative traditions of historical Christianity. Other groups could be imagined to share in rational religion of the requisite sort because of the sheer thinness of contact with such groups.

The point is easily made in reference to America circa 1800. Almost 90 per cent of the citizens of the US at that time who belonged to a religious community identified themselves with some Protestant group. About 10 per cent were Roman Catholics and only 0.5 per cent were Jewish.[6]

---

[6] See Edwin Scott Gaustad, *Historical Atlas of Religion in America*, 2nd edn (New York, 1976).

If we focus more narrowly on Jefferson's own state, whose Statute for Religious Freedom became the model for the first amendment of the US Constitution, the homogeneity is even more staggering. In the whole of the Commonwealth of Virginia at the turn of the century, there was not a single Roman Catholic church, and the nearest Jewish congregations were in Philadelphia to the north and Charleston to the south. In such circumstances, maximizing common ground may well have been a reasonable and practical strategy for containing the damage that might be done to the public good by the fact of religious diversity. But this is not the sort of religious diversity that occupies us today, whatever the level of magnification used in our enquiries, whether we focus on the local, regional or global scene.

Contrast the sort of diversity that concerned Jefferson and his generation with the sort of diversity evident today in a city like Boston or in a major research university like Boston University. Contrast it also with the kind of diversity evident today in the very European countries that produced the leading architects of the rational religion embraced by classical liberalism. In Britain today, for instance, there are more Hindus than Jews and more Muslims than Methodists.[7] Nor is Britain in this respect unique among European lands. The precise mix may be different, but the sort of religious diversity experienced in many European countries today is not that different. *What kind of strategy would be effective in respect to this sort of diversity, so that it has a chance of becoming a positive good rather than a detriment to the stability of an open society?*

In recent academic debates about the role of religious differences in threatened culture wars and impending clashes of civilizations, too much attention has been given to destructively conflictual consequences of difference and too little to the positive benefits of diversity or to the complex strategies that religions themselves develop to accommodate difference, whether it exists within a single religious community or among a plurality of religious communities that may have existed for some time alongside one another, cheek by jowl.

Sometimes these strategies are purely local, partial and inconsistent with a given community's 'official' polity and practice. They may nonetheless be effective strategies, which, without external interference, can have long-term local benefit. In 1992, the world's attention was focused on Ayodhya, an inconspicuous village in India, where a mob of Hindu

---

[7] See A. H. Halsey, ed., *British Social Trends since 1900*, 2nd edn (Basingstoke, 1988).

nationalists destroyed the sixteenth-century mosque that in times of Islamic ascendancy had been built over the legendary birth spot of the God Rama. Press coverage of this event and the violence that ensued throughout India was intense and unremitting. Less well covered was the fact that local Hindus and Muslims had long ago reached an accord that allowed a corner of the mosque to be used by Hindus to honour Rama.

Local accommodation is more widespread 'on the ground' among religious populations than might be imagined, as are extensive syncretism and a variety of pick-and-choose combinations. A successful Japanese family might follow certain Shinto practices, opt for a Christian wedding for their daughter, but at death find comfort in a Buddhist funeral. It is not unusual for contemporary Christians to experiment with a wide variety of meditative and spiritual practices belonging properly to other paths, legitimated by narrative traditions, grounded in doctrinal schemes and directed at goals quite different from their own path, narrative, doctrine and goal, and to conduct such experiments with the expectation of spiritual insight that somehow goes beyond what is otherwise available to them in their own tradition's spiritual practices. In some areas of Nepal, Buddhism and Hinduism are so intermingled in popular belief and practice that a credible difference can no longer be found. If one were to examine the classical polemical texts of Buddhist and Brahmanical philosophers, however, it would be hard to imagine that such syncretism could be possible in principle, much less that it could be sustained in practice. Yet it is.

We academics, notoriously susceptible to the mental hobgoblins identified by Emerson, find it easy to dismiss examples from popular religion as intellectually uninteresting. I protest. I would go on to suggest that such muddling efforts may even contribute more to peace and human flourishing than does professorial hand-wringing over domestic culture wars and global clashes of civilizations. But I will not labour that point here. Instead, I will retreat to academically more comfortable territory and remind us that strategies for accommodating difference occur not just at the popular level. At more reflective levels, spiritual and intellectual elites of religious groups develop means for dealing with difference inside and beyond their boundaries. Some may even be philosophically interesting in their capacity to suggest models of public reason at odds with the dominant paradigm of classical liberalism that continues to inform academic ideals of public reason.

Rather than viewing religions as inherently 'irrational' because they fail to conform to the style of tradition-free reasoning idealized in classical liberal or Enlightenment accounts of rationality, it may be better to see religions as *localized rationalities*, that is, as largely coherent instances of group-specific reasoning.

Reasons do matter intensely to religious communities, but what counts as a good reason in what circumstance may be tradition-specific and itself be a matter of controversy within a community. To discern what count as 'good reasons' in a given situation requires one to get one's intellectual fingernails dirty: that is, one must root out particular cases for closer scrutiny. To be maximally effective, this digging about will need to be comparative, so one has to root around under more than one tree; otherwise, there is a danger of attaching general import to a single and possibly atypical instance. It is also necessary to shift the focus of attention from rationality in general to the practical operations of reason in specific contexts, contexts in which reasons as ends and reasons as motives will almost certainly be pertinent to identifying the role of reasons as grounds, contexts in which the boundaries between – say – logic, rhetoric and dialectic are not nearly as well formed as they are in philosophy textbooks.

Attending to the practical operations of reason in differing varieties of traditional religious discourse opens up a complex and fascinating world of local knowledge and local rationality. We can visit that world, but we may not want to live there. Even so, a visit to this exotic world may expose us to previously unimagined possibilities that might enable us to extrapolate fresh ways to theorize the practical operations of reason in the public world of political discourse.

When uncertainties arise or claims are contested in religious communities, complex strategies typically come into play, with differential weightings assigned to authoritative sources (sometimes textual, sometimes oral, sometimes personal), recognized precedents and traditions of interpretation, contemporary experience of narrowly religious or broadly secular kind, and other local circumstances. The kinds of reasoning found in such contexts typically resemble legal argument more closely than the mathematical-experimental reasoning idealized in classical liberal notions of public reason.

The comparison with jurisprudence, however, should not lead us to assume that the operations of reason in religious contexts are always conservative. There are loose and strict constructionists among canon lawyers as well as among constitutional lawyers. As in jurisprudence, however, innovation is frequently disguised as embodying the 'spirit' of the tradition, or as a recovery of the 'true meaning' of some authoritative text or tradition of interpretation, or as a reassuring means of resolving a seeming conflict between competing authorities. Religious traditions renew themselves and reshape themselves through these complex operations of practical reason. By such operations, they rarely achieve community-wide consensus. But they do sometimes manage thereby to confine the destructive consequences of internal dissonance and in the process redefine the limits of credible difference in the community. They may also transform internal diversity into positive energy that enables communities more effectively to adapt to constantly changing circumstance.

One common mechanism for defining the limits of credible difference inside religious groups has been the controlled conflict allowed by formal disputation. Formal public debate has been a feature of traditional education in a number of groups, including Islam, Christianity and Indo-Tibetan and Chinese religions. I focus here on Islamic and Indian practice.

In Islamic cultures, *kalam* emerged as a method of arguing, but also as a structure for formal disputation in and among the disparate schools of law that centred on the principles developed by eminent jurists (who have traditionally been occupied as much with philological, hermeneutical and philosophical issues as with narrowly legal ones). Muslims recognized from early days that *shariʾa* would require interpretation, since it is not reasonable to expect to find explicit guidance to cover all cases that can arise. In a *hadith* from the formative phase of Islam, there is a remarkable exchange between the Prophet and a companion, Muʾadh, who was about to be made a provincial governor.[8] As governor his duties would include settling disputes and offering legal judgments from time to time. The Prophet asked Muʾadh how he would render judgments. 'According to God's Scriptures', was his reply. And if the answer is not found there? Then, he said, 'according to the traditions of the Messenger'. And if the answer is not found there? 'Then I will rely on my reason.' The Prophet is reported to have expressed his approval and to have offered a prayer of thanksgiving. The use of reason being encouraged in this *hadith* is not the tradition-free reason of the classical liberal paradigm, but a reason infused with the controlling authority of *shariʾa* as given in the Qurʾan, the cycle of *ahadith* that surround the life of the Prophet, the learned consensus (*ijma*) of prevailing tradition. It is in short an intricately textured reason.

Even such richly textured reason could not guarantee uniformity of case law in Islam, however, and jurists developed individual approaches to interpreting the obligations of *shariʾa* in new circumstances, approaches that may have had considerable local influence but no overall authority.

---

[8] Cited in Noel J. Coulson, *Conflicts and Tensions in Islamic Jurisprudence* (Chicago, 1969), p. 4.

By one count, there were at the beginning of the ninth century over five hundred competing systems of legal interpretation with at least local influence. The winnowing effects of history, however, together with the vagaries of political patronage – and, not to be forgot, the weight of reasoned argument in legal disputation – resulted by the thirteenth century in a narrowing down of these local authorities in orthodox Islam to just three or four generally recognized approaches to the law, ranging from the relatively liberal Hanafi to the traditionalist Hanbali, with two moderate schools (Maliki and Shafiʿi) occupying the middle ground. Each school had a coherent and cohesive approach to the law; its decisions embodied their distinctive jurisprudential principles. All four of them came to be recognized by orthodox or Sunni Muslims as legitimate. What they agreed upon came to be accepted as the orthodox consensus or *ijma*; what they disagreed about was still tolerated as conceivable within orthodoxy without threatening its stability. These four schools, in my terms, mark the limits of credible or defensible difference within Sunni Islam. Diversity of legal perspectives in Islam also helps account for its remarkable ability to manage change by adapting itself to new circumstances without losing a sense of identity.

Disputation or *vada* arose in Brahmanical circles in India well before the beginning of the Common Era, out of the question-and-answer methods of instruction used to elucidate the intricacies of Vedic ritual or to solve metaphysical puzzles in Vedic scripture. Disputation between learned experts may have developed also from ancient Brahmanic methods of resolving legal disputes and from medical practitioners' methods of arriving at an agreed diagnosis or method of treatment. In addition, philosophical dialectic had independent origins outside Brahmanic circles within Jaina and Buddhist groups, each of which had developed its own distinctive procedures and categories which eventually fed into the main-stream traditions of *vada* disputation.

The Buddhist influence in particular on that wider tradition was considerable. Despite the Buddha's warning against engaging in any doctrinal dispute that could risk schism, Buddhist *pitakas* abound in reports of controversy inside their circles regarding the correctness of rival doctrinal interpretations. Such controversies had over time a certain winnowing effect on Buddhist positions, so that certain schools emerged with widespread credibility, so much so that their existence was attributed to the Buddha's intention to make provision for different levels of spiritual attainment, a tale told by Madhyamikas, who would have placed themselves at the highest level.

Since Buddhist schools differed in their conception of the nature of reality, debates about ontology and cognition presented practical obstacles. How do you run a debate between someone who believes that our perceptions mirror external objects and someone else who is persuaded that every theory about the nature of things collapses by virtue of insurmountable internal contradictions? You could only do so if the latter person were willing *for the sake of the debate* to posit the reality of external objects. You must learn to see things as an elephant sees them, the great Dharmakirti advised, if you want to debate with an elephant. The acquired capacity to think as the opponent thinks is a key to the practical operation of reason in the Indian paradigm of public reason. For the willingness and skilful means to reflect systematically on the Other's perspective from within that perspective as if it were one's own perspective not only enabled internal Buddhist debates between the Madhyamikas and the Sautrantikas; it also enabled external debates with non-Buddhists.

Religious groups in long-term contact with other religious groups typically develop discourses for debate across their respective borders. The type of argument that had been used for *intra*-traditional debate was also adapted for *inter*-traditional use. In Persia and elsewhere, *kalam* provided a framework for public debate among Muslims, Jews, Christians and other local groups. As a style of argument, *kalam* had much influence within the Jewish and Christian communities, as well as becoming *the* discourse of public debate in the region. The popular success of open debate in cosmopolitan Baghdad alarmed more conservative Muslims from elsewhere. Ibn Saʾdi, a tenth-century visitor from Spain, went to a public debate at which he found gathered together not only members of disparate Islamic sects, but also non-Muslims of all sorts, including 'Magions, materialists, atheists, Jews, and Christians'. Upon his return to Spain, ibn Sa'di described what he had witnessed abroad as a calamity (in an evident pun on the word *kalam*) by virtue of the fact that the Muslims present at the debate did not insist on everyone's accepting the authority of the Qurʾan as a condition of participation.[9]

A century later, however, the Muslim ruler of Moorish Saragossa, in correspondence with a certain 'monk of France' who was inclined to try to trump arguments by quoting the New Testament, reminded him that all religions make such appeals, and argument [*kalam*] is the only means we

---

[9] Cited in Moise Ventura, *La philosophie de Saadia Gaon* (Paris, 1934), p. 93. I am grateful to Paul Morris, Victoria University (New Zealand), for having supplied me with this reference.

have of distinguishing possibility from absurdity.[10] I do not know what
the *monk* from France replied, but it would not be long before *friars* from
France would be touting also in Spain the value of scholastic discourse as a
vehicle of disputation between Christians, Muslims and Jews.

If ibn Saʾdi had been concerned that Muslims had not pressed their
numerical and political dominance in debates in Baghdad, he would have
been equally alarmed at the readiness with which Christians regularly
pressed their dominant position of power in the Latin West. Sometimes
there was an effort at fairness, sometimes not, and even in those cases
where the ruler swore his protection, he was not always in a position to
make good his promise. As the distinguished Nahmanides realized before
engaging in debate in Barcelona (1263), it was 'catch-22'. If he did badly
and lost, his people would suffer added pressure and humiliation at the
hands of the triumphant Christians; if he did well and won, his people
might suffer even greater retaliation. Who won? It depends whether you
believe the summary of the debate written by the Christians or the one
written by Nahmanides, the publication of which led directly to his exile.[11]

From these examples, we see not only that religious communities
develop a language for arguing across their confessional boundaries, but
also that the asymmetry of political power in Islamic and Christian lands
meant that in practice these discourses were in constant danger of being
subverted politically as discourses of domination.

In regions where political advantage was more randomly distributed,
however, debating traditions led to more interesting results over time. In
India, for instance, *vada* became a public discourse for defining defensible
difference between competing groups able to survive public scrutiny. To
say that political advantage was more randomly distributed does not of
course mean that political factors were absent from the Indian debating
tradition or that debates were not a means of one local group gaining
political advantage over another. This is especially true of court debates,
where royal patronage and prejudice were often decisive to the outcome
of the disputation. In a wonderful exchange in the *Milindapanha*,[12]

---

[10] D. M. Dunlop, 'A Christian Mission to Muslim Spain in the 11th Century', *Al-andalus* 17 (1952),
273ff.

[11] For the Christian and Jewish texts relating to the Barcelona disputation, see Hyam Maccoby, ed.,
Judaism on Trial: Jewish–Christian Disputations in the Middle Ages (London, 1982), pp. 97–150. See
also Robert Chazan, *Daggers of Faith: Thirteenth-Century Christian Missionizing and the Jewish
Response* (Berkeley, 1989), pp. 71ff.

[12] Adapted from *The Questions of King Milinda*, 2.1.3, trans. T. W. Rhys Davids (Delhi, 1960), vol. 1,
p. 46.

King Milinda asked the Buddhist pandit Nagasena if he would debate with him. Nagasena replied that he would debate with the king as scholars debate, but not as kings debate.

How is it that scholars debate? 'When scholars debate with one another, Your Majesty, there is a winding up, an unravelling; one or other is convicted of error, and mistakes are acknowledged; distinctions and counter-distinctions are drawn; there is also defeat, and yet they do not lose their temper. Thus, Your Majesty, do scholars debate.'

And how do kings debate? 'When kings debate, Your Majesty, they state a proposition, and if anyone differs with them, they order his punishment. "Away with him!" they shout. Thus, Your Majesty, do kings debate.' In response, King Milinda graciously agreed to debate with Nagasena in the idealized manner of scholars.

Representatives of any philosophical perspective – Brahmanic or Buddhist or Jaina or even Carvaka – had free access to the forum of public debate, providing, that is, that they were willing to have their school's claims publicly challenged according to the rules of *vada*. Contest-ability, not *neutrality*, was the price of entry to the public arena in the Indian *vada* tradition. One could enter public space and participate in public reason without pretending to rise above difference or to abstract oneself from one's entanglements with the communities of interest that make us who we are. Unlike classical European liberalism, the Indian debating tradition did not require one to give up one's own grounds in order to participate in public reason; public reason is open to all, but a share in 'common ground' is not required. Reasons given in debate do not have to be reasons for everyone, but they must be contestable by anyone with requisite knowledge and an interest in the topic.

In any given debate, there were of course a winner and a loser. And opponents from different *darsanas* typically engaged in debate in order to defeat their opponents and to establish the superiority of their own perspective. Buddhist logicians nonetheless typically insisted that it is unworthy to enter into debate in order to win or defeat an opponent, that one should enter into the dialectic of debate to arrive at the truth. Assuming the conditions of defeat and victory were met, however, there would be a winner and there would be a loser. Egos were at risk – even, one suspects, in the case of Buddhists, who theoretically had no ego to be threatened. To be defeated in an important debate involved loss of face and, depending on the wager, maybe more. Some groups, notably the Naiyayikas, had the reputation of being ready to use any means, fair or foul, to win debates.

However important winning was to most of those who engaged in public debate, the long-term effect of the debating tradition was not to arrive at an overall World Cup-winning team or to achieve a general consensus on matters in dispute. Nor was it, as Adam Smith might have expected, for the rough edges of difference to be worn away as once-strong positions became more moderate. The long-term effect was quite the opposite: not to diminish but precisely to specify difference. The lines separating the emerging *darsanas* were firmed up by a gradual sharpening of the points of difference that distinguished them.

Preparation for debate forced each competing *darsana* to reflect systematically on its own position and also on the opponent's, since they would have to defeat the opponent on his or her own grounds. In the process, it became clear that their difference – their *alterity* – was not simply a difference about this or that issue; it was systemic. Their difference was *darsanic*; it was perspectival. But the *darsanas* that survived this process gained credibility and earned thereby a place in the set of *darsanas*. They were regarded as worthy opponents in debate.

None of the *darsanas* was left unaffected by their extended process of polemic and debate, but each one was affected differently. At one time independent perspectives, Nyaya and Vaisesika moved toward each other until they finally merged, with the combined *darsana* integrating the logical and dialectical skills of the one with the realist ontological commitments of the other. And the Naiyayikas, once non-theistic, became forceful apologists for what might be called somewhat anachronistically 'rational religion'. At one time subsidiary to Mimamsa, Vedanta came to have a separate existence from what then came to be Purva-Mimamsa. And, as Vedanta became conceptually more variegated within and eventually acquired political advantage without, it assumed an increasingly prominent place in accounts of the *saddarsanas*.

Not all perspectives survived having their basic claims contested in debate. Although evidently regarded at one time as equal in standing to Samkhya and Yoga, the Carvaka may have failed to clear the hurdle of public contestability, surviving not in its own right as a living *darsana*, but only as a stereotyped image in the polemical texts of other *darsanas*. Why then did it continue to be treated as a possible perspective even after it had ceased to be an active presence within Indian philosophy? The Carvaka represented a philosophical position that is not otherwise present among the *darsanic* systems. Only the Carvaka represented materialism in ontology; only they rejected inference as a *pramana*; only they denied the cycle of rebirth and the moral basis of world-order. In short, without the Carvaka the construction of philosophical systems would have been left unfinished and the outer limit of credible philosophical reflection would have been left undefined.

This gives us a clue to the way that the set of philosophical *darsanas* achieved definitive shape. Each surviving *darsana* represented a possible point of view, without which the 'set' would have been incomplete. Collectively, they possess a kind of coherence based not on their being built on 'common ground' but on together constituting the sum total of defensible possibilities that could be conceived within the Indian *imaginaire*. Sa-Skya Pandita, the eminent thirteenth-century Tibetan scholastic philosopher, insisted that the traditional Indian *darsanas* exhaust the possibilities philosophically.[13] A worthy opponent stands in one of the four main Buddhist lineages or belongs to one of the recognized non-Buddhist sects. There are these and no others. Anyone who holds a coherent point of view holds one of these positions, whether or not they realize it. If there is any merit in this remark, then one product of the practice of *vada* could be said to have been a determinate set of recognized *darsanas*. In my language, the process produced a clarification of publicly defensible difference.

Earlier, I suggested that the notion of public reason in classical liberal theory is not able to cope with the kind of radical religious diversity that confronts us today, whether we look at matters more regionally or more globally. Latterly, I have been suggesting that attending to the strategies religious communities themselves have developed to accommodate the Other in their midst may offer an alternate way of conceiving public reason – one in which reason lies open to all, to be sure, but does not require abandonment of group-specific reasons as the price of entry to the public arena. In the mediaeval Indo-Tibetan tradition of public debate between different perspectives, for instance, we encountered a conception of public reason that allowed public debate in which tradition-specific reasons might be offered and which resulted not in general consensus but in the clarification of publicly defensible difference.

I now want to suggest that what we found there is in fact nearer to the actual operations of public reason in modernity than is the idealized account of rationality found in most classical and much recent liberal

---

[13] David P. Jackson, ed., *The Entrance Gate for the Wise*, Wiener Studien zur Tibetologie und Buddhismuskunde, 17 (Vienna, 1987), vol. II, pp. 343ff.

theory. To make my point, I want to refer to selected aspects of the contemporary global debate about human rights.[14]

Just as academics may have worried too much about religious diversity as a cause of local or global violence and may have attended too little to ways that religious communities might contribute to a better understanding of the positive role of diversity in public reason, so academics may have concentrated too much on the violation of human rights in traditional religious communities and may have looked too little at what traditional religious communities might contribute to a richer understanding of human flourishing than has historically been the case within the modern secular discourse of rights.

One reason why the positive role religions might play in defining and enforcing human rights has tended to be ignored in international discussions on human rights must surely be sought in the popular presumption that the public discourse of rights is universal in scope and ideologically neutral in respect to underlying principles. The private discourses of religious communities are perceived in contrast as parochial or local in scope and as being grounded in group-specific commitments. The moral discourses of the disparate religious communities carry conviction for some people at some time and in some place, but they cannot be expected to carry conviction for all people at all times or in all places. At most, they express the tradition-constituted values of a limited community of interest and thereby fail to achieve the generality of moral discourse required for the recognition and implementation of human rights. For human rights – entitlements all persons are supposed to possess simply by virtue of being persons – would seem by definition to be rights whose authority cannot be contingent upon limiting circumstances, historical or cultural. Human rights are presumed to trump group-specific privileges and duties.

The diverse moral discourses of religious groups more typically spell out duties which are specific to the members of their own communities and which often could not even in principle be reasonably extended as requirements for persons beyond their borders. And legitimation of group-specific duties derives ultimately from some authority that is accepted as authority by that group alone. Such discourses can be said to express group-specific norms, but not universal maxims.

---

[14] The position sketched here is elaborated more fully in John Clayton, 'Universal Human Rights and Traditional Religious Values', in *Human Rights and Responsibilities in a Divided World*, ed. Jaroslav Krejci (Prague, 1997), pp. 29–46.

Any talk of 'human rights' and 'religious values' must, therefore, deal with the dilemma of universal and local in at least these two interrelated aspects: first, how group-specific duties relate to human rights, and second, how human rights are legitimated. In regard to legitimation, the issue is whether human rights claims must always be backed by reasons that can be reasons for everyone, or if they might also be backed by reasons that are accepted as such only by participants in some localized community of interest.

This dilemma faces anyone engaged in discussion of human rights, but it is made more acute by the extravagant claims religious groups often make for their moral code and its unique authority. Of course, all religious codes are in a weak sense unique in that each is the code of one religious community and not another. Yet some religious groups claim for themselves uniqueness in a strong sense: namely, their code exclusively provides a reliable guide to the good life by virtue of its authority as revealed law. Their code is claimed to have universal validity, even if its authority is not acknowledged beyond the community's edge. But when a religious group claims universal validity for its own code, its authority is in practice still restricted to the group that acknowledges its laws as binding. However sweeping the claim on the code's behalf, its authority remains localized to the group for which it is acknowledged as revealed law. For such religious groups, therefore, the tension persists between the universal entitlement to human rights and more localized group-defined duties and liberties.

The way this tension has been stated assumes that secular rights discourse is in some strong sense universal and objective, whereas the competing moral discourses of determinate religions are local and partisan, being confined to the communities of interest that embrace them. Yet the secular discourse of rights (including human rights) is itself a construction of a specific historical and cultural circumstance, as is the concept of the autonomous self as rights-bearer. And the idea of rights encoded in such discourse is also tied to the place in which it is formed or gains endorsement. Human rights are historical constructions, not natural kinds. For instance, John Locke, a major architect of the modern formation of rights discourse, could without violating his understanding of rights defend in his *Second Treatise of Government* the institution of slavery. A later upholder of the Lockian tradition of human rights may have been ambivalent in his attitude toward the institution of slavery, but Thomas Jefferson cannot have had foremost in mind his own slaves when he extolled in one of the most eloquent documents of his age the inalienable rights of life, liberty and the pursuit of happiness.

Surely none could claim that Locke's or Jefferson's understanding of rights was 'universal', whether in the sense of being an equal entitlement to everyone or in the sense of gaining general endorsement by everyone. Nor could one reasonably think that its underpinning was ideologically neutral. Human slavery may not have been eradicated in the world (indeed, it may be more widespread today than it has been at any time in human history), but it no longer has morally earnest defenders. What has changed since Locke's or Jefferson's time to make slavery indefensible, however, is not just that a further item or two has been added to the short list of so-called 'core rights'. What has occurred, more crucially, is a transformation of our vision of what constitutes a human right and of what entitles someone to be a rights-bearer.

Every understanding of 'rights' is bound to a time and place. This holds for our own notion of human rights as much as it does for that of Locke or Jefferson. Over time, the concept of rights may develop or be stretched or be altered to fit some new circumstance or it may be finally abandoned as outmoded. But it does not stay fixed. The discourse of human rights is itself temporal and not eternal, local and not universal. And this applies to the Universal Declaration of Human Rights, no less than it does to the American Declaration of Independence or the French *Déclaration des droits de l'homme et du citoyen*, the datedness of which may be more readily evident. The 1948 Universal Declaration was a historic document. It is rightly regarded as a key moment in shaping the postwar world. In the meantime, however, it has become also a historical document. It can now be seen to mirror the concerns of that time and to embody its asymmetry of political power. The understanding of what count as human rights presumed by it has now been altered and stretched and developed by ensuing Charters, Conventions, Declarations and Protocols. The discourse of rights has continued by this means to construct itself anew. And rival conceptions of human rights compete for wider endorsement within an increasingly global culture of rights.

This feature of the modern discourse of rights ironically brings it nearer to the competing moral discourses of sectarian religious groups which, according to the idealized Enlightenment self-image, the tradition-neutral language of rights was itself supposed to supersede. The dilemma of universal and local seems, therefore, to end in a proliferation of localized norms, vying with one another in the world's market place.

Does this not leave us awash in a sea of relativism? There is another way of explaining what is going on, a way that brings together the argument of this paper. More significant than the perceived threat of relativism in matters moral is the simple fact that the discourse of rights has become in modern times, and pre-eminently since the Second World War, the shared public language in which to differentiate the defensible from the indefensible in our behaviour toward others. It has effectively become the most widely accepted global currency in which to negotiate differing views about what weighting attaches to competing entitlements due to persons as persons. In this fact, rather than in pseudo-intellectual shilly-shallying over problems of incommensurability and relativism (problems which are themselves functions of an unimaginative and flat-footed theory of public reason), is to be found the key to undo the deadlock between local and universal in regard to religious values and human rights, religious diversity and public rationality.

This is not to say that there is a consensus about the rights we have or the values that underpin them. Nor is it to ignore the fact that the spread of the language of rights from West to East and from North to South was both enabled and tainted by colonialism, whether political or economic or cultural. The discourse of rights has nonetheless established itself as the language in which competing values are publicly justified and, in the face of opposition, publicly contested. The language of rights provides a public frame within which disparate communities of interest, religious and non-religious alike, can test the soundness of the Other's position and have their own position contested in return. The outcome of the process is unlikely to be moral consensus; but we may reasonably hope for an emerging sense of the credible limits of what is and what is not defensible human behaviour toward others.

Such debates do not occur in some neutral space. Nor are they generated by value-free reasoning. There is no place that is not some place in particular, and there are no reasons that are not reasons for someone. Such debates cannot be expected to lead to global consensus on 'core rights' or on prioritization in the hierarchy of rights. But they remain strategies that can be pursued within a public discourse of rights. The price of gaining access to that language is not agreement to set aside all attachments and commitments in order to achieve universality and neutrality. The price of entering into that realm of discourse is no more than a willingness to be a reasonable partisan, that is, to abide by the rules of engagement. Testing and being contested – by this means the discourse of rights constructs itself anew and the hierarchy of rights is subjected to public scrutiny. By this means, from different motives and disparate grounds, specific limited goals may be tactically agreed upon by culturally diverse groups who share no common historical narrative and occupy no 'common ground' save only the fragile and threatened planet that fate has destined as our shared home.

We must of course learn to be good neighbours. But the New England poet Robert Frost reminded us years ago that neighbourliness can also be shown in mending walls that mark off boundaries: *it is not so much common ground as good fences that make good neighbours.* In a similar spirit, I want to suggest that clarifying defensible difference may help build up a sense of community and encourage a variety of liberal virtues, including civility toward the stranger and toleration of otherness. It may also contribute to the recognition of cultural and religious diversity as a positive good.

CHAPTER 4

Religions, reasons and gods*

Philosophers have tended to discuss theistic proofs (and theistic disproofs) largely in abstraction from their specific roles within the religious traditions in which those proofs were cultivated and in which, until modern times, they flourished. As a result, the traditional theistic proofs of the West are generally presented in the philosophical literature as no more than (failed) attempts to demonstrate or within tolerable limits to establish the probability of the existence of at least one god. Whatever the history of philosophy may suggest, the history of religions shows that theistic proofs have been developed from a variety of motives and have been employed to a variety of ends, only one of which is to persuade someone not already so inclined to believe that god/s exist. Indeed, this latter purpose is fairly subsidiary in the history of religions. A survey of the place and roles of theistic proofs and disproofs within a range of religious traditions, Eastern as well as Western, suggests that in the main they were used to serve intra-traditional ends. Their principal function seems to have been more nearly *explanatory* than *justificatory.*[1] Even when they aimed them outside the tradition and used them to apologetic ends, purveyors of the proofs tended to assume prior belief in god/s on the part of their intended audience.

I

The specifically *religious* significance of theistic proofs has been too little explored in recent philosophy of religion. In some cases, the very people

---

* This article originated as a paper read in Michaelmas Term 1983 to the Philosophical Society at the University of Lancaster. For their criticisms and suggestions, I am indebted to a number of colleagues, most especially the following: John Benson, R. L. V. Hale and Colin Lyas of the Department of Philosophy; Paul Morris, Patrick Sherry, Ninian Smart and David Waines of the Department of Religious Studies; and John Bowker, now Dean of Trinity College, Cambridge.
[1] Cf. Michael Dummett's use of this distinction in 'The Justification of Deduction' (1973), in *Truth and Other Enigmas* (London, 1978), pp. 290ff.

who have been best equipped to do so have appeared most unwilling
to undertake such exploration. The author of *Reasons and Faiths*, for
instance, might have been expected to develop his observations there into
a more systematic analysis of the religious import of theistic proofs.
Yet, despite the beginning made in *Doctrine and Argument in Indian
Philosophy*, when Smart came later to discuss some theistic proofs in
Philosophers and Religious Truth and in *The Philosophy of Religion*, he
did so in a surprisingly conventional way. It is not merely that he made
little reference in those volumes to non-Western deployments of proofs,
but that he attended so little to their specifically religious functions and so
much to their strictly philosophical features. Smart, of course, allows that
proofs for the existence of god/s have a properly religious import, even if
he has never worked out this insight in any detail. A sizeable number of
contemporary philosophers of religion, however, would appear to deny
even this basic point. Those philosophers who are most self-consciously
influenced by Wittgenstein, for example, have been almost uniformly
reluctant to allow that theistic proofs have a legitimate role in religious
'forms of life'. With the notable exception of the so-called 'ontological
argument', the traditional theistic proofs have tended to be eschewed by
such philosophers as no more than illicit attempts to justify playing 'the
religious language game'. Wittgenstein himself, of course, had little time
for theistic proofs; and it might be reasonably suggested that aversion to
such proofs belongs inextricably to any philosophy of religion undertaken
in the Wittgensteinian mode. But it could also be argued that such
aversion is occasioned more by the way these arguments have been used
in the history of modern philosophy than by any considered analysis of
the function of such arguments within religious forms of life. When
viewed from this perspective, the traditional arguments may more plausibly be regarded as *moves within* religious language games proper than
as antecedent attempts to justify the playing of such games. Three points
will help illustrate what I mean, although none of the three can be fully
supported here.

First, theistic proofs are not 'tradition-neutral'. They cannot be pressed
without some modification into the service of incompatible doctrinal
schemes. Such proofs are themselves already aspects of a particular doctrinal scheme, and their specific meaning is shaped by their place within
that scheme. Some theistic proofs, including the mediaeval *ratio Anselmi*
(as it was then known), originated within the scheme in which they
continued to exercise their principal influence. Certain other theistic
proofs originated outside the doctrinal scheme/s onto which they were

later grafted. This grafting, however, was by no means a simple process. The suitability of candidate proofs seems to have been measured, not so much by their ability to provide grounds which might lead to belief as by their ability to confirm an already held belief. Historically, those 'proofs' were favoured which expressed support for or which could be adapted to provide support for the specific idea of god/s which the tradition already embraced. To take one familiar example from the history of Western religious thought: Thomas Aquinas is famous for his 'five ways', but these five are merely a selection made from the numerous arguments in circulation within mediaeval Europe. At one point or other in his writings, Thomas himself commended no fewer than eleven separate proofs for God's existence. More importantly, he rejected as many as thirteen others, which were adjudged either formally invalid or theologically inadequate or both. His short list of five 'ways' represents those which he judged to be both logically valid and theologically sound.[2] His favourite proof was the argument from 'motion' or 'change', the *argumentum ex parte motus*. It figures prominently both in the *Summa Theologiae* and in the *Summa contra Gentiles*, and it is the only proof endorsed in his *Compendium Theologiae*, which was written in the year before he died. Tracing briefly the 'pre-history' of this one proof will illustrate the way in which proofs are sometimes adapted to the requirements of particular religious traditions.[3]

The proof from 'motion' can be traced back to Aristotle. In books H and Θ of the *Physics*, he (or his school) offered two separate arguments from motion (κίνησις) in order to demonstrate, not the existence of the God of theism, but the existence of some immanent first cause or causes within the universe or at its very edges. By creatively misreading Aristotle, however, the mediaeval Muslim philosophers managed to conflate these two arguments into a single proof which they held to be compatible with the requirements of a somewhat deterministically inclined monotheism. And their reinterpretation of Aristotle was further modified by the Jewish philosopher Moses ben Maimon, who was more attracted to their monotheism than he was to their determinism, which ran counter to the

---

[2] Cf. esp. Joseph Owens, *St. Thomas Aquinas on the Existence of God*, ed. J. R. Catan (Albany, 1980); J. A. Baisnée, 'St. Thomas Aquinas' Proofs for the Existence of God Presented in their Chronological Order', *in Philosophical Studies in Honor of the Very Revd. Ignatius Smith, OP*, ed. J. K. Ryan (Westminster, MD, 1952), esp. pp. 63–4; and also R. L. Patterson, *The Conception of God in the Philosophy of Aquinas* (London, 1933), pp. 21–39.

[3] For additional details of the history of this (and other) theistic proofs, see my article on 'Gottesbeweise' in *Theologische Realenzyklopädie* XIII (Berlin and New York, 1984), pp. 724–76, and the extensive bibliography of standard and recent literature which is published on pp. 776–84.

voluntaristic tendency in the Jewish idea of God. Thomas Aquinas attributed the proof to Aristotle, but presented it basically in the form in which he found it in Maimonides, with the result that the ancient argument from motion came to be used in defence of the existence of a single First Cause whose attributes differed significantly both from those adduced by Aristotle and from those ascribed to the God of Islam. This brief sketch suggests one way in which the requirements of different religious traditions acted as a control on the formulation of a theistic argument. The resistance within mediaeval Islam to the proofs of the Arab philosophers further suggests that the grafting of a novel argument onto a vigorous tradition is not without danger. Be that as it may, the ways in which the argument from motion was adapted to the needs of traditions to which it always remained subservient show that theistic proofs are more integrated than is sometimes supposed into specific doctrinal schemes.

Secondly, theistic proofs exhibit clearly the religious 'form of life' in the range of experiences which they express. Their significance lies, not merely in their compatibility with specific doctrinal schemes, but also in their ability to express the range of religious experiences and the sorts of religious piety which are tolerated within the tradition of which they form a part.[4] Each of the traditional arguments for God's existence which have persisted in the West – the ontological, the cosmological, the ideological, and the moral proof – expresses the sorts of experience which have drawn people, not only to belief in what they took to be God, but also to worship of the deity. This holds equally for proofs *a priori* and *a posteriori*, proofs from pure reason and from practical reason. The ontological argument in at least its Anselmian form expresses a quiet but deep sense of awe before God as God; the various cosmological arguments express in different ways the sheer uncanniness that there should exist anything at all; the teleological arguments communicate that sense of wonder which can be evoked by even the most ordinary regularities or goal-directed tendencies exhibited in the world-order; the moral argument articulates that sense of oughtness which drives as if by divine imperative toward the highest good.

Each of these sorts of experience can be correlated with different styles of religious piety and forms of worship. There is one style of piety which looks inward in prayerful contemplation in order to know the very being of God and which tends to favour the rather cerebral language on

---

[4] In section II below, I suggest that this observation holds equally for the theistic disproofs attributed to the Buddha, but here I confine my remarks to theistic proofs common in the West.

ontology, without any admixture of the merely 'empirical'. There is a second, more devotional style which sees the hand of God in all that is and which tends to favour the more anthropomorphic language of popular religion. As one would expect, this sort of piety is most at home with the quasi-empirical proofs and most especially with the design argument. And there is a third style of piety which holds the practice of virtue to be the only worship required or worthy of the Author of all good.

These brief examples, each of which could be elaborated at length, suggest some ways in which types of theistic proof might be correlated with types of religious experience and practice. The question arises, of course, whether these links are 'strong' or 'weak'. In at least some cases, the links would seem to be strong. The design argument seems most intimately connected with popular piety, so that it is hardly surprising that this proof is the most widespread in the history of religions. It has flourished in the ancient and in the modern world, and in Eastern and in Western religions alike. As one would expect, it is especially strong in those traditions which stress worship or devotion (*bhakti*). It is at least implicit in the Hebrew Bible (Psalm 19) and, in modern times, it was set to music in the hymn 'The Spacious Firmament'. It seems quite natural for the design argument to be sung as a hymn. Not so the ontological argument. It expresses a very different sort of religious experience and is typical of quite another style of religious piety. The sort of piety expressed in Anselm's argument is of the contemplative (*yoga*), not the devotional variety. Anselm's aim, as expressed in the *Proslogion*, is immediate and direct knowledge of God's very being (*Op. Om.* I, 100). This he hopes to achieve through a proof grounded in pure reason, for – as he had already said in the earlier *Monologion* – it is through reason alone that we come nearest to knowing God's true essence (*Op. Om.* I, 77f.). Anselm was not, of course, commending the 'unaided reason' of later invention. Anselm held that it is God who draws us to that understanding which we seek (*Op. Om.* I, 104). His is a 'faith-full reason', and it is not irrelevant to his purposes that his proof was altered in the form of a prayer addressed to the very God who is its subject. The argument in any other form would not be Anselm's proof.

Thirdly, theistic proofs of some sort have featured in virtually every major religious tradition, Eastern no less than Western. This suggests that the presence of theistic proofs in Western religions is not simply a consequence of Greek influence on Western theologies. Indeed, allowing for a certain amount of local variation, all of the theistic proofs which we tend to regard as peculiarly 'ours' can be found duplicated in the Indian and Far Eastern religious traditions. Both the design argument and the cosmological argument are common in Indian thought. And Udayana even anticipated some moves we associate with the ontological argument in his attempt to convince Buddhists that it is impossible for God (Isvara) not to exist.[5] Although the moral argument seems not to have been used in classical Indian thought, something akin to its Kantian version can be found prefigured in China in the writings of Mo Tzu. Mo's ethical thought is a curious mixture of seemingly incompatible motives: he proposed on largely utilitarian grounds an ethic of love (*Ai*), but insisted that the practice of universal love conforms to the Will of Heaven. He argued for the existence of ghosts and spirits on the ground that such beings are required to witness the practice of righteousness (*Li*) amongst humankind, so that the worthy can be rewarded and the evil-doer punished, thereby ensuring that happiness is proportional to virtue, according to the Will of Heaven.[6] Although further examples could be offered, these few would seem to be sufficient to show that constructing arguments about the existence of god/s is a general feature of humankind's religious quest, and not merely an accident of Western intellectual history.

But this is not the whole story. Theistic proofs may be widespread in the world's religions, but opposition to such proofs is equally widespread in those same religious traditions. Strong opposition to rational proofs arose within both Judaism and Islam, as well as within Western Christianity. And, in India, Ramanuja developed a strong case against all possible theistic proofs as being both religiously dangerous and philosophically unsound (e.g. *Sri Bhasya*, I, i, 3). This would seem to suggest that theistic proofs, in addition to belonging to the heart of religious piety, are also perceived by many believers to represent some danger to theistic religion's sacred centre.

II

The standing of theistic proofs within religious traditions is radically ambiguous. They seem capable with almost equal force of both attracting and repulsing the religious spirit. But this very ambivalence heightens, rather than diminishes, their religious significance. And it suggests that we should enquire more closely into their place within the history of

---

[5] Cf. Book Three of *Nyayakusmanjali*. I am grateful to Professor B. K. Matilal for having suggested this interpretation to me.
[6] Cf. Mo Tzu, §31.

religions. Within the limits of this article, it is obviously impossible to do more than offer a preliminary survey of the territory that would require careful exploration in any proper analysis of the religious significance of arguments for and against the existence of god/s. Present purposes will be served, however, by indicating something of the variety of roles played by theistic proofs (and disproofs) within different types of religion. Brief attention is given in this section to three dissimilar types of religious tradition: a radically monotheistic tradition (Islam); a theistically more pluralistic tradition (Hinduism); and a more or less 'atheistic' tradition (Theravada Buddhism). The older Indian traditions will be introduced before turning to Islam, the tradition which has most directly influenced the role of theistic proofs within Judaism and Christianity (the religions from which are borrowed most of the examples to be cited in section III of this article).

(1) It is important at the outset to emphasize that discussion of theistic proofs, though widespread, was very much subordinate to other concerns within Indian religions. Indeed, 'right doctrine' was never accorded the sort of priority within Indian religious thought that it has sometimes been given in the West.[7] But, for our purposes, this makes Indian religion all the richer as a resource for arguments concerning the existence of god/s. Enormous diversity necessarily developed there in regard to theistic proofs because a wide range of theologies or even atheologies has flourished within the theistically permissive ambience of the *astika* or 'orthodox' systems of Hindu thought. Several orthodox Hindu sects have taught the existence of a single, uncreated and eternal Lord of the world, Isvara, variously conceived as Brahma, Visnu, Siva (to recall one common triad). Existence of Isvara has sometimes been affirmed by a straightforward appeal to the revelation (*sruti*) which is recorded in Vedic or other holy scripture. Ramanuja, for instance, repudiated all possible divine proofs as illicit attempts to establish rationally something which can be known through scripture alone. God's self-revealing activity, not our intellectual cunning, is the proper means whereby God is known in his grace (*prasada*). By way of contrast to Ramanuja, the somewhat earlier Udayana held that

---

[7] This point is rightly emphasized by Ninian Smart in his book *Doctrine and Argument in Indian Philosophy* (London and New York, 1964). Despite being in some respects now dated, Surendranath Dasgupta's five-volume *History of Indian Philosophy* (Cambridge, 1922–54) remains the standard English-language survey of Indian approaches to the philosophy of religion, including theistic proofs and disproofs. The various volumes which have appeared so far of *The Encyclopedia of Indian Philosophies*, ed. Karl H. Potter, are also indispensable guides to the arguments of the texts of the main schools.

the authority of the Vedas is not self-authenticating. Their authority is derived instead from their general trustworthiness as shown in part by the success of the theistic proofs, by which means the existence of Isvara can be demonstrated (*anumana*) with certainty. Philosophically intermediate between Udayana and Ramanuja stood Madhva, the thirteenth-century Vaisnavite opponent of the Advaita Vedanta position which had been propounded by Sankara in the ninth century. Madhva defended the view that, although they had no independent power to convince the sceptic or doubter, the arguments for God's existence could indeed be used to confirm the faith of one who had already affirmed the authority and uncreatedness of the Vedic scriptures (cf. *Tarka-tandava*).

Initially, Madhva's position appears to be quite similar to one which is familiar enough within Western theology. But, when viewed in relation to the other 'orthodox' schools within Indian religion, Madhva's position gains new significance. For mere acceptance of the Vedic authority did not entail that the message of the Vedas would be interpreted in a theistic manner. Some who accepted that same authority, most notably representatives of the Samkhya and of the Mimamsa, had interpreted the Vedas in a thoroughly atheistic way. It would be quite important, therefore, for Madhva to be able to produce arguments that would help resolve the issue whether the tradition's sacred scriptures espouse atheism or theism (*Isvaravada*).

Even though this particular doctrinal dispute cannot be said to have had the sort of central import that it might have gained had it occurred in one of the Western monotheistic traditions, it is for us an illuminating example of the intra-traditional application of theistic proofs. The principal purpose served by arguments for and against the divine existence was in this instance to help settle a hermeneutical dispute that had arisen within Hindu orthodoxy about the proper interpretation of its own revelation, the final authority of which was equally acknowledged by all sides. These particular arguments, it seems, were not designed primarily to convince someone who stood without the tradition or who simply refused to acknowledge the Vedic authority. Disagreement about the existence of Isvara had arisen within the tradition itself. But it was not a purely 'speculative' dispute, or even simply a matter of correct interpretation. At issue was the fundamentally soteriological question: is our liberation from *samsara* furthered or is it hindered by the existence of Isvara? And contrary answers to that question were tenable within Hindu orthodoxy.

(2) The atheistic answer to that question favoured by Siddharta Gautama, the 'Buddha', was made in the first instance within Brahmanism. And it

could well have been tolerated within that tradition had his own way of giving that answer not been entailed by his repudiation of other orthodox teachings which were more generally agreed among Hindus, including their somewhat deterministic interpretation of *karma* and *samsara* and also their doctrine of the 'soul' (*atman*). The Buddha's atheology is in fact a function of his repudiation of these and other views more constitutive of Hindu revelation and tradition (*smrti*). What may have begun as an *intra*-traditional disagreement, therefore, soon escalated into an *inter*-traditional dispute. And the Buddha's atheological proofs gained thereby an importance and an impetus that they would not have had within Hindu orthodoxy. They became part of a wider repudiation, not merely of a particular interpretation of (say) the *Vedanta*, but also of the authority of the Vedic revelation as such.

Repudiating the Vedic authority did not mean for the Buddha that everything found in the Vedas is thereby repudiated. But it did mean that nothing found there has more authority than something found elsewhere. The Buddha commended the view that everything, including his own teaching, should be measured by its conformity to experience and practical reason alone. The Buddha's *dhamma* is not regarded as a new ideology in the same series as other ideologies. It is intended merely as a guide to understanding. For this reason, he refused to become embroiled in purely speculative disputes. They simply distract us from our chief aim and duty.

If that was the Buddha's view, why then did he consider it worth while to construct theistic disproofs? Their place in his thought is clearly limited. He did not bother, for example, to deny the existence of gods (*devas*) conceived as contingent beings. But he did deny the existence of anything which a monotheist would allow to count as a God who is worthy of worship. And he did this for entirely religious/practical reasons. In order to be free, we must be liberated from the bondage to gods as well as from the bondage to other humans (*Dhammapada*, §417). This 'existential' concern explains the Buddha's preference for two theistic disproofs in particular, although he is reported also to have resorted to others. First, he argued that if the God of theism (Issaro) exists, then we are not masters of our own destinies and cannot, therefore, be responsibly free in our choices of action (*Jataka*, v, 238). By making the attainment of *nibbana* depend in some measure upon God, theism at least partially undermines individual responsibility and thereby impedes enlightenment (*bodhi*) and prevents release. The second main disproof said to be favoured by the Buddha is an argument based on the problem of evil and suffering

(*Jataka*, vi, 208). If God is creator of the world, then God must also be the author of all things, including evil and misfortune and injustice, all of which are obstacles to our salvation.[8] The Buddha's apparent preference for just these two disproofs is telling. They suggest that he opposed theism, not because belief in God was thought to be untenable owing to the limits of human reason etc., but because belief in God is morally repugnant to the requirements of practical religion. Human salvation is at stake. Even these theistic disproofs, therefore, express a deep religious sensitivity to which one should not be blinded by their explicitly atheistic character. The 'piety' which they embody, however, is of the contemplative or *yoga*, rather than of the devotional or *bhakti* variety.

(3) Islam stands at the opposite extreme of the religious spectrum. Variety of opinion is not unknown within Islam, but the opinions that are tolerated are confined within the bounds of radical monotheism. In order to give coherence to the presentation of Muslim attitudes toward arguments for God's existence, one can usefully adapt a three-fold classification that was first suggested by the mediaeval Spanish philosopher ibn Rushd:[9] the traditionalists or Qur'anic 'literalists', who adamantly rejected philosophical argument altogether and who professed that true knowledge of God comes through authoritative revelation alone; the 'scholastic' thinkers, who affirmed the possibility of a rational demonstration of God's existence, whether from temporality (*huduth*) or from possible being (*jawaz*); and the Sufis, who claimed direct knowledge of God's being through mystical insight.

Rational proofs for God's existence obviously found favour neither within narrow traditionalism nor within fully developed Sufism. Representatives of the former were of the opinion that, for followers of Islam, belief is an obligation, so that raising questions of Qur'an is a heresy that is possibly more dangerous than unbelief itself. The so-called 'consolation of philosophy' was said to be an illusion and any inclination toward philosophy was said to be clear evidence of deficient faith. Although Sufism in its early period of development at least tolerated (without necessarily

[8] For an elaboration of these two disproofs, see K. N. Jayatilleke, *Early Buddhist Theory of Knowledge* (London, 1963), and, more popularly, his posthumously published *The Message of the Buddha* (London, 1975). See also Helmuth von Glasenapp, *Buddhismus und Gottesidee* (Mainz, 1954).

[9] See *Al-Kashf'an Manahij al-Adillah*. For helpful surveys of Islamic philosophy, including approaches to theistic proofs, see Oliver Leaman, *An Introduction to Medieval Islamic Philosophy* (Cambridge, 1985), and Majid Fakhry, *A History of Islamic Philosophy* (New York, 1970), as well as the latter's 'The Classical Islamic Arguments for the Existence of God', *Muslim World* 47 (1957), 133–45. See also chapter 3 of William Lane Craig, *The Cosmological Argument from Plato to Leibniz* (London, 1980).

encouraging) the scholastic style of argument known as *kalam*, it gradually grew to emphasize the exclusive sufficiency of mystical experience.

Within historical Islam, therefore, the proofs for God's existence played a positive role in the strategies of two groups: the 'scholastic theologians' (*mutakallimun*) and the 'scholastic philosophers' (*falasifa*). But these two groups favoured very different sorts of theistic proof. And their different preferences betray deeper differences in their respective positions regarding the proper function of theistic proofs. These differences can be explained as follows.

The *kalam* had its origins within early attempts by Muslim theologians to understand the meaning of Qur'an and its application to Islamic life and thought. Although it degenerated later, this sort of Muslim 'scholastic theology' produced at least one philosophically astute proponent: namely, al-Ghazali. The *mutakallimun* may have moved beyond the literalism of their more radically conservative co-religionists, but they did not ever question the truth of Islamic faith or the unique authority of Qur'an for Islam. Faith was indeed as much their starting-point as it had been for, say, Augustine or Anselm within the Christian tradition. Rational argument had for the *mutakallimun* a purely ancillary function. They were favourably disposed toward the *huduth* argument for God's existence on two grounds, both of which derived from principally religious motives: first, the proof from temporality alone adequately preserved their Qur'an-based belief in God as *creator ex nihilo*; and secondly, the Aristotle-inspired argument from contingency was thought to encourage a theologically defective view of God that, according to some *mutakallimun*, differed insignificantly from atheism, to which it would inevitably lead. They reasoned that an eternal universe, whether uncaused or self-caused, had no need for a God causally to sustain it in existence. An eternal universe, according to the *mutakallimun*, is necessarily self-sufficient. Their over-riding concern, therefore, was by means of rational argument to protect the Qur'anic doctrine of God as creator and sustainer of all that is.

Although such philosophers as al-Farabi, ibn Sina and ibn Rushd were no less faithful followers of Islam than were al-Kindi and al-Ghazali, these *falasifa* adopted a very different strategy in respect to theistic proofs. Their over-riding concern was to construct on the basis of universally agreed principles an argument for the existence of an eternal God who acts as cause and sustainer of all that is. For the purposes of their argument, the authority of Qur'an was momentarily suspended. The various philosophers attached differing degrees of importance to the doctrine of creation in time, but all were agreed that this doctrine was consequent to affirming God's existence and not prerequisite to it, as the *mutakallimun* argued. The philosophers further countered that God's priority over the world is in any case a causal priority and not simply a temporal one. Using Aristotle as their guide, the Islamic philosophers insisted that God's causal priority over the world could be adequately protected without recourse to a doctrine of temporal creation.

There were genuine philosophical differences between the *mutakallimun* and the *falasifa*, to be sure, but there was also between them an essentially religious difference. They represent in the end two varieties of Muslim piety expressed in two different attitudes toward the relation of reason and faith, as well as toward the nature of Qur'anic authority. The Islamic 'scholastic theologians' can be said to have held that firm faith leads naturally to rational reflection about the divine nature and exist-ence as revealed in Qur'an; the ecclesiastically more independent-minded philosophers, on the other hand, can be said to have held that only those doctrines which can be rationally demonstrated are finally worthy of belief, even if this procedure sometimes leads to deviation from views clearly taught in Qur'an and in Muslim tradition. Al-Ghazali and others used theistic proofs in order to *confirm* traditional doctrine; ibn Sina and ibn Rushd, however, used them at least in part to *correct* or to *reform* traditional doctrine. Within the community of the faithful, the *mutakallimun* were triumphant over the reforming philoso-phers, whose influence nonetheless was keenly felt within Judaism through Moses ben Maimon and within Christianity through Thomas Aquinas, amongst others. Nor did the Muslim philosophers' influence within Christianity go unchallenged, as is shown by the condemnation of the 'errores Averrois' in edicts of 1270 and 1277. This all serves to show, moreover, that in the mediaeval period the so-called 'truths of reason' tended to be held in check by the theological requirements of particular religious traditions. And that suggests that what was expected of the theistic proofs in the Middle Ages was quite different from what came to be expected of them in the modern era. Just what was expected of them before the modern period?

III

In modern Western philosophy, the traditional theistic proofs have tended to be treated in isolation from the religious traditions in which they were developed. Once abstracted from their properly religious context, theistic proofs came to be expected to bear greater weight than they had been designed to bear when they were merely part of a larger theological strategy. They came to be expected without additional support to establish with certainty or at least high probability the existence of the God of theism. This, it is widely (but by no means universally!) agreed within contemporary philosophy, they have failed convincingly to do. But, one might argue, what they have failed to do is not what they were designed to do. Just what tasks were these alleged 'proofs' assigned in those religious traditions which have most intimately shaped Western religious thought?

Within traditional Judaism and Christianity, theistic arguments were used to more than one end. They were more frequently than not aimed at individuals or groups within their respective communities of faith in order to correct heresy, confirm true belief or simply express awe or wonder. But theistic arguments were also sometimes aimed apologetically at persons outside the community. This particular usage, which appears to be largely unknown within Judaism, is widespread within traditional Christian thought, whether Catholic or Protestant.

From the fact that theistic proofs were sometimes used to apologetic ends, however, one should not assume that they were necessarily intended to convince the sceptic or the atheist that there is a God. Theistic proofs were sometimes used by Christian apologists in order to establish some point of contact with non-Christian theists. One thinks especially of Thomas Aquinas. In the *Summa contra Gentiles*, for example, he laid out five ways in which pagan philosophers and Catholic teachers alike were said to have demonstrated God's existence (I, 13). His principal aim, however, seems not to have been to convince total sceptics or atheists that God exists and can be known to exist; the five ways outlined there were, rather, part of his strategy to convince mainly Muslims of the truth of the Catholic faith. Although it might have been *useful* in relation to heretics and Jews, rational argument was thought by Thomas to be *necessary* in any successful attempt to persuade Muslims to follow the path of Christian faith. Against heretics, Thomas commended the use of the New Testament as sufficient to convince them of the error of their ways; against Jews, he recommended appeal to the Old Testament; but against Muslims, it would be necessary to use natural reason, since they accepted the final authority neither of the Old nor of the New Testament (I, 2, 3). But, since the Muslims already believed in God, Thomas cannot have wanted by means of rational argument to convince them that God exists. So what did he intend? It would seem more likely that he had hoped through rehearsing such proofs (together with other proofs about God's nature) to establish with Muslims a positive basis upon which additional, more specifically Christian, arguments could be built.

Thomas had suggested that rational proofs were necessary in dealing both with Muslims and with those whom he called 'pagans'. The latter were not in fact a major problem for the Spanish Catholic missionaries for whose benefit Thomas had prepared his *Summa contra Gentiles*. The so-called 'pagans' were more directly a concern of the pioneering Catholic missionaries, such as Roberto de Nobili and Matteo Ricci, who later served the missions in India and in China. To take but one example, de Nobili adapted Thomas's technique to the needs of the India mission.[10] Initially and unsuccessfully, de Nobili attempted to use the Vedas directly as a foundation upon which to construct a Christian 'natural theology' and to do so in a way similar to the way Thomas had used Aristotle. Eventually and more successfully, however, he came simply to adopt Thomas's own natural theology, including the 'five ways'. And, as Thomas had done in relation to Spanish Muslims, de Nobili used those proofs wholly irenically in order to establish a groundwork of agreement with at least theistic Hinduism upon which could then be built a theologically Christian superstructure. By means of the Thomistic proofs, de Nobili hoped to convince theistic Hindus, not that God exists, but that their God and the Christians' God are one and the same. This, it was hoped, would provide a positive point of contact between these two religious traditions and thereby make the Hindus more receptive to the Christian message. The theistic proofs were being used apologetically, to be sure, but more to establish a common basis of shared belief than to convince anyone that there is a God.

This specifically Roman Catholic *positive* point of contact can be contrasted sharply with the more characteristically Protestant *negative* point of contact which features in John Calvin's 'apologetic' use of theistic proofs. He argued in his *Institutes of the Christian Religion* that, although some knowledge of God is by nature implanted in all of us, such knowledge is wholly without benefit and serves only to condemn us for having failed to respond to God as manifest in our consciousness and in God's works (I, 3). Calvin commended without apparent reservation the Ciceronian *argumentum e consensu gentium* and even went so far as to

---

[10] Editions of de Nobili's relevant works include the following: *Ajnana Nirvaranam* (Trichinopoly, 1891); *Atuma Nirunayam* (Madras, 1889); *Jnanopadesam*, vols. I–II (1775; Madras, 1891), vol. III (Trichinopoly, 1907); and *Premiere Apologie* (1610), ed. with French trans. by Pierre Dahmen (Paris, 1931). The only book-length study of de Nobili in English known to me is Vincent Cronin's *A Pearl to India* (London, 1959).

recommend one form of the ideological argument (I, 5). In both cases, however, he insisted that such knowledge, although in principle accurate enough to convict us for having failed to respond, is not in fact 'true' knowledge since it derives not from God's own initiative but from our own. Calvin called special attention to the inability of human 'religions' to lead us to true knowledge not merely of the divine nature but also of God's very existence (II, 18).

This style of apologetic is clearly worlds away from the gently irenical apologetic of someone like de Nobili. Despite the obvious differences, however, there is at least one important similarity: although theistic proofs were being aimed by de Nobili and Calvin alike at individuals who stood outside their communities of faith, neither man used them with the intention of convincing anyone that God exists. De Nobili presumed that 'true' knowledge of God's existence already prevailed within at least theistic Hinduism, so that it would be unnecessary to 'prove' it; Calvin presumed that 'true' knowledge of God's existence could be obtained only in obedient response to God's self-disclosure in revelation, so that it would be quite impossible to 'prove' it by any other means.

Although theistic proofs have been used apologetically, they have also been used to serve needs wholly internal to a religious tradition. So common are these non-apologetic uses that one is tempted to claim that they are in fact more typical uses of the proofs than is their more strictly apologetic usage.

First, theistic proofs have been employed in order to correct false or heretical beliefs about the nature of God. The clearest examples of this sort of usage can be found in mediaeval Jewish and Islamic thought. The Jewish theologian Saadia ben Joseph, for instance, constructed theistic proofs in part to correct the erroneous views of 'many believers whose belief is not pure and whose convictions are not sound'.[11] Who were these 'many believers'? To be counted among them was most certainly anyone who purported to profess God's existence whilst failing to affirm the temporality of the universe. This was also the sort of Muslim 'believer' against whom al-Ghazali aimed his own philosophical (as well as political) skills. 'Unbelievers' in the sense of atheists posed less a direct threat to the mediaeval Muslim and Jewish world than did the *falasifa*, whose adaptation of Aristotle threatened to undermine belief in a doctrine most certainly enjoined by both the Qur'an and the Hebrew Bible. Theistic proofs were used in both traditions in order to protect a teaching which

---

[11] *The Book of Beliefs and Opinions*, trans. and ed. Samuel Rosenblatt (New Haven, 1948), p. 7.

was held to be fundamental by each against a contrary position which had been gaining ground within both Islam and Judaism. An essentially intra-traditional controversy was being conducted by means of arguments which at least superficially seemed to be aimed primarily at 'the unbeliever'. The practitioners of *kalam* seem to have held that if the doctrine of *creatio ex nihilo* were denied, then one might as well be an unbeliever, since the universe would then be self-sufficient. Begin with Aristotle, it was purported, and you will end with Strato. Not only did the Jewish and Islamic *mutakallimun* attempt to refute all who denied the doctrine of creation, but they also sought rationally to ground the doctrine of a temporal creation. But this suggests a second possible use of theistic proofs.

Proofs for God's existence have commonly been used in order to confirm to the understanding something that is already a matter of firm faith. Anselm's *Proslogion*, which for a time circulated under the title *Fides Quaerens Intellectum*, provides one fairly obvious example of this use of a theistic proof. But such examples are not restricted to Christianity. Within Judaism, for instance, Saadia put proofs to a not dissimilar usage. Saadia rejected the sufficiency of reason in matters religious, but insisted nonetheless that reason can properly be used to corroborate revelation in order to show the essential reasonableness of the belief. His procedure was to develop parallel arguments within a single proof. He typically began a proof with a doctrine found in Jewish scripture and then proceeded to show that, not only is it true to faith by divine revelation, but it is also intelligible to reason through philosophical proof. A good example of this technique is found in his defence of the doctrine of *creatio ex nihilo*, which he in turn used to prove God's existence.[12] The presence of the teaching in Jewish scripture was itself sufficient for Saadia to conclude that we have no choice but to accept its truth on divine authority. But he held that it can also be confirmed by rational argument. Saadia offered in surprisingly short space four separate proofs for the temporality of the universe: from its finitude, from its composite nature, from the inherence in it of accidents, and from its existence in time. Having demonstrated to at least his own satisfaction that the universe had a beginning in time, Saadia then set out to determine whether it was self-caused or created by some external cause. He argued that nothing could be self-caused, so that the universe must have been caused by some external agent. He then sought to show that this external cause, the necessity of which had been demonstrated

[12] *Ibid.*, pp. 38ff.

speculatively, conforms exactly to that which could also be proved from scripture alone, namely

Before the mountains were brought forth, or ever thou hadst formed the earth and the world, from everlasting to everlasting thou art God. (Psalm 90:2 RSV)

This verse was used by Saadia as more than a mere illustration. It was itself *a move in the argument*. By citing from the ninetieth Psalm, he thought that the argument had been sealed, that he had been able to return to the point whence he had begun. Only then was the proof complete. Saadia's proof was being asked to serve more than one end, but at least one of those ends was to confirm to the understanding a doctrine that had already been accepted on very different grounds. Closely associated with this aim, Saadia moreover intended to help shore up wavering faith in God on the part of any doubter within the Jewish community. Amongst the ends served, however, does not seem to have been included that of persuading someone not already so inclined to believe that God truly exists. He did occasionally refer to 'unbelievers', but they seem to have been individuals who held false opinions about God, not people who denied altogether the existence of God.

Finally, theistic proofs have been used to express a sense of awe or wonder. This usage, which seems quite appropriately expressed in prayers or hymns or poetry, comes perhaps nearest to the heart of the religious sensibility of the more devotional or *bhakti* variety. A particularly powerful non-argumentative expression of such wonder in response to God's creation can be found in the first, and apparently original, half of the Hebrew Bible's Psalm 19:

> The heavens are telling the glory of God;
>   and the firmament proclaims his handiwork.
>
> Day to day pours forth speech,
>   and night to night declares knowledge.
> There is no speech, nor are there words;
>   their voice is not heard;
> yet their voice goes out through all the earth,
>   and their words to the end of the world.
>
> In them he has set a tent for the sun, which comes forth
> like a bridegroom leaving his chamber,
>   and like a strong man runs its course with joy.
> Its rising is from the end of the heavens,
>   and its circuit to the end of them;
>   and there is nothing hid from its heat.   (RSV)

The earthiness and directness of this early form of 'natural theology' possibly caused the Hebrews to have second thoughts, so that it was felt necessary later to add a similar number of verses praising the Law as the only sure and perfect revelation of God's will.[13] This Psalm was perhaps not far from Kant's mind when at the end of the *Critique of Practical Reason* he wrote: 'Two things fill the mind with ever new and increasing admiration and awe, the oftener and more steadily we reflect on them: the starry heavens above me and the moral law within me.'[14] The original six verses alone, however, seem to have inspired 'The Spacious Firmament', the hymn in which Addison eloquently expressed his generation's awe before 'the works of an almighty hand':

> The spacious firmament on high,
>   with all the blue ethereal sky,
> and spangled heav'ns, a shining frame,
>   their great Original proclaim.
> The unwearied sun from day to day
>   does his Creator's power display,
> and publishes to every land
>   the works of an almighty hand.
>
> Soon as the evening shades prevail
>   the moon takes up the wondrous tale,
> and nightly to the list'ning earth
>   repeats the story of her birth;
> whilst all the stars that round her burn,
>   and all the planets in their turn,
> confirm the tidings, as they roll,
>   and spread the truth from pole to pole.
>
> What though in solemn silence all
>   move round the dark terrestrial ball;
> what though nor real voice nor sound
>   amid their radiant orbs be found;
> in reason's ear they all rejoice,
>   and utter forth a glorious voice,
> for ever singing as they shine,
>   'The hand that made us is divine.'[15]

---

[13] However much they may have differed from one another about details of interpretation and basic approaches to the text, this century's leading commentators on the Psalms – including Briggs, Kraus, Mowinckel and Weiser – have agreed that verses 7–14 are a later addition to 19.1–6.

[14] Immanuel Kant, *Critique of Practical Reason*, trans. Lewis White Beck (Indianapolis and New York, 1956), p. 166.

[15] *Hymns Ancient and Modern*, 662.

In respect to content, it is quite near to the nineteenth Psalm; in respect to form, however, it is nearer to a non-inferential version of the modern design argument. Both the Psalmist and the poet, however, are taken more by the evidence of God's 'ordinary' presence and activity in the workings of the creation than by the evidence of God's 'extraordinary' presence and activity in mighty saving acts or direct intervention in human affairs. The wonder of the ordinary is what attracted also Luther, who was not by nature well-disposed toward theistic proofs, to the teleological argument:

We have very obvious proof that God exists, in the exact and perpetual move-ment of the heavenly bodies: we find that the sun rises and sets from year to year in its regular place. We reach the same conclusion from the certainty with which those things, which are a part of our daily experience, do not excite our wonder; they are hardly deemed worthy of notice. But if a person should be educated from his youth up in a dark place, and after twenty years released, he would be astonished at the sun and wonder what it was and why it always took a certain course at any given time![16]

Luther is not here putting forth an argument for God's existence with a view to demonstrating to an unbeliever that there is a God. Surely, he is attempting instead to evoke from his listener, who already believes and trusts in God, greater sensitivity to the divine presence in the ordinary events of life which we too commonly take for granted. His aim is not far removed from that of the author of the nineteenth Psalm, or from that of the composer of 'The Spacious Firmament'; but it is far removed from many a philosopher's pre-understanding of the aims of theistic proofs.

---

[16] *Conversations with Luther*, ed. Preserved Smith and H. P. Gallinger (Boston, 1915), p. 119.

PART II

Theistic arguments in pre-modern contexts

Part II offers three exploratory demonstrations of how comparative philosophy of religion might proceed, if oriented by the study of theistic arguments as embedded in religious forms of life. In these chapters Clayton discusses the degrees and kinds of difference that become visible through such comparative historical projects. He also provides examples of pre-modern theistic argument in relation to which the distinctive character of modern uses of such argument might be measured. Chapter 5, 'Ramanuja, Hume and "Comparative Philosophy": Remarks on the *Sribhasya* and the *Dialogues concerning Natural Religion*', develops a comparison of Hume and Ramanuja by analysing their theistic arguments with respect to the interpretative communities to which they belonged. Differentiation between the grounds, motives and ends of argument for Ramanuja and Hume provides the philosophical structure through which Clayton historicizes instances of rationality.

Chapter 6, 'Piety and the Proofs', continues Clayton's attention to the operations of theistic argument within specific religious traditions and communities, here described as forms of life. In this chapter we see an intensification of interest in the genres within which theistic proofs occur, and the audiences for such genres, topics which receive yet more explicit treatment in Chapter 7, 'The Otherness of Anselm', and in Part III. All of the essays in Part II (Chapters 6 and 7 most explicitly) approach the comparative philosophical study of theistic proofs by analysing them within contexts of composition and reception. On Clayton's view, without such contextual analysis one risks making mistaken philosophical claims. This approach receives sustained attention in Chapter 7, where Clayton emphasizes the distinctiveness of the modes of experience and learning characteristic of Anselm and his *Proslogion*. In this essay we see with great clarity the historical and literary strategies on which Clayton draws in order to emphasize the particularity of instances of reasoning and argument. In this sense, Part II prepares the ground for Clayton's more explicitly genealogical method in Part III. Moreover, the final pages of Chapter 7 gesture toward Clayton's reading of Kant as ally in the work of historically informed refinement of philosophical concepts, a topic that recurs in the final chapter of the volume.

CHAPTER 5

Ramanuja, Hume and 'comparative philosophy': remarks on the Sribhasya and the Dialogues concerning Natural Religion

In an article on the current state of Indology, first published in *Hochland* in the late 1960s, Paul Hacker made a plea for a new kind of philosophizing, one grounded in an immediate knowledge of both Indian and European sources.[1] This quotation was later used as the epithet for the much-respected book *India and Europe* by Wilhelm Halbfass, whose work as a whole can be said to have exemplified just that kind of philosophizing.

However dubious one may be that it is ever possible to have *immediate* knowledge of any text,[2] one cannot but agree that doing philosophy would be greatly enriched by immersion in the main texts of a variety of reflective traditions, including – of course – the reflective traditions of India. Ideally, one would want to be open to more than just the traditions of India and 'the West', intricately differentiated though each of them may be in itself. The ideal would be, from intimate knowledge of several traditions, to develop a reflective style that is global and not simply bi-cultural. The ideal, however, is just that – *an ideal*. It is for most of us hardly possible to master the varieties even of Western and Indian thought in tandem, to discern the points of real (not just *apparent*) difference and similarity, much less to add to that the full range of other indigenous styles of reflection it would be necessary to master in order to earn a right to philosophize in a global mode or a right to

---

[1] 'Es müsste ein Philosophieren geben, das auf unmittelbarer Kenntnis von indischen *und* europäischen Quellen gründet.' Paul Hacker, 'Die Indologie zwischen Vergangenheit und Zukunft', *Hochland* 60 (1967–8), 155.

[2] This holds especially for historically and culturally remote texts, which may have been part of a complex context that is for us largely inaccessible. The more remote the reader is from the context in which the text was produced, used and transmitted, the greater the difficulty. But no text – even the most proximate – is in this respect problem-free. However careful our approach to texts in an effort to read and understand or to weigh and assess what they say, we can never do so wholly unconditioned by those things we bring to them. Nor can we gain access to remote texts unlimited by our necessary lack of direct acquaintance with some, if not most, of the things tacitly assumed by the author or redactor of the text under scrutiny. 'Reading' texts is mediated and partial. But it is still worth while. For understanding and knowledge also admit of degrees.

undertake what is now grandly called 'world philosophy'. It is no doubt good that some philosophers dare to attempt to approximate the ideal in reality. Nothing that has been said here should be taken to dissuade from the attempt. On the other hand, it is good that some philosophers become specialists in the history, texts, languages of two historically developed and internally differentiated traditions of intellectual reflection, such as Indian and European traditions. And it is also good that philosophers aim in their cross-cultural enquiries, whether of the more 'local' or of the more 'global' variety, to move beyond a level of just 'knowing that' such and such views are held by diverse thinkers in different traditions to a level of 'knowing how' to engage their varied insights in the kind of intellectual enquiry which, in Western academic cultures, has been called *philosophizing.*

Wilhelm Halbfass was keenly aware of the need, the dangers and the possibilities of just such philosophizing. He had himself early attempted to construct a methodologically self-aware 'comparative philosophy'[3] and eventually held a chair by that name. But he came to be much vexed by the excess baggage the history of that phrase carried with it.[4] He opted eventually for a more modestly styled 'dialogic comparison' in philosophy, which was defined by 'listening as well as speaking' and by abrogating for itself all claims to be able to occupy a 'superior standpoint' or an 'objectifying distance' from the enquiry.[5] Halbfass came to conceive of *dialogue* quite literally. Although he did not live to carry out his plans, he indicated that he wanted to pursue dialogic comparison by constructing imaginary conversations between major thinkers of the European and Indian traditions on philosophical topics.[6] He mentioned, as examples, Samkara and Descartes (on whom he had written his dissertation[7]) on the foundations of knowledge or Nagarjuna and Aristotle on the nature of argument and debate. Here, I intend to follow Halbfass's lead partially in this direction, metaphorically if not literally, by engaging in conversation on a major topic two thinkers from the Indian and the European philosophical traditions. This essay is also dialogical in a further sense. I will endeavour to engage *Halbfass* himself, inasmuch as he remains present to us in memory and in print, in an extended dialogue on the

---

[3] 'Indian and Western Philosophy: Preliminary Remarks on a Method of Comparison', *Journal of the Bihar Research Society* 54 (1968), 359–64.

[4] See his remarks in *Beyond Orientalism: The Work of Wilhelm Halbfass and its Impact on Indian and Cross-Cultural Studies*, ed. Eli Franco and Karin Preisendanz (Amsterdam, 1997), pp. 297ff.; also his entry on comparative philosophy in *Historisches Wörterbuch der Philosophie* 7 (1989), cols. 922–4.

[5] Franco and Preisendanz, eds., *Beyond Orientalism*, p. 298.

[6] *Ibid.*, p. 302.

[7] *Descartes' Frage nach der Existenz der Welt: Untersuchungen über die cartesianische Denkpraxis und Metaphysik* (Meisenheim am Glan, 1968).

nature and aims of philosophical enquiry and on the nature and aims of cross-cultural philosophy.

I

The claim to be able to know the being and nature of God/Brahman by rational means was made widely both in Ramanuja's India of the eleventh century and in David Hume's Europe of the eighteenth. It is a claim that made each of them suspicious of its pretensions and concerned for its consequences. Their extended critiques of the professions of natural theology in Ramanuja's *Brahmasutrabhasya*[8] and in David Hume's *Dialogues concerning Natural Religion*[9] have become classic statements of religious scepticism in their own traditions of reflection. But, so far as I am aware, neither text has made any impact on the other's followers. Nor do these texts seem ever to have been subjected to 'dialogic comparison'.

Though Ramanuja and Hume are not here brought directly into dialogue with each other, they both of them in the texts that are our focus engaged in an imaginary dialogue with their peers and adversaries. This is most obvious with regard to Hume, who adopts a dialogic form of philosophizing that had both ancient and modern precedent in Western thought.[10] It is a genre that was quite variable, but dialogues have had a persistent history in Western philosophy, the dialogues of Plato being only the best known. The platonic dialogue is often cited as a model of philosophical reflection, in which truth is arrived at through dialectic – a series of 'yes' and 'no' exchanges until a final 'yes' emerges by consensus. If one looks at Plato's dialogues in detail, however, what happens in them is rather different. Socrates has all the good lines and makes all the persuasive arguments. His hapless interlocutor is typically left to utter propositions that are demolished one by one and is left to utter lines akin to, 'How stupid of me not to have seen that myself, great Teacher!' However much the Socratic dialogue may be idealized in philosophy textbooks, it is

---

[8] I will be citing from George Thibaut's edition (referred to here as the *Sribhasya*), published first in 1904 by the Oxford University Press, as part of the Sacred Books of the East series, edited by F. Max Müller.

[9] Originally published in London in 1779, three years after Hume's death. I will be citing from the edition prepared by Norman Kemp Smith (London, 2nd edn, 1947).

[10] On the place of dialogue as a genre in eighteenth-century British elite culture, see Michael Prince, *Philosophical Dialogue in the British Enlightenment: Theology, Aesthetics and the Novel* (Cambridge, 1996). On Hume and the art of dialogue, see the article of that title by Michel Malherbe in *Hume and Hume's Connexions*, ed. M. A. Stewart and John P. Wright (Edinburgh, 1994; University Park, PA, 1995), pp. 201–23.

hardly the stuff of lively debate between what the celebrated thirteenth-century Tibetan dialectician Sa-skya Pandita, or 'Sa-Pan', would have called 'worthy opponents'.[11]

The so-called 'Socratic dialogue' is not the only model available in Western philosophy to have been transmitted from classical times. There is, for example, the more even-handed form proffered by the Roman philosopher Cicero, most famously in his *De Natura Deorum*, after which Hume fashioned his own *Dialogues concerning Natural Religion*. The topic of the two productions is similar – so are some of the characters and the positions they represent and, in many cases, the arguments they advance. The most striking similarity, however, is that no one character occupies the privileged place of Socrates in dialogues constructed by Plato. There is an attempt by Cicero to build up the best case for each participant in the conversation, with no character left to utter lines like, 'How stupid of me not to have seen that myself!' Dialogue in the style of Cicero is a kind of invitation to a conversation that is projected beyond the text at hand. Which is to say, it is an invitation to participate in a process of philosophizing, rather than just a rhetorical artifice for a single philosophical position. A winner may be declared and it may be quite clear who in the dialogue speaks for its author. A serious attempt is nonetheless made to state opposing positions with as much vigour and conviction as the proponents of such positions would have done had they been speaking for themselves in their own 'voices'.

David Hume's *Dialogues concerning Natural Religion* are more akin to a Ciceronian than to a Socratic dialogue, even if – perhaps as a protective ruse – Hume chooses to be more coy about which character speaks for him. In the text, Cleanthes – a proponent of rational theology and defender of the design argument – is declared the winner on points.[12] Such a declaration would incline one to presume that Cleanthes must be Hume's spokesman. If it were his intention by this manoeuvre to distract critics, he did not wholly succeed. From the very beginning, a number of readers – including Joseph Priestley[13] – have, with good reason, recognized Philo (identified in the text as 'a careless

---

[11] See David Jackson, ed., *The Entrance Gate for the Wise: Sa-skya Pandita on Indian and Tibetan Traditions of Pramana and Philosophical Debate* (Vienna, 1987), II, pp. 343ff. Cf. John Clayton, 'Religious Diversity and Public Reason', in *Perspectives in Contemporary Philosophy of Religion*, ed. Tommi Lehtonen and Timo Koistinen (Helsinki, 2000), pp. 204f.

[12] *Dialogues*, §XII, p. 228. It was left to the youthful Pamphilus to issue the verdict: 'upon a serious review of the whole, I cannot but think, that Philo's principles are more probable than Demea's; but that those of Cleanthes approach still nearer to the truth.'

[13] *Letters to a Philosophical Unbeliever: Part I containing An Examination of the principal Objections to the Doctrine of Natural Religion, and especially those contained in the Writings of Mr Hume* (Bath, 1780), p. 108; cf. pp. 105–33. Contemporary reviews and reactions to the *Dialogues* have been

sceptic'[14]) as projecting the thinly disguised voice of Hume himself, a voice which is sounded more firmly in writings such as the *Enquiry concerning Human Understanding* and *A Treatise of Human Nature.*

If Philo is to be heard as the voice of Hume, for whom – if anyone – do Cleanthes and Demea speak in the *Dialogues?* Much ink has been spilt over this question. Cleanthes and Demea are undoubtedly in a sense ideal types, comprising elements of a number of individuals from the past and from Hume's own time. Even so, it is possible that these two protagonists in the *Dialogues* take on core characteristics of identifiable individuals writing in Hume's day. Hume's biographer, Ernest Campbell Mossner, tried long ago to establish that Hume's Cleanthes is modelled on Bishop Butler.[15] More recently, Professor M. A. Stewart[16] has argued that the figure more nearly approximates Henry Home Kames, author of *Essays on the Principles of Morality and Natural Religion* (1751). And the inept Demea seems to have been modelled, though with less sophistication and subtlety, on the English natural theologian Samuel Clarke, whose much-heralded Boyle Lectures were circulated as *A Demonstration of the Being and Attributes of God* (1705, 6th edn 1725).[17]

If, as now seems most likely, Cleanthes and Demea have many core features of identifiable contemporaries (though their images might be embellished for the sake of the dialogue), this would tie the dialogues more inextricably to actual debates of his day. It would also suggest that we should read Hume, through Philo ('a *careless* sceptic' in the sense of being *detached* and *uninvolved*), as setting himself up to adjudicate in controversies that he may have feared would otherwise lead to more confusion and to greater dogmatism. By this strategy he managed to tease out in a congenial literary genre the defects of the perennially popular argument from order to design (the experimental argument *a posteriori*) and also of the philosophers' favoured argument from contingent effects to their necessary causes (the metaphysical argument *a priori*).

Given that Ramanuja was writing his *Sribhasya* in 'commentary' and not in 'dialogue' mode, one would have expected it to be easy to identify

collected and reprinted in *Early Responses to Hume's Writings on Religion*, ed. James Fieser (Bristol, 2001), II, pp. 191–288.

[14] *Ibid.*, Prologue, p. 128.

[15] 'The Enigma of Hume', *Mind* 45 (1936), 334–49.

[16] 'Hume and the "Metaphysical Argument *A Priori*"', in *Philosophy: Its History and Historiography*, ed. A. J. Holland (Dordrecht, 1985), pp. 243–70.

[17] Demea's vulgarized version of Clarke's proof *a priori* is dismissed by Philo in *Dialogues*, §IX, pp. 188ff.

his voice within the text. Take, for example, his other great commentary, the *Gitabhasya*. It is simple enough in it to identify his authentic voice in the *bhakti*-style piety and practice there expounded. In the parts of the *Gitabhasya* that are written in the form of questioning and answering, one recognizes more nearly the style of catechesis than of apologetics or polemics. The *Gitabhasya* also aims, of course, to dislodge established readings of the *Bhagavadgita*, but without naming those who have interpreted it awry or considering their arguments. In the *Sribhasya*, by contrast, Ramanuja calls opponents by name and sets out to refute their arguments. He hits out most forcefully against the Mimamsakas for their views on the nature of language and the connection between ritual action and theological insight; against the Naiyayikas, on the authority of logical inference in matters theological; and, most extensively, against the Advaitins, on the necessary conditions for achieving release, on the reality of the world, on the nature of the self and on the nature of Brahman.

Attack them, he does. But his strategy requires Ramanuja first to expound their views in full, often with an enthusiasm that an inattentive reader can easily mistake for endorsement. Ramanuja can be brusque in dismissing views that he regards as untenable. Yet he more commonly presents his opponent's case in the opponent's voice. This rhetorical strategy makes reading at least this *bhasya* more like reading a 'dialogue' than one might initially have imagined. The careless reader (in the everyday sense of 'careless') can be misled about whose voice is being heard. Even if one occasionally wanders down a wrong path when working through the *Sribhasya*, one will eventually find the proper way back and rediscover who is speaking for Ramanuja. *Ramanuja is speaking for himself.*

Though true, this statement must be qualified in two ways. First, Ramanuja is not writing as a free agent, in the manner of a modern philosopher (even one who participates through individual choice or institutional appointment in an ongoing interpretative community). Ramanuja is writing self-consciously in the lineage of Yamuna, and this serves as an active constraint on the mental moves that are possible for him to make. This does not mean, of course, that he slavishly repeats what the earlier *acarya* had said. In textual communities, innovation and originality occur precisely through commentary on texts made from within a particular lineage of received interpretation. The mode of introducing novelty in such communities as these is through purported recovery of the original meaning of textual or traditional authorities. In reflective communities that are text-based, the most far-reaching changes are typically introduced, not as innovations (which tend to varying degrees to be discouraged, if not forbidden altogether), but as recoveries of some essential meaning that is said to have been distorted or obscured by later accretions. Second, Ramanuja in the *Sribhasya* is commenting on a foundation text of the Vedantan tradition. In it, he seeks above all to justify his lineage's distinctive interpretation of that text over against older and established *bhasyas*, most especially the renowned commentary by Samkara. Among other things, the way a *bhasya* is tied to *sutra* texts controls the sort of topics that are covered, the particular emphases given them, and the order of their discussion. If we want properly to understand what Ramanuja is arguing and what is at stake in his argument, we must examine his views closely in the context of *Brahmasutras* and the controversies over their meaning for different groups, all of whom regarded that text as binding on their obligation to act responsibly on its opening words: *athato brahmajijnasa.*

Ramanuja's *Sribhasya* and Hume's *Dialogues* both achieved canonical status in the educational practices of their respective interpretative communities, the Srivaisnavas, on the one hand, and Anglo-American philosophers of religion, especially of the analytic variety, on the other. The nature of that status and the process of achieving it were, of course, different in each case. All Ramanuja's literary productions were bound to become special for Srivaisnavas from the moment Gosthipurna pronounced him to be the proper successor of Yamuna. But the *Sribhasya* holds a unique place for Srivaisnavas, just because *bhasyas* occupy a unique place in the system of layering of commentaries and meta-commentaries in the Brahmanic traditions of reflection. They are, for all those who accept them as authoritative, the lens through which the normative *sutras* are read by elite members of an interpretative community; they are the filter through which other levels of commentary – *varttika, paryatika, paryaparisuddhi* – receive the essential meaning of the *sutras*. Large parts of an authoritative *bhasya*, along with the group's *sutras* in their entirety, are typically committed to memory by students as part of their education.

Though many passages in it are quite familiar to students and their tutors alike, Hume's *Dialogues concerning Natural Religion* (in my educational experience) is most unlikely to be engraved in the memory of even his most faithful devotee. The slim volume nonetheless has become part of the informal or 'practical canon'[18] of philosophical texts in faculties

---

[18] A phrase I borrow happily from Anne M. Blackburn, 'Looking for the Vinaya: Monastic Discipline in the Practical Canons of the Theravada', *Journal of the International Association of Buddhist Studies* 22/2 (1999), 281–309. *Philosophical* canons do not function precisely like *religious* canons, but they

where philosophy of religion is taught. It was not always so. For much of his life and for almost a century after his death, Hume was more often remembered as English historian (*genitivus objectivus*) than as Scottish philosopher (*genitivus subjectivus*).[19] Even in the circles where Hume was read as a philosopher, his *Dialogues* had been largely ignored in Britain and America – somewhat less so on the Continent[20]– until the new edition of his *Philosophical Writings* appeared in 1874.[21] Even so, Hume's now standard text did not become part of the working canon until well into the twentieth century.[22] The Norman Kemp Smith edition was both sign of and impetus for this change in status of *Dialogues* that only rarely had been in print for nearly a century after initial publication. But now, there is hardly a Philosophy programme in Great Britain or North America that would not as a matter of routine include Hume's *Dialogues concerning Natural Religion* on its reading list in the philosophy of religion. The volume continues to attract admirers (who claim that it demolished for good the design argument) and also quibblers (who claim that it is a seriously flawed piece of analysis). In either case, the book is still read. And it remains part of the normal working canon, at least among Anglo-American analytic philosophers of religion.

In a volume honouring the memory of Wilhelm Halbfass, neither this selection of thinkers nor this choice of topic is self-evident. Hume and Ramanuja figure neither singly nor as a pair in the grand narrative of *India and Europe*. If Halbfass had ever chosen to address the topic central to this paper, he would have been more likely to have chosen the likes of Samkara and Descartes. Halbfass was, in any case, unlikely to have focused his energies directly on the knowability of God. In his productions as a writer, Halbfass was not much occupied with the debates in

---

do act as reference points for a tradition of reflection. They become points of departure for the discussion of major philosophical issues, and intellectual lineages are defined by reference to them. The formation of textual canons in interpretative communities of philosophers has in the past twenty-five years or so itself become a topic of detailed research and reflection. See, e.g., Bruce Kuklick, *The Rise of American Philosophy* (New Haven, 1977), and his essay in *Philosophy in History: Essays on the Historiography of Philosophy*, ed. Richard Rorty *et al.* (Cambridge, 1984).

[19] His reputation as 'English historian' derives from his six-volume *History of England from the Invasion of Julius Caesar to the Revolution of 1688* (Edinburgh and London, 1754–62).

[20] There was a French edition in 1780 and an edition appeared the following year in Germany, where it was given a boost in 1787 by the appearance of *David Hume über den Glauben* by Friedrich Heinrich Jacobi.

[21] *The Philosophical Writings of David Hume*, ed. T. H. Green and T. H. Grose, eds., 2 vols. (London, 1874).

[22] This is a complex story, which cannot be told here, but I intend to do so elsewhere in the near future. Editors' note: See also Chapter 10 of the present volume.

India or Europe about specifically religious questions.[23] This is not to say that he was not in his way occupied with questions that might reasonably be called 'religious'. In response to Frank Clooney's contribution to *Beyond Orientalism*, Wilhelm insisted that – though not himself a practitioner of any religion – he shared with those who are 'a realm of religious meaning'. He added that he regarded the religions as indispensable ways of formulating 'questions which continue to be my own questions, and which no science can even comprehend as questions',[24] much less have power to silence with unassailable answers.

Not just in the context of the present volume do Ramanuja and Hume seem an odd couple to be nudged into conversation.[25] Their differences are clear and easy enough to catalogue. Moreover, even among his Enlightened peers, Hume held all non-European cultures in unusually low esteem.[26] His references to India are rare, casual, and as caustic as they are ill-informed. In his *Natural History of Religion*, with neither apparent embarrassment nor evident knowledge, Hume speaks indiscriminately of Indians, Africans and Japanese as being 'very barbarous and ignorant nations . . . who can form no extensive ideas of power and knowledge' and as idolaters, among whom 'worship may be paid to a being, whom they confess to be wicked and detestable; though they may be cautious, perhaps, of pronouncing this judgment of him in public, or in his temple, where he may be supposed to hear their reproaches'.[27] Later in the *Natural History*, he complains of the 'excessive penances of the [superstitious] Brahmans' who seek divine favour in ritual acts rather than 'in virtue and good morals'.[28] At the conclusion of part VII of the *Dialogues*, the Hume-like Philo introduces what he calls the 'ridiculous' view of the Brahmins that an infinite spider spun the universe from its own bowels and 'annihilates afterwards the whole or any part of it, by absorbing it again, and resolving it into his own essence'.[29] This is the same Philo who elsewhere commends to Cleanthes as thinkable the view that

[23] The main exception being, 'Indian Philosophers on the Plurality of Religious Traditions', in *Identity and Division in Cults and Sects in South Asia*, ed. Peter Gaeffke and David Utz (Philadelphia, 1984), pp. 58–64.

[24] Franco and Preisendanz, eds., *Beyond Orientalism*, p. 146.

[25] Ramanuja has more typically been compared to modern Western Idealists, whether of the Bostonian or the Berliner species. See F. K. Lazarus, *Ramanuja and Bowne: A Study in Comparative Philosophy* (Bombay, 1962), and Rama Prasad, *Ramanuja and Hegel* (Delhi, 1983).

[26] For a survey of contemporary dispositions, see David Pailin, *Attitudes to Other Religions: Comparative Religion in Seventeenth- and Eighteenth-Century Britain* (Manchester, 1984).

[27] *The Natural History of Religion*, ed. H. E. Root (Stanford, 1956), §XIII, p. 66.

[28] *Ibid.*, §XIV; Root, pp. 70f.

[29] *Hume's Dialogues concerning Natural Religion*, ed. Norman Kemp Smith (London, 2nd edn, 1947), pp. 180f.

the world might have arisen from vegetation or generation, rather than manufacture.[30] This is the same Philo who also expresses sympathy for the view that the world could be imagined as being God's body.[31] But he may have shown a dash less sympathy for such a view had Hume learned of it first from reading Ramanuja, instead of from reading classical Greek writers.

It is not among such speculative and metaphysical cobwebs that we find the most engaging parallels between Hume and Ramanuja in matters pertaining to philosophy of religion. If we turn, rather, to epistemology we find important and unexpected points of resemblance, but – upon examination – it turns out that the points of difference are more determinative in their thought than points they seemingly held in common. Ramanuja and Hume both hold experience or 'perception' (*pratyaksa*) and inductive reasoning or 'inference' (*anumana*) as proper ways of coming to know and at the same time as grounds for claiming to know things appropriate to each *pramana*. Ramanuja also holds *sabda* or testimony as reliable. In restricted instances, Hume, too, trusts human testimony as reliable, but he does so with caveats not likely to have been found congenial by Ramanuja.

Hume famously reduced all true propositions to two kinds: those that express relations of ideas and those that express matters of fact.[32] The former are analytically true, in the sense that their negation is self-contradictory; whereas the latter are contingently true, in the sense that they can be negated without entailing self-contradiction. That is to say, matters of fact – including the existence of mango trees, fires on mountains, cats on mats, unicorns and also gods – must be established, if at all, by sense experience or observation. Rational proof alone, however valid it may be formally and however elegant it may be aesthetically, can never establish a matter of fact. There are these two possibilities, and no others: abstract reasoning regarding relations of ideas; experimental reasoning regarding matters of fact. On these principles, Hume believed that he could determine which claims might be deemed worthy candidates for examination, and which claims should be avoided altogether. The *Enquiry concerning Human Understanding* ended with words that might be moderately chilling for most metaphysicians, but must make the blood run cold for all librarians:

When we run over libraries, persuaded of these principles, what havoc must we make? If we take in our hand any volume; of divinity or school metaphysics, for

---

[30] *Ibid.*, pp. 176ff.; cf. pp. 144f.   [31] *Ibid.*, pp. 171f.

[32] *Enquiry concerning Human Understanding*, §IV: 'Sceptical Doubts concerning the Operations of the Understanding'. In the Selby-Bigge edition, pp. 25ff. This is known popularly as 'Hume's fork'.

instance; let us ask, Does it contain any abstract reasoning concerning quantity or number? No. Does it contain any experimental reasoning concerning matter of fact and existence? No. Commit it then to the flames: For it can contain nothing but sophistry and illusion.[33]

Even though Hume appears to recognize two ways of coming to know things – experience and inference – in respect of matters of fact, there is only one way: *experience*.[34] Even though Ramanuja recognizes inference and experience, in respect of matters of fact, he also holds that inferences must be confirmed by experience. With regard to matters of fact, in Hume's texts and in Ramanuja's, arguments will be made and inferences will be drawn in order to ground epistemic judgments. But arguments and inferences have no epistemic authority independent of the experiences and observations that give them warrant. In the *Sribhasya*, Ramanuja reports in a cursory way his views on the legitimate ways of coming to know, which also serve as proper grounds for claiming to know.[35] Within the accepted boundaries of what Vedantan *acaryas* profess, Ramanuja has nothing especially novel to say about the *pramanas*, not as a class or singly. And, like those *acaryas*, Ramanuja holds that experience and inference may be reliable in optimal circumstances in the world of facts, but with regard to all divine things, testimony or *sabda* is the only reliable *pramana* and, therefore, authoritative in all matters to do with Brahman. In the spiritual realm, scriptural authority trumps wherever our senses may lead us by observation or our reason, by formal argument:

Apprehension of Brahman – which is mere intelligence, eternal, pure, free, self-luminous – is effected by Scripture which rests on endless unbroken tradition, cannot therefore be suspected of any, even the least, imperfection, and hence cannot be non-authoritative; the state of bondage, on the other hand, with its manifold distinctions is proved by Perception, Inference, and so on, which are capable of imperfections and therefore may be non-authoritative.[36]

With all his intuitive suspicion of the claims of traditional religion, Western or not, David Hume is most unlikely to have been inclined to acquiesce in such a bold claim. He would have been more inclined to insist that we use our senses to correct our senses whenever they mislead us; that

---

[33] *Ibid.*, §XII.3, S-B, p. 165.   [34] Cf. §XII.3, S-B, pp. 163ff.

[35] Cf. *Sribhasya*, §I.1.3; Thibaut translation, pp. 162ff. A more systematic account of Visistadvaita views on epistemology was elaborated by Srinivasdasa in his *Yatindramatadipika* (Poona, 2nd edn, 1934), the basis for the account in Anima Sen Gupta, *A Critical Study of the Philosophy of Ramanuja* (Varanasi, 1967), pp. 25–61.

[36] *Sribhasya*, §I.1.1; Thibaut, p. 25.

we use our reason to correct our reason whenever it leads us astray. There is no other means of greater certainty than those means made available by nature to human understanding. In limited cases, Hume allows, it is even reasonable to accept *as certain* testimony about matters of fact that runs counter to our cumulative experience of the way things go in the world. Ironically, perhaps, one such case is cited in the course of his celebrated attack on miracles in the *Enquiry concerning Human Understanding* [§X]. Having catalogued from the history of religions a list of miraculous claims he regarded as patently absurd, Hume goes on without much fanfare to mention an apparent counter-example to his generally sceptical stance toward knowledge of past unique events:

Suppose all authors, in all languages, agree, that, from the first of JANUARY 1600, there was a total darkness over the whole earth for eight days: Suppose that the tradition of this extraordinary event is still strong and lively among the people: That all travellers, who return from foreign countries, bring us accounts of the same tradition, without the least variation or contradiction: It is evident, that our present philosophers, instead of doubting the fact, ought to receive it as certain, and ought to search for the causes whence it might be derived.[37]

That is to say, reports of a strikingly unique event, which is contrary to our cumulative experience of the world, may be judged to have happened for sure without our knowing its causes, if it is (a) universally and (b) invariably attested and if it has (c) no supernatural agency ascribed to it! These are hardly caveats that Ramanuja would happily allow in respect of the authority of scriptural *sabda*.

Belief, for Hume, is a matter of evidence: wise persons proportion their belief to evidence. Belief, for Ramanuja, by contrast, is more a matter of authority: wise persons proportion their belief to the teachings of the Vedas and the Upanisads. Both Hume and Ramanuja concur that God/Brahman is not a possible object of sense perception, or an entity whose nature and existence could ever be established by inference or 'reason'. Their respective reasons, in the sense of *grounds*, for repudiating every possible rational proof of the being and character of God/Brahman are remarkably similar. But their reasons, in the sense of *motives*, for undermining every possible inference to the Deity are rather less akin. And their reasons, in the sense of *ends* for which such a critique is undertaken in the service of their respective communities of interpretation, are altogether different.

---

[37] *Enquiry*, §X, S-B, pp. 127–8.

II

The knowability of the gods or Brahman is a topic that has historically exercised the best minds of both Indian and Western cultural traditions of self-reflection. In both traditions, the topic has been debated with regard to at least three distinct issues: the soundness of individual proofs for the existence of the gods/Brahman; the provability of the existence of the gods/Brahman by rational or other means; the actual existence of the gods/Brahman.

These three issues tend often to be conflated in discussion, but they need to be separated out for the purposes of analysis in order to avoid confusion. For instance, Brahman or the gods may well exist, even if their existence cannot be established rationally; their existence may be provable rationally, but some specific proofs may be logically unsound. Although these issues have all been discussed in Indian and Western traditions of philosophy, there remain differences of importance. The so-called Indian syllogism is not just different in detail from the Aristotelian syllogism or its more modern alternatives; it is also different in kind. For instance, the formal 'syllogism' in an Indian sense cannot simply be identified with 'deduction' in a Western sense, or *anumana* with 'inference'.[38] Moreover, Indian philosophy makes use of 'property-location' logic, rather than the 'subject–predicate' logic that is typical in traditional Western thought.[39] And the Indian syllogism shows in its very form that it was designed to meet the particular needs of public debate (*vada*). As a result, Indian 'logic' is less easily separated from 'rhetoric', the art of persuasion, than is Western logic, which – for good or ill – traditionally draws the lines more sharply between formal logic and rhetorical skills.

The more important sort of difference between discussions of the knowability of gods or Brahman in India and in the West arises out of differences in their historically dominant religious models. The dominance in the West of theistic, typically monotheistic, religious models has meant that discussion about the knowability of gods, more often than not, has tended to bear the weight of religion *versus* irreligion. The spiritual ambience of India, where one could be *astika* or 'orthodox' in Brahmanic terms and still be non- or even anti-theistic, has meant that the debate about gods/Brahman has in effect been for the most part a debate *within*

---

[38] See V. K. Bharadwaja, 'Implication and Entailment in Navya-Nyaya Logic', *Journal of Indian Philosophy* 15 (1987), 149–54. Contrast Mohini Mullick's article by the same title in *Journal of Indian Philosophy* 4 (1976), 127–34.

[39] Bimal Krishna Matilal, *Logic, Language and Reality* (Delhi, 1985), pp. 6ff.

religion, not between religion and irreligion. This state of affairs has affected, among other things, the strategy in Indian debate of arguing for and against the existence of gods. Many of Udayana's proofs of God in the *Nyayakusumanjali*, for instance, are philological or grammatical and seem to have been intended to persuade Mimamsakas that the Vedas – whose eternity and authority Mimamsakas accepted, if anything, more firmly than Naiyayikas – had an author and that their author was God.[40]

Denial of God/Brahman in the non-Brahmanic sects of South Asia also tended to be motivated by religious concerns. The Carvaka were the exception that proves the rule. The Buddha, for instance, repudiated the existence of a creator God (*paramesvara*) for reasons that are essentially soteriological. He and his followers did not bother to deny or seek to disprove the existence of *devas* or *devatas*, because they were not spiritually very bothersome. But he and those who came later to develop his thought formulated several arguments against the existence of a Supreme Being,[41] upon whom devotees depended to deliver them from the cycle of *samsara*. Such a belief is considered to be spiritually more dangerous. It is danger-ous most plainly because it ultimately hinders liberation. So long as we depend on some power other than ourselves to attain final release, according to the Buddha's words as reported in the *Dhammapada*, we will never achieve release.[42] Belief in a *paramesvara* or *mahesvara* must, therefore, be opposed by all rational means.

Neither Ramanuja nor Hume calls into question the fact of God's existence. Although they do not conceive the divine Being in precisely the same ways, there is quite enough similarity in their conceptions, at least at a gross level of magnification, to make it worth our while to hold up for comparison their respective strategies regarding the knowability of God/Brahman.

Ramanuja conceives the Supreme Being to be possessor of all perfections and of no defects. Most succinctly, Ramanuja identifies Brahman or Visnu[43] as 'highest Person (*purushotta*), who is essentially free from all imperfections and [who] possesses numberless classes of auspicious qualities of unsurpassable

[40] See *Nyayakusumanjali*, stabaka V.

[41] George Chemparathy, 'Two Early Buddhist Refutations of the Existence of Isvara as the Creator of the Universe', *WZKSO* 12/13 (1968/9), 85–100; Richard P. Hayes, 'Principled Atheism in the Buddhist Scholastic Tradition', *Journal of Indian Philosophy* 16 (1988), 5–28; Roger R. Jackson, 'Dharmakirti's Refutation of Theism', *Philosophy East and West* 36 (1986), 315–48; and also K. N. Jayatilleke, *Early Buddhist Theory of Knowledge* (London, 1963).

[42] *Dhammapada*, §417.

[43] *Sribhasya*, pp. 89, 91. See also the *Vedantasamgraha*, where Ramanuja attempts to establish from scriptures that Visnu (Narayana) is none other than this Supreme Person.

excellence'.[44] He is much more elaborate in his characterizations of Brahman's many qualities[45] than Hume would think is warranted by the evidence, but Hume would perhaps allow Ramanuja's short statement as an account of what people commonly take God to be.[46] The most important metaphysical difference between them – a difference to which I will want to return later – is that for Hume, God and world are *externally* related, whereas for Ramanuja, they are *internally* related. Both men accepted the existence of such a Being, and occupied themselves rather with the issue whether the existence and nature of that Being can be discerned by rational means. Hume was indeed reluctant to make strong claims about the attributes proper to his God, but he still remained a believer of sorts, and was reportedly deeply shocked at the bold claims of atheists he encountered among Parisian philosophers.[47] Belief in God was for Hume almost a 'natural belief', akin to belief in other minds or the external world.[48] The only question in doubt is *how much* we are able to know about the nature of such a Being. Hume is less occupied with the claims of atheists, real or imagined, than he is with the claims of theists who proffer putative proofs of the existence of the Deity or who claim detailed knowledge of divine being by other means. In his writings, Ramanuja does consider the claims of non-theists – namely, of Mimamsakas – but he has mainly in his sights the claims of Advaita Vedantins, whose system he tends to oppose wholesale, and the claims of the Naiyayikas, who specialized in logic and debate and who had developed an elaborate rational defence of the existence of a Supreme Being. For each man, the main issue is the possibility of some rational knowledge of Brahman or God. To that end, each tests at least one of the locally most popular theistic arguments of his day: the argument from regularity to design(er).

---

[44] *Sribhasya*, p. 4. [45] *Ibid.*, pp. 88–9, 156 *et passim*.

[46] Cf. *Hume's Dialogues*, p. 141 *et passim*.

[47] Regarding his encounter with avowed atheists at d'Holbach's *salon*, see Diderot's *Lettres à Sophie Volland*, ed. André Babelon, II (Paris, 1938), p. 77. Cf. Ernest Campbell Mossner, *The Life of David Hume* (Oxford, 2nd edn, 1980), pp. 483ff.

[48] The matter is more complex (and also more controversial) than this simple statement suggests. Could such a 'belief' have any religious significance? It all hangs on what kind of 'belief' one thinks is required for a belief in some God to have religious significance. What Hume allows is clearly not sufficient to sustain a robust belief in the 'God' of traditional Judaism, Christianity or Islam, or even of philosophical theism. It may still, nonetheless, be sufficient to sustain belief in some kind of 'God' – say the kind which has evoked a sense of wonder at it all seemingly sufficient to serve the religious needs of an Albert Einstein or of a Stephen Hawking. For a useful survey of the literature and issues involved, see Beryl Logan, *A Religion without Talking: Religious Belief and Natural Belief in Hume's Philosophy of Religion* (New York, 1993). See also Miguel A. Badía Cabrera, *Hume's Reflection on Religion* (Dordrecht, 2001), pp. 297ff.

Arguments of this kind are among the most ancient and widespread proofs of God/s in the history of humankind.[49] In the Indian context, it was a favourite proof of Naiyayikas, almost from the moment of their taking a more theistic turn.[50] It figures in classic texts of the Nyaya tradition, including the *Nyayamanjari* by Jayanta, the ninth-century admirer of the Buddhist logician Dharmakirti, and the *Kiranavali* and *Nyayakusumanjali* by Udayana, a contemporary of Ramanuja in remote Mithila, though the two were evidently unknown to one another. The proof (with many variations) runs along the following lines in Naiyayika texts: (a) this universe had an intelligent being as its cause; (b) because it consists of many parts that are arranged purposefully; (c) things that consist of many parts that are arranged purposefully, like a chariot, have an intelligent being as their cause; (d) this [universe] is like that [chariot]; (e) hence, it has an intelligent being as its cause.

In a world that was increasingly shaped by Newtonian principles of physics, there were in seventeenth- and eighteenth-century Britain variations on what was often called 'physico-theology', but which was known by Hume as 'the argument *a posteriori*' and which has now come to be called more commonly 'the design argument'. At a time when the Germans inclined to *a priori* demonstrations and the French, to versions of what Kant named the *cosmological proof*,[51] most British philosophers, scientists and theologians were irresistibly drawn to embrace the less formal and more intuitive design argument, which was generally held to be persuasive, even if it was admitted to lack the force of a demonstration. This feature of the design argument suits present interests well, in that this less rigorous sort of argument is much more akin to the informal style of proof favoured by the 'natural brahmalogians' of India. It is Cleanthes in the *Dialogues* who iterates, on behalf of mainstream philosophers and scientists and theologians of Hume's day, the experimental argument *a posteriori*:

Look round the world: Contemplate the whole and every part of it: You will find it to be nothing but one great machine, subdivided into an infinite number of lesser machines, which again admit of subdivisions, to a degree beyond what human senses and faculties can trace and explain. All these various machines, and even their most

---

[49] See John Clayton, 'Gottesbeweise', in *TRE*, XIII (1984), pp. 751ff.
[50] C. Bulcke, *The Theism of Nyaya-Vaisesika: Its Origin and Early Development* (Delhi, 2nd edn, 1968), pp. 35–45. Cf. Gerhard Oberhammer, *Wahrheit und Transzendenz: ein Beitrag zur Spiritualität des Nyaya* (Vienna, 1984).
[51] *Der einzig mögliche Beweisgrund zu einer Demonstration des Daseins Gottes* [1763], in *KA* 2:160.

minute parts, are adjusted to each other with an accuracy, which ravishes into admiration all men, who have ever contemplated them. The curious adapting of means to ends, throughout all nature, resembles exactly, though it much exceeds, the productions of human contrivance; of human design, thought, wisdom, and intelligence. Since therefore the effects resemble each other, we are led to infer, by all the rules of analogy, that the causes also resemble; and that the Author of nature is somewhat similar to the mind of man; though possessed of much larger faculties, proportioned to the grandeur of the work, which he has executed. By this argument *a posteriori*, and by this argument alone, we do prove at once the existence of a Deity, and his similarity to human mind and intelligence.[52]

Neither Philo nor his creator doubts the existence of God, in some non-anthropomorphic and non-specific sense 'maker of heaven and earth'; nor does either one of them doubt (except methodologically) that this Being bears at least a remote resemblance to human intelligence. Hume makes clear his own acquiescence to such a belief in the *Natural History of Religion* (1757). 'The whole frame of nature', he declares there, 'bespeaks an intelligent author; and no rational enquirer can, after serious reflection, suspend his belief a moment with regard to the primary principles of genuine Theism and Religion.'[53] This belief is given here and elsewhere in the *History* as something impossible to doubt (*contra* Descartes), rather than as a belief established by inference. It seems almost a natural disposition or intuition, not an inductive inference or the conclusion to a formal demonstration. Nor can it be a belief based on religious experience or biblical authority. Hume was as suspicious of the claims of religious enthusiasts as had been John Locke before him or was Immanuel Kant after him. And the weight Hume attached to the authority of scripture is easily surmised from his celebrated attack on miracles in §X of the *Enquiry concerning Human Understanding*. An irrefragable quality to basic belief in God is consistent with what Hume has all his characters agree in the *Dialogues*, namely, that the sorts of problems under discussion there concern the *nature* of God, not the *being* of God. But just *what* each of them does believe about the *God* in whom they are content to believe is quite considerably different. In Philo's (and also of course Hume's) case, for instance, the content of their belief is minimalist in the extreme. None of the traditional moral (e.g. goodness, mercy, justice) or metaphysical (e.g. omnipotence, unity) attributes can be established for the Supreme Being by what we might justifiably infer of such a Being by analogy from the world as we have experienced it.

---

[52] *Dialogues*, part II, p. 143. Philo's restatement and initial objections follow on pp. 145ff.
[53] *The Natural History of Religion*, p. 21; see also §XV, Root edition, pp. 74f.

Is Hume's 'God' then empty of all attributes? If so, how would such a God differ from no God at all?

Hume adopts the principle that like effects imply like causes. If the putative 'cause' is not available to inspection, no more can be inferred about it than is sufficient to account for observable effects.[54] Since the world's cause or causes are not possible objects of sense perception, what we can know of it or them, if we can know anything at all, is limited to what can be warranted by observation statements about the world of sense experience. A number of consequences follow from this stricture that might well be thought generally unhelpful to purveyors of the argument from regularity to design. But, insists Philo, the principle cannot be doubted, nor can its consequences be resisted.[55] Since the world is finite, we cannot infer that the cause(s) of the world is infinite; since there is multiplicity in the world, we cannot infer that its cause(s) is one; since there are defects in the world, we cannot infer that its cause(s) is perfect; since there is evil and gross suffering in the world, we cannot infer that its cause(s) is good.

Of all these difficulties, the last named – the ever daunting 'problem of evil' – receives the most extended consideration in the *Dialogues*.[56] If we look at the world, with its many sufferings and ills, natural and moral, and without prior assumption of a benevolent creator and governor, reasons Philo, then we are bound to see that 'the whole presents nothing but the idea of a blind nature, impregnated by a great vivifying principle, and pouring forth from her lap, without discernment or parental care, her maimed and abortive children'.[57] Moreover, Hume argues, even if the world were perfect in every way, we still could not know for certain that the excellences of the work could legitimately be ascribed to the cause of its construction.[58] Defects in the world, on the other hand, suggest shortcomings in the cause of the world. Perhaps it was the early effort of a young and inexperienced godling, or maybe it was the late production of an ageing and incapacitated divinity?[59]

In the first set of objections, Hume did not directly call into question the authority of the 'artisan–artifact' analogy that is the basis of the

---

[54] See *Enquiry*, §XI, S-B, pp. 135ff.

[55] *Dialogues*, §V, p. 165. The main consequences are relentlessly elaborated by Philo on the ensuing pages.

[56] *Ibid.*, §§X–XI, pp. 193–213. Though the 'problem of evil' does not figure in Ramanuja's *Sribhasya* as centrally as it does in Hume's *Dialogues*, it is not altogether absent from the great *acarya's* work. See P. B. Vidyarthi, *Divine Personality and Human Life in Ramanuja* (New Delhi, 1978), pp. 1–26.

[57] *Dialogues*, §XI, p. 211.   [58] *Ibid.*, §V, p. 167.   [59] *Ibid.*, §V, p. 169.

particular type of design argument under scrutiny in the *Dialogues*. He goes on, secondly, to object that the analogy required by this type of argument is too weak to support the theists' desired claims about the nature of the world's cause(s). The design argument assumes that the world as a whole resembles a human artifact, such as a watch. Just as an artifact of such precision and purpose implies a skilled and intelligent artificer, regularity and purpose evidenced in the world as a whole and in its parts imply also an intelligent maker. The artisan–artifact analogy itself has no intrinsic authority, however, and its success depends upon the similarity of the world as a whole to a human artifact. Much in the world-order does not resemble a human artifact.[60] For instance, plants and animals do not replicate themselves by manufacture. They do so by natural processes of vegetation and generation. One could quite plausibly argue that the world as a whole more nearly resembles a vegetable or an animal than it resembles a vast machine. All three are merely analogies or models, if one prefers, and none of the three has intrinsic authority. Each of the three is equally plausible and equally implausible as a potential explanatory hypothesis of the way things go in the world as a whole. There is no reason to infer that the cause of the world, therefore, resembles human intelligence; it could as easily resemble a seed or an egg. It is human arrogance to believe that the cause of the world resembles the principle that moves our own minds.[61]

Thirdly, any attempt at all to talk about the 'cause(s) of the world as a whole' raises for Hume insurmountable difficulties. We can infer things about *causes* of effects only when we are certain that they are *effects*, that is to say, when we are certain that they have been *caused*. We infer skills and qualities attributable to the watchmaker of a particular watch, because we already know from numerous comparable cases that watches are made, and do not come into being spontaneously or by vegetation or generation. Likewise, we infer the building activity of workers from a half-finished house, because we have seen many other houses in the process of being built by workers. Houses, too, are constructed and neither vegetate nor generate themselves. But the world as a whole is quite different from these examples. We have no prior knowledge of how worlds come to be. We have never seen other worlds being made. We do not know if they are manufactured or if they come to be by some other means. The world as a whole, Hume asserts, is unique in experience.[62] In order to make a plausible

---

[60] *Ibid.*, §§VI–VII, pp. 170ff.   [61] *Ibid.*, §III, p. 156; cf. *Enquiry*, §XI, S-B, pp. 145ff.
[62] *Dialogues*, §II, pp. 149ff. Here Demea is speaking, but he is later supported by Philo.

analogy about the origin and order of this world, we would also need to have acquaintance with other cosmogonies, whence we might accumulate enough data to speculate about the likely nature of the cause(s) of this world. The sting of this point may have been eased by advances in more recent astronomy and physics, but there was no effective antidote for it in the scientific cupboard of Hume's day and, as a result, Cleanthes' response to Philo on this point is feeble and misguided.[63]

Finally, Hume argues that the order evident in the world as a whole and in its parts may in any case have a purely naturalistic explanation. Theistic explanations are not the only ones available to the philosophical imagination.[64] Hume's Philo holds up the belief of Epicureans that the world, being composed of a finite number of atoms in random motion in infinite time, eternally produces every conceivable combination an infinite number of times. The world moves eternally in and out of periods of formation, stability and dissolution. At the moment, we happen to be living in a period of relative stability. But this orderly state is merely transitory; the world has been produced and destroyed before and it will be again and again, *ad infinitum.* Philo, ever careless, has nothing riding on the acceptance of this view. He is merely claiming that such an account of the apparent regularity in the world as a whole has just as much to commend it as has the theistic account preferred by those to whom the argument from order to design(er) seems plausible.

Scepticism in such matters is the viewpoint more nearly being commended by Philo and his literary designer. Our natural tendency is to scepticism, Hume speculates, but within the bounds of sense, this tendency is kept in check by brute facts. We stumble over chairs; we fall down stairs; we bang into doors. But when we move beyond the bounds of sense experience, there is no such check on our natural tendency to scepticism. To claim some rational knowledge of the nature of gods, who dwell beyond the reach of human perception, is for humankind simply not warranted, 'except we call in the assistance of exaggeration and flattery to supply the defects of argument and reason'.[65] In such matters, Hume says with heavy irony, one listens with greater expectation to priests than to philosophers![66] What do we hear when we turn, not to a Christian priest, but to a Srivaisnavite *acarya*?

[63] See *Dialogues*, §II, p. 150.   [64] *Ibid.*, §VIII, pp. 182ff.
[65] *Enquiry*, §XI, S-B, p. 137.   [66] *Ibid.*, p. 138.

III

Issues to do with natural theology were the main topic of conversation in the *Dialogues* of David Hume. Not so, in the *Sribhasya* of Ramanuja, who harboured no doubts about the fact of Brahman's existence or about knowability of that existence or about knowability of Brahman's attributes. For Ramanuja, the only question to be settled was the proper and reliable means of such knowledge, the certainty of the knowledge itself not being a matter of doubt. The point to establish firmly, according to Ramanujacarya, is that Brahman is knowable reliably and solely from Vedic scriptures, including the Vedantan Upanisads. He makes his case when attempting to elucidate the meaning of the third *Brahmasutra*, which in Sanskrit is a single word – *sastryonitvat* – the meaning of which was a matter of intense dispute among diverse Vedantan schools, especially between the *advaita vedanta* of Samkara and the *visistadvaita vedanta* of Ramanuja.

The first *adhyaya* of the *Brahmasutras* lays the general basis of the Vedantan doctrine of Brahman, with liberal citations and allusions to the more theologically inclined Upanisads – especially the Brhadaranyaka, the Chandogya, the Katha and the Mundaka.[67] For our present purposes, the first four *sutras* are most important. Having already enquired into *dharma* in the *Mimamsasutras*, one is enjoined by the first *Brahmasutra* then to enquire into Brahman: *athato brahmajijnasa*. *That* Brahman is to be enquired into is established, but *what* precisely is the nature of the object of such enquiry? That is elaborated in the second *sutra*: *janmadyasya yatah*. Which is to say, Brahman is cause of the creation, subsistence and dissolution of the world. If one were to encounter a discussion of theistic arguments in the *Sribhasya*, this would seem the most likely place. Indeed, Samkara had introduced the proofs here, asserting that at best they confirm to our limited reason what is already more certainly known from *sabda*.[68] But Ramanuja did not. Such proofs do not for Ramanuja have any part in establishing, confirming or even clarifying the nature and existence of Brahman. Brahman is for Ramanuja already known from scriptures. There is little left for Ramanuja to do in his commentary but to

---

[67] Additional aspects of the doctrine are explicated later in *adhyaya* 3.2.11–41.

[68] By insisting that the contexts of Samkara's arguments are not philosophically relevant [121–2], Paul Deussen in *The System of Vedanta* (Chicago, 1912; repr. New York, 1973) grossly misrepresented Samkara's view on the place of reason or inference with regard to the knowability of Brahman. See pp. 124ff.

iterate what is to be learned from sacred writings about Brahman's attributes. From them, one learns that Brahman is

> that highest Person who is the ruler of all; whose nature is antagonistic to all evil; whose purposes come true; who possesses infinite auspicious qualities, such as knowledge, blessedness, and so on; who is omniscient, omnipotent, supremely merciful; from whom the creation, subsistence, and reabsorption of this world proceed – he is Brahman: such is the meaning of the *Sutra*.[69]

In a sense, the whole of the *Sribhasya* elaborates this *credo*. Ramanuja has relatively little to say further about the second *sutra*, other than to make preliminary comments on what he has just said about Brahman and to insist that it is not self-contradictory (as some had claimed) for all these attributes to coinhere in one entity. If he has relatively little to say about this *sutra*, he has rather a lot to say about the next one.[70] In connection with his commentary on the third *sutra*, Ramanuja lays out his critique of the putative proofs of God/Brahman.

The word *sastrayonitvat* was read by Samkara as 'because it is the source of scriptures'. That is to say, Brahman is the source or speaker of Vedic scriptures. Whatever Samkara's philological justification may have been for rendering the *sutra* in this way, it enabled him to engage in polemic against the Mimamsakas, who denied that the Vedas had an author, human or divine. The third *sutra*, therefore, provides Samkara with a very convenient point to clarify a matter of some difference between the so-called 'old Mimamsaka' and the 'new Mimamsaka' or *Vedantan* perspective on scriptural authority. With a different opponent in mind, Ramanuja insisted that *sastrayonitvat* be rendered quite differently. He read it to mean 'because the scriptures are the source' of all knowledge of Brahman. He read it, in effect, as a Vedantan version of *sola scriptura*. We have no way of coming to know of Brahman or of undertaking 'an enquiry into Brahman' but through *sabda*, especially the key Upanisadic passages which, when threaded together, form the basis of the thirty-two *sutras* that comprise the first *adhyaya* of the *Vedantasutras*.

---

[69] *Sribhasya*, §I.1.2; Thibaut, p. 156.

[70] Things are reversed in the *Vedantasara*, in which Ramanuja's comments on 1.1.2 extend over sixteen pages, but his comment on 1.1.3 is one short paragraph, with no attack on Naiyayika proofs of Brahman: 'The Brahman, who has as His body all the sentient and non-sentient beings, is the material cause and also the efficient cause of the Universe. This fact could not be apprehended by reasoning, but could be proved by scriptures alone. Therefore, it is established that the scriptural text "From whom, all these things are born" (Tait., III.1) discerns the *Brahman*, who is the only cause of all the world.' *Vedantasara*, edited by V. Krishnamacharya and translated by M. B. Narasimka Ayyangar (Adyar, 1953; 2nd edn., 1979), pp. 6–22, p. 22.

In order to substantiate his reading of this *sutra*, over against Samkara's rendering of it, Ramanuja rehearsed all the *pramanas* that were acknowledged by all Vedantan schools, eliminating each in turn, save *sabda*, as a possible way of coming to know Brahman.[71] Ramanuja has nothing particularly new to say about the *pramanas*. His account of them is brief and perfunctory. Indeed, he could easily have had before him any number of treatises on *pramanas* by earlier writers of a variety of *darsanas*. In his *bhasya*, Ramanuja takes up the standard Vedantan line that we ordinarily come to know all that we can know by three and only three means: by *pratyaksa* or perception, which includes not just the five senses, but also yogic insight and inner feeling-states, such as pleasure and pain; by *anumana* or inference, which in practice means inductive reasoning about matters of putative fact; and by *sabda* or testimony, which includes testimony both of trustworthy witnesses and of authoritative scripture (*sruti*). All three ways are ordinarily reliable ways of coming to know what we know within the world of human experience, but *sabda* alone is reliable with regard to the knowledge of Brahman. Brahman is not a possible object of human perception in any of its specified senses. Nor is Brahman in principle knowable by means of inference, which is capable of establishing a proof only with regard to things that are in principle knowable by means of perception or experience.

That leaves *sabda* as the only remaining way of our possibly coming to know Brahman, if Brahman is to be known at all. Ramanuja does not in the commentary on the third *sutra* presume that Brahman can be known even by this means. He does not set out to establish *sabda* as a reliable way of coming to know Brahman until his commentary on the fourth *sutra*: *tattu samanvayat*.[72] For his overall argument, it is of course critical that Ramanuja establish this claim, but it is not the part of his argument that concerns us most directly. Our attention is directed, instead, to his grounds (*hetu*) for scepticism about the possibility of knowledge of Brahman by means of *anumana*. As it happens, many of those grounds closely parallel grounds given in the *Dialogues concerning Natural Religion* by Hume and his creation, Philo, for scepticism about the knowability of God by inductive reasoning.

---

[71] Ramanuja's comments on *Sribhasya*, §I.1.3, including his extended critique of *anumana* as a means of divine knowledge, is found in Thibaut, pp. 161–74, which is the source for most of what follows.

[72] However, he argued in relation to the first *sutra* that scripture alone is absolutely reliable in all things, so that when our perception and scripture stand in conflict with one another, we are to place our trust not in our direct experience but in the testimony of scripture. *Sribhasya*, §I.1.1; Thibaut, pp. 24ff.

First, Ramanuja concurs with Hume that, in the case of inferential knowledge of the cause or causes of this world, we are limited in what we can rightly claim to know by what can be warranted by observation statements about the world of sense experience. Even if we were to grant, for the sake of argument, that it is possible to regard the world as an effect and that it is possible to infer from it the nature of its cause, there are a number of limitations on the sorts of inferences we could draw from our experience of the world.[73] To say that the land, oceans and so forth are all 'effects' of some 'cause' is not in itself a sufficient reason to claim that it must have been the *same* cause. We have no grounds for claiming that all the discrete parts of the world are made and destroyed at the same time by a single cause. If we are tempted to make such a claim, it is because we are predisposed by what is taught in scripture about the maker, sustainer and destroyer of the world.

Even if it were a single cause, that could not be shown by inference from what is directly known by observation of the world or its parts. Our experience of the world generally is that things come into being and pass out of being in succession from a variety of causes, in much the same way that things like pots and chariots are made by diverse agents and are destroyed, whether intentionally or not, by equally diverse means. From experience of the world, we could never infer a single agent with the attributes of Brahman as the world's maker, sustainer and destroyer. Brahman's 'marks' or attributes are not instantiated in the parts that make up the world, nor can they be inferred from an examination of all the parts that make up the world. A bare minimum may be known from the world as available to us; namely, that its cause is an intelligent agent somewhat akin to ourselves. This is known to everyone already and is doubted by no one, he says in a vein similar to Hume. But we could never know anything for certain about it, not even if it is incorporeal or corporeal. If incorporeal spirit, *how* could it act as an agent, since our experience of sentient agents is that they act through their bodies? On the other hand, if corporeal spirit, it is composed of parts, as is the world. If it is imagined that the existence of the world requires explanation because it consists of parts, then why does an embodied spirit not require explanation for its own existence? And, if not, why should the world's existence require explanation?

Moreover, Ramanuja argues in a manner that often evokes Hume's Philo that the 'artifact–artisan' analogy has no intrinsic authority. If we consider the world as it is manifest to us in everyday experience, we have

---

[73] *Sribhasya*, §I.1.3; Thibaut, pp. 170ff.

no alternative but to concede that its composite parts fit together according to different principles. The parts cannot be presumed to be 'effects' in the same sense, or to be governed by the same principles. It must be allowed that some of them are governed by principles that more nearly resemble organic principles and others, by those that more nearly resemble mechanical ones. But the world as a whole cannot be said entirely to resemble an artifact, because its parts are not conjoined just as they are in manufactured products. Nor can it be said as a whole entirely to resemble an animated body, because it does not in all of its parts resemble an organism. We cannot, therefore, determine by *anumana* if the world is a manufactured product or if it is an embodiment of the supreme Soul. Human reason is no help in deciding such matters.

Ramanuja's argument here is particularly interesting. Not only does he insist that reason is unable to establish the existence of Brahman on 'artifact–artisan' models, but he also insists that reason is unable to show the existence of Brahman on 'body–soul' models, a version of which he himself embraced.[74] Ramanuja is, if anything, harder on the latter view of the world than he is on the former view. The world does not in all its parts closely resemble embodied spirit. Animate bodies breathe, but land, seas and mountains, for instance, do not breathe. Ramanuja was himself firmly convinced that the world is best regarded as the embodiment of Brahman. He was equally firmly convinced that this could not be known by *anumana*. It could be known by the testimony of scripture alone. One might observe that Ramanuja is free to embrace scepticism so enthusiastically because he could fall back on *sabda* as a source of invariably reliable knowledge – a move not available to Hume in his attempts to determine the possibility and limits of knowledge of God and God's ways.

Thirdly, all talk of 'the cause of the world as a whole' also raises for Ramanuja the same sort of difficulties for inference-based knowledge of a creator God that we have already seen it raised for Hume. Both men operate with the principle that like effects prove like causes. Ordinary experience of the way artifacts as diverse as pots and palaces are made is sufficient to allow us to infer from any given pot or palace, whether under construction or already finished, that it is a product of the activity of one or more appropriately skilled persons. We have no similar experience of the way the world was made or the way it will be destroyed, because we have not seen how other worlds come into and go out of being, whether

---

[74] *Sribhasya*, §II.1.1ff.; Thibaut, pp. 408ff. See Eric J. Lott, *God and the Universe in the Vedantic Theology of Ramanuja: A Study in his Use of the Self–Body Analogy* (Madras, 1976), pp. 146–64.

all at once or progressively. We are in the case of the world as a whole unable to infer similar causes, because we have no similar effects. Ramanuja, likewise, has difficulty with the idea of treating the world 'as a whole': that is, as one thing, akin to a pot or jar. There is no basis for the assumption that all the disparate sorts of things that collectively make up the world have a sufficiently uniform character to be able to speak of them all as making up a single thing, in the way that various material parts can make up a single jar.

Fourthly, Ramanuja considers also the plausibility of something akin to the 'naturalistic' accounts of the existence and order of the world mooted by Hume in his *Dialogues*. The Mimamsaka account of the world is that the cause of its being and governance effectively resides in itself, not in some external agent. It is thus improper to call the world an 'effect' for which a 'cause' needs to be identified. Though Ramanuja does not embrace such a view and does not believe that we are without witness (*sabda*) to a true view of the origination and destruction of the world, he firmly insists that reason alone cannot show the Mimamsaka explanation to be untenable. Were it not for the testimony of the scriptures, in the full Vedantan sense, we would be left without any reliable ground for deciding if the world had a point of origin or if its cause or causes were divine or wholly naturalistic.

Finally, there are a number of objections to the use of *anumana* as a means to knowing the being and nature of Brahman that apply so specifically to the South Asian context, they make relatively little contact with the framework within which Hume was working. For instance, Ramanuja reflects on the necessary connection between agency and *karma*, without which nothing could be the cause of some effect. Some aspects of Ramanuja's analysis of causality have parallels to what can also be found in the writings of Aristotle, which would have been known to Hume, but which would have had more direct import for Ramanuja than they did for Hume as a result of options present in Indian metaphysics. When Hume discusses causality in the *Dialogues*, he is drawing on what he had written in the *Treatise*.[75] He seems not to feel the need there to take up the battle again in detail. Nor would it have been natural to him to differentiate its possible senses along Aristotelian lines. If we put it in those terms, however, he is most directly concerned with efficient causality in the governance of the universe. When Ramanuja discusses causality, he does need to deal with what Aristotle would have named material and

---

[75] Cf. *A Treatise of Human Nature*, Selby-Bigge edition, pp. 155–72.

formal causality, as well as with efficient or instrumental causality. If God and world were *internally* related – as they would be if the world were conceived, à la Ramanuja, as God's body – then it would make sense to ask about the stuff from which the world may have been made (its *material* cause) as well as the means by which it was made (its instrumental or *efficient* cause), if it were made at all. A major difference between Samkara and Ramanuja, for instance, had to do with the reality of the material world, which raises in an acute form the question of the stuff of which the world is made. This is clearly not an immediate issue for Hume. He is more concerned with what, if anything, can be inferred about the efficient causality of a physical and inanimate world, the order of which may or may not show signs of intelligent design and purpose. Whether the evidence of order is considered sufficient to infer an intelligent designer, it would have been assumed by Hume and most of his contemporaries that such a putative designer would be externally related to the physical world. An alternative view had been proffered by the seventeenth-century Dutch philosopher Spinoza, who had spoken so easily of *deus sive natura* as interchangeable that his critics, including Pierre Bayle in France and David Hume in Scotland, had difficulty distinguishing between 'Spinozism' and 'atheism'.[76]

If God and world were externally related, then there would be such a metaphysical gap between the two that much would ride on reason's ability to bridge that gap. Hence, the impassioned interest in proofs of God and their reliability. If, however, there were no such gap, then less would ride on the ability of reason to establish foundations for belief. In fact, Cleanthes the Stoic, the historical prototype for Hume's 'Cleanthes', held a view of the relationship between God and world that is much nearer to Ramanuja than it is to his Humean namesake. If we look at his *Hymn to Zeus*, in which the presence of Zeus in the active governance of the world is a major feature, there is no *inference to Zeus* from such governance; rather the *presence of Zeus* is unmediated in dramatic events of nature.[77] Such 'physico-theology' is miles away from the metaphysical assumptions of Hume and most of his peers. It is much nearer to the metaphysical assumptions at play within Ramanuja's thought. Yet it

---

[76] Pierre Bayle, 'Spinoza', in *Dictionnaire historique et critique* (Amsterdam, 1697; 2nd edn, 1702; 3rd edn, 1740). An English translation – based on the second edition and known to Hume – was published in London in five volumes between 1734 and 1738 as *Dictionary, Historical and Critical*. 'Spinoza' appears in that edition, vol. V, pp. 199–244.

[77] A. A. Long and D. N. Sedley, eds., *The Hellenistic Philosophers* (Cambridge, 1987), I, pp. 326–7; II, pp. 326–7.

would be as wrong to identify the theology of the Stoic Cleanthes with the theology of Ramanuja, even if there should be such unmistakable parallels, as it would be to identify the mitigated scepticism of Hume's Philo with that of Ramanuja, even if there should also be such conspicuous parallels.

Parallels between Ramanuja and Hume's Philo exist in the similarity of their reasons in the sense of *grounds*. But reasons are reasons only in connection with the *ends* to which and for which they are directed. No parallel exists between the ends served by Ramanuja's sceptical arguments and the ends served by Philo's. Ramanuja's scepticism is in no sense a 'careless' scepticism. His scepticism serves in the end explicitly spiritual interests. He in effect sides with the hapless Demea in Hume's *Dialogues*, when he contends that we could never infer a religiously adequate cause of all that is by an argument that is based on the similarity of an infinite cause and its finite effects:

What Scripture tells us of is a being which comprehends within itself infinite, altogether unsurpassable excellences such as omnipotence and so on, is antagonistic to all evil, and totally different in character from whatever is cognised by the other means of knowledge: that to such a being there should attach even the slightest imperfection due to its similarity in nature to the things known by the ordinary means of knowledge is thus altogether excluded.[78]

On this account, the needs of religion require *dissimilarity* between the cause of the world and anything we encounter in the world, including human agency; the needs of the design argument, based as it is on analogical reasoning, require significant *similarity* between the cause of the world and human agency. If the needs of religion are adequately protected, the design argument is substantially weakened; if the conditions necessary for the success of the design argument are satisfied, however, the requirements of religion cannot be met. So Ramanuja. He finds in Vedic scriptures sufficient ground for a full-bodied belief in the being and attributes of his God. Not so Philo and Hume. They seem to need no ground in addition to raw experience of the world for their rather minimalist belief in cosmic purpose or intention, inexplicable and incomprehensible though it may finally be to human reason.[79] For the content of their belief, neither Ramanuja nor Hume nor his careless *Doppelgänger* requires an experimental argument in the mode of their orthodox interlocutor, Cleanthes.

---

[78] *Sribhasya*, I.1.3; Thibaut, p. 173.   [79] *The Natural History of Religion*, §XV; Root, p. 74.

CONCLUDING REMARKS

In the introductory remarks to this essay, I mentioned the need for philosophers engaged in cross-cultural reflection to move beyond *knowing that*
thinkers in diverse traditions hold certain views to a level of *knowing how*
to engage their insights in the process of critical self-reflection. It could easily
appear that I have in my essay here confined myself to the more rudimentary
level of comparison, and have not made the move to those deeper and more
productive levels of reflection. If so, what has been written in these pages
would seem to fall under the interdict promulgated by Wilhelm Halbfass in a
powerful passage toward the end of *India and Europe*:

> If 'comparative philosophy' is supposed to be *philosophy*, it cannot just be the
> comparison of *philosophies*. It cannot be the objectifying, juxtaposing, synoptic,
> comparative investigation of historical, anthropological or doxographic data.
> Comparative philosophy is philosophy insofar as it aims at self-understanding.
> It has to be ready to bring its own standpoint, and the condition and the horizon
> of comparison itself, into the process of comparison which thus assumes the
> reflexive, self-referring dimension which constitutes philosophy.[80]

What have we been engaged in here if not that which Halbfass says is
not philosophy? But then, again, what was he doing in *India and Europe*,
if not that which he himself says is *not* philosophy? Perhaps. One way to
read his remarks cited above is to imagine that he is not wanting to claim
that such activities are themselves unnecessary to proper philosophizing,
only that they do not of themselves constitute philosophy, which entails
something more.

Whether there is 'something more' and, if so, what it might be hangs
on what we take the aims of philosophy to be. And that depends considerably on one's philosophical lineage, so to say. Wilhelm was inclined
toward a 'Continental' or hermeneutical perspective on the philosopher's
craft, though not to the unbending exclusion of all other *darsanas*. Some
fellow Continental thinkers worried, in particular, that he might be too
open to insights of analytic philosophy, the 'Western *Nyaya*'. Anyone so
inclined who had read carefully his book on the Vaisesikas[81] must surely
have realized that such fears were utterly groundless.

---

[80] Wilhelm Halbfass, *India and Europe: An Essay in Understanding* (Albany, 1988), p. 433. Cf. Franco
and Preisendanz, eds., *Beyond Orientalism*, p. XI.

[81] *On Being and What There Is: Classical Vaisesika and the History of Indian Ontology* (Albany, 1992),
despite what is reported on p. 14 about the analytic movement in philosophy.

It is, of course, easy enough to list the failings of analytic philosophers – and it is, after all, *philosophers*, not *philosophies*, who 'do things' or fail to do them. Analytic philosophers, especially in the days of their hegemony, tended to be provincial in their philosophical interests, mistaking *local* rationality ('what we mean by. . .') for *natural* rationality, and assuming that nothing is to be gained philosophically by engaging culturally or historically 'other' intellectual traditions. Philosophers who trace their intellectual lineage back to Hume have too often shared his limited grasp of the philosophical import of non-Western traditions of critical reflection. Antony Flew, author of two books on Hume,[82] made little advance over the master's embarrassingly thin knowledge of the 'Eastern' philosophical traditions. In his *Introduction to Western Philosophy*, Flew justified his focusing on just *Western* philosophy on the grounds that 'Eastern philosophy' did not fall within what he understood by 'philosophy':

For philosophy, as the word is understood here, is concerned first, last, and all the time with arguments (it is, incidentally, because most of what is labelled *Eastern philosophy* is not so concerned – rather than for any reasons of European provincialism – that this book draws no materials from any sources east of Suez. . .).[83]

The irony of it all, of course, is that *this* understanding of *Eastern* philosophy is based on the neo-Vedantan construction of Indian philosophy by Radhakrishnan, onetime Spalding Professor in Oxford University and later President of India, who had in *Eastern Religions and Western Thought* and elsewhere presented Indian spirituality as an antidote to an over-rationalized Western philosophy that had substituted argument for direct experience and had in consequence failed to meet our deepest spiritual needs. However much this neo-Vedantan construction may have appealed to a then burgeoning Indian nationalist sentiment or to a then prevailing Western cultural pessimism, it is hardly an accurate portrayal of the classical Indian philosophical tradition. Hume's view of Indian thought had the advantage of being based on no acquaintance at all; Flew's had the disadvantage of being based on an acquaintance with one dubious construction. Flew was not alone in accepting this modern construction, and it still retains popularity in India and in the West. The neo-Vedantan system is often assumed by devotees and critics alike to

---

[82] Antony Flew, *Hume's Philosophy of Belief: A Study of his First Inquiry* (New York, 1961) and *David Hume: Philosopher of Moral Science* (Oxford, 1986).
[83] *Introduction to Western Philosophy: Ideas and Arguments from Plato to Sartre* (Indianapolis, 1971), p. 36.

be the quintessential expression of the Indian tradition of philosophical reflection. But their construction hardly represents what one discovers by wider acquaintance with the classical commentarial and doxographical literature of South Asia. Neo-Vedantan emphasis on experience takes no account of the long tradition of logic and debate in Indian philosophy, especially as it was practised by Buddhists and Naiyayikas. Nor does it take account of detailed polemic found in treatises and commentaries produced by philosophical *darsanas* of every persuasion, not least the commentary-hungry varieties of traditional Vedanta. To earn the right to enter the arena of philosophical debate in classical Indian culture, it was necessary to be able to give reasons for one's claims, to submit those reasons to public scrutiny, and also to be able to defend them against critique with additional arguments. This feature of Indian philosophy, which is neglected by Radhakrishnan and Flew equally, establishes a congenial point of departure for analytic philosophers who may wish to engage in cross-cultural intellectual reflection.

Not all analytic philosophers have been equally narrow or blinkered in their pursuit of the aims of philosophy. It should be remembered that the late Ninian Smart was and remained an appreciative pupil of J. L. Austin, and that his book *Reasons and Faiths* (London, 1957) originated as an Oxford dissertation in Philosophy. And John Hick's vision may seem neo-Vedantan in its inspiration, but it arises out of issues first addressed within a well-trodden analytic approach to philosophy.[84] On the more rigorous end of the analytic spectrum, the recent work of Keith Yandell comes to mind for its breadth of understanding of the textual resources available for philosophical analysis.[85] Most recently, Matilal's former student Jonardon Ganeri has produced a philosophically sophisticated introduction to Indian philosophy, which applies analytic techniques to the arguments found in its formative and classical texts.[86] Of the books mentioned here, this volume comes closest to exemplifying, albeit in an Anglo-American and not a Continental mode, the ideal of philosophizing based on a direct acquaintance with primary texts in both Western and Indian reflective traditions. Each of these volumes, in its own way, moves beyond showing *that* such and such views are held in a variety of cultural

---

[84] Cf., e.g., *An Interpretation of Religion: Human Responses to the Transcendent* (New Haven, 1989).

[85] See, e.g., *Philosophy of Religion: A Contemporary Introduction* (London, 1999). Yandell's cross-cultural interests are less prominent in his analysis of Hume's views on religion in the volume *Hume's 'Inexplicable Mystery'* (Philadelphia, 1990), though they are not wholly lacking. See, e.g., pp. 120f., 334.

[86] Jonardon Ganeri, *Philosophy in Classical India: The Proper Work of Reason* (London, 2001).

traditions to showing *how* at least some that is found there can inform the way we do philosophy.[87] This is done in a generally unselfconscious way, so that it is made to seem increasingly 'natural' to engage in critical reflection in the company of Samkara as well as Descartes, Nagarjuna as well as Aristotle, Ramanuja as well as Hume.

For the Hume–Flew lineage, however, it must be at least mildly embarrassing to discover that most of Hume's clever case against the modern 'design argument' had already been put together some six hundred years earlier by a barbarous and superstitious Indian. Nor were the building blocks of Ramanuja's case especially original to him. They had already been available in India for centuries before Ramanuja put his characteristic stamp on them in the *Sribhasya*. They had been well debated by proponents and opponents of theism and design in South Asian philosophy, since before the days of Dharmakirti and Jayanta. This long reflective process did not lead to perspectival consensus in India, any more than it has done in Europe. Philosophical reflection can be judged in both cases to have contributed to a winnowing of proposals, with only the most substantive of them remaining, and to have contributed to a gradual clarification of what might be called 'defensible difference'.[88]

The rationality of it all lies less in the triumph of one perspective over another and more in the process itself of critical reflection and clarification. In order for this process to achieve its aims, 'difference' or alterity is neither accidental nor regrettable; it is, rather, essential. Engaging the 'other' is the very stuff of philosophy, which lives or dies by argument and debate. That this seems to many philosophers today self-evident owes something to the passion with which Wilhelm Halbfass engaged so persistently in a kind of philosophizing that was grounded in an intimate knowledge of both Indian and European sources.

---

[87] See also in this regard Rom Harré, *One Thousand Years of Philosophy: From Ramanuja to Wittgenstein* (Oxford, 2000).

[88] See John Clayton, 'Common Ground and Defensible Difference'. Editors' note: This appears as Chapter 3 of the present volume.

CHAPTER 6

Piety and the proofs*

Religious piety and proofs of God's existence have not in modern times invariably sat so happily beside one another as the attempted euphony of my title may at first appear to suggest.

In the seventeenth and eighteenth centuries, the existence and nature of God came to be conceived as a purely philosophical question that could be answered, if at all, without recourse to 'narrowly religious' considerations.[1] Philosophers and sympathetic theologians agreed that a religiously independent philosophy is itself competent to demonstrate the Deity's existence and nature by means of formally valid and generally convincing rational proofs.

Motives varied. Some philosophers may have desired that a common rational religion would eventually displace the diverse 'positive religions', which – as the then recent religious wars in Europe and the invasion of the Turks from the South had shown – tend toward divisiveness, intolerance and bloodshed. Some Jewish thinkers may have hoped via a confessionally neutral 'rational theology' to win an equal place within Europe's intellectual mainstream. And a few Christian theologians may have joined in the 'Enlightenment project' – as it has been called – in the belief that 'natural theology' itself already contained the best that is in Christianity, whilst

* A shorter version of this paper was read to the Christian Philosophers' conference on 'Philosophy and Other Religions' held in September 1989 at Pembroke College, Oxford. It embodies research undertaken during my tenure as a Visiting Fellow of Wolfson College, Cambridge, and during an extended research visit to the Institute of Indology at the University of Vienna. I am deeply grateful to the President and Fellows of Wolfson College, to the Lancaster University Research Committee and to the British Academy for their support of the research programme of which this paper forms a part. For their patience, encouragement and specialist knowledge, however, I am most deeply indebted to my Lancaster colleagues, Drs David Smith and David Waines, to Professor David Burrell, CSC, of the University of Notre Dame, and to Professor Gerhard Oberhammer and his associates in Vienna.
[1] For a detailed attempt to retrace the steps of this modern transposition, see Michael J. Buckley, *At the Origins of Modern Atheism* (New Haven, 1987).

others may have been confident that the independent foundation would be sufficient to support a robustly Christian superstructure.

Whatever the motives of their backers, theistic proofs attained in the process a philosophical importance that they had not previously enjoyed as well as an unprecedented independence from the several religious traditions in which they had been fostered and in which they had earlier flourished. Now separated from the constraints of every religious tradition, autonomous reason was expected to find independent reasons for belief in the Supreme Being, reasons which would warrant assent from all rational beings everywhere.

This image of theistic proofs – although an image first forged in the European Enlightenment – is so firmly fixed in our minds that we find it difficult to imagine that it could ever have been otherwise. Whether we are by disposition inclined to think well of such proofs, or to question their philosophical soundness, or even to avoid them altogether as religiously suspect, we tend on the whole to do so in terms of the image that I have just sketched. This same image also shapes and distorts our understanding of the place of theistic argument in pre-modern traditions – both mediaeval and ancient, Western and Eastern.

So far as the capacity in us lies, let us set aside this modern prejudice, at least momentarily, in the hope that we may rediscover the religious uses to which reasoning was once commonly put. Let us aim to determine the extent to which theistic arguments were at one time embedded in religious traditions by enquiring into the pieties they expressed, the doctrinal schemes they supported, the spiritualities they engendered, the God/s they honoured. In the process, we may begin to guess why at least this aspect of the 'Enlightenment project' was bound to founder. And we may even pick up some clues about what to do next.

In this paper – which continues the argument begun in 'Religions, Reasons and Gods'[2] – I want to focus attention on the place of theistic argument in the work of two eleventh-century contemporaries of Anselm: from Persia, the Muslim jurist al-Ghazali (1058/9–1111) and from India, the Brahmanic *srotriya* Udayana (c. 1025–c. 1100). Each has been chosen for his recognized spiritual qualities, as well as his acknowledged intellectual accomplishments. Each of them proffers in his writings, albeit expressed in different logical systems, a version of what since Kant we have called 'the cosmological argument' for God's existence. But each of them represents a religious tradition with a markedly different concept of God, and each of them displays in his work

---

[2] Editors' note: See Chapter 4 of this volume.

quite a different use of theistic argument. Even so, the pattern which exhibits itself in their work is strikingly similar at just those points where 'the Enlightenment project' appears for present purposes most dubious.

AL-GHAZALI

Al-Ghazali is rightly remembered as a mystic and a saint, as well as a skilled polemicist and a theologian of the first rank. Some of his most important writings, however, were produced during his tenure as professor of Islamic law (*fiqh*) at the Nizamiyah *madrasa* or 'university' in Baghdad, which had been established by Nizam al-Mulk to counter the growing influence of extremist and sectarian groups within Islam.[3]

Islam, it has been observed, is first and foremost a nomocracy.[4] Moreover, 'the highest expression of its genius' is said to be found in its law, which effectively holds together the Muslim community. Through the study of law – 'the queen of the Islamic sciences' – the gradually evolved concept of traditional 'consensus' (*ijma*) was made more precise and also dialectical skills and logical categories were greatly refined.[5] By the eleventh century, orthodox Islam had achieved as a consequence of the study of jurisprudence a certain balance between commitment to tradition, on the one hand, and respect for reason, on the other.[6] This balance is exemplified historically in the theory of law elaborated by al-Shafi'i in the ninth century, the most outstanding exponent of which in the eleventh century was Abu Hamid Muhammad b. Muhammad al-Ghazali al-Tusi.

Having become professor of law in 1091, Ghazali resigned his chair in 1095, and returned to the leaching of law once again in 1105. The reason for his having abandoned the lecture hall, as well as for his having decided later to return to teaching, is a matter of some uncertainty.[7] However much scholars may disagree with one another on that issue, there is virtual unanimity amongst them that the ten years in between his professorial appointments were for Ghazali a time of spiritual self-discovery. Through mystical experience, Ghazali says, he came to know by acquaintance what he had previously

---

[3] For my understanding of law and legal education in eleventh-century Islam, I am greatly dependent upon the work of George Makdisi, especially his book *The Rise of Colleges: Institutions of Learning in Islam and the West* (Edinburgh, 1981). See also Jospeh Schacht's two books, *An Introduction to Islamic Law* (Oxford, 1964) and *The Origins of Muhammadan [sic] Jurisprudence* (Oxford, 1950).

[4] Makdisi, *The Rise of Colleges*, p. 8.   [5] *Ibid.*, pp. 105ff.   [6] *Ibid.*, pp. 6ff.

[7] Ghazali's own explanation is given in his *al-Munqidh min al-Dalal*, translated by R. J. McCarthy as *Freedom and Fulfillment* (Boston, 1980). See pp. 89ff.

known only by description.[8] Whatever the details of his experience, it clearly added new spiritual dimensions to his attempt to forge reason into an instrument of the heart.[9] Although none could deny that his Sufi experience led him to refashion some views, there is nonetheless a remarkable consistency of perspective in his legal opinions over the two periods at the *madrasa*, as there is in his attitude toward basic philosophical issues, such as the value and limitations of theistic proofs.[10]

Ghazali insisted that a reasoned proof (*burhan*) for the existence of God, creator of heaven and earth, is quite superfluous.[11] The testimony of the Qur'an and the wonders of the creation are themselves sufficient grounds for sure knowledge of God's existence and nature. The Qur'an itself declares,

> Surely in the creation of the heavens and the earth
> and the alternation of night and day
> and the ship that runs in the sea with profit to men,
> and the water God sends down from heaven
> therewith reviving the earth after it is dead
> and scattering abroad in it all manner of
> crawling thing, and the turning about of the winds
> and the clouds compelled between heaven and earth –
> surely there are signs for a people having understanding.[12]

But common sense tells us, and the Qur'an also concurs, that not everyone who sees such things sees them as 'signs' of divinity. Some through ignorance or inattentiveness and others through wilfulness or unbelief have looked but have not seen. Is it then perhaps for such people as these that al-Ghazali constructed rational proofs for the existence of God?

It is not difficult to imagine that his main proof of God, a version of the cosmological argument, might have been designed for just such persons. The proof is stated syllogistically in Ghazali's summary of the fundamentals of Muslim belief which has come to be known as 'The Jerusalem Tract' or *Kitab ar-Risalah al-Qudsiyyah*:

---

[8] *Ibid.*, pp. 90f.
[9] Cf. Ghazali's main late work, the *Ihya'*, a key section of which (*Kitab Sharh 'Aja'ib al-Qalb*) has been translated by McCarthy and included in *Freedom and Fulfillment*. See especially pp. 363ff. See also David Burrell, 'The Unknowability of God in al-Ghazali', *Religious Studies* 23 (1987), 171–82.
[10] This remarkable consistency has also been stressed by Iysa A. Bello in the only recently published study of *The Medieval Islamic Controversy between Philosophy and Orthodoxy* (Leiden, 1989).
[11] 'The Jerusalem Tract', ed. and trans. A. L. Tibawi, *Islamic Quarterly* 9 (1965), 97–8.
[12] *Qur'an*, sura 2; translated by A. J. Arberry, *The Koran* (Oxford, 1983), p. 21

It is self-evident to human reason [begins Ghazali] that there must be a cause (*sabab*) for the origination (*huduth*) of anything originated (*hadith*). Since the universe is originated, it follows that there was a cause for its origination.[13]

He then offers a series of arguments to support the proof in order to show that the universe must have had a temporal beginning and that it therefore must also have had an originator or creator. Since our immediate interest is in the uses to which the proof was put, and not in the merits of the proof itself, it is not necessary here to test the strength of its support. Instead we ask: what was the job that Ghazali's proof was designed to do?

Looked at in isolation, with total disregard for its wider context, Ghazali's proof could be thought to have been constructed to convince any reasonable person – regardless of prior disposition – that the existence of God is capable of being demonstrated with apodictic certainty from the temporality or 'originatedness' of the universe. Its principal intent, therefore, would be seen as apologetic. One can easily understand why some present-day 'creationists' have developed a fresh interest in Ghazali and have attempted to exploit for evidently apologetic purposes his argument from the temporal contingency of the universe.[14]

What, however, do we learn of Ghazali's proof and its intended purpose if we contemplate it, not from our perspective today, but from that of the eleventh-century Muslim world? Ghazali put theistic proofs to work in his writings in a variety of ways. But there seem to be no instances in his writings when he specifically constructed proofs for God's existence to be aimed apologetically at unbelievers who were outside the Muslim community. This is not to suggest that Ghazali was unconcerned about 'unbelief' as it was encountered in Judaism, Christianity and Brahmanism – the three 'other' religions that he knew best.[15] The form of 'unbelief' that concerned him most directly, however, was that which he detected within the Islamic community itself.

Ghazali was more specifically worried by the insinuation of Greek and Hellenistic ideas into Islam through the more speculative of the Shi'ites, not least through Ibn Sina, the most distinguished thinker to have been

---

[13] 'The Jerusalem Tract', p. 98. For a discussion of this proof, based on the version included in Ghazali's *Ihya*', and a comparison with Thomas's *viae*, see S. de L. de Beaurecueil and G. C. Anawati, 'Une preuve de l'existence de dieu chez Ghazali et S. Thomas', *Mélanges de l'institut dominicain des études orientales* 3 (1956), 207–58.

[14] See William Lane Craig, *The Kalam Cosmological Argument* (London, 1979).

[15] See, e.g., *Faysal al-Tafriqa bayn al-Islam wa l-Zandaqa* ('The Clear Criterion for Distinguishing between Islam and Godlessness'), in McCarthy, *Freedom and Fulfillment*, p. 150, and regarding Christians as 'unbelievers' see esp. pp. 170ff.

produced by the sectarians. That it was through the Shi'ites that Hellenistic philosophy had taken strongest hold within Islam may have been fortuitous, since it had already entered through the writings of al-Farabi before they had become a major force in Islam. But it was among the Shi'ites that it had received the warmest welcome.[16] From an 'orthodox' or Sunnite point of view, the Shi'ite system of authority – which gave to their Imam an infallibility in matters of law and doctrine, even when his pronouncements went against the orthodox 'consensus' of Islamic tradition – made the sectarians more vulnerable to error from within and to alien influence from without.

Added to this first concern about the doctrinal unreliability of the Shi'ites was Ghazali's entirely understandable uneasiness about the Shi'ites' increasingly successful encroachment on traditionally Sunnite territory through an effective combination of religious propaganda and political assassination.[17] This worry provides the political 'subtext' of much that Ghazali said and did.

When taken together, these two worries may help explain the strength of Ghazali's determination in – for example – his *Tahafut al-Falasifa*[18] to put to rout 'the atheists of our day' by prosecuting for unbelief certain philosophers who were long out of harm's way, such as al-Farabi and Ibn Sina. Against the philosophers – and against Ibn Sina most systematically – Ghazali's whole arsenal of argument was directed. And in that arsenal was his cosmological proof for God's existence from the temporal contingency of the universe.

'Unbelief' is in Islam a *legal offence*, which may result in formal accusation (*takfir*) and prosecution if the crime is particularly serious. If such a prosecution were successful, the guilty party's property could be confiscated, his life taken, and his soul condemned to the Fire for eternity.[19] Despite the seriousness of the charge, the accusation was often made casually in Muslim polemical writings.

---

[16] One possible explanation for this welcome has been proposed by Majid Fakhry: 'since throughout Muslim history the Shi'ites had been forced into the position of a disgruntled minority whose political ambitions were repeatedly thwarted, it was natural that they should rebel intellectually against the facts of religio-political reality and seek in the realm of abstract constructions a spiritual haven to which they could turn in adversity. This tendency would probably account not only for the revolutionary spirit that fired many Shi'ite leaders throughout Muslim history and the occultism characterizing Shi'ite thought and attitude, but also for their association with the leading school of rationalist theologians in Islam, i.e. the Mu'tazilah, their recognition of the validity of the independent judgment (*ijtihad*) of qualified jurists in matters of jurisprudence, even to the present day, and their readiness to assimilate Greek philosophy without any hesitation.' *A History of Islamic Philosophy* (London and New York, 1983), p. 41.

[17] *Ibid.*, pp. 217f.　　　[18] Trans. S. A. Kamali (Lahore, 1958).

[19] *Faysal*, pp. 149–50, 164.

Ghazali, one of the most respected jurists of his day, is most unlikely to have made such an accusation recklessly or without weighing carefully its possible consequences. In one of his important tracts on the issue of *takfir*, written during his second period as Professor of Law, Ghazali rebuked those who hurled the term 'unbelief' too readily at everyone with whom they disagreed, no matter how inconsequential the point under discussion.[20] In keeping with its gravity, the charge should be restricted – according to Ghazali – to matters that go to the root of the Islamic faith: namely, belief in God, in the Prophet, and in the Last Day. Everything else is secondary. Though dissent in such matters may attract the lesser charge of heresy or 'innovation' (*bid'ah*), it should not result in a formal charge of unbelief or 'infidelity' (*takfir*).

With a caution that befits the distinguished academic lawyer he was, Ghazali expressed the opinion that the accusation – where possible – is best avoided altogether, because legal opinion is divided over matters of detail and the rules of evidence are, in any case, so strict that proving a case is extremely difficult.[21] His cautious approach to the legal aspects of *takfir* makes even more poignant his determination to prosecute the philosophers for unbelief.

The bill of indictment, drawn up at the *madrasa* in Baghdad and published in 1095 as the *Tahafut al-Falasifa* or 'The Destruction of the Philosophers', specified twenty separate charges against the Muslim philosophers, most of which were adjudged as no more than 'innovations'.[22] Three of the charges were nevertheless serious enough to be treated as instances of 'unbelief': (i) they had denied the world's creation *ex nihilo* by affirming the universe's eternality, past and future; (ii) they had effectively eliminated not only the possibility of miracle and prophecy, but also the necessity of God's active sustaining power by denying that God has knowledge of particulars, and affirming that such knowledge is of universals only; and (iii) they had denied the resurrection of the body and physical rewards and punishments by affirming that the soul alone is immortal and that rewards and punishments are spiritual only.[23] All three

---

[20] *Ibid.*, pp. 150ff.   [21] *Ibid.*, p. 166.

[22] The full list of charges appears in Kamali's edition of the *Tahafut* on pp. 11ff. See also *Freedom and Fulfillment*, pp. 76f.

[23] For a balanced discussion of these three issues as disputed between Ghazali and the philosophers, see Oliver Leaman, *An Introduction to Medieval Islamic Philosophy* (Cambridge, 1985), pp. 25–120. Among older works, see Louis Gardet's study of *La pensée religieuse d'Avicenne* (Paris, 1951), which was published to commemorate the one-thousandth anniversary of the birth of Ibn Sina.

of these claims are intertwined and concern the heart of Muslim belief in the nature and agency of God.

'No [true] Muslim', Ghazali states emphatically in another essay, 'ever professed any of their views on these questions.'[24] Moreover, they had not only flaunted the consensus of orthodox opinion, but had in these views also blasphemed the revealed law or *shariʾa*. By so doing, they had accused the Prophet and his Companions of lying. And this, according to Ghazali's legal opinion on the matter, constitutes unbelief.

Had they been available to speak in their own defence, the accused philosophers might have been expected to reply somewhat along the following lines: although the reported views on the above-mentioned points were arrived at and are supported by reason, they are also entirely harmonious with the revealed texts cited against them by Ghazali, providing that the relevant texts are interpreted allegorically and not literally.

Deciding the issue of unbelief, therefore, reduces itself in this instance to the question of the proper interpretation of sacred texts, the revelatory authority of which is not itself challenged by either party. Any other arguments that may have been given by either side were intended to help settle the text's proper interpretation. This, in fact, conforms perfectly to the paradigm case of unbelief elaborated by Ghazali in his legal essay on *takfir*.

Suppose some Muslim claimed that a given text in the Qurʾan – some text that was heretofore always held to be literally true by the consensus of the community of faithful – is in fact to be interpreted allegorically. Suppose some Muslim claimed that the following text is to be taken allegorically so that it is compatible with the view that the universe is eternal, without beginning or end:

> Surely your Lord is God, who created
> the heavens and the earth in six days.[25]

According to the legal opinion written by Ghazali, five conditions would have to be met before it would be safe to convict such a person of *takfir*.[26] First, it would have to be decided on largely linguistic grounds whether the text is susceptible of anything other than literal interpretation. Second, the question of the text's authenticity and the trustworthiness of its transmission would have to be settled. Third, it would have to be ascertained if the proposer of the allegorical interpretation were in a position to know that the text is authentic, its transmission impeccable, and its interpretation

[24] *Freedom and Fulfillment*, p. 77.
[25] *Qurʾan*, sura 10; Arberry translation, p. 196.   [26] *Faysal*, pp. 164–6.

agreed by consensus of the community. Only then – and this is the fourth condition – would the arguments offered in support of the allegorical interpretation be weighed. Among the arguments discussed at this point might be competing theistic proofs, one allowing the eternality of the universe and the other requiring its creation *ex nihilo*. Even if all four of these conditions were met, however, the matter could still be dropped unless it were determined – as the final condition – that publication of the novel interpretation would do great harm to true religion.

Within these hermeneutical limits was fixed the legal disposition of the charge of unbelief. Within these limits Ghazali accused the philosophers of unbelief on three counts. And within these same limits he argued against their theistic proofs which presupposed the eternality of the universe and argued for his own alternative proof which had built into it the necessary temporality of the universe.

The issue between Ghazali and the philosophers, however, goes beyond the questionableness of interpreting an isolated verse allegorically, when the orthodox consensus is to interpret it literally. And it goes beyond any differences they may have had over the archaeology of the universe, so to speak. These are symptoms, but are not actually the source of their disagreement. Their disagreement issues instead from their competing conceptions of God and of divine activity in relation to the world. The question on which they divided was whether God is to be conceived, with the philosophers, as necessary cause or, with Ghazali, as voluntary agent. According to one recent interpreter of the dispute,

if the world should be eternal, and a deity is recognized, the deity's relationship to the universe would likewise be eternal. Since eternity and necessity are, by virtue of an Aristotelian rule, mutually implicative, an eternal relationship is a relationship bound by necessity; and necessity excludes will. The eternity of the world thus would imply that the deity is, as the cause of the universe, bereft of will. A beginning of the world would, by contrast, lead to a deity possessed of will. Should the world be understood to have a beginning . . . the existence of a creator can be inferred; and the decision on the creator's part to bring a world into existence where no world existed before would constitute a supreme and paradigmatic act of volition. Will in the deity would, therefore, be ruled out by the eternity of the world and entailed by [its] creation.[27]

Ghazali is obliged to repudiate the philosophers' preferred proof, adapted from Aristotle, because it proves the existence of the wrong 'God'. The God

[27] Herbert A. Davidson, *Proofs for Eternity, Creation and the Existence of God in Medieval Islamic and Jewish Philosophy* (Oxford, 1987), pp. 1f.

of the philosophers, lacking Will amongst its attributes, cannot be the personal agent required of Islamic belief. And, in consequence, no such argument could ever be used to warrant the allegorical interpretation of any sacred text. Moreover, an alternative proof – one which *is*, as it happens, wholly compatible with the Islamic understanding of God as voluntary agent – can be constructed in order to show that a literal interpretation of the verse in question is not contrary to reason.

Not that Ghazali would ever allow the issue of proper interpretation to be decided by rational proof alone. The consensus of the Muslim community is itself infallible in such matters.[28] Rational proof could have at best an ancillary function, its role being tightly controlled in the case of the prosecution of the philosophers by the requirements of due process.

But Ghazali also used theistic proofs outside the juridical context. I cited at the beginning of this section a proof found in 'The Jerusalem Tract', a document supposedly written at the request of members of the Jerusalem mosque at a time when they may have felt under threat from different quarters.[29] This little summa opens with a prayer which flows so smoothly into the text proper that it is less than obvious where, if at all, the prayer ends. The fundamentals of belief are organized in such a way that they could be more easily committed to memory: the edifice of Muslim belief is supported by four pillars – namely, the 'nature', 'attributes', and 'works' of God, plus a number of beliefs accepted on authority, such as the bodily resurrection and the day of judgement; each of these pillars, in turn, rests on ten foundations. In his exposition of the 'first pillar' – the nature of God – Ghazali sets out the syllogism cited earlier. That proof – though valid – is said, however, to be of little consequence in itself:

The foremost guiding light, and the path most likely to lead to [knowledge of God's existence,] are indicated in the Qur'an, since all guidance beyond that of God is superfluous.[30]

---

[28] For a discussion of Ghazali's concept of 'consensus', see Bello, *Medieval Islamic Controversy*, pp. 29–43.

[29] In addition to Islamic 'sectarians' and other 'heretics', the pious Muslims of Jerusalem had also to contend with the First [Christian] Crusade to 'liberate' the Holy City. Support for the Crusade was incited by Pope Urban in an address at Clermont in Auvergne on 25 November 1095, and Jerusalem finally capitulated to the invaders on 15 July 1099. George Hourani reckons that 'The Jerusalem Tract' cannot have been written before 1098. See 'The Chronology of Ghazali's Writings', *JAOS* 79 (1959), 229.

[30] 'The Jerusalem Tract', p. 96.

Why, one may wonder, does Ghazali bother to construct a theistic proof, only to belittle its importance? One possibility suggests itself. It may have been intended to shore up the faith of 'true believers' against the threat of any who would mislead them 'into the ways of the atheists' and who would attempt to dazzle them with a great show of learning. In short, he may have wanted to reassure the faithful that they had a proof for God's existence at least as sophisticated as those being proffered by the heretical philosophers.[31] The same proof that had been employed in order to confound the heretical was now being commended in order to edify the faithful. In both cases, however, its use was restricted to the house of Islam. It was a proof intended 'for a people having understanding', for a people who could say with the Qurʾan:

> Surely your Lord is God, who created
> the heavens and the earth in six days,
> then sat Himself upon the Throne
> directing the affair. Intercessor
> there is none, save after His leave.
> That then is God, your Lord; so serve Him.[32]

UDAYANA

Tradition has it that at the height of his popularity, Udayana made a pilgrimage from his native Mithila, near the border with Nepal, to the shrine of the God Jagannatha in the temple at Puri, on the Bay of Bengal.[33] Jagannatha, represented in the temple by a crudely carved wooden figure, had once been a minor tribal deity of no obviously great significance, despite the expectations raised by his name, which means 'Lord (or "Protector") of the World'. By the end of the eleventh century, however, Jagannatha – in consort with his brother (Balarama) and sister (Subhadra) – had come to be the focus of a burgeoning cult which, whilst retaining some more primitive features, effectively synthesized the main components of the three major cults – Vaisnavism, Saivism, and Saktism.

---

[31] *Ibid.*, p. 98. See also *Tahafut*, trans. Kamali, pp. 1–10.   [32] *Qurʾan*, sura 10.

[33] Legends about Udayana derive mainly from chapter 30 of the *Bhavisyatpuranaparisista*, though Dineshachandra Bhattacharya reports that anecdotes are still narrated with great delight by Mithila scholars. *History of Navya-Nyaya in Mithila* (Darbhanga, 1958), p. 6. For variant tellings of the legends recounted here, see – in addition to Bhattacharya – Visweswari Ammi, *Udayana and his Philosophy* (Delhi, 1985); Karl Potter (ed.), *Indian Metaphysics and Epistemology: The Tradition of Nyaya-Vaisesika up to Gangesa*, volume II of *The Encyclopedia of Indian Philosophies* (Princeton, 1977), p. 522, and the additional sources mentioned by Potter (see p. 706).

Having begun at Puri, the new cult spread throughout the region until it became the dominant religion of Orissa.[34]

Whatever may have occasioned Udayana's association with the temple at Puri, the narrative of events following his arrival there takes an unexpected turn. Instead of being allowed into the shrine, the doors to the temple had been barred to prevent his entry. From within, so the legend continues, the voice of Jagannatha himself called out that Udayana would have to atone for his sin before he could come into the divine presence. According to one of several variant endings to the story, Udayana then performed the penitential rite of *tusanala*,[35] his dying words to the God Jagannatha being more nearly defiant than penitent: 'Intoxicated with your own greatness, you treat me ignominiously. But you forget that when the Buddhists reigned supreme, you depended upon me for your very existence!' One version has it that Jagannatha soon afterwards appeared in a dream to a priest of the temple to say that Udayana had been his own incarnation and that by Udayana's efforts alone had the existence of God been firmly established.

Udayana's success as an apologist for theism is celebrated in another legend, one in which he occasions a man's death – the sin, mentioned above, for which atonement was required. A clever Buddhist logician is said to have visited Mithila with a view to challenging Udayana to a philosophical contest concerning the existence of God. The disputation, which is said to have been held at court before the king, who served as 'referee' or *saksin*, seems to have been evenly matched. When it had gone on for several days, with neither side willing to concede ground, Udayana suggested a dramatic way to settle the issue. Having gained the king's consent, he and the Buddhist climbed a high mountain and, upon reaching the top, declared their belief or non-belief in God's existence. They then each jumped – the Buddhist to his death, and an unharmed Udayana to a warm reception by his supporters.[36]

---

[34] On the origins, character and spread of the Jagannatha cult, see Thomas E. Donaldson, *Hindu Temple Art of Orissa*, 3 vols. (Leiden, 1985–7); Anncharlott Eschmann *et al.* (eds.), *The Cult of Jagannath and the Regional Tradition of Orissa* (New Delhi, 1978); and Ulrich Schneider, *Der Holzgott und die Brahmanen*, 2 vols. (Wiesbaden, 1984).

[35] That is, he burned himself to death over a slow fire.

[36] It is a pity that John Wisdom evidently did not know this story, because it would have served his purposes in 'Gods' much better than the Elijah legend he cited to show that 'the existence of God is not an experimental issue in the way it was' [*Philosophy and Psycho-Analysis* (Oxford, 1953), p. 149]. For one forceful account of the point of the 'experiment' on Mount Carmel, and of its abuse in the writings of Wisdom and others, see Emil Fackenheim, *Encounters between Judaism and Modern Philosophy*, 2nd edn (New York, 1980), pp. 9–29.

The fact that such fantastic legends grew up around him no doubt itself indicates the esteem in which Udayana was held as a defender of theistic belief. Of Udayana himself, however, very little is known. It is not even known for certain when he lived – though a number of scholars now locate him in the eleventh century.

1. From his being accepted as a *srotriya*, we know that Udayana must have been a *brahmana*. As such, his day-to-day life would have been regulated down to the smallest detail by the requirements set out in the *Manusmrti* and in other Brahmanic scriptures.[37]

2. From what is taken to be a contemporary description of him, we learn that Udayana had a razor-sharp wit. His thoughts were uttered with clarity and force and were, moreover, written with great elegance. In consequence, Udayana's works – especially the *Parisuddhi* [38] – were judged to have eclipsed those of his predecessors. Whether or not exaggerated in detail, this portrait by an unknown contemporary admirer squares with the respect in which Udayana came to be held by friend and foe alike within the various philosophical systems of India.[39]

3. From his series of authoritative commentaries on the normative scriptures of both the Nyaya and the Vaisesika philosophical systems, it becomes evident that Udayana occupied a unique place in the assimilation of the Vaisesika categorical scheme into the Nyaya-system.[40] The resulting Nyaya-Vaisesika system integrated within itself the logical and epistemological strengths of the one with the 'realist' ontological pre-occupations of the other. So armed, Udayana was able more forcefully than his predecessors amongst the Naiyayikas or Vaisesikas to mount an effective response to the mainly Buddhist challenge to the coherence of their 'realist' doctrines of causality and substance, the self and God.

---

[37] 'Brahmanic culture is essentially textual, for the entire way of life – personal, social and ritual – of a Brahman *is* basically guided by scriptures . . . To a Brahman, there is hardly anything in his life and ways of living which escapes the body of scriptures. The brahmanic scriptural text has thus built up an autonomous culture which is coherent, self-consistent, and distinctive.' Baidyanath Saraswati, *Brahman Ritual Traditions in the Crucible of Time* (Simla, 1977), p. ix. Cf. Rajendra Nath Sharma, *Brahmins through the Ages: Their Social, Religious, Cultural, Political, and Economic Life* (Delhi, 1977).

[38] The *Parisuddhi* – or, to give it its full title, The *Tatparyaparisuddhi* – is the final link in the five-member chain, beginning with Gautama's *Nyayasutra*, which together constitutes 'orthodox' Nyaya-doctrine. According to Dineschachandra Bhattacharya, who cites the above 'pen-picture' of Udayana, 'it was probably written by an admirer who actually saw him alive'. *History of Navya-Nyaya*, p. 37. (For his assistance with the translation of the Sanskrit verse on which this paragraph is based, I am grateful to Uni.-Doz. Dr Roque Mesquita.)

[39] *Ibid.*

[40] See Bimal Krishna Matilal, *Nyaya-Vaisesika*, vol. VI of *A History of Indian Literature*, ed. Jan Gonda (Wiesbaden, 1977), p. 96. See also Potter, *Indian Metaphysics and Epistemology*.

In addition to the theological treatise, the *Nyayakusumanjali* (which we will discuss later in some detail), a good example of his effectiveness is his monograph the *Atmatattvaviveka*, a sophisticated defence of the doctrine of the permanent self or 'soul' against its rejection by the Buddhists, who held a kind of 'bundle-theory' of the self.[41] So effective was Udayana's polemic that the work has come to be known as the *Bauddhadhikkara* or 'The Disgrace of the Buddhists'.

From the salutations and other tell-tale signs in his writings, we know for sure that Udayana was a devotee of the god Siva, though we do not know for certain to which Saivite sect he may have belonged. Even so, we can reasonably surmise that, as a pious Saivite, much of Udayana's time would have been given over to meditating on Siva and his various forms, whilst murmuring a prescribed formula, such as *om namah sivaya*. His writings also show him to have been religiously quite eclectic. They exhibit in different ways important affinities with the Vaisnavism of the Vedantins and with the sorts of spirituality that are more often associated with the Buddhists or with the *Yogasutras* of Patanjali. And, whilst holding that the supreme yoga or union with God is most nearly approximated via the path charted by the Nyaya-Vaisesika system itself,[42] Udayana also allowed that all sects – including those that are overtly atheistic – somehow have as their focus and object of worship the one Supreme Being or Isvara,[43] the maker, maintainer and destroyer of all worlds:

> He is the One who, spreading wide His net,
> Rules with His sovereign powers . . .
> Over against (His) creatures stands He, protector;
> All worlds He emanated ['made' or 'brought forth'
> (*samsrjya*)],
> (All worlds) will He roll up at the end of time.[44]

This Upanisadic hymn to the Vedic god Rudra, traditionally identified with the god Siva, nicely encapsulates the essential functions of God in the

---

[41] For a philosophically brilliant analysis of Udayana's defence of the doctrine of the 'soul' (*atman*) and of his critique of the Buddhist's 'no-soul' (*anatman*) doctrine, see Claus Oetke, '*Ich' und das Ich: Analytische Untersuchungen zur buddhistisch-brahmanischen Atmankontroverse* (Stuttgart, 1988).

[42] See, e.g., the end of the *Atmatattvaviveka*, where Udayana ranks the various systems of salvation as steps leading to the Nyaya-Vaisesika system, which he cheekily calls – no doubt to the chagrin of the Vedantins – 'the final Vedanta'.

[43] *Nyayakusumanjali*, stabaka I, karika 3. See Johannes Bronkhorst, 'God in Samkhya', *Weiner Zeitschrift für die Kunde Süd- und Ostasiens* 27 (1983), 159f.

[44] *Svetasvara Upanisad*, III, 1–2 [trans. R. C. Zaehner, *Hindu Scriptures*, 2nd edn (London, 1966), p. 207)].

Nyaya-Vaisesika system as it had evolved by Udayana's time. And, as we shall see, the theistic proofs preferred by him and the other Naiyayikas were all of them expressive of the various functions that they had ascribed to God.

According to the Nyaya-Vaisesikas,[45] God – conceived as one soul amongst other souls, albeit as the 'supreme soul' or *paramatman* – desires above all else the final release of every human being (*jivatman*) from the cycle of suffering that is *samsara*. According to the law of *karma*, however, the fact and circumstance of our birth are determined by the residual effects of past deeds. Within the limits of that law, over which not even Isvara has power, God is enabled by perfect wisdom to fashion a world so that each soul can enjoy the fruits of past deeds and, quite possibly, find salvation as well. As one cause amongst several, God makes the world from eternally pre-existing 'atoms' (*paramanus*) and other 'substances' (*dravyas*), including the also eternally pre-existing souls.

The world having been so fashioned, God then teaches the first embodied souls the Vedas, certain traditional crafts and any other information essential for life's tasks. Those first souls then pass what they have heard (*sruta*) to the next generation, and they to the next, and so on. Some individual souls will find release by following the path originally taught by God. Others will become distracted or confused and will lose their way. God, however, will continue to maintain and direct the world process so long as salvific possibilities remain.

But after one hundred Brahma-years (calculated as 311,040,000,000,000 calendar-years)[46] and at a precise moment of God's own desiring, the universe will disintegrate back into its constituent parts, the atoms and other substances. Though all souls become separated from their bodies, which also dissolve back into atoms, their accumulated merits and demerits will remain with them. Then, after another one hundred Brahma-years, the desire arises in God to fashion a fresh world out of the same material, so that all the souls that remain bound by *karma* can be given another chance to find release. According to the Nyaya-Vaisesika scheme of things in Udayana's day, this cyclic process will be repeated under God's guidance until all souls have been freed from the round of existence.

---

[45] This account is based largely upon Udayana's *Kiranavali*, a commentary on the Vaisesika text *Padarthadharmasamgraha* by Prasastapada. For a summary of the Nyaya-Vaisesika cosmology, see Hans-Georg Türstig, *Über Entstehungsprozesse in der Philosophie des Nyaya-Vaisesika-Systems* (Wiesbaden, 1982).

[46] George Chemparathy, *An Indian Rational Theology: Introduction to Udayana's Nyayakusumanjali* (Vienna, 1972), p. 145, n. 309.

This, then, is the God worshipped by Udayana, the God in whom alone he places his trust; namely, the God Siva, whose magical powers he praises at the end of a chapter in the *Nyayakusumanjali*:

Him who in sport having repeatedly made this strangely wonderful world by his illusive [i.e. 'conjuror's'] power, again causes it to collapse, and having destroyed it again remakes it as a magic show. – that Deity, Siva, the might of whose will bursts forth unhindered into accomplishment – him I salute, the sole ground of confidence, and may I continue to pay him homage even unto the end.[47]

This is the God whose Name is invoked at the beginning of Udayana's writings, including the *Atmatattvaviveka*, where we read:

Reverence to the father, the Lord of the worlds [Siva], whose lordship over the worlds is spontaneous at first when they were produced and thereafter (their) protection as well, which gives rise to the knowledge which brings into existence the injunctions and the prohibitions about the beneficial and the harmful act (respectively), whose statement of truth is inherent, whose favour unconditional, and (all of) whose effect is for their sake (alone), and who is the first and best of (all) teachers.[48]

And this is also the God whose existence Udayana defended with all the logical tools and dialectical skills provided by the Nyaya-Vaisesika philosophical system which he followed.

In his various writings, Udayana put forward around two dozen different arguments in proof of this God's existence.[49] All of them – without exception – are based on the several functions of Isvara within the Nyaya-Vaisesika scheme. He argued from the world's being an effect or a product to the necessity of a cause of its production; from the world's contingency to the necessity of some being to sustain it in existence, lest it self-destruct; from the existence and nature of the Vedas to the necessity of a supranatural author; and from the knowledge of traditional skills and crafts to the necessity of a first teacher.

Some of his arguments – particularly those to do with the capacity of 'dyads' (*dvyanuka*) to form into 'triads' (*tryanuka*) and with the significance of special numbers – are inaccessible to anyone not reasonably *au fait* with

---

[47] Stabaka 2, karika 4 [trans. E. B. Cowell (Calcutta, 1864), p. 31].

[48] Translated by Chitrarekha V. Kher and Shiv Kumar (Delhi, 1987). Contrast what Udayana says here in praise of God with what al-Ghazali says in praise of God in the laudatory preface (*khutba*) to the *Fada'ih al-Batiniyya wa Fada'il al-Mustazhiriyya* (*Freedom and Fulfillment*, pp. 175f).

[49] They appear principally in the *Nyayakusumanjali*, but also in the *Atmatattvaviveka* and in the *Kiranavali*. The best summary of Udayana's proofs is found in Chemparathy, *An Indian Rational Theology*, to which the reader is referred.

the finer points of the Vaisesika theory of number (*samkhya*) and size (*parimana*) on which they are based. Other proofs, though readily accessible in one sense, require of us assumptions about certain classes of activity – such as weaving – that we would not normally expect to entertain. About one half of the arguments proffered by Udayana concern God as author or 'speaker' of the Vedic scriptures. For instance, the proof which is expounded at greatest length in the *Nyayakusumanjali* is based on a specific (and, one gathers, controversial) interpretation of a particular verb form in Sanskrit, an interpretation which is then used to justify the claim that the injunctions contained in the Vedas entail a speaker whose wish they express and that this speaker is God, whose existence is thereby proven.[50]

All of the proofs for God as author of the Vedas are built on linguistic and grammatical points. This may strike us – who are not 'orthodox' by Hindu standards – as curious, but it makes more sense if the authority of the Vedic scripture and the supranatural origin of the *devanagari* alphabet are already presupposed. Since Udayana's *Nyayakusumanjali* is in some measure a compendium of arguments that had attained a certain standing amongst the Naiyayikas, the preponderance of such philological proofs must indicate the importance attached to them and may well reflect the course and intensity of the centuries-long debate between the orthodox Naiyayikas and the equally orthodox Mimamsakas over the existence of God and the nature of Vedic authority.

The debate about God's existence was far more variegated in Udayana's India than it was in Ghazali's Persia or, for that matter, in Anselm's Europe. At issue in eleventh-century India was not simply the provability of God's existence, nor even was it just the appropriateness of a given proof to the being of a particular God. Such issues were also discussed in Udayana's India – an India in which his contemporary Ramanuja, for example, argued vigorously against any possible proof of God's existence as religiously illicit and, in the process of so doing, managed to anticipate by roughly seven hundred years most of Hume's objections to the argument from design.[51]

In addition to the provability of God's existence, the fact of God's existence was much debated in the India of the eleventh century – as it had been for over a thousand years before that. The 'heterodox' (*nastika*) systems – the Carvaka, the Jainas and the Buddhists – had all denied the

---

[50] *Nyayakusumanjali*, stabaka 5, karikas 6–14 (Cowell translation, pp. 71–82). See Chemparathy, *An Indian Rational Theology*, pp. 122–5.

[51] See his *Sri-Bhasya*, I, i, 3.

existence of a creator God or Isvara, even one with the rather limited 'job description' allowed by the Nyaya-Vaisesika system. That denial was not the cause of their heterodoxy, however. They were excluded from the orthodox *darsanas*, not by their 'atheism', but by their repudiation of the authority of the Vedas and by their failure to perform the sacrifices and other rituals required by the Vedas and other Brahmanic scriptures.

Even within the 'orthodox' (*astika*) systems – of which there were six – there was a variety of stances adopted toward the God-question. Of the orthodox *darsanas*, only two were unambiguously theistic: the Vedanta system (whose most famous followers were Samkara, Ramanuja and Madhva) and – from a certain point in time – the Nyaya-Vaisesika system, though the earliest Naiyayikas were evidently non-theistic. Only later was the Vaisesika doctrine of God annexed onto their otherwise naturalistic scheme based on the law of *karma*. Whether this new development was more in reaction to criticism from without (possibly from the Buddhist logicians, who questioned the coherence of Nyaya teachings) or in response to a need felt from within the Nyaya circle itself, the attention of their leading *srotriyas* from about the sixth or seventh century onwards turned increasingly to the task of elaborating and defending their conception of God.[52] But the remaining orthodox systems – the Yoga, Samkhya and Mimamsa – were with varying degrees of conviction largely atheistic.

The question of 'orthodoxy' turned, not on belief in God, but on acceptance of the authority of the Vedas, which could be read either non-theistically or theistically. The non-theistic Mimamsakas, against whom Udayana directed most of his arguments in the *Nyayakusumanjali*, are best understood as a group of 'hermeneutical a-theologians' devoted solely to the interpretation of the Vedic scriptures, which they believed to be without origin, without author, without error, and – as such – self-authenticating in authority.[53] The debate between the Naiyayikas and the Mimamsakas, therefore, was a debate about how to read the Vedic scriptures, the authority of which was disputed by neither side. Should the Vedas be read theistically or atheistically? – that was the question. Into this essentially hermeneutical debate Udayana introduced a long string of philological and grammatical

---

[52] See Gerhard Oberhammer, 'Zum Problem des Gottesbeweises in der indischen Philosophie', *Numen* 12 (1965), 1–34. For a sensitive comparison of the doctrinal schemes and styles of spirituality which characterized non-theistic and radically theistic expressions of early Nyaya philosophy, see the same author's *Wahrheit und Transzendenz: Ein Beitrag zur Spiritualität des Nyaya* (Vienna, 1984).

[53] See Jean-Marie Verpoorten, *Mimamsa Literature*, vol. VI of *A History of Indian Literature* (Wiesbaden, 1987).

reasons why the Vedas should be read theistically, as the Naiyayikas now held, rather than atheistically, as the Mimamsakas still insisted.

There was in Udayana's India a degree of religious pluralism that would not be experienced in Europe until several hundred years later, if at all. Moreover, there had also developed in India a tradition of public disputation that provided (at its best) an orderly procedure for representatives of the various competing standpoints to confront each other and to test the soundness of each other's claims before a mutually acceptable 'arbiter' or 'referee' (*saksin*) and a body of witnesses.

With roots that go deep into the Brahmanical ritual of Vedic times, *vada* or public disputation on philosophical topics was an important feature of the Indian intellectual tradition from its formative period.[54] As a consequence, dialectical dexterity was greatly prized amongst the 'orthodox' and the 'heterodox' alike. It has even been asserted that the distinction between 'orthodox' and 'heterodox' can itself be traced back to the one who affirms (*astika*) and the one who denies (*nastika*) the proposition in a philosophical debate.[55] Whatever the merits of this claim, it does seem certain that Indian logic in the formal sense – especially as systematized by the Buddhists and the Naiyayikas – grew out of centuries of reflection on the rules which governed such disputations.[56] Some of the most important early milestones in the history of Indian logic dealt with the kinds of difficulties which can arise in the course of such debates.[57]

Even the *Nyayasutras*, the foundation text on which was built the philosophical system of which Udayana was a foremost exponent, are occupied in the main with the accepted means of cognition, forms of proof, and techniques of argument relevant to the conduct of philosophical disputation. But disputation was not entered into for its own sake by the Naiyayikas. Rather, philosophical debate – conducted according to established principles of argument – was regarded by the Naiyayikas as the most certain means of arriving at the kind of reliable knowledge required to achieve the *summum bonum* of life, which the Naiyayikas (in common with every other classical system, whether orthodox or heterodox) held to be the final release from the round of existence (I.i.1–2).

---

[54] See J. C. Heesterman, 'On the Origins of the Nastika', *WZKSO* 12–13 (1968–9), 171–85, and Michael Witzel, 'The Case of the Shattered Head', *Studien zur Indologie und Iranistik* 13 (1987), 363–415.

[55] See Heesterman, 'On the Origins of the Nastika', pp. 171f.

[56] See Gerhard Oberhammer, 'Ein Beitrag zu den Vada-Traditionen Indiens', *WZKSO* 12 (1963), 63–103.

[57] Cf. Michael Torsten Much, *Dharmakirtis Vadanyayah* (Diss. phil.: University of Vienna, 1983).

This clarifies to some extent the import attached in the *Nyayasutras* to the licit means of knowledge (I.i.3–8 *et passim*), the possible objects of knowledge (I.i.9–22 *et passim*), and also to sound argument as the proper means of removing doubt and establishing truth (I.i.23–41 *et passim*). It may even go some way toward explaining the significance of knowing twenty-four kinds of futile rejoinders (V.i.1–42) and twenty-two ways in which an inference may be faulty and an argument lost (V.ii.1–24).

The essence of the Nyaya system *as a system of salvation* is the use of argument as an instrument of eliminating ignorance and arriving at knowledge necessary for obtaining release from the cycle of rebirth.[58]

These three things – the extent of religious pluralism, the tradition of public disputation, the salvific purpose of argument in the Nyaya scheme – all help us understand why theistic proofs might occupy a key place in Udayana's writings. But they do not tell the whole story. A fourth factor must also be taken into account: namely, Udayana's use of argument as a form of *bhakti* or worship of the God whose existence he had taken it upon himself to defend.

This devotional application of philosophical argument is most prominent in Udayana's remarkable theological monograph, the *Nyayakusumanjali*, in which he mounts a determined defence of the Nyaya-Vaisesika doctrine of God against a variety of non-theistic opponents, including of course the Buddhists, but more systematically the Mimamsakas. As this description implies, the book is at one level an exercise in polemics/apologetics.

This adversarial quality of the tract is underscored by Udayana's having chosen to set out the case he is defending according to the rules and conventions of the *vada*-debating tradition. Those rules require, amongst other things, the winner of a disputation both to demolish the opponent's case and to construct successful positive arguments in support of the position being defended. If either of these conditions fails, the outcome of the disputation is indecisive.[59] Udayana's reputation as a fierce debater was not won on well-played 'draws' at the *vada*-equivalent of Lord's or Old Trafford. The structure of the *Kusumanjali* shows that he had every

[58] See Satischandra Chatterjee, *The Nyaya Theory of Knowledge: A Critical Study of Some Problems of Logic and Metaphysics*, 3rd edn (Calcutta, 1965), pp. 1ff.; V. A. van Bijlert, *Epistemology and Spiritual Authority: The Development of Epistemology and Logic in Old Nyaya and the Buddhist School of Epistemology* (Vienna, 1989).

[59] See, e.g., Michael Torsten Much, 'Dharmakirti's Definition of "Points of Defeat" (*Nigrahasthana*)', in *Buddhist Logic and Epistemology*, ed. B. K. Matilal and R. D. Evans (Dordrecht, 1986), pp. 133–44.

intention of satisfying both the required conditions. First, he enumerates the main objections that have been raised to belief in God and he then rebuts them each in turn, according to established *vada*-principles. Having, at least to his own satisfaction, undermined his opponents' position in the first four chapters of the work, Udayana then sets about in the final chapter establishing his own position by constructing and adequately supporting a number of positive arguments drawn from reason and scripture. These, too, are set out in accordance with prevailing *vada*-principles.

Had he done no more than this, Udayana's book would still no doubt have become the classic defence of the Nyaya-Vaisesika doctrine of God. That on its own would probably have been enough to earn for the book and its author the kind of pre-eminence which they in fact enjoyed and, indeed, have continued to enjoy in some parts of India up to the present day.[60] But Udayana did more than that in the *Kusumanjali*, and it is this 'more' which lifts the book above the level of mere polemics or apologetics.

The clue to determining wherein this 'more' lies is given already in the title of the *Nyayakusumanjali*. *Nyaya* in this instance simply means 'arguments', though it is possible that a playful Naiyayika, like Udayana, may even here have intended a *double entendre*, as a way of alluding to the name of his school's philosophical system. *Kusuma* means a bunch of flowers, and *anjali* is the quintessential gesture of respect or devotion in India. It is the gesture of reverential greeting when the hands are cupped together and held before the face, and it is the gesture of pious supplication which is made when, for example, flowers are brought to the altar and offered in worship to a God. *Nyayakusumanjali*, then, means a bouquet of arguments offered to God. But it is a bouquet whose fragrance should also bring benefit to the reader, who is urged to hover bee-like over each blossom in search of its nectar.[61]

The metaphor given in the title – which is in one sense already more than 'mere' metaphor – is extended by Udayana into the text as well. Each of its five chapters, for instance, is called a *stabaka* or a 'cluster' of flower blossoms. Each argument is itself a flower and we are invited to imagine that each argument unfolds like a blossom opens, until the argument-flowers are all fully displayed. The final cluster – the point in the book where Udayana gives his positive arguments for God's existence – is a horticultural (or perhaps horti*logical?*) treat. Not only does he set out nine

---

[60] See Bhattacharya, *History of Navya-Nyaya in Mithila*.
[61] *Nyayakusumanjali*, stabaka 1, karika 1.

arguments for God's existence, but when the nine are fully unfolded, they all turn out to be double-blossoms. Through a linguistic conjuring trick that might well have evoked shrieks of pure delight from Siva – the master conjuror – the nine proofs turn magically into eighteen or more proofs for God's existence, with each pair of the nine growing from the same ground (*hetu*), so to speak.[62] The resulting display of colour is such as to bring joy to the faithful and pause for thought to the unbeliever.

Moreover, the way that the *Nyayakusumanjali* is organized encourages the reader to imagine that the five clusters of blooms are braided together to form a daisy-chain of arguments or perhaps a garland of logic-flowers, which Udayana then lays at the feet of Siva. That the arguments themselves might have salvific value to a Naiyayika has already been established above. Here, however, there is a new dimension – for the arguments are being offered to Siva for the deity's sake alone, and not just for any benefit that may accrue to the credit of the one who hears and understands and meditates on them. And this new dimension is the 'more' that constitutes the uniqueness and the beauty of the *Nyayakusumanjali*.

The three final verses of the book, when read together, reinforce the interpretation which I have been offering of the *Kusumanjali*.[63] The first of the three is a prayer offered on behalf of those unbelievers who, having hardened their hearts, fail to be persuaded by the truth of the arguments presented for their benefit. Udayana suggests that 'in time' – meaning through the repeated cycle of rebirth – God in mercy and goodness 'canst save even those who oppose our propositions, and make them undoubting in their conviction of Thy existence'. The next verse is a prayer made on behalf of those who already believe, but who may waver in their certainty or wander in their concentration. Udayana asks of God mercy, so that with 'our minds fixed only on Thee, we may no more be subject to Yama's [i.e. death's] continual inflictions'.

These two verses, taken on their own, suggest strongly that the *Nyaya-kusumanjali* was written with the dual purpose of persuading the un-believer and of edifying the faithful, to the end that both might find final release from suffering. And so it no doubt was. But the final verse, when read in the light of the two that precede it, suggests that even this dual purpose is in the end subordinated to a higher purpose; namely, to the loving worship of Siva for Siva's sake alone. It does not matter, Udayana confesses, whether the flowers of logic perfume the 'right' hand or the

---

[62] See Chemparathy, *An Indian Rational Theology*, pp. 199ff.
[63] Stabaka 5, karikas 17–19 (Cowell translation p. 85).

'left' – the pure or the impure, the righteous or the wicked, the believer or the unbeliever – so long as they are acceptable as a gift to the Lord Siva, so that 'the Guru of Indra's Guru' – as Siva was sometimes represented – 'may be pleased by my presenting it as an offering at his footstool'. Udayana seems to be content that his efforts would have achieved their ultimate purpose, if only they are received by the Lord Siva. But, if the *Bhagavad Gita* warrants the respect that Udayana paid it as sacred scripture, then he could have been confident that his wish would be granted, and he could also have been confident of much more besides:

> For those who meditate upon Me, no other [thought in mind],
> Who do Me honour, ever persevere,
> I bring attainment
> And possession of what has been attained.
> . . .
>
> Be it a leaf, or flower, or fruit, or water
> That a zealous soul may offer with love's devotion (*bhakti*),
> That do I [willingly] accept,
> For it was love (*bhakti*) that made the offering.
> . . .
>
> So from (those) bonds which works (of their very nature forge),
> Whose fruits are fair or foul, thou shalt be freed:
> Thy self (now) integrated by renunciation and spiritual
> exercise (*yoga*),
> Free, thou shalt draw nigh to Me.
> . . .
>
> In all contingent beings the same am I;
> None do I hate and none do I fondly love (*priya*);
> But those who commune (*bhaj-*) with Me in love's devotion (*bhakti*)
> (Abide) in Me, and I in them.[64]

CONCLUSION

At one level, it would be difficult to select two more contrasting contemporaries than al-Ghazali and Udayana, or two more varied agendas for theistic argument than those itemized in their respective writings. Even what they initially appeared to have in common – namely, a preference

---

[64] IX.22, 26, 28–9 (*Hindu Scriptures*, p. 288).

for some version of the cosmological argument – turns out on closer inspection to have been only superficial, so substantial are the differences in their cosmologies, in their conceptions of causality and of divinity. At another level, however, one is profoundly struck by points of similarity in their handling of theistic argument. And it is these very points which distinguish their intellectual projects from those of the modern era.

First, theistic proofs function in Ghazali's and Udayana's writings in a variety of ways in addition to being used polemically and apologetically. (*a*) They were used by both men for the edification of members of their respective communities. Theistic proofs may form part of instruction in the fundamentals of the faith, or they may be used to reassure those whose faith is uncertain or to encourage greater commitment from those who are too casual about their religious obligations. They may also play a central role in such spiritual exercises as devotion and meditation. This latter use is particularly prominent in Udayana's *Nyayakusumanjali*. And though I would not wish to claim that this devotional dimension is wholly absent from the way theistic proofs were used on the fringes of the Enlightenment – one thinks, for example, of John Ray, Jonathan Edwards and also of Addison's hymn, 'The Spacious Firmament' – the cultivation of such spiritual disciplines did not figure centrally in the Enlightenment's search for confessionally independent reasons to warrant belief in the existence and nature of God.[65]

(*b*) Normally in connection with their polemical or apologetic aims, both Ghazali and Udayana also used theistic proofs hermeneutically in order to determine the proper interpretation of some sacred text, whether to clarify the sense of an obscure passage or to settle the meaning of a disputed one. For reasons to do with the legal requirements in prosecutions for 'unbelief' within Islam, this was a prominent feature in Ghazali's use of theistic argument, but it also figured significantly in Udayana's defence of theism against the Mimamsakas. In addition, both men regularly cited sacred texts in association with their theistic proofs, presumably to give the proof an enhanced authority, though it may also have been just to show the concurrence of reason and scripture. Whatever the specific aim, the plenitude of such references in association with their proofs gives an added 'texture' to the place of theistic argument in their writings which is absent from more modern attempts to find tradition-independent warrants for belief in the existence of some God. It also suggests a second point of difference, to which I now turn.

---

[65] Editors' note: See further, in relation to this final point, Chapter 10 of this volume.

Theistic argument was enlisted by Ghazali and Udayana alike in order to defend their tradition-specific partisan beliefs about God, and not in order to negotiate some tradition-free common ground where all theists could with equal comfort gather. Neither man seems to have had the least interest in establishing the rationality of some general belief in 'God'. They were each of them very intent, however, on establishing by formally valid argument the existence of the God as worshipped by Sunnite Muslims or as worshipped by Saivite Naiyayikas. They expressed their proofs, to be sure, in syllogistic form – whether of Aristotelian or of Nyayan origin[66] – and they both affirmed the authority of the rules of logic in matters theological, but the actual reasons adduced by each in support of his God were more directly what would count as reasons within their individual traditions than they were generally convincing or 'tradition-neutral' reasons.

Given that Ghazali directed his theistic proofs exclusively at elements within the Muslim community, it is perhaps only to be expected that his choice of reasons would reflect that rather specific audience. But what holds for Ghazali in this regard holds also for Udayana, who addressed his theistic proofs mainly to elements outside the Nyaya-Vaisesika school. For all of Udayana's proofs for God's existence were built on the functions of Isvara within the Nyaya-Vaisesika theological scheme.

I do not mean to suggest that their intended audiences had no effect on the fashioning of theistic argument by Ghazali or Udayana. There is evidence enough that both of them slanted their proofs according to their immediate objectives. For example, Ghazali uses his argument from the 'originatedness' of the world when he has the likes of Ibn Sina in his sights, but earlier, when quarrelling with the Batinites, he resorted to an argument from 'necessary being', which he possibly judged to be more effective against them.[67] And it is perhaps understandable that so many of Udayana's proofs in the *Nyayakusumanjali* would be based on grammatical or philological issues arising from the study of the Vedic scriptures, since the primary target in that work seems to have been the Mimamsakas, for

---

[66] Despite Satischandra Vidyabhusana's having asserted in his influential *History of Indian Logic* (Delhi, 1971 [1920]) that the Indian syllogism was 'greatly influenced by, if not based on' Aristotle (p. 511; cf. pp. 497–513), scholars today are inclined to stress their independent origins and their distinctive features, whilst allowing some affinities. Cf., e.g., Bimal Krishna Matilal, *Logic, Language and Reality* (Delhi, 1985), pp. 1–8.

[67] *Fada'ih al-Batiniyya*, §§166–9 (*Freedom and Fulfillment*, pp. 224–5). See Lenn E. Goodman, 'Ghazali's Argument from Creation', *International Journal of Middle Eastern Studies* 2 (1971), 75f., 187.

whom the Vedic scriptures had special authority. More significantly, however, when defending the Nyaya-Vaisesika doctrine of the Soul against the Buddhist no-soul doctrine, Udayana built much of his case in the *Atmatattvaviveka* on the fact that the Vedas clearly and consistently teach the doctrine of the Soul which he is propounding.[68]

Even though there was some adapting of proof to intended target, both the choice and the construction of theistic arguments in the writings of Ghazali and Udayana were controlled by the specific teachings about the divine nature and activity in their respective religious traditions. There are in this sense no 'general' proofs for God's existence in their writings. Nor do they ever adduce as warrants any reasons which are not reasons for their own religious communities, though they do regularly introduce as warrants reasons that would not be regarded as such by those targeted by their particular proofs. This reliance on tradition-specific reasons is curious from a modern point of view, conditioned as we are by the expectations raised in the minds of friend and foe alike by the place of theistic proofs in what we have been calling 'the Enlightenment project'.

From a pre-modern perspective, however, the bond between rational argument and authoritative textual tradition is more self-evident. For the likes of Ghazali, Udayana and also their contemporary Anselm stood in an immediate relation to texts that we have quite lost and would find it hard to recover. Every day of their lives was in large part filled with 'listening to', 'thinking about' and 'meditating on' sacred texts as a path to holiness, as it says in a scripture of uncertain origin that Udayana was fond of quoting.[69] Moreover, their authoritative texts and other significant writings – in Ghazali's case, his entire library[70] – would have been

---

[68] Udayana's Buddhist opponents – being 'heterodox' – would not be inclined to accept an appeal to Brahmanic scripture as a reason for granting the truth of any doctrine. In order to establish the reasonableness of his appeal in Vedic scripture, therefore, Udayana offered arguments for their authoritativeness. One such argument was built on their having been 'spoken' by a trustworthy person, namely, God, whose existence can be inferred by means of theistic proofs. In other words, the existence of God is demonstrated in the *Atmatattvaviveka* in order to show that the Vedas are authoritative, so that they can be cited as evidence for the existence of the soul. But, since none of these arguments would count as reasons amongst the Buddhists, one might be better advised to regard them as Udayana's attempt to show the reasonableness of Nyaya-Vaisesika doctrine (in this case, of the soul) than to treat them as apodictic proofs which any rational person, including a Buddhist, would be expected to accept.

[69] The verse is cited in – and is, therefore, older than – Vyasa's *Yogabhasya* on Patanjali's *Yogasutra*, 1.48. Even though he would have known Vyasa's *Bhasya*, Udayana more likely adopted the interpretation given that verse by his fellow Naiyayika Vacaspati Misra, who in his gloss on Vyasa transposed the possibly yogic verse into a Nyayan key. See Rama Prasada (trans.), *Patanjali's Yoga Sutras*, 3rd edn (New Delhi, 1982).

[70] See Makdisi, *The Rise of Colleges*, p. 100.

committed to memory. Texts in this way were internalized and became part of them. They not only *cited* the texts, they *thought* and *spoke* the texts, they *lived* the texts. And this not merely as isolated individuals, but as whole communities.

This being the case, it is not at all surprising that their rational reflections should have been so prompted and so guided by their tradition's authoritative texts. Nor should it be astonishing that their rational reflections should have found an important place in the devotional and other spiritual exercises of the members of their communities. That 'The Jerusalem Tract', including the theistic argument it contains, might be used devotionally by members of the Jerusalem mosque is no more astonishing than that the works by Udayana of Mithila or by the Prior of Bee might be used as aids to meditation on the divine nature by members of their communities.

It is we, not they, who find such uses of theistic argument out of the ordinary. And if it is mainly the 'otherness' of their intellectual projects (which, incidentally, were more accurately life projects) which we find most striking, this may not simply be because of our philosophical or theological differences, though these no doubt also come into play. It may be because we have lost, through the effects of the Fall of Modernity, the kind of immediacy with which they lived their texts and because we have concurrently lost any sense for the styles of spirituality and the modes of experience in which their 'projects' were embedded. To appropriate for ourselves what they were doing with theistic arguments may, therefore, require a rediscovery of those modes of experience, those spiritual disciplines, those forms of life which seemed to them second nature.

For a few of us this may well be possible. For many of us, however, this way may be cut off, whether by personal temperament or by conscious choice. For such of us to whom this applies, the mediaeval world – whether Western or Eastern – offers no welcome refuge from the modern. Even so, those of us who are still committed to some form of 'natural theology' may feel reassured to be reminded that the use of theistic proofs is widespread amongst the religions of the world and may also be emboldened by these examples from the past to combine a commitment to public argument about basic religious issues with a more confident use of tradition-specific reasons. And those of us who are not so well-disposed toward 'natural theology', but who still cling to the now old-fashioned idea that the primary purpose of the philosophy of religion – including also the comparative philosophy of religion – is the clarification of meanings and the analysis of concepts may have caught a whiff of the hint running throughout this paper that a close inspection of theistic proofs may show them to be most usefully approached as indirectly stated forms of conceptual analysis.

But all of us are bound to allow that the force of these proofs in pre-modern times comes from the extent of their embeddedness in the religious forms of life which they express; and it is the lack of this embeddedness in modern proofs, more than any philosophical deficiencies which they may also have, which in comparison makes them look so thin.

CHAPTER 7

The otherness of Anselm*

Anselm's *Proslogion* is an obvious resource for anyone wishing to reflect on 'the otherness of God'. The mediaeval monk's desire to be allowed to know and love and rejoice in the being of his God (§26) was in no way fed by a desire to deny God's otherness. His strategy was rather to confirm what we already believe about God's utter difference by making the divine 'otherness' intelligible to the human mind; that is, by making otherness *thinkable.*

God's way of being is one kind; ours, quite another. For instance, I know that my existence is contingent. I can easily think of myself as not existing. I can imagine a time in the past before I came into being, and I can also imagine time in the future after I shall cease to be. If I put my mind to it, I can even imagine my never having existed at all.

But that is not the way God is, according to Anselm. Unlike ourselves, God can only be conceived as being without beginning and without end, as being 'inoriginate' and 'imperishable'; that is, as being *necessary* in one mediaeval sense of that term. In chapter 22 of the *Proslogion*, Anselm hymns his God:

You are that being who exists truly and simply, because you neither were nor will be but always already are, nor can you be thought not to be at any time. And you are life and light, wisdom and blessedness, eternity and many other such good things, indeed you yourself are nothing other than the one and highest good, entirely sufficient to yourself, needing nothing, but he whom all things need for their being and well-being.[1]

Such a God is not just 'aliquid quo nihil maius cogitari possit' (§2), to recall Anselm's famous phrase, which played so central a part early in his

---

* Originally given as a paper at the international conference on 'The Otherness of God' held at the University of Virginia in April 1994 to commemorate Professor Robert Scharlemann's sixty-fifth birthday.

[1] Quotations from the *Proslogion* follow, with minor emendations, the fluent translation of Benedicta Ward in *The Prayers and Meditations of Saint Anselm* (Harmondsworth, 1973), pp. 238–67. For the Latin text, see the *Opera Omnia*, ed. F. S. Schmitt, 6 vols. (Rome and Edinburgh, 1938–61; repr. Stuttgart-Bad Cannstatt, 2nd edn, 1984), I, pp. 93–122.

argument. This God, as he had come to see by chapter 15, is even greater than can be conceived: '*Ergo domine, non solum es quo maius cogitari nequit, sed es quiddam maius quam cogitari possit.*' Anselm's God is radically other, dwelling 'in light inaccessible', eluding our senses and our understanding alike (§§17, 16), but in whose dazzle we are made aware of overwhelming greatness and fullness of being (§14).

There would seem to be good reason, therefore, to include the *Proslogion* on the reading list of works to consult when contemplating the otherness of God. If we should pick up the *Proslogion*, however, we must do so not just with an expectation of learning something of the necessary *otherness of God*. We must be prepared also to find in it evidence of the possible *otherness of Anselm*.

And this for at least two reasons.

First, God was not 'other' for Anselm in just the sense that God has become 'other' for many of us. In our time (whether we be disposed to see it as more nearly 'modern' or 'post-modern'), we find it difficult to think about 'otherness' in God without being mindful of the darker side of that projection as exposed in the reflections of Feuerbach, Freud and – more recently – some feminists. Once such suspicions have been aroused about our projections, otherness can never be the same again.

By contrast, God's not-being was for Anselm in a strong sense of the term *inconceivable*. I do not mean to suggest, of course, that from his perspective it was impossible for the non-being of God to be experienced emotionally. For even a model monk, in a moment of deep distress born of bereavement, may have been tempted to deny God's existence. But it was impossible from Anselm's perspective for the non-being of God to be conceived rationally. The sense of 'atheism' to which we have become accustomed in modern times was for Anselm a kind of square-circle. The possibility of God's not being was for him quite simply *unthinkable*: 'Sic ergo vere es, domine deus meus, ut nec cogitari possis non esse' (§3).

For many of us, however, the necessity of God's *being* has become more nearly unthinkable than is the possibility of God's *not-being*. The story of how that which for Anselm had been so utterly inconceivable has come to be culturally so well established in the modern imagination is too long to tell here.[2] But the twist for us in this serpentine tale is that we would

---

[2] For narratives stressing the complicity of theologians themselves in creating the conditions for that kind of cultural change, see Michael J. Buckley, *At the Origins of Modern Atheism* (New Haven,

most certainly find it difficult not to feel out of place in Anselm's cosmologically enclosed world of thought, the monastic world in and for which the proof of the *Proslogion* was first conceived.

Of course, I do not mean thereby to suggest that everyone who shared Anselm's space in time shared also his perspective on the utter unthinkability of God's not being, or shared also his elation at having invented (in the mediaeval sense) the proof of the *Proslogion*. Anselm's most celebrated early critic was likewise a monk, to whom he wrote a detailed reply protesting that his argument had not been reported fairly or understood properly. Ironically, by responding at length to Gaunilo's critique of chapters 2–4,[3] Anselm himself may unwittingly have colluded with his critic in guaranteeing that future commentators would also focus on just those three chapters, to the neglect of the rest of the *Proslogion*, with the result that later generations of philosophers would almost uniformly read those chapters ignorant of any sense of their place in a line of argument the very thought of which gave Anselm such joy.

Nor was Gaunilo the first monk to have harboured doubts about Anselm's argument, even if those becowled sceptics registered their suspicions with less sophistication than his clever defence of 'the Fool'. Their own insipience was acted out in more foolishly direct ways; namely, by the theft and wanton destruction of the wax tablets on which Anselm had first made a rough draft of his proof. And this was done not just once, but twice.[4] Clearly, not everyone at Bec welcomed the argument known at the time simply as the *ratio anselmi*.

1987), and Alan Charles Kors, *Atheism in France, 1650–1729*, vol. I: *The Orthodox Sources of Disbelief* (Princeton, 1990).

[3] Gaunilo, it seems, had no quarrel with the remainder of the book: 'Cetera libelli illius tam veraciter et tam praeclare sunt magnificeque disserta, tanta denique referta utilitate et pii ac sancti affectus intimo quodam odore fragrantia, ut nullo modo propter illa quae in initiis recte quidem sensa, sed minus firmiter argumentata sunt, ista sint contemnenda; sed illa potius argumentanda robustius, ac sic omnia cum ingenti veneratione et laude suscipienda.' *Pro Insipiente*, §9.

[4] See Eadmer, *The Life of St Anselm*, ed. and trans. R. W. Southern, 2nd edn (Oxford, 1972 [1962]), pp. 30–1. Having written his new argument on wax tablets and given them to a fellow monk for safe-keeping, Anselm later 'asked the monk who had charge of them for the tablets. The place where they had been laid was searched, but they were not found. The brethren were asked in case anyone had taken them, but in vain. And to this day no-one has been found who has confessed that he knew anything about them. Anselm wrote another draft on the same subject on other tablets, and handed them over to the same monk for more careful keeping. He placed them once more by his bed, in a more secret place, and the next day – having no suspicion of any mischance – he found them scattered on the floor beside his bed and the wax which was on them strewn about in small pieces. After the tablets had been picked up and the wax collected together, they were taken to Anselm. He pieced together the wax and recovered the writing, though with difficulty. Fearing now that by some carelessness it might be altogether lost, he ordered it, in the name of the Lord, to be copied onto parchment.'

Second, the *Proslogion* preserves a mode of cloistered reflection that predates the birth of academic theology and philosophy in Latin Europe and that is quite unsuited to the mode of learning that became established in the two centuries following Anselm's authorship.[5] Anselm's *Proslogion* is a book that one should read complete, and in a prayerful mood with the heart-felt intention of finding one's way to God. 'Come', Anselm coaxes his reader,

turn aside for a while from your daily tasks, escape for a moment from the tumult of your thoughts. Put aside your weighty cares, let your burdensome distractions wait, free yourself awhile for God and rest awhile in him . . . Enter the inner chamber of your soul, shut out everything except God and that which can help you in seeking him, and when you have shut the door, seek him. (§1)

A book like that was spiritually too personal, stylistically too rhetorical and structurally too complex to be of much use to compilers of theological textbooks, then or now.

The work was too lacking in pithy summaries to catch the eye of twelfth-century collectors of theological 'sentences'. Indeed, for most of the twelfth-century renaissance of learning and culture, when professional theology and theological education can be said to have been formed to the needs of the new cathedral schools, the *Proslogion* was simply ignored,[6] even if other works by Anselm did attract the attention of the new academics.[7] Nor were the ends for which the *Proslogion* was designed commensurate with the objectives of the thirteenth-century compilers of theological 'summae', academics who were intent on constructing new modes of theological reflection suited to the challenges that were felt to be pressing in on Christendom.[8] Neither, it would seem, is Anselm's little

---

[5] See Marcia L. Colish, *Peter Lombard*, 2 vols. (Leiden, 1994), for a major new study of the beginnings of academic theology and revaluation of Lombard's innovative role in its formation.

[6] In the hundred years between the passing reference by Gilbert Crispin (c. 1045–1117?) to Anselm's famous characterization of God in his *Disputatio Iudei et Christiani* (§81) and the elegant summary by Alexander Nequam (1157–1217) of the *ratio anselmi* in his *Speculum Speculationum*, the surviving texts from the twelfth century are remarkably silent about the argument now regarded as Anselm's principal contribution to Western intellectual life. See *The Works of Gilbert Crispin*, ed. A. S. Abulafia and G. R. Evans (Oxford, 1986), p. 27, where Gilbert embellishes Anselm's language to read 'quo nihil maius siue sufficientius cogitari potest'. See also *Alexander Nequam Speculum Speculationum*, ed. Rodney Thomson (Oxford, 1988), where Nequam summarizes Anselm's proof as follows: 'Qui ergo recte intelligit Deum, intelligit Deum esse' (p. 56).

[7] See, e.g., G. R. Evans, *Anselm and a New Generation* (Oxford, 1980), and the survey of the reception of Anselm's writings in the twelfth century by Michael J. P. Robson in the introductory chapter of 'Saint Anselm's Influence upon Saint Bonaventure's Theology of Redemption' (Ph.D. diss., Cambridge University, 1988), pp. 1–41.

[8] For a helpful digest of such concerns, see R. W. Southern, *Western Society and the Church in the Middle Ages* (Harmondsworth, 1970).

book well suited to the commercial constraints under which today's academics edit paperback textbooks trimmed to the needs (and means) of students pursuing introductory courses in philosophy of religion.

With rare exceptions,[9] editors restrict their selection from the *Proslogion* to chapters 2–4, in which (we are informed) is to be found complete a proof almost uniformly called the 'ontological argument' – a name first given it in the late eighteenth century by Immanuel Kant, and then principally in reference to a proof perfected by Leibniz but designed by Descartes[10] for use in a new project that Anselm himself would not have recognized, even if it be outlined in a book of *Meditations*. Friend and foe alike have credited Anselm ever since with having invented (in the modern sense) the ontological proof in three chapters of a book that he himself will have conceived in its entirety as a single if circuitous proof of the way God is.

Thus disembedded from Anselm's text, this so-called 'ontological argument' has been interpreted in lectures, analysed in essays, and anthologized in textbooks wherever theistic proofs form part of the undergraduate syllabus. Concentrating attention on this small, dislocated fragment of a text has meant that philosophers have typically tried to interpret the argument in *Proslogion* 2–4 without much feel for its place in the strategy of the book as a whole: indeed, without much sense of the purpose of Anselm's book. And all this has quite often occurred without any thought of its being important to identify that purpose or strategy in order to understand the point of the argument even in the few chapters that have been the single-minded focus of their professional attention.

Further dismemberment occurred in the middle of our own century when Anselm's new-found friends 'discovered' that not even chapters 2–4 amount to *unum argumentum*.[11] Apparently incapable of sustaining an argument over more than a single chapter, Anselm was now claimed to have begun but abandoned an abortive argument in chapter 2, in order to make a fresh and logically independent start in chapter 3. This line of interpretation was widely discussed and frequently applauded at the time

---

[9] E.g. Patrick Sherry, ed., *Philosophers on Religion* (London, 1987).

[10] In the account of the 'ontological proof' in the *Critique of Pure Reason*, Kant does not mention Anselm at all [A592–602/B620–30]. In his *Vorlesungen über die philosophische Religionslehre* [ed. K. H. L. Politz, 2nd edn (Leipzig, 1830; Darmstadt, 1982)], however, Kant ascribes that proof to Anselm, whom he calls 'der erste, der aus bloßen Begriffen die Nothwendigkeit eines höchsten Wesens darthun wollte . . .' (p. 18).

[11] See Norman Malcolm, 'Anselm's Ontological Arguments', *Philosophical Review* 69 (1960), 41–62, and Charles Hartshorne, *Anselm's Discovery* (LaSalle, 1965), as well as numerous articles and rejoinders to critics.

by an audience that had been long conditioned to confine attention to chapters 2–4 (regarded as the *philosophically* relevant bit) and to ignore the rest of the *Proslogion* (regarded as the embarrassingly *religious* bits). Such a novel interpretation as offered by Hartshorne and Malcolm, imaginative though it may have been, had little to do with Anselm's project in the *Proslogion*, and betrayed the then widespread disregard in philosophy for an argument's locality within a text and within the wider context.

Even those who have attempted to do justice to the place of the *ratio anselmi* within Anselm's project have approached his *Proslogion* with expectations more appropriate to other times and other places, so that distinctions are drawn and intentions ascribed that do not quite fit Anselm.

One thinks, for instance, of Karl Barth, whose study of *Anselm: Fides Quaerens Intellectum* remains one of the most sensitive attempts to view the argument of the *Proslogion* from the inside, so to say.[12]

For all Barth's talk of the importance of viewing Anselm's project in the *Proslogion* from its own perspective, however, he pushes the 'context' of Anselm's authorship – and of Anselm's proof[13] – most firmly into the background. We learn in passing, for instance, that in Anselm's day the prevailing architectural style was Romanesque.[14] And we are reminded that Anselm's authorship overlaps with the era of the Crusades.[15] But we are not told even in passing what it may have been like to be a monk in the monastery at Bec under Lanfranc, its Abbot. Nor do we learn what purposes a book like the *Proslogion* may have been designed to serve within the spiritual disciplines of monastic life.

Even more curiously, however, Barth would appear to have managed to write his book without once finding it necessary to mention that Anselm was a monk. Perhaps so obvious a fact as *that* was simply *too* obvious to

---

[12] *Anselm: Fides Quaerens Intellectum*, trans. Ian W. Robertson (London, 1960). The subtitle of Barth's volume, first published in 1931, is *Anselms Beweis der Existenz Gottes im Zusammenhang seines theologischen Programms* [page references are to the English edition followed in square brackets by page references to the German text edited by Eberhard Jüngel and Ingolf U. Dalferth and published in the *Karl Barth Gesamtausgabe* (Zurich, 1981)].

[13] Following the convention of philosophical commentators, whose approach he sets out to counter, Barth neglected the first chapter of the *Proslogion* and failed to extend his exposition beyond the fourth, evidently thinking that Anselm's proof of God was by then complete. Once again following philosophical convention, Barth divided the text of the *Proslogion* into two parts, the one concerning the *existence* of God and the other concerning the divine *nature*. *Ibid.*, pp. 13f., p. 73 [*KB-GA*, pp. 1f., p. 75].

[14] *Ibid.*, p. 16 [13].   [15] *Ibid.*, p. 65 [65].

require mention even in passing. But surely it would have been at least as obvious *to Barth* that Anselm was a 'theologian'. And yet *this* putative feature of Anselm's authorship is scrutinized from virtually every angle in his book.

It is not as if Barth were simply ignorant of the fact that Anselm was a monk; and it is not as if Barth (who in 1933 pointed approvingly, if mistakenly, to the un-political existence of the monks at Maria Laach[16]) were uninformed about Benedictine spirituality. Rather, it would appear that Anselm's being a monk was just not perceived by Barth as being relevant for understanding the Prior of Bec's authorship of the *Proslogion*. And it would also appear that Karl Barth – the dogmatic theologian – was so intent to show us that Anselm was not a *philosopher* in the modern, professional sense, he failed to see that neither was Anselm a *theologian* in the sense Barth was and so dearly wished Anselm also to be.

Barth can be seen in retrospect to have read Anselm's text with agendas before him that were more pressing for Barth than they were or could have been for Anselm. At the time he wrote the *Fides Quaerens Intellectum,* Barth was much preoccupied with defending the 'scientific' character of dogmatic theology and the legitimacy of confessional theology's presence within the academy. Barth's concerns may follow from a crisis in the Modern project, but they were of no concern to Anselm. Analogous questions could also have concerned the thirteenth-century scholastic theologians who disputed among themselves whether God's existence is a properly basic belief (to apply out of season Plantinga's currently much-bandied phrase) or, better, whether God's existence can be known *per se nota* (to use terms that would have been used by the scholastic theologians themselves).

But this is not a question that would have exercised the eleventh-century Prior of Bec. Nor is it a question that would have worried the immediate audience of the *Proslogion*. Anselm was a monk, and the *Proslogion* was meant foremost to benefit other monks. That obvious, all-too-obvious fact is regularly overlooked by philosophers and theologians

---

[16] 'At Bonn here', Barth wrote in June, 'I endeavour to carry on theology, and only theology, now as previously, and as if nothing had happened', a strategy he likened to 'the chanting of the hours by the Benedictines near by in the Maria Laach, which goes on undoubtedly without break or interruption, pursuing the even tenor of its way even in the Third Reich' [*Theological Existence Today* (London, 1933), p. 9]. Whatever Barth may have done at Bonn, the monks at Maria Laach did more than chant the hours in the Third Reich. They also secreted fugitives to safety, including most famously Konrad Adenauer.

alike in their efforts to examine the authorship of the *Proslogion* or to see the point of the *ratio anselmi*.

Having reduced Anselm's project to a professionally *theological* project, Barth may have felt excused from the requirement to enquire more closely into how the monastic life shaped Anselm's work as an author. By *not* asking *that* question, however, Barth limited the success of his attempt to situate Anselm's argument within its context.

Barth was right to insist that the *ratio anselmi* must be understood in relation to Anselm's other writings. He was right to make connections (and dis-connections) between the *Proslogion* and the *Monologion*, just as he was right to deal carefully with Anselm's reply to Gaunilo's defence of the Fool. And he was also right to point to the import of the text's prayer structure for understanding Anselm's objective in the *Proslogion*, even if he conspicuously showed no inclination to investigate the specific role of prayer and meditation in the regular life of those cloistered in the monastery at Bec.

Barth did make some reference to Anselm's devotional writings, winnowing out what might be called their 'dogmatic' kernel. But he showed no real interest in exploring the connections between them and the *Proslogion*, despite the fact that they are written in a similar literary genre and date from roughly the same period.[17] Why did Barth not make more of them?

Could it be that their typically mediaeval Catholic piety was less congenial to Barth's more austere Reformed theological sensitivities than was the 'dogmatic'(!) essay *Cur Deus Homo* (to which he makes repeated reference)? Or could it be that their painfully introspective tone reminded him of the pietists and Romantics nearer to his own time? Whatever the ultimate cause of Barth's avoidance, close attention to just such writings may actually be more crucial for locating the *ratio anselmi* within the Prior of Bec's corpus than are the later 'biblical-ecclesiastical-dogmatic'[18] writings by the Archbishop of Canterbury. For the very style and form of the *Proslogion* may be said to betray its origins in monastic life. The Latin cadences of the *Proslogion* bear resemblance to the Psalms and thus would have been well suited for monks to read silently in moments of private meditation or to sound aloud in acts of communal devotion.

---

[17] See Benedicta Ward's introduction to her collection of Anselm's *Prayers and Meditations*. See also Richard Southern, *Saint Anselm: A Portrait in a Landscape* (Cambridge, 1990), pp. 91ff.

[18] This inelegant phrase is Barth's own. See *Anselm: Fides Quaerens Intellectum*, p. 58 [58].

Even if Barth was wrong to presume that Anselm could be read as if he were a professional 'theologian' like himself, Barth was right to protest that Anselm's purpose in the *Proslogion* did not include the construction of some free-standing 'rational theology', in the manner of the Modern project. Nor is the 'God' addressed in the *Proslogion* the generic God of Enlightenment theism. The God addressed there is the Triune God of Christian faith (§22, 23).

The *ratio anselmi* must nonetheless still be regarded *in some sense* as a proof of God. But in what sense? *That* is the issue. But so much has been written on just *this* issue, is there anything left to be said? One way to redirect discussion away from the hackneyed disputes that rumble on in the journals and the set battles that get re-enacted in the textbooks is to step back a little and ask instead what end or ends the *ratio anselmi* was designed to serve.

To understand an argument is to understand what it is used to do. At least, that is a maxim I would wish to commend. But it must seem unnecessary to ask what a theistic proof is meant to do. Surely, it is supposed to prove to any reasonable person on rational or empirical grounds that some God exists. In modern times, that is certainly what has been expected of any sound proof of God. Those who have endorsed such proofs, as well as those who have opposed them, have done so with just such an expectation in mind. Before modern times, however, theistic arguments were used to serve a rather richer array of ends, only one of which shows much kinship to their supposedly 'standard' usage in modern philosophy.

Theistic proofs can be seen in pre-modern times to have had at least four main uses: apologetical, polemical, hermeneutical, edificatory. I will characterize each usage briefly and give an example or two, drawn from various religious traditions, Eastern and Western.

First, theistic proofs might be used to persuade 'unbelievers' of the truth of a given religious community's doctrine of God. This can be called an apologetical use of argument, in which the proof is aimed outside the community in order to persuade the 'other' of the soundness of the community's own view of God or the Gods. We must remind ourselves that, before modern times, 'non-believer' was commonly a designation for persons, however pious, who belonged to an out-group: for a Christian, Muslims were unbelievers; for a Muslim, Christians were. So, to aim proofs of God at 'unbelievers' (in that sense) meant to aim them at members of another religious community. In such a circumstance, a Christian might use theistic proofs in order to persuade or possibly to reassure a Jew or Muslim that they all believe in the same 'one God'. This is arguably the strategy adopted by Thomas Aquinas in the *Summa contra Gentiles.*

Second, theistic arguments have been used to correct deviant views of God within a given religious community. If theistic proofs have been aimed apologetically at the 'other' outside the community, they have also been aimed polemically at dissident elements *within* the community in order to correct heretical or otherwise defective views of the nature of God. Examples of this sort of usage are common in mediaeval Judaism and Islam. The likes of Saadya Gaon and al-Ghazali, for instance, formulated proofs for the existence of God from the necessary temporality of the creation in order to counter the growing influence of Aristotle's causal proofs within Judaism and Islam.[19] The fact of God's existence was not directly at issue, but proofs for God's existence served as a way of showing an opponent's concept of God to be defective and dangerous to the life of faith. Begin with Aristotle, it was sometimes said, and you will end with Strato.

Third, theistic proofs have been used to assist the interpretation of sacred texts. Within text-based religious traditions, Eastern and Western, theistic arguments (or their critique) have been applied hermeneutically to help establish the meaning of an ambiguous text, to reinforce the traditional interpretation of a controversial text or to legitimate a novel interpretation of a well-established text.

Whilst insisting that scripture is the proper way to come to know Brahman, for instance, the Vedantin Sankara allowed the use of theistic proofs if they help an understanding of scripture, but not if they be taken as independent grounds for knowledge of the existence and nature of Brahman. In his *bhasya* on *Brahmasutra* 1.2 ('Brahman as cause of the universe'), he insists we know that Brahman is cause of the origin, preservation and destruction of the universe because scripture declares it. But he allows that theistic proofs can still be used to confirm the interpretation given to authoritative texts, since inference is an instrument of right knowledge and since inference is also commended by the Upanisadic scriptures themselves. By way of contrast, in his own *bhasya* on the notoriously ambiguous *Brahmasutra* 1.3, Ramanuja used all his

---

[19] See Saadia ben Joseph, *The Book of Beliefs and Opinions*, trans. Samuel Rosenblatt (New Haven, 1948), and al-Ghazali, *Tahafut al-Falasifa*, ed. S. A. Kamali (Lahore, 1958); cf. Herbert A. Davidson, *Proofs for Eternity, Creation and the Existence of God in Medieval Islamic and Jewish Philosophy* (Oxford, 1987).

dialectical skills to undermine confidence in inference as a way of coming to know Brahman in order to show that the *sutra* should be read to speak not of '[Brahman] as the source of the Vedas' (as Sankara and his school had held), but of 'the Vedas as the [only] source of [knowledge of] [Brahman]'.

The Islamic tradition provides further examples of theistic proofs being used to limit the interpretation of disputed texts.[20] In the *Tahafut al-Falasifa*, for instance, al-Ghazali applied 'kalamic' proofs against al-Farabi, Ibn Sina and other Islamic philosophers to show that it is not contrary to reason to affirm the traditional, literal interpretation of the Qur'anic *suras* referring to the creation of heaven and earth in six days. In the *Tahafut al-Tahafut*, on the other hand, Ibn Rushd (Averroes) appealed to Aristotelian proofs to show that reason in fact supports a metaphorical reading of those same suras.[21]

Fourth, theistic proofs have been widely used to build up the members of a community, their sense of well being and their sense of solidarity. This final and most complex group of ends served by theistic argument can be called edificatory, to adopt a term reintroduced into Anglo-American philosophical discourse by Richard Rorty.[22]

Theistic proofs have been used within a wide range of religious communities, Western and Eastern, as aids to prayer and devotion or as a basis for meditation. Bonaventura's *Itinerarium Mentis in Deum* leads the reader nearer and nearer to the object of devotion, pausing briefly to review the *ratio anselmi* before finally entering mystically into the being of God.[23] One thinks also of the remarkable *Nyayakusumanjali* by the eleventh-century Naiyayika Udayana, whose theistic arguments were directed toward several ends, but which were finally given as an offering in praise of Siva, whose existence they purport to prove.[24]

Theistic proofs have occasionally been used to encourage members of a religious community to remain faithful to its basic beliefs in the face of persecution. Al-Ghazali included a proof of God in his concise summary of the Islamic faith known as 'The Jerusalem Tract'.[25] Traditionally it was

---

[20] See my 'Piety and the Proofs'. Editors' note: This appears as Chapter 6 of the present volume.

[21] *Averroes' Tahafut al-Tahafut*, trans. Simon van den Bergh, 2 vols. (London, 1954). Cf. *On the Harmony of Religion and Philosophy*, trans. George F. Hourani (London, 1961).

[22] *Philosophy and the Mirror of Nature* (Oxford, 1980), pp. 357ff.

[23] 'The Soul's Journey into God', in *Bonaventure*, ed. and trans. Ewert Cousins (New York, 1978), pp. 51–116.

[24] *Nyayakusumanjali*, trans. E. B. Cowell (Calcutta, 1864), p. 85. See again my 'Piety and the Proofs'.

[25] A. L. Tibawi, 'Al-Ghazali's Tract on Dogmatic Theology', *Islamic Quarterly* 9 (1965), 65–122.

said to have been written at the request of members of the Jerusalem mosque to bolster their courage as they made themselves ready for the arrival of the first Christian crusaders.

Theistic proofs have been used in addition to exhort someone to live a more pious life. Socrates, for instance, is reported once to have detailed a version of the 'design argument' in a conversation with Aristodemus, not in order to convince him that the gods exist (for he did not deny that), but in order to persuade Aristodemus (who was known not to engage in cultic practices) that he should fulfil his civic duty by making sacrifices to the gods.[26]

And, finally, theistic proofs have often been rehearsed simply to express awe and wonder at the marvels of nature. Tokens of this type are widespread. They are found in the Hebrew Bible (Psalm 19) and *Qur'an* (sura 2) alike, in Luther's table-talk,[27] in Jonathan Edwards's letters[28] and in the hymns of Cleanthes[29] and Addison.[30] In none of these cases, however, is the fact of God's existence in question. The proofs of God in each case are meant instead to make one more attentive to the divine good pleasure manifested in the vastness of creation or hidden in its lesser parts.

There are no doubt other ends that might be served by proofs of God in religious traditions, but this brief list surely contains sufficient variety to stimulate our enquiry. What end or combination of ends can Anselm's argument be said to serve in the *Proslogion*?

We will not get very far in finding an answer to that question if we simply follow philosophical or (mindful of Barth!) theological convention and concentrate on the logic of chapters 2–4 or 2 and 3 or just 2 or 3, oblivious to the role those few chapters play in the structure of the *Proslogion* as a whole. Nor will we get very far in finding an answer to that question if we try to read the *Proslogion* without some awareness of its being a production of the form of life that was cultivated in the monastic community at Bec. For it was while he was engaged in the quintessentially monkish activity of meditating on the meaning of sacred texts that Anselm discovered the proof which at the time gave him such delight and which ever since has caused logicians such anguish.

---

[26] Xenophon, *Memorabilia* I, iv, 1–19.   [27] *WA*, TR 5, 155, pp. 30–9; Nr. 5440, 1542.

[28] 'The "Spider" Letter', *Scientific and Philosophical Writings*, ed. Wallace E. Anderson (New Haven, 1980), pp. 163–9.

[29] 'Hymn to Zeus', *The Hellenistic Philosophers*, ed. A. A. Long and D. N. Sedley, 2 vols. (Cambridge, 1987), I, pp. 326f.

[30] 'The Spacious Firmament', *Hymns Ancient and Modern*, §662.

Although 'scripture' for Anselm would have meant the whole of the Christian Bible and the bulk of the Fathers, the Hebrew Psalms had for him special import, owing to the prominence given the Psalter in the devotional life laid down by Benedict's *Rule*. The Psalms of the Hebrew Bible would have been read by Anselm as properly Christian scripture, in which is presaged the Christ event to come. Even so, the place of the Psalter in Benedictine practice gives quiet testimony to the Hebrew religious tradition's profound influence on Christian spirituality through the mediaeval monastic communities.

But the Psalms were not for Anselm something read as you and I might read a book. The Psalms were for Anselm sounded text.[31] They were for him the base text of theological discourse. Meditating on them and other scripture is what Anselm would have understood by 'theology'. He chanted the Psalms; he meditated on the Psalms; he reflected on the Psalms. He may be said to have lived the Psalms, and to have done so with an immediacy which we could not possibly hope to replicate, but which would have seemed natural to his near contemporaries, including Ghazali and Ramanuja and Udayana.

Within this context of lived textuality we must locate Anselm's concern about the Fool. For he would have lived with the Fool and reflected on his foolishness every week of his life as a monk, simply because the Fool who said in his heart there is no God appears twice in the Psalms: first in the thirteenth and again in the fifty-second, to use the numbering system of the Latin Vulgate that would have been familiar to Anselm (or the fourteenth and the fifty-third, to use the numbering system of the Hebrew Bible itself). These psalms each began in Anselm's Psalter with the words 'dixit insipiens in corde suo non est Deus . . .'.

Even if he had done no more than follow the minimal recommendations of the *Rule of Benedict*, which suggested that monks try to chant through the entire Psalter at least once a week, Anselm would have been faced with the Fool twice a week, once at Prime on Thursday when the fourteenth Psalm was chanted second and again at the week's end when the fifty-third would have been chanted in order to complete the cycle of Psalms before beginning again at Matins on Sunday.[32]

Benedict expected more than this from diligent monks, and Abbot Lanfranc demanded more than this from the monks at Bec when he

---

[31] For an exploration of the importance of oral aspects of scripture, drawing on a variety of religious traditions, see William Graham's *Beyond the Written Word* (Cambridge, 1987).
[32] *The Rule of St Benedict*, ed. Justin McCann (London, 1952), p. 63.

reformed their routine to allow even more time for the divine office, for personal prayer and devotion and – yes – for chanting and meditating on the Psalms.[33] We do not know for sure how often Lanfranc required those in his charge to complete the cycle of Psalms. But we know that Benedict held up to earnest monks the model of the 'Fathers of old', who each day chanted the full Psalter.[34] If Anselm had followed their example, then he would have encountered the Fool twice a day or fourteen times a week – and not just one day or one week, but each day and every week for as long as he was a monk at Bec.

This meeting, however frequently it may have occurred, created for Anselm a dilemma which the *Proslogion* was meant to resolve. We believe God to be a being whose non-existence cannot be conceived. But we read in scripture about some Fool who appears able to deny God's being. How can this be? Are you like we believe you to be? If so, then why does scripture allow the Fool to say otherwise?

The place of the Fool is often misunderstood. The Fool is not simply a foil or 'hypothetical Other' against whom Anselm could test the strength of his own reasoning. For Anselm's proof of God is rare amongst theistic arguments in having been aimed at no 'Other': not apologetically at unbelievers outside the community, or polemically at heretics within. The only 'Other' in the *Proslogion* is the radically Other, the God to whom it is addressed in prayer. Anselm's problem in this phase of the argument is more nearly hermeneutical: if you are as we believe you to be, how then are we to make sense of the fact that in holy scripture there is reference to at least one person who says you do not exist?

On this question Anselm prayed and meditated, until the argument of the *Proslogion* came to him. And it fittingly came to him as he was doing what was required of him by the *Rule of Benedict*. For it came to him one night at Matins as he meditated on the meaning of the Psalms that were set for that office.[35] It came to him when he was engaged in what he understood by 'theology'. It came to him as he was seeking to know God. And it should not be forgot that the aim of the *Proslogion* is to guide those who follow its lead to know God as God truly is, that is, to know God 'face to face'.

---

[33] Details of Lanfranc's reforms at Bec are surmised in part from what is known of his later reforms at Canterbury. See *The Monastic Constitutions of Lanfranc*, ed. David Knowles (Edinburgh, 1953), pp. xxxv–xxxvi. Cf. David Knowles, *The Monastic Orders in England*, 2nd edn (Cambridge, 1963), pp. 448ff., pp. 714f.

[34] *The Rule of St Benedict*, p. 64.   [35] See Eadmer, *Life of Anselm*, p. 30.

This desire to see God's face is expressed in the crucial first chapter of the *Proslogion*, a chapter that anthologists usually skip in order to get more quickly to the 'ontological argument'. Anselm, lamenting human-kind's estrangement from its divine ground, asks that he be allowed, 'whether from afar or from the depths', to catch at least a glimpse of God. He does not disguise his deepest and most audacious wish: to know God as God is. His quest is undertaken by means of the contemplative use of reason.

This is entirely in keeping with his having stated in the *Monologion* that through reason alone we come nearest to knowing God as God is.[36] But, it must be emphasized, Anselm is not here commending the 'unaided reason' of later invention. The *ratio anselmi* is constructed instead in terms of a 'believing reason'. Anselm seeks more profound understanding of God's being – 'that you exist as we believe you exist and that you are what we believe you to be' – but still recognizes that such understanding can come only as gift.

Unless we first believe, we will not be able to understand. The *ratio anselmi*, then, far from providing some 'foundation' for faith, is itself grounded in the very faith which it is intended to make intelligible. Anselm's God draws him to the understanding which he seeks: 'Teach me to seek you, and I shall seek you. Show yourself to me, for I cannot seek you unless you show me how, and I will never find you unless you show yourself to me' (§1, p. 243).

The structure of the *Proslogion* surely, but unhurriedly, draws the reader along a path leading toward the divine Light, deeper and deeper into the mystery of God's innermost being: 'Tell me what you are, beyond what I have seen', Anselm petitions, 'so that I may see clearly what I desire':

I strive to see more, but I see nothing beyond what I have seen but darkness . . .
Are my eyes darkened by my weakness, or dazzled by your glory?
The truth is, I am darkened by myself and also dazzled by you. I am clouded by my own smallness and overwhelmed by your greatness; I am restricted by my own limitedness and mastered by your expanse.
How great is that light from which shines out every truth that lightens the reasoning mind! . . . What purity, what simplicity, what certainty and splendour, are here! It is more than a creature can comprehend! (§21)

Anselm exudes joy at having arrived at the understanding that God is as we believe God to be, and more: 'Lord, you are then not only that than

---

[36] *Opera Omnia*, I, pp. 77f.

which nothing greater can be thought; you are something greater than that which can be thought' (§15).

Anselm's quest has then a paradoxical outcome. The nearer he comes to understanding God, the more he sees that God is not to be understood. The result of the desire to see God as God is, is to be confronted with God's otherness. And in that otherness, Anselm discovers joy and peace, though there is greater joy to come and peace that passes all understanding.

Anselm's *Proslogion* was aimed at a specific audience, who lived their lives according to specific *regulae,* and who had specific kinds of aims in this life and beyond. Books like the *Proslogion* were not first read for reasons appropriate to the intellectual life of the academy; they were read more nearly for reasons cultivated by the spiritual life of the monastery. Academic philosophy and academic theology had not yet been invented, so they did not yet order their reflections about divine things in ways governed by the adversarial structure of scholastic disputation. Theology was for them the knowledge of God which is to be gained through prayer and meditation on the Psalms and other scriptures. The *ratio anselmi* was invented for just that sort of audience with just those aims.

Few moderns or, if one prefers, *post*-moderns can easily count themselves among that kind of audience or readily share their goal-specific aims. So what can we, whose fate it is to live our lives under the conditions of late modernity, make of Anselm's argument?

We dare not idealize the past and its securities. We may visit past times and far away places, but we cannot live there. We visit them not in search of a lost paradise or a golden age to which we can repair. For paradise, once lost, cannot be regained except in imagination and in story. We might still learn some things from the past. Indeed, the exercise in which we have been engaged in this paper would hardly be worth the effort if there were *nothing* to be learned from other times and other places. But there is one thing I am most doubtful of our ever being able to share with Anselm's original audience: namely, the immediacy with which they related to, and formed themselves in and through, their sacred texts. As a result of what might be called *the Fall of Modernity,* we have lost the capacity for that kind of immediacy. And therein lies much of our problem with pre-modern uses of theistic proofs, including or perhaps especially the one that has been under scrutiny here.

If the religious uses of argument I have been trying to elucidate in this essay are not uses with which we ourselves can identify, that may be because we do not identify with the kinds of activities with which those uses of argument were associated. Indeed, if theistic arguments no longer make sense to so many of us today, this may be because we no longer find it possible to participate fully in the forms of life in which they were once so firmly embedded.

That, I say, rather than the reverse.

It is not because they make no sense to us that we no longer participate, but because we do not participate, they no longer make sense. Understanding can often be gained more readily in *doing* than in *thinking*. To recover a taste for these proofs and their earlier uses, therefore, may require not just or not even principally a change of mind. That recovery may require more radically a change of life. For some that may well be possible, and I would not want anything I have said to discourage them. But for many others that way is cut off, whether by historical fate or by personal choice.

What remains for those among us to whom this last remark may apply? Even if theistic proofs no longer have for such persons a specifically religious import, they might still have for them a properly philosophical import. But, we must enquire, wherein lies their philosophical import? In modern times, their philosophical value has typically derived from the role they have played in the foundationalist programme. If that were the sole basis on which their value should be measured, then they must surely be judged failures – failures not just in detail, but also in principle. 'Merely so much labour and effort lost', as Kant said of the ontological argument (A602/B630), on which he thought all other speculative proofs of God were built.

If the proofs of God fail to provide what is required of them in the foundationalist programme, what remains for them to do? Have they no other philosophical import?

Even discredited theistic proofs must be allowed to have an antiquarian value. They still have a place (perhaps a distinguished and honourable place) in the history of philosophy, even if their time is past and they have no place in philosophical thinking today. They could continue to be studied for their historical interest. As a historicist of sorts, I have no wish to discourage curiosity about the past. But this seems a feeble reason to subject students in philosophy of religion courses to detailed study of the proofs of God. One is tempted to liken it to the mindlessness of the philosophical syllabus at Paris in the late eighteenth century, when students were required to demonstrate their proficiency in all the arguments for and against the Ptolemaic theory, even though Copernicanism was already firmly established, amongst even the stodgiest of philosophers![37]

However deficient they may be as proofs, theistic proofs might still serve perversely demonstrative ends. Not only do they fail to establish the reasonableness of belief in God, it might be claimed, but they can be twisted so as to reinforce the reasonableness of disbelief. Think, for instance, of Findlay's ontological proof for the necessary non-existence of God[38] and of Dawkins's timely reversal of Paley's most famous analogy in order to defend a Darwinian sense of design.[39] Their clever appeal to *reductio ad absurdum* could have amused even Anselm. But their confidence in theistic disproof, like the apologetic certainty it mimics, rests on an intellectualist misunderstanding of the place of proof in religious traditions. Living religions are neither first formed nor long prolonged by rational proof. Their life is fed from more characteristically religious sources of empowerment. Rational reflection in religion is always an afterthought, so to say.

Thirdly, theistic proofs could be judged unsound as proofs and still be allowed to have a place in sound philosophical training. They might be held up to students as good examples of bad arguments,[40] by being used to exemplify common fallacies in logic: as warnings against the assumption that analogy can bear more weight than it can safely sustain or as warnings against confusions that arise when reason extends its activities beyond its natural bounds. From a foundationalist perspective, theistic proofs may indeed be seen as no more than good examples of bad arguments, but it may not be necessary to privilege that particular view of 'RC' or *rational correctness*.

In recent years, there has been no shortage of monographs and articles, written from often opposing vantage points, advocating this or that view of the residual value of theistic proofs. Rather than entering directly into these discussions, however, I want in conclusion to point out a regularly overlooked feature of the viewpoint advocated in a very familiar text: namely, Kant's *Critique of Pure Reason*, the book in which confidence in

[37] See L. W. B. Brockliss, *French Higher Education in the Seventeenth and Eighteenth Centuries: A Cultural History* (Oxford, 1987), p. 189.

[38] J. N. Findlay, 'Can God's Existence be Disproved?', in *New Essays in Philosophical Theology*, ed. Antony Flew and Alasdair MacIntyre (London, 1955), pp. 47–56.

[39] Richard Dawkins, *The Blind Watchmaker* (New York, 1986).

[40] See Stephen M. Cahn, 'The Irrelevance to Religion of Philosophic Proofs for the Existence of God', *American Philosophical Quarterly* 6 (1969), 170–2.

the foundationalist pretensions of theistic proofs was so devastatingly undermined. Perhaps it is overlooked because Kant no more than hinted at it in the selections regularly anthologized. He seems no better served by his editors than was Anselm! If one continues reading after the sections usually excerpted in the textbooks (A590–630/B618–58), Kant will be found feeling his way beyond the common sense of what theistic proofs are built to do and discovering a possible function for them outside the recognized boundaries that defined their use in the Modern project.[41] Compounding irony with paradox, Kant fixed his vision of their licit use on the discredited ontological proof, the necessary underpinning of 'transcendental theology' in his critique of the knowability of God.

The novelty of Kant's position lies in his having distinguished between what the traditional proofs can contribute to our knowledge of the *existence* of God and what they can contribute to our understanding of the *concept* of God. Such proofs may not be equal to the task of establishing God's existence, but their necessary failure in that respect did not in Kant's view limit their possible success in helping clarify or – to use his image – 'purify' the concept of God. The same discredited proofs can still show what it would be for God to be God, and to free the concept of God from anything out of keeping with the idea of 'a necessary and supremely real being'.

So, it seems, Kant can after all find room for the ontological argument in his scheme, providing it is confined to issues about the *nature* of God's being and is not expected to establish the *fact* of God's existence. But Anselm's proof is itself said by many, including his fellow monk who knew his mind best,[42] to be concerned more with the *nature* than with the bare *existence* of God. Would it not be the height of irony if in the end Immanuel Kant, who thought that he had discredited anything resembling Anselm's proof, could be shown to have mapped out for himself a position located not that far from Anselm?

Things are not always just as they seem. And, alas, this finely balanced *coincidentia oppositorum* is only apparent. Kant's interests and Anselm's interests in the nature of God are embedded in different programmes and

---

[41] See A631–42/B659–70, especially A639–42/B667–70.
[42] Eadmer epitomizes the *Proslogion* without mentioning the issue of God's *existence*. After writing the *Monologion*, he says, Anselm attempted to prove 'by one single and short argument the things which are believed and preached about God, that he is eternal, unchangeable, omnipotent, omnipresent, incomprehensible, just, righteous, merciful, true, as well as truth, goodness, justice and so on; and to show how all these qualities are united in him' [*Life of Anselm*, p. 29]. See also Southern, *Saint Anselm*, pp. 117, 127ff.

are pursued to different ends. 'Purifying' the concept of God meant for Kant removing from that concept all residual impurities left behind by the idiosyncrasies of particular religious traditions; but 'understanding' the doctrine of God meant for Anselm making intelligible to reason precisely such idiosyncrasies that he had received in faith through his own tradition. However much Kant may be said to have moved beyond its conventional limits, his programme still remains tied to the fortunes of the Enlightenment project and its notions of religion in general, Utopian reason and the generic God of 'theism'.[43] Anselm's programme, by contrast, was pursued inside a specific community, using reasons that counted as reasons in that community, out of a desire to know its particular God. Finally, one can no more imagine Kant's argument about the possible value of the ontological argument being expressed as a prayer to his God without its ceasing to be *Kant's* argument than one can imagine Anselm's proof being expressed in any other way without its ceasing to be *Anselm's* proof.

If we can see why this should be unimaginable, we can begin to grasp something of the Otherness of Anselm – and, to anticipate an argument for another day, something also of the Otherness of Kant.

---

[43] 'Religion in general', 'Utopian rationality' and 'generic God' were used to characterize the philosophy of religion typically done within the frame allowed by the Enlightenment project in my Stanton Lectures, given at Cambridge University in 1992.

PART III

Theistic arguments in early-modern contexts

As noted earlier, the essays in Part II explore instances of theistic proofs from the mediaeval period with particular attention to the 'forms of life' within which such proofs were embedded, and to the literary genres and rhetorical structures within which they functioned. Those essays also provide treatments of theistic proofs in pre-modern contexts to be used as points of orientation in a consideration of the degree and character of difference between the work of rationality within which the proofs participated in *pre-modern* and *modern* contexts. In Part III of this volume, Clayton provides three histories of the transitions from pre-modern to modern philosophical and theological uses of reason. Here he investigates uses of theistic proofs in a variety of discursive and institutional contexts, developing a regionally and temporally comparative account focused on France and the Netherlands in Chapter 8, Germany in Chapter 9 and Britain in Chapter 10.

In these essays, Clayton attends closely to intellectual debates within which theistic proofs figured, from the late seventeenth century into the nineteenth. He provides histories of 'natural theology' and of 'atheism' in relation to the early-modern lives of theistic proofs. In doing so, Clayton offers focused studies of particular thinkers and moments of debate. These are examined in connection with generational and regional trends in the relationships that obtained between philosophy, theology and natural science. Our own distinction between 'philosophy', 'theology' and 'natural science' in the last sentence is, as Clayton's work in Part III suggests, in some ways anachronistic. A central aim of Chapters 8, 9 and 10 is to trace the development of these disciplines and forms of knowledge in contexts as varied as Paris, Rotterdam, Halle and Cambridge. Clayton also questions accounts of the 'Enlightenment project' and the emergence of 'modernity' which stress the natural unfolding of a unified modern rationality. As Clayton remarked shortly before his death, these essays indicate that 'similar engagements with rationality' (i.e. uses of theistic proofs) 'yield different results because of different historical roots of argument and different institutional arrangements and inclinations'. Moreover, as these chapters make clear, uses of theistic proofs (and, thus, of rationality) *varied* in *both* pre-modern and modern contexts, including uses that Clayton (in Chapter 10) terms 'apologetic-justificatory' and 'expressivist'. Clayton emphasizes a broadly modern movement toward uses of theistic proofs disembedded from earlier forms of rationality specific to religious traditions and their practices. At the same time, however, he underscores the variability of the processes through which such disembedding occurred as well as the importance of local patterns of religious belief and practice to that variation.

These essays reveal Clayton's preoccupation with developing richly historical accounts of the uses of argument and the origins of 'thinkable positions'. Such accounts were of intrinsic interest to him. Importantly, however, he also uses them in order to develop a comparative modern history of public uses of theistic proofs. This comparative history emphasizes both the local character of such uses of reason and the ways in which this 'localized rationality' relates to other conditions of possibility in the spheres of economy, demography, confessional culture, pedagogy, institutional patronage, and so on. In these chapters, as in Part II, Clayton tends to the contexts of creation *and* reception in historical treatments of proofs and arguments. In Clayton's view, the methodological practice of empathy discussed in Chapter 1 is crucial to the historical work undertaken in *Religions, Reasons and Gods*.

Part III reveals with particular clarity the ways in which this methodological principle drew Clayton toward an integration of philosophy with what he sometimes called 'historical sociology', in the attempt to view both the roots and the branches in the 'patterns of the Other's scheme'. As Chapter 11, the 'Epilogue', indicates, Clayton's historical studies of theistic proofs in early-modern contexts provide an ironic but suggestive location from which to reconsider the roles to be played by philosophy of religion in our time. Some might argue that Clayton's proposal to move toward a principle of defensible difference in philosophical responses to contemporary religious pluralism breaks with the privileged secularism of modern rationality. The essays in Part III, however, offer one rejoinder: forms of modern rationality are themselves the result of debate embedded within traditions; they are themselves the result of non-secular processes through which the means and ends of arguments were clarified.

CHAPTER 8

The debate about God in early-modern French philosophy*

Parameters of the debate about God in eighteenth-century France had been set by the middle of the seventeenth century in France and the Netherlands. Disagreement among scholastics, rationalists and sceptics as to the provability of God effectively defined both the terms and the stakes in the eighteenth-century debate about the Deity. In those earlier disputes, however, the fact of God's existence was not an issue; even so, the outcome of their quibbling about the provability of divine existence was a heightened expectation of the proofs of God as *évidence* and a diminished confidence in the ability of any given proof to satisfy that expectation. The corrosive effects of protracted wrangling surfaced with some surprises in the debate about God among the philosophes from mid-century to the Revolution, a debate in which the fact of God was a material question in more than one sense.

PRE-ENLIGHTENMENT IN FRANCE AND THE LOW COUNTRIES

Proofs of God's existence had been integral to the scholastic project since the twelfth century; but the traditional proofs gained new prominence and authority in early-modern France and the Netherlands. Where they had been used in mediaeval scholasticism typically as *viae* to express the prior consensus among Christians and Muslims and Jews, they came to be treated in early-modern scholasticism as independent evidence adequate to convince 'atheists' of God's being.[1]

---

* Editors' note: A version of this material (presumably much briefer) was presented as a lecture to the British Society for Philosophy of Religion at King's College, London, in 1998. This chapter shows some signs of research undertaken between 2000 and 2002.
[1] For recent accounts of the changing role of theistic proofs in early-modern French thought, see A. C. Kors, *Atheism in France, 1650–1729*, 2 vols. (Princeton, 1990, 1997), and Michael J. Buckley, *At the Origins of Modern Atheism* (New Haven, 1987).

'Atheists' became an obsession of early-modern scholastic philosophers, at a time when speculative atheism was held in theory to be unthinkable and professing atheists were in practice nowhere to be found locally. Absence of open unbelief is hardly surprising in an era when atheism was still a capital crime punishable by burning! Theologians and politicians were equally convinced that excessive immorality, such as portrayed in Molière's *Dom Juan*, was itself a sure sign of secret atheism. Up to the time of Bayle and sporadically thereafter, immorality and atheism were imagined to imply each other.

Before the clandestine literature that circulated in the first half of the eighteenth century, the only instances of professed atheism likely to be encountered in early-modern France or the Low Countries were confined to texts of ancient philosophy that were available in modern editions and to the reports of explorers, traders and above all of Christian missionaries to far-away lands like China and the Caribbean. From ancient texts and distant reports, supplemented by suspicions of secret unbelief among social deviants at home, priests and politicians, theologians and philosophers formed an image of a larger-than-life enemy of God that must be defeated by every means available to the defenders of faith and public order.

In these circumstances, proofs of God were increasingly asked by early-modern scholastics to serve as sure grounds to make credible God's being and providence to an elusive but dreaded opponent that had been constructed largely out of their own imaginations. The evidentialist turn, typically associated with philosophers leading the opposition to scholasticism, was in fact already made within scholastic circles in the first half of the seventeenth century, as exemplified in *De Providentia Numinis et Animi Immortalitate* (1613) by Louvain Jesuit Leonard Lessius, who mustered nineteen proofs against atheists,[2] and in *L'impiété des déistes, athées, et libertin de ce temps* (1624) by French Minim Marin Mersenne, who contented himself with nine. By the mid seventeenth century, philosophical proofs were well on the way to becoming necessary grounds for belief, rather than being merely sufficient means of coming to know God in the absence of revelation.[3] It is not surprising that some philosophers had taken up such a position; it is more surprising that scholastic theologians themselves came to do so, even if their adopted strategy indicates an underlying confidence in theistic proofs as *évidence* of God.

---

[2] Including four proofs refuting denials of divine providence. In the same treatise, Lessius demonstrated the immortality of the soul with twenty-two proofs.

[3] Cf. especially Kors, *Atheism*, I, pp. 110–31.

When added to the mix of ideas in circulation at the time, this baroque strategy contributed to the irony of the conclusions drawn by some philosophes a century later.

Rationalist and sceptical opponents of scholasticism added to that curious mixture. Rationalism and scepticism are two sides of the same coin, each committed to equally rigorous conditions of cognitive certainty. The difference between them lies in the fact that, for the one, the conditions are in principle attainable; whereas, for the other, they are incapable of being met in all or some areas of putative cognition. Scepticism was not always viewed as an enemy of philosophy or theology: Descartes subverted scepticism to rationalist ends, whilst the Jansenists and the Huguenots gave scepticism a 'fideistic' twist in pre-Enlightenment France and the Netherlands.[4] As opposed as their positions may otherwise have been, René Descartes (1596–1650) and Blaise Pascal (1623–62) shared a determination to defeat scepticism by attacking it on its own terms by devising strategies that would allow it to be diverted to their chosen ends. Their adopted strategies, however, entailed diametrically opposed attitudes to the provability of God by reason alone.

Assuming nothing to be true that could be doubted, Descartes turned sceptical doubt into systematic method by building confidence in cognitive claims from the ground up. The movement in the *Meditations* is from self-certainty to certainty of God, which is then used to warrant cognitive credibility of ideas derived from experience. Given this movement, God's existence cannot be proved *a posteriori* without Descartes being trapped in circularity. Although his critics then and now have remained unconvinced that he had avoided just such circularity, Descartes himself was confident that God's existence can be shown *a priori* from the innate thinkability of God (§III) and from the necessary unthinkability of God's non-existence (§V). God is arguably instrumentalized in Descartes's *Meditations*. If another means could be found to justify the move from the thinking subject to the objects of thought, the need for God would have been eliminated altogether, as Pascal recognized, thus anticipating one direction Cartesianism would be taken by the philosophes.

In contrast to Descartes, Pascal insisted in his *Pensées* that we know even first principles by intuition or feeling, not reason. When we are awake, we know

---

[4] Harry M. Bracken presses the difference between Catholic and Calvinist 'sceptical fideism' in 'Bayle's Attack on Natural Theology: The Case of Christian Pyrrhonism', in *Scepticism and Irreligion in the Seventeenth and Eighteenth Centuries*, ed. Richard H. Popkin and Arjo Vanderjagt (Leiden, 1993), pp. 254–66.

that we are not dreaming; if reason cannot prove it, then this shows the frailty of reason, not the uncertainty of the knowledge.[5] Reason's frailty prevents also its being able either to prove or to disprove the existence of God.[6] Pascal proposed instead a more pragmatic justification for the rationality of believing in God and living a godly life. 'Pascal's wager', as it has come to be called, is not a proof of God, not apodeictic or probabilistic; yet it was still meant to justify to a sceptic the rationality of belief in God in the absence of *évidence*.[7]

It may be that sustained attack by Jesuits and Jansenists was sufficient to stymie Descartes's influence into the eighteenth century, but that attack did not go unchecked in the seventeenth. Cartesian physics gained ground steadily in the final decades of the seventeenth century.[8] And Cartesian confidence in one's power to establish metaphysical claims with a certainty equal to that of mathematics was buoyed by the work of Benedict Spinoza (1632–77). In his posthumously published *Ethica Ordine Geometrico Demonstrata*, he applied to the proof of God the method of serial deduction from definition, axiom and proposition that Descartes had professed, whilst not formally practising it. Rather than proceeding, as Descartes had done in his *Meditations*, from self-certainty to certainty of God, Spinoza began his *Ethica* immediately in Part I with the deduction of God as necessary and infinite Substance, whose self-caused existence is the indwelling cause of all that is. Only after demonstrating the existence of God was Spinoza able in Part II to deduce the human mind and its attributes as modifications of being within this one Substance. *A posteriori* proofs were no more use to Spinoza than they had been to Descartes, even if Spinoza sometimes set out his *a priori* proofs in *a posteriori* form for the convenience of readers.[9] In the *Ethica*, he outlined three proofs of God: from the absurdity of God's non-existence; from causality; and from the infinite power of necessary being.

It was less Spinoza's actual proofs of God, however, than the God whose existence he proved that generated heat in the debate over the *Ethica*. Since there seemed to be no place in his system for God as an

---

[5] *Pensées*, §§14, 7.
[6] *Pensées*, §§378, 49 (cf. §§449, 315), 736. In keeping with his Jansenist principles, Pascal held that God can be known only by the way commended in scripture, namely, by faith [§§737, 376, 343]; the true proofs of religion are those sanctioned by scripture, namely, prophecy, miracles, morality, etc. [§§38, 459].
[7] *Pensées*, §343; cf. §§800, 837.
[8] See L. W. B. Brockliss, 'Aristotle, Descartes and the New Science: Natural Philosophy at the University of Paris, 1600–1740', *Annals of Science* 38 (1981), 33–69, and *French Higher Education in the Seventeenth and Eighteenth Centuries: A Cultural History* (Oxford, 1987), pp. 337ff.
[9] See note to the proofs of God given in *Ethica*, part I, prop. 11.

independent being, Spinoza's position was popularly reduced to pantheism or more radically to atheism. 'Spinozism' soon became a term of abuse, hurled indiscriminately at anyone with little obvious inclination to religion or at anyone whose views of God and the world were perceived to deviate from local norms. Few philosophers before Mendelssohn read carefully Spinoza's major works once they became widely available in the *Opera Posthuma* (1677). Most depended for their knowledge of Spinoza upon secondary accounts, such as polemical tracts or clandestine work or one of the new treatises on atheism that began to appear at the end of the seventeenth century or Pierre Bayle's new *Dictionnaire*, where Spinoza was portrayed as the first person to have reduced atheism to a system and formed it into a body of doctrine ordered and connected by the principles of geometry.[10]

FROM BAYLE'S *DICTIONNAIRE* TO MESLIER'S *TESTAMENT*

The debate about God reached crisis point in the early decades of the eighteenth century. Articles in Bayle's *Dictionnaire* made atheism seem less dangerous than previously thought at just the time that the warfare between Jesuits, Cartesians and Jansenists made the rational foundations of belief seem less solid than previously hoped. It was left to an obscure *curé* named Jean Meslier to draw the conclusion that would be debated more openly in the second half of the century.

Bayle's Dictionnaire *and the debate about God*

The first major production of the French Enlightenment, the *Dictionnaire historique et critique* by Pierre Bayle (1647–1706), was virtually a proto-*Encyclopédie*. First in two volumes and then in four, Bayle gathered together from his place of exile in Rotterdam what was known of ancient philosophy at the end of the seventeenth century and what he took to be the most important developments in philosophy since the Renaissance.

---

[10] Amsterdam, 1697, 2nd edn, 1702, 3rd edn, 1740. An English translation – based on the second edition and known to Berkeley, Hume and Jefferson alike – was published in London in five volumes between 1734 and 1738 as *Dictionary, Historical and Critical*. 'Spinoza' appears in that edition, vol. v, pp. 199–244. A one-volume, abridged edition was translated by Richard H. Popkin as *Historical and Critical Dictionary: Selections* (Indianapolis, 1965). Alas, Bayle's attitude to theistic arguments was not foremost in Professor Popkin's mind when he made his choices. All my references are to the 1734–8 edition of the *Dictionary*, though spelling and punctuation have been modernized.

More importantly, Bayle brought the two together in a subtly systematic engagement with the central issues of philosophy as viewed at the dawn of Enlightenment, including the limits of reason and faith and the provability of God's being and providence. Even though most of the information contained in the *Dictionnaire* was widely available elsewhere, Bayle synthesized it all with cunning irony and tested the evidence with a critical perspicuity that left sophistry and prejudice exposed. Although he laboured the weaknesses of everyone else's position, Bayle sometimes managed to keep his own views skilfully masked, so that commentators then and now have struggled to discover his true position. Whatever Bayle's own intentions may have been in compiling his *Dictionnaire*, it became a veritable arsenal for the likes of Voltaire, Diderot and d'Holbach in their battle against the dominant religious ideology of what by the end of the century would be called the *ancien régime*.

Though not simply a 'Cartesian',[11] Bayle possibly owed more to Descartes than he did to any other modern philosopher, and the method of enquiry followed in his *Dictionnaire* was a development or 'transposition' of the Cartesian method.[12] But it was less the Cartesian promise of mathematical certainty in metaphysics than the Cartesian style of disinterested enquiry itself that appealed to Bayle. Unlike the scholastic method, which he said had served only to multiply opinions or to reach predictable results that merely confirmed prior prejudices,[13] the Cartesian method was supposed to facilitate public contestability of disputed claims by reducing them to questions that could guide genuinely open enquiry to achieve *évidence*:

we must not suffer our preconceived opinions to add any weight to the arguments that favour them nor to weaken their contrary reasons. We must examine everything as if we were a tabula rasa. It is not necessary actually to doubt, and much less to affirm, that all we have believed is false: it is sufficient to keep it in a

---

[11] Bayle's early attraction to Descartes shows itself in his exposition of Cartesian metaphysics in the *Système de philosophie en quatre parties*, written in Sedan between 1675 and 1677, where he also summarizes without critique Descartes's proofs of God, and in his alliance between Cartesian and Calvinist doctrines in his *Dissertation* (1680) in defence of certain Cartesians against Jesuit critics [*Œuvres diverses*, IV (The Hague, 1731; Hildesheim, 1968), pp. 479ff.; pp. 3ff.]. Even if Bayle could continue to use Cartesian discourse to clarify and augment traditionally Calvinist arguments in his later *Commentaire philosophique*, he could also be doggedly(!) persistent in his criticism of Cartesian doctrines, including the paradoxes created by mind–body dualism when applied to men, beasts and Calvinists. See the entry on 'Rorarius' in the *Dictionnaire*.

[12] See Elisabeth Labrousse, *Pierre Bayle*, vol II: *Hétérodoxie et rigorisme* (The Hague, 1964), pp. 39ff.

[13] 'Euclid', E; 'Maldonet', M. Though Bayle showed in his *Commentaire philosophique* (1686) that he, too, could master *and subvert* the rules of scholastic disputation in defence of civil religious tolerance against then current Catholic arguments against toleration.

kind of suspense; that is, not to suffer our persuasion to bias us in the judgement we are to pass on the proofs of the existence of God and the difficulties and arguments of the Atheists.[14]

Bayle was as insistent of the necessity as he was aware of the risks of applying such a method of enquiry to God's existence. Philosophy may not be competent to penetrate Christian *mystères* such as the Trinity[15] or to intervene substantively in intra-Christian doctrinal disputes over the Eucharist,[16] but Bayle still held in keeping with the times that the existence of God is a properly philosophical and not a specifically theological issue.[17] Even professors of divinity, according to his *Thèses philosophiques*, must establish the existence of God by *la lumière naturelle* alone.[18] Bayle was keenly aware that the conventions of public enquiry, which required theism and atheism to be presumed equally credible, might create doubts in the minds of some where none had previously existed and could contribute over time to weakening of belief in God by scepticism's corrosive effects.[19] But such dangers were not sufficient to make Bayle draw back from testing the claims of theist and atheist with rigour and detachment.

Bayle did much to transform 'atheism' from an emotional epithet to a definite description of a position that can be publicly and rationally contested. There were in his estimate degrees of atheism, ranging from the denial that God created the world by 'an inducement of free will', to the denial that this world is the work of God, to the denial that God exists as an independent and immutable being.[20] All three 'degrees' were present in the *Ethica* by Spinoza, which then became for Bayle the standard by which other putatively atheistic systems were measured. In general, Bayle handled ancient atheists more sympathetically than modern atheists, on the grounds that they were struggling to know God without the aid of revelation, whereas modern atheists had rejected what could be known

---

[14] 'Maldonet', L. The passage concludes: 'This is doubtless what Descartes intended when he would have his philosopher doubt of everything before he examines the reasons for the certainty of it.'

[15] 'Perrot', L.

[16] But both the *Pensées diverses* (1682) and the *Commentaire philosophique* (1686) show Bayle's willingness to use philosophy polemically in intra-Christian debates between Protestants and Catholics. See *Essays on Pierre Bayle and Religious Controversy* by Walter Rex (The Hague, 1965) for a useful study of these two works, which both complement and correct impressions left by the *Dictionnaire*.

[17] 'Eclaircissement', 3:1; 'Maldonet', L.

[18] §XII, in *Œuvres diverses*, IV, p. 143; 'Maldonet', M. For a helpful account of Bayle's 'quirky attitude to the grounds of faith', see Ruth Whelan, 'The Wisdom of Simonides', in Popkin and Vanderjagt, eds., *Scepticism and Irreligion in the Seventeenth and Eighteenth Centuries*, pp. 248ff.

[19] 'Euclid', E; 'Maldonet', M; 'Rufinus', C; cf. 'Acosta'.   [20] 'Thales', D.

with the aid of true revelation. For instance, Anaxagoras was excused for failing to disentangle God and matter, since he had achieved greater understanding of God than previous philosophers, whereas this was the chief complaint made against Spinoza.[21] Despite the demonology of the day, however, Bayle insisted that Spinoza, albeit an atheist, remained 'a sociable, affable, honest, friendly, and a good moral man'.[22]

Bayle's sympathetic portrait of Spinoza the man and of other atheists in classical texts and in far-away places led to his being accused of atheism himself by some Dutch Calvinists and French Catholics. The Huguenot Bayle's motive in picturing atheism as less dangerous and more agreeable than imagined was quite possibly to persuade the French authorities to allow French Protestants to return from the exile into which they had been forced in 1685 when Louis XIV revoked the Edict of Nantes that had guaranteed them freedom of religion: if atheists pose no danger to the moral fabric of society, how much less a danger are mere heretics![23] In retrospect, however, the unwitting effect of Bayle's strategy is more likely to have been to contribute to the further domestication of 'atheism' by making it intellectually imaginable and morally credible in an era when it was conventionally presumed to be irrational and immoral. Bayle's composite picture of virtuous atheists in distant lands may also have hastened the inevitable demise of the venerable *argumentum e consensu gentium*, popularly called Aquinas' sixth way and the one straightforwardly falsifiable argument for God ever to have been taken very seriously by philosophers and theologians.[24]

The combined effect of Bayle's abandoning two arguments traditionally held to give moral certainty of God's existence – from presumption and from universal consent – did much to shift the burden of proof in the unfolding debate about God in eighteenth-century France.

Most of the other arguments for God's existence fared no better than those two in the *Dictionnaire*, as Bayle built up over its successive volumes a sort of cumulative case against their foundationalist credibility by

---

[21] Contrast what Bayle says of Spinoza in remarks N and CC with what he says of Anaxagoras in remarks D and E.

[22] Cf. also 'Spinoza', B and E, where Bayle attacks the stereotype that all atheists are immoral.

[23] What he says in the *Dictionnaire* in defence of the toleration of all religious persuasions and none is argued more fully in his *Commentaire philosophique*, published in Holland the year after the Revocation of the Edict of Nantes.

[24] On that proof's demise in the seventeenth century, see A. C. Kors, '"A First Being, of Whom We Have no Proof": The Preamble of Atheism in Early-Modern France', in A. C. Kors and Paul J. Korshin (eds.), *Anticipations of the Enlightenment in England, France and Germany* (Philadelphia, 1987), pp. 50ff.

showing how they crumble from internally generated difficulties. As one would expect from an author whose sympathies lay generally with Descartes, the causal arguments preferred by the Jesuits came under particular pressure in the *Dictionnaire*. Their proof *ex parte motus* is said to collapse unless motion is eternal, but if motion is eternal, it requires no external cause;[25] no proof can establish God as creator and governor of the world;[26] the concept of causality required by all causal arguments generates perplexities and confusions that reason cannot resolve.[27] Even so, Bayle allowed the reasonableness of the intuition that gives rise to causal proofs and proofs from order in the world,[28] whilst insisting in the spirit of Jean Calvin that 'this beautiful regularity' can be seen as the work of God only to those who begin with that belief and not to those who attempt to infer it from experience of the world.[29] Anyone attempting to base a proof of God on the details of experience will expose themselves to ridicule.

What of the proofs *a priori*? The one proof not to be completely destroyed by Bayle's cutting wit is the Cartesian proof from the thinkability of God. Bayle handled this proof gingerly from his time as Professor in Sedan to his years of decline in Rotterdam.[30] Even so, in at least one entry in his *Dictionnaire* Bayle does not distance himself from a cited critique also of that proof.[31] Though Bayle's private position on the knowability of God by *la lumière naturelle* is a little obscure, the overall impression he left in the *Dictionnaire* and elsewhere suggests a strategy of using reason critically to undermine reason's pretensions by showing how our finest arguments collapse on themselves through internally generated contradictions.

Bayle's lack of confidence in the proofs derives not so much from an accumulation of individual faults as from a pervasive suspicion about reason's power to settle so great an issue. Reason is by its deepest nature weak and indecisive; it can prove one thing, but it can just as easily prove the contrary;[32] finally, it is able to prove nothing. The role of reason in religion is critical, not constitutive.[33] It can show what cannot be known; if more than that is expected from reason, it leads astray and stands in need of correction by tradition or revelation.[34] On its own, reason leads to perplexity and doubt about God; scepticism, however, can lead to faith in

[25] 'Zabarella', G.   [26] 'Thales', D.   [27] 'Chrysippus', H; 'Paulicians', F.
[28] 'Anaxagoras', G.   [29] 'Anaxagoras', R.
[30] See, e.g., *Système de philosophie en quatre parties*, IV, pp. 474ff., and *Thèses philosophiques*, §XII.
[31] 'Zabarella', G.   [32] 'Bunel', E; 'Hipparchia', D; *et passim*.
[33] 'Acosta', G.   [34] 'Simonides', F.

God.[35] True religion is grounded in revelation, not reason.[36] On purely rational grounds alone, there is little to choose between opposing views; atheism and Manichaeism appear equal to Christianity.[37]

If we take at face value what Bayle says on faith and reason, then it is possible to read him as a 'sceptical fideist', similar to Pascal,[38] whom Bayle called 'one of the sublimest geniuses in the world'.[39] But Bayle has not always been taken at face value. Even his traditionally Calvinistic emphasis upon the authority of revelation and the insufficiency of reason was regularly presumed by Dutch Protestants and French philosophes alike, albeit from very different motives, as little more than subterfuge to distract from his covert strategy in the *Dictionnaire* to undermine belief in the God of Abraham, Isaac and Jean Calvin. Bayle was not an atheist within the terms of his own definition, and indeed rejected atheism as an absurd position to hold.[40] Moreover, he lived his life and faced his death with a sense of vocation as a 'Christian philosopher',[41] and protested to his critics that he had never endorsed in print a view that was in conflict with confessional statements of the Reformed Church.[42]

Bayle's *Pensées* and *Commentaire* as well as his more popular *Dictionnaire*, nonetheless, all contributed to a new climate of opinion in which atheism was gradually gaining cultural credibility. The orthodox theologians and the heterodox philosophes were both right to recognize the import of Bayle's having conceded the intellectual and moral possibility of atheism. If God's existence is a matter of dispute in the modern (not mediaeval) sense, then the evidence against and for God's existence must be examined dispassionately and without prejudice to the eventual outcome of the enquiry. But let us assume – as Bayle himself held – that reason is incapable of settling the question in dispute. Scholastic philosophers and their heirs, including Leibniz, held that in the absence of decisive evidence for or against the existence of God, the presumption

---

[35] 'Pyrrho', C. [36] 'Bunel', E.

[37] See entries on China and Japan, and also on the 'Manichaeans'.

[38] See, e.g., Terence Penelhum, 'Skepticism and Fideism', in *The Skeptical Tradition*, ed. Myles Burnyeat (Berkeley, 1983), pp. 287–318.

[39] 'Pascal', I. [40] See not least the entry on Spinoza in the *Dictionnaire*.

[41] Richard Popkin has surveyed the options, and defended a sense in which Bayle is to be regarded as a religious thinker.

[42] 'Eclaircissement', preliminary remarks, IV. Bayle's Calvinist credentials in the *Dictionnaire* are considerably strengthened if the *Pensées diverses* and *Commentaire philosophique* are also taken into account. But whether it is right to call him simply 'naïf et pieux produit d'un village protestant des Pyrénées' is another matter. See J. Solé, 'Religion et conception du monde dans le *Dictionnaire* de Bayle', *Bulletin de la Société de l'histoire de protestantisme français* 118 (1972), 96.

of theism would prevail since atheism was contrary to the general consensus that God exists. But Bayle, among others, had given good reasons to reject the traditional *argumentum e consensu gentium* that underlay the presumption of theism. Fideism may have provided a 'ground' for someone who was already a firm believer, but it offered no evidential foundation for anyone whose faith was shaky or lacking altogether. By insisting on the necessity of *évidence* that could not be reasonably attained, the Enlightenment project in France was from the time of Bayle's *Dictionnaire* forward tilted against the presumption of theism.

Cartesians versus Jesuits versus Jansenists

Arguments advanced by the scholastics, rationalists and their sceptical critics in 'pre-Enlightenment' France and the Netherlands led willy-nilly to surprising outcomes in the *siècle des lumières*. Ironic results are exemplified no more clearly than in the prolonged wrangling between Cartesians, Jesuits and Jansenists over the question whether any rational proof were adequate to refute atheism and to establish theism. From Rotterdam, Bayle avidly followed this controversy, at one point compiling some essays and a chronicle of the debate for the French audience.[43] Perhaps it was this debate, likened to an 'inquisition' in his *Recueil*, that Bayle had foremost in mind when he warned in the *Dictionnaire* against getting involved in querulous disputation for its own sake or when he cited with evident sympathy the view that the learned professors who had set about defending by reason the existence of God had instead instilled doubt in divine existence.[44] For at least some members of the urban professional elite in Enlightenment France, belief in God died the death of a thousand disputations.

The debate about God in the France of the Enlightenment was a very public affair, conducted in the pages of proliferating journals, magazines, books and encyclopaedias, but prepared for in the lecture halls of the universities and *collèges* in which future *professeurs, avocats, conseillers* and *curés* were prepared for their intended professions. It was in the leading *collèges de plein exercise*, a number of them Jesuit or Jansenist, that actors and audience alike were prepared for the Enlightenment debate about

---

[43] *Recueil de quelques pièces curieuses concernant la philosophie de Monsieur Descartes* (Amsterdam, 1684).

[44] 'Maldonet', M. He also warned that repudiation of all proofs of God *could* but not necessarily *would* lead to rejection of God. See 'Rufinus', C; 'Anaxagoras', E.

God conducted in the second half of the century between deists and atheists.[45] There they would have been made aware of the issues that divided Cartesians and Aristotelians both in theory and by the example of those who taught them in physics (where Aristotelianism had been largely replaced by the newer mechanistic approach by the final decades of the seventeenth century) and in metaphysics (where scholasticism still held the upper hand in the first half of the eighteenth century). In the study of metaphysics and in theology, where traditional methods of education persisted despite the success of the more experimental approach used in the sciences, scholastic and Cartesian approaches to the existence of God would have been regularly subjected to the rigours of formal disputation. *Utrum Deum esse sit demonstrabile* had been disputed by scholastic masters since the twelfth century, but before a more restricted audience of would-be theologians, not before one of pre-professional doctors and lawyers and such. The soundness of each other's proofs of God had also been contested by Dominicans and Franciscans since the thirteenth century, but in circumstances very different from those in which Cartesians, Jesuits and Jansenists engaged in open warfare before an educated public in an early-modern France heading toward Enlightenment.

The real object of their struggle was power in the church and a right to shape ideology in the public sphere: to over-simplify matters only a bit, the Cartesians wanted to replace what they perceived to be the outdated Aristotelian framework of Catholic doctrine (not least 'transubstantiation'); the Jesuits were intent on stopping them at all costs; and the Jansenists were equally determined to halt what they saw in both as an over-dependence on philosophy instead of the resources of faith to explain the mysteries of Christianity. Whoever won the day would win also the right to teach in the name of the church. Their three-way dispute over the provability of God's existence was simply one battle in a wider war. But it was a battle in which their essential differences were peculiarly well exhibited. It was also a battle the aim of which was as much to eliminate the opponent's position as it was to establish their own.[46] On the one hand, Cartesian objections to scholastic proofs of God centred mainly on the difficulty of moving from

---

[45] See Brockliss, *French Higher Education*, pp. 1–107, 444–58.

[46] Kors, *Atheism in France*, I, pp. 297–356, cites the most influential contemporary works containing the most common objections to the newer Cartesian and to the traditional scholastic proofs of God. When the references in Kors are used in conjunction with the relevant appendices in Brockliss, *French Higher Education*, pp. 459ff., a three-dimensional image of the institutional context of battle begins to take shape.

observation statements about the world to God as transcendent cause of it all.[47] On the other hand, most scholastic objections to Cartesian proofs of God flowed from the assumption that they were no more than variations on Anselm's proof, the errors of which had been fully exposed by Thomas Aquinas.[48]

Arguments and counter-arguments were marshalled in a war of attrition that dragged on for half a century. Where did this prolonged and bitter dispute lead? The battles were set pieces and, despite the carnage, no ground changed hands; all parties remained entrenched in their original positions. The Jesuits skilfully used their political dominance in the educational system from school to university to enforce scholasticism as 'normal philosophy'.[49] The philosophical significance of the wrangling lay more in the vehemence with which each of the warring parties insisted that the other's position would inevitably result in the triumph of atheism. If the only evidence of God were the proofs adduced by the Cartesians, there was from an Aristotelian perspective no evidence at all. For this reason, the Jesuit Gabriel Daniel (1649–1729) warned, it would be imprudent of the Cartesians to persist in their attempt to refute the time-tested Aristotelian-Thomistic *viae*: 'Car s'il était vrai que les autres n'eussent pas d'évidence, en comparaison de celles-là, on tirerait de ce principe de fort méchantes conséquences contre l'existence du Premier Etre.'[50] But from a Cartesian perspective, sense experience could never yield sure *évidence* of God: if the only 'proof' of God were induction from the senses, which are inherently unreliable, there would be no *évidence* at all; an imagined atheist would surely not be persuaded by so weak an argument. Indeed, the Benedictine François Lamy (1636–1711)

---

[47] See François Lamy, *Les premiers éléments des sciences* (Paris, 1706) and *L'incrédule amené à la religion par la raison* (Paris, 1710); Pierre-Sylvain Régis, *Système de philosophie*, 3 vols. (Paris, 1690) and *Réponse aux Réflexions de M. Du Hamel sur le système cartésien de la Philosophie de M. Régis* (Paris, 1692).

[48] Descartes's repeated insistence that he had no prior knowledge of Anselm's proof only made his scholastic opponents think that he was deceitful and untrustworthy. See Pierre-Daniel Huet, *Nouveaux mémoires pour servir à l'histoire du cartésianisme* (Paris, 1692), p. 7. See also Pierre Barbay's earlier but influential *Commentarius in Aristotelis metaphysicam*, 2nd edn (Paris, 1676), pp. 368–72, which is representative of the view that Descartes had done nothing to repair the faults of Anselm's proof that had been revealed by Thomas; Barbay's work was widely used in the subsequent debates between Cartesian and scholastic philosophers on the provability of God.

[49] The formal condemnations of Cartesian philosophy were gathered together and published by Jean du Hamel in *Quaedam Recentiorum Philosophorum ac Praesertim Cartesii Propositiones Damnatae ac Prohibitae* (Paris, 1705). The polarization of standpoints was formally enforced by the Jesuits; those who made an explicit effort to reconcile Thomist and Cartesian principles were quickly censured, though subtle efforts often went unpunished. See Brockliss, *French Higher Education*, pp. 206ff.

[50] Gabriel Daniel, *Voyage du monde de Descartes* (Paris, 1702), pp. 174–5.

foresaw, *cette philosophie toute sensuelle* would more likely end in atheism.[51]

Theism's foundations undermined?

It would be tempting to suggest that the result of the warfare between scholastics and Cartesians was mutual self-annihilation: it does not matter whether one begins with one's innermost intuitions or with one's experience of the world, neither can yield sufficient *évidence* of God to refute atheism. This conclusion was endorsed in time by materialists in defence of atheism, but it was embraced first of all inside the Catholic fold itself by those with affinity to the sceptical fideism of the Jansenists. Their having entered the fray against their fellow religionists on both sides helped consolidate the case against the provability of God's existence in eighteenth-century French philosophy. Nicolas l'Herminier (1657–1735), a Sorbonne Jesuit sympathetic to the Jansenist cause, had warned that feeble arguments can do great damage to faith and strengthen unbelief, whilst insisting that neither the Cartesian nor the scholastic proofs of God were in the least convincing. Using the scholastic refutation of Cartesian proofs and the Cartesian refutation of scholastic proofs, he insisted that all *a priori* proofs of God were circular and that no *a posteriori* proof can arrive at the supremely perfect being or God.[52] Claude-François Houtteville (1686–1742) and Claude Buffier (1661–1737) similarly argued that neither set of arguments could demonstrate what it purported.[53] The mutual refutation of the Cartesian and scholastic positions was taken by all of them as a healthy reminder of the frailty of reason and of our dependence upon faith (l'Herminier) or sentiment (Buffier) or Pascal-like reasons of the heart (Houtteville) in averting the destructive consequences of scepticism. In an age of religious fervour, such as that experienced in Pascal's day, this line of defence may have resonated with the public *mentalité*; but in an age of disquiet about corruption and injustice arising from the alliance of church and crown, the residually Jansenist appeal to sentiment and revealed authority was decidedly inopportune. It arguably contributed to further weakening of the rational foundations that had been deemed necessary to support belief in God.

[51] Lamy, *Premiers éléments des science*, pp. 68ff.
[52] Nicolas l'Herminier, *Summa Theologiae*, 3 vols., 2nd edn (Paris, 1718), I, pp. 24ff.
[53] Claude-François Houtteville, *La vérité de la religion chrétienne prouvée par les faits* (Paris, 1722); Claude Buffier, *Traité des premières vérités et de la source de nos jugements* (Paris, 1724) and *Eléments de métaphysique* (Paris, 1725).

This three-sided warfare within Christian theology itself produced arguments which, in other hands, would be made to support the very atheism they had been constructed to refute. With tongue firmly in cheek, the Baron d'Holbach would later record in his entertaining *Théologie portative* that the harmony that reigned supreme among the Christian theologians is the most compelling argument for the truth of that religion.[54] The protracted debate among Cartesians, Jesuits and Jansenists about the provability of God is an example of the kind of '*concorde*' applauded by d'Holbach. In *Christianisme dévoilé*, he made much of the fact that Christians did not agree among themselves about the proofs of God, or about the soundness of particular proofs or even about God's provability in principle. Each of the warring parties moreover regularly accused all others of atheism when they did not agree with its own preferences. The cause of this discord, however, lay for d'Holbach in the incoherence of the concept of God, which though unable to be instantiated was still able to be refuted. For this reason, all three parties might be justified in the case levelled against their opponents, even if their own positive arguments were untenable. Whatever the starting-point – be it Aristotelian or Cartesian or Jansenist – atheism necessarily follows.

The urbane *philosophe* d'Holbach was not the first person to have come to this view. An obscure village *curé* from the Champagne named Jean Meslier (1664–1729) had done so some thirty years previously in a remarkable *Testament* in which he repudiated not only the Christian religion and its Triune God but also 'natural religion' and its generic God.[55] And he built up his case against God from books that had been written in the Deity's defence by combative Jesuits, Cartesians and Jansenists. Their inability to agree on a single proof for God's existence becomes for Meslier a good reason to presume that there is no compelling ground for belief in God. In effect, he embraced the scepticism of the Jansenists, but not their fideism. The significance of Meslier's rejection of God does not lie in the originality of his arguments (for each of them is derivative) but in the fact that he was able to prosecute his case against God in utter dependence upon the works of orthodox theologians such as the pro-Cartesian Archbishop François Fénelon, the learned scholastic René-Joseph Tournemine and the pro-Jansenist Nicholas l'Herminier.[56]

---

[54] 'Concorde', *Théologie portative ou Dictionnaire abrégé de la religion chrétienne* (London, 1768).

[55] Jean Meslier, *Œuvres complètes*, ed. Roland Desné, 3 vols. (Paris, 1970–2), II, pp. 149–525.

[56] See Meslier's notes in the margins of Fénelon's *Démonstration de l'existence de Dieu* and de Tournemine's *Réflexions sur l'athéisme*, edited by Jean Deprun and printed in Meslier, *Œuvres complètes*, III, pp. 209–388. Though direct evidence is less strong, it has been suggested that Meslier's case was developed in close dependence on l'Herminier's critique of the proofs of God in his *Summa Theologiae*. See Kors, *Atheism in France*, I, p. 374, n. 60.

Jean Meslier's name was exploited by the philosophes, but to their own ends. At the time of his death in 1729, Meslier left three copies of his *Testament*; by 1760, more than 100 copies circulated furtively among the philosophes in Paris.[57] Voltaire 'edited' an *Extrait des sentiments de Jean Meslier* (1761), but omitted all reference to his denial of the existence of God, with the result that the atheist *curé* was transformed into a rational deist like himself;[58] Diderot was inspired to write a dithyramb;[59] and d'Holbach published a summary of his own system under Meslier's name, giving a materialist elaboration of Meslier's thought that was wide of his mark and beyond his means.[60]

FROM THE *ENCYCLOPEDIE* TO THE REVOLUTION

The debate about God continued unabated in French philosophy in the second half of the eighteenth century, but not in just the same terms as in the by then exhausted debate between the Jesuits and the Cartesians. The Cartesian proofs *a priori* had few proponents in the latter half of the eighteenth century, and the traditional scholastic proofs were deprived of their most persuasive advocates after the expulsion of the Jesuits from France in 1762. As Newtonian physics gradually took hold in France and as a medley of English philosophers found their admirers there, a new set of ready-made *a posteriori* proofs and disproofs was brought into play in the French debate about a God who had by then become the God of Locke, Newton and Clarke. The distinctive flavour of this phase of the debate can be sampled in the work of Voltaire, Rousseau, Diderot and d'Holbach.

These four representatives of French thought between the start of the *Encyclopédie* and the outbreak of the Revolution held divergent views on religion. All four strongly opposed the existing alliance of church and crown, and with differing degrees of vehemence attacked religious superstition, intolerance, cruelty and corruption. They were divided in their

---

[57] Ira O. Wade, *The Structure and Form of the French Enlightenment*, 2 vols. (Princeton, 1977), I, pp. 189f. and *The Clandestine Organization and Diffusion of Philosophic Ideas in France from 1700 to 1750* (Princeton, 1938).

[58] *Testament de Jean Meslier* (Geneva, 1762), reprinted in Meslier, *Œuvres complètes*, III, pp. 431–90, together with additional remarks from the 1768 edition [pp. 481–5] and 'Voltaire sur Meslier', pp. 486–90. The atheist priest was transfigured by Voltaire in his *Bolingbroke* into a person who on his deathbed could plausibly beg God's forgiveness for ever having taught Christianity, when the late *curé* in fact knew no such being from whom it was possible or necessary to ask forgiveness.

[59] 'Les eleutheromanes ou les furieux de la liberté' (1772), in Meslier, *Œuvres complètes*, III, pp. 493–9.

[60] *Le bon-sens, ou Idées naturelles opposées aux idées surnaturelles* (London, 1772).

personal views of the social and moral merits, if any, of 'natural religion' and the provability, if at all, of at least one God. They did agree, however, that the question of God's existence was a matter of *évidence*, to be settled by rational proofs, foremost amongst which were those from the motion of matter and from the order of the universe. The issue that divided them into pairs was whether, as Voltaire and Rousseau claimed, those purported proofs supported the existence of a God or whether, as Diderot and d'Holbach concluded, the same proofs undermined all theistic claims.

The rational deism of Voltaire and Rousseau

However great their personal animosity or their intellectual differences on other points, Voltaire and Rousseau regarded the proofs of God as bulwarks against superstition and atheism. Even so, they aimed their proofs at different ends in divergent projects and, from one point of view, in the defence of incompatible Gods.[61] Here as elsewhere in their writings, it is the profound differences, not the superficial similarities, that finally prove determinative.

Although he seems neither to have feared the one nor hoped for the other for himself, Voltaire (1694–1778) was persuaded that the threat of hell and the reward of heaven are necessary incentives for most people to avoid wickedness and to live morally upright lives. Voltaire was more and more concerned about the danger to public order posed by unbelief as atheism became more open in French society from about mid-century, from which time his God increasingly resembled a magistrate, who hands out rewards to the virtuous and punishments to the wicked.[62] He disagreed with Bayle that atheists can be good citizens; if they pose no danger to public order, it is only because they are too few and not in positions of political power.[63] This conviction may explain why Voltaire abridged Meslier's testament in the way he did, so that the attack on the church was treated in full but the attack on God was suppressed altogether. Voltaire's conviction that belief in God is necessary for public order may also have motivated his attempt to rehabilitate the *argumentum e consensu gentium*, the seemingly fatal weaknesses of which had been catalogued long ago in Bayle's *Dictionnaire*.

---

[61] 'Though Voltaire has always appeared to believe in God, he has really only believed in the Devil, because his so-called God is nothing but a malicious being who, according to his belief, only takes pleasure in doing harm.' *Confessions*, trans. J. M. Cohen (Baltimore, 1953), p. 399.

[62] H. T. Mason, *Pierre Bayle and Voltaire* (Oxford, 1963), p. 84.

[63] *Homélies*, §1; cf. 'Athée, athéisme', *Dictionnaire philosophique*.

In response, Voltaire allowed the existence of isolated pre-theistic primal communities and of individual atheists of virtuous character, but he disputed the example of China and insisted that all civilized societies in human history have grounded their morality in God.[64]

Knowledge of this God is implanted by reason's master in every heart and is demonstrable by reason and experience. Like the Jesuits who had taught him at the Collège Louis-le-Grand, Voltaire treated the proofs of God as foundational and showed a clear preference for *a posteriori* arguments. Despite his merciless ridicule of Leibniz in *Candide*, Voltaire adopted the Leibnizian proof from contingency as one of two proofs of God endorsed in his *Homélies*. Voltaire's other proof there was the argument from regularity in nature, which he had taken over from English authors, particularly Samuel Clarke, whom he came to admire during the three years he lived in England (1726–9). In the course of defending the design argument in the *Homélies*, Voltaire found it necessary to refute the materialism of La Méttrie, to defend teleology in the natural order[65] and to skirt round the problem of evil, resigned to one's fate in this world and hoping for better in the next.[66] On none of these fronts did he make an original contribution to philosophy, but Voltaire's writings – filled as they were with witty anecdotes and biting humour – did much to popularize the issues raised in the debate about God. One supposes from official reaction, however, that it was his avant-garde attack on *l'infâme* more than his *arrière-garde* defence of God against the materialists that left the deeper impression in the public mind.

Jean-Jacques Rousseau's (1712–78) most eloquent statement of his religious convictions is found in book IV of *Emile* in the famous 'Profession de foi du vicaire savoyard', the passage in his book that received more attention from the reading public (and from public officials!) than did any other.[67] There we also find an elaboration of the two proofs of God that, in Rousseau's view, can withstand sceptical doubts and materialist claims: from causality and from order.

---

[64] To say of some primal community that it is atheistic when the question of God had not yet arisen for it is judged by Voltaire no more appropriate than to say of the same community that it is anti-Cartesian. After some dithering on the question of the alleged atheism of the Chinese, Voltaire eventually came to the view that belief in the will of heaven was tantamount to belief in God. On the latter point, see Mason, *Pierre Bayle and Voltaire*, pp. 19f., 81, 84f.

[65] See also 'Fin, causes finales', *Dictionnaire philosophique*.

[66] See also 'Méchant', *Dictionnaire philosophique*.

[67] Despite his (feigned?) belief that it would be universally acclaimed by readers and public officials alike, his 'Profession de foi' forced Rousseau instead into prolonged periods of exile in Neuchâtel, Geneva, and then England. See Jean-Jacques Rousseau, *Œuvres Complètes*, ed. Bernard Gagnebin and Marcel Raymond, 5 vols. (Paris, 1959–95); cf. *Confessions*, 1:534, 574.

In order to understand the place of those proofs in Rousseau's strategy, however, it is necessary first to note his inversion of the Cartesian method of enquiry.[68] Descartes had assumed nothing to be true except that which was absolutely known to be true, but Rousseau assumed everything to be true except that which was the subject of real doubt. Descartes subjected his deepest intuitions to sceptical doubt and rational proof, whereas Rousseau tested sceptical arguments by his most deeply held intuitions, which he regarded as stronger and more reliable than rational proof.[69] This strategic difference preserved for Rousseau the presumption of theism. It also eased the requirements for any successful proof of God and tightened up the requirement for any putative disproof of God. The burden of proof was shifted dramatically from believer to sceptic in Rousseau's inversion of the Cartesian method. In these circumstances, believers need only show that their imaginative intuitions of God are not contrary to reason and experience, whereas sceptics must demonstrate the truth of what were for Rousseau entirely counter-intuitive claims. The *évidence* produced by sceptical proofs must be sufficient to persuade him against his will to abandon his inner feelings and intuitions; the odds against this occurring Rousseau reckoned at infinity-to-one.[70]

Unlike Descartes, Rousseau's Savoyard priest (protesting all the time that he was not a philosopher, only a man of *bon sens*) had no problem with the certainty of his own existence or the reliability of his senses. He had great difficulty, however, with metaphysical theories about material bodies in motion built on claims about 'blind force' and the like. Rousseau's physics may have been modern, but the structure of his proof remained the Thomistic *ex parte motus*,[71] except that it flowed unbrokenly into a design argument stressing the orderliness rather than the purposefulness of the universe.[72] From both arguments, Rousseau concluded that materialism is incoherent and that no good reason had been found that would lead him to question his original intuitions. Indeed, everything he had found confirmed the inner feeling that the universe is governed by a wise and powerful will,[73] appropriately called God, even if the nature and purposes of that Being remain unknowable to humankind.[74]

---

[68] *Emile, OC*, IV, pp. 567f.
[69] *Ibid.*, p. 569. The imperative to trust one's 'inner light' is a leitmotif that runs through *Emile*.
[70] *Ibid.*, p. 579.   [71] *Ibid.*, pp. 575f.   [72] *Ibid.*, pp. 576ff.
[73] *Ibid.*, pp. 578f.   [74] *Ibid.*, pp. 578, 624ff.

The rational atheism of Diderot and d'Holbach

What Rousseau had called the *coterie holbachique* acquired a reputation as a *salon* of atheists, a reputation d'Holbach himself may have done little to discourage, but one which is still an exaggeration.[75] The circle gathered around the German-born *maître d'hôtel de la philosophie française* embraced a wide diversity of religious opinion, from critically orthodox to militantly atheistic. Only a few – the most enduring being Diderot and d'Holbach – wrote openly atheistic works for public dissemination; but even here there was difference. According to one observer, Diderot can be likened to someone who cannot be bothered to pursue the dragon because he has more important pursuits, whereas le Baron d'Holbach was like a relentless knight who would 'drive the beast to its deepest lair and slay it'.[76] Undermining theistic proofs figured in both strategies.

Though he early repudiated Christianity's supernatural and miraculous claims, Denis Diderot (1713–84) seems to have come to atheism slowly and even reluctantly, but eventually unreservedly. In his polemic against Pascal, published as *Pensées philosophiques*, for instance, Diderot allowed the Atheist to raise the hard questions of the day regarding the explanation of motion or the problem of evil,[77] but seemingly engineered his defeat by the Sceptic (who argued that the Atheist, in casting doubt on the deistic explanation of motion, had not proved an alternative explanation) and by the Deist (who was permitted to argue without refutation that the results of experimental physics confirm that the order of the universe requires an intelligent cause).[78] This was for Diderot the only possible ground of God.

Doubts about that argument, however, surfaced shortly in the *Lettre sur les aveugles* (1749), which created scandal in England and France and

---

[75] See Alan Charles Kors, *D'Holbach's Coterie: An Enlightenment in Paris* (Princeton: Princeton University Press, 1976), pp. 41ff.

[76] James Byrne, *Glory, Jest and Riddle: Religious Thought in the Enlightenment* (London, 1996), p. 168. Kors also contrasts d'Holbach's (and Naigeon's) proselytizing zeal for the atheist cause with Diderot's 'quieter and less impatient' strategy. *Coterie*, p. 47. Despite his single-minded militancy, however, d'Holbach welcomed *abbés* into his *salon* and, when they were banished from the Kingdom of France in 1762, even gave sanctuary in his home to exiled Jesuits!

[77] *Œuvres philosophiques*, ed. Paul Vernière (Paris, 1964), pp. 15–16.

[78] *Ibid.*, pp. 17ff., where he appeals to Newton and Nieuwentijt, among others. Cf. Bernard Nieuwentijt, *L'existence de Dieu, démonstrée par les merveilles de la nature* (Amsterdam, 1714). In the same passage, Diderot also undercuts the Cartesian *a priori* proofs of God with the observation that 'Les subtilité de l'ontologie ont fait tout au plus des sceptiques; c'est à la connaissance de la nature qu'il était réservé de faire des vrais déistes.' *Ibid.*, p. 18. The Jesuit masters who taught him at the Collège de Langres would have been pleased!

earned for Diderot a stay in the prison at Vincennes. The discussion of the provability of God's existence caused particular offence. Nicholas Saunderson (1682–1739) was a blind but brilliant algebraist at Cambridge who was appointed to the Lucasian Chair of Mathematics formerly held by Barrow and Newton. In Diderot's *Lettre*, the pious Saunderson is made to have had doubts about God's existence on his deathbed. A minister was summoned and a dialogue on divine things ensued, during which Saunderson reminded the minister that *le spectacle de la nature* celebrated by Newton and Clarke in the design argument had little force to one who cannot see and, moreover, that the very existence in the universe of beings born blind or with other deficiencies is itself contrary to the perfection of nature so adored by theists.[79] But Diderot may have pulled back even here from adopting the conclusion of the Atheist in the *Pensées philosophiques*; for he had Saunderson cry in delirium at the moment of death, 'O Dieu de Clarke et de Newton, prends pitié de moi!'[80]

By the time he penned the *Pensées sur l'interprétation de la nature* (1753), however, Diderot was overcome by the 'grande révolution dans les sciences' and no longer required a God to explain order in the universe; Philosophy herself would by experiment and reason lift the veil and discover nature's hidden Truth. In struggling toward an immanent explanation of the unity, movement and order of the universe, Diderot in effect reinterpreted Spinoza's phrase 'Deus sive Natura' as expressing disjunction, $a \lor b$, and not logical equivalence, $a = b$. For Diderot, the naturalistic disproof of God would run: *Deus sive Natura; non Deus; ergo Natura.*[81] Nature's force is itself endlessly creative and eternally in motion, without recourse to transcendent cause or to immanent spirit. *La matière se mouvoir et le chaos se débrouiller.*[82] From this point onwards, Diderot had no need of God as an explanatory principle; God had been made redundant before the future Marquis de Laplace (1749–1827) had entered school.

---

[79] *Ibid.*, pp. 118ff.

[80] *Ibid.*, p. 124. Buckley interprets Saunderson's words ironically, despite Diderot's protestation to Voltaire that the cry for mercy was sincere and that Diderot did not share the doubts about God expressed in the *Lettre*. *At the Origins of Modern Atheism*, pp. 224f.; p. 410, n. 92.

[81] See *Ibid.*, pp. 224ff.

[82] Diderot's defence of a materialist philosophy is developed further in the dramatic trilogy known collectively as *Le rêve de d'Alembert* (c. 1769, but published posthumously in 1831). The three pieces are individually entitled: *Entretien entre d'Alembert et Diderot*, *Le rêve de d'Alembert* and *Suite de l'entretien*. They are most readily available in *Œuvres philosophiques de Diderot*, pp. 246–385. Buckley attaches considerable importance to the *Rêve* for the critique of the design argument on materialist principles. See *Origins*, pp. 225–48.

Diderot's objections to God were moral, not just intellectual. In his Nietzsche-like aphorisms, appearing eventually as *Addition aux pensées philosophiques* (1762), belief in such a God, which had led to endless disputation and pointless warfare, must have been visited upon humankind as a vengeful act by some spiteful misanthrope.[83] Diderot also repeated Meslier's wish to see the last king strangled with the entrails of the last priest. Even so, he never became so militant or systematic in his atheism as did d'Holbach, who had also fed on the clandestine *Testament* for his *Le christianisme dévoilé*.

Paul-Henri Thiry d'Holbach (1723–89) aimed not just to eradicate Christianity, with its supernatural claims and privileged position in French society, but also to eliminate natural religion as well. The idea of God as an independent, spiritual being was for him incoherent and incredible. This held for the God of deism no less than for the God of theism.[84] Tongue in cheek, he called the material (and unspiritual) focus of idol worship the only 'true God'.[85] Idolaters at least bow before *ce qui existe*, namely, physical nature: eternal, unoriginate and imperishable; the cause of all causes, self-moved and self-moving; self-existing, its own sufficient reason for being; self-regulating and without need of *un ouvrier inconnu* to assist or intervene in its operations.[86]

God is nature, the cause of all that is. The worship of God is displaced wonder before nature. The attributes of God are misattributed qualities of nature, which lead to paradoxes when predicated of a single being but not when predicated of nature as a whole. The proofs of God can likewise be subverted as proofs of nature – not as proofs of the existence of nature, for that is simply *un fait*, but as proofs of the attributes of nature in so far as they can be known. Nature may be ultimately as incomprehensible as its divine projection, but the simple and general laws by which bodies move are knowable. And from them we learn that the metaphysical properties traditionally predicated of God belong instead to nature. Clarke had used Newton-like proofs from causality and order to demonstrate the metaphysical and moral attributes of God.[87] In his *Système de la nature*, d'Holbach mimicked those theistic proofs in order to show that the metaphysical attributes are right, but the subject is wrong; and in order

---

[83] *Œuvres Philosophiques de Diderot*, p. 72.
[84] *Le bon-sens*, p. 141. See also *Système de la nature; ou, Des loix du monde physique & du monde moral, par M. Mirabeaud* (London, 1770), II.5, pp. 159ff.
[85] 'Idolâtrie', *Théologie portative*. Cf. also Bayle's *Dictionnaire*!
[86] *Système de la nature*, II.3, p. 118; II.4, p. 154.   [87] See p. 211 below.

to show that the moral attributes apply neither to God nor to nature itself, but that they emerge out of nature.[88] Throughout the *Système de la nature*, arguments set up by Clarke to refute materialism are turned round by d'Holbach in its defence.

D'Holbach directs to his own ends not only Clarke's proofs from causality and order but also Descartes's proof from the thinkability of God in the third *Meditation*.[89] He makes the usual point that the existence of *x* cannot be inferred from the idea of *x*; then he argues that the idea of God is itself incoherent, because we cannot form a 'clear and distinct' idea of a disembodied spirit or being without matter or extension; and, finally, he points out that attributes like 'infinite', 'immense' and 'eternal' are empty and devoid of content. The subversion of Descartes is made possible by presuming mechanistic physics as the theoretical foundation of materialism and by displacing the incoherent Cartesian God with a pantheistic Spinozan God, which through its identification with nature acquires matter and extension and, thereby, the power to cause change or movement. But it does so at the cost of becoming material and mutable as well. Ever since Bayle's authoritative article on Spinoza, however, such a God had been widely thought to be indistinguishable from no God at all. This is indeed the conclusion that d'Holbach would have us draw; it is also the conclusion that provides an additional warrant to predicate of nature properties customarily predicated of God. So: it matters little whether one begins with the *a posteriori* arguments of Clarke and Newton or the *a priori* arguments of Descartes and Spinoza, atheistic materialism is the inevitable conclusion.

The end of Enlightenment in France

All the intellectual strands traced in this section are woven together in the work of Diderot and d'Holbach. It would be tempting to say that this is the goal toward which the Enlightenment was heading all along. Others have drawn just this conclusion.[90] Such one-sided triumphalism (or, for that matter, defeatism) must be resisted. And this for two main reasons: their

---

[88] *Système de la nature*, II.2, pp. 39–97. D'Holbach resists the temptation to anthropomorphize nature in the manner that all theists and some deists project essentially human qualities onto their God. For instance, nature does not 'think', but it produces through an unceasing chain of causes and effects the organizations of matter from which intelligence emerges. *Système de la nature*, II.2, pp. 64ff.

[89] *Ibid.*, II.3, pp. 97ff.   [90] Most recently, Michael Buckley.

work was very much a 'minority report' which did not go unchallenged at the time; the same strands were woven together by others inside and outside France to make a very different cloth.

The textbooks sometimes leave the impression that Diderot and d'Holbach carried the day without significant opposition. This is an exaggeration. To restore some sense of proportion, it is perhaps worth noting that in 1770, the same year that the *Système de la nature* appeared, over seventy monographs were published in France defending the existence of God. More followed in 1771, including *Observations sur le livre intitulé Système de la nature* by Johann von Castillon, Professor of Philosophy in the University of Utrecht, and *Examen du matérialisme, ou Réfutation du Système de la nature*, by the remarkable Nicolas-Sylvestre Bergier (1713–90), a canon of Notre-Dame, Confessor Royal and author of previous apologetic works that were well regarded within both ecclesiastical and philosophical circles.[91] More remarkably, he was himself *un des familiers du salon holbachique*! Not only could he match their wit, but he would not betray their confidence even in his official capacity. For instance, he discussed an early draft of *Examen du matérialisme* with Diderot and d'Holbach, but did not reveal to the public that the true author of the *Système de la nature* was not, as announced on the title page, the late Jean-Baptiste de Mirabaud – a revelation that would inevitably have led to arrest and imprisonment for d'Holbach.[92]

Bergier agreed with d'Holbach & Co. that the dispute between theists and atheists should be decided on empirical grounds; the hypothesis that has fewer difficulties should be embraced by both sides of the dispute. The fate of God would be decided by natural philosophy. Abbé Bergier himself had no doubts about the outcome:

As soon as it is evidently proven that movement is not essential to matter, that the latter is purely passive by its nature and without any activity, we are forced to believe that there is in the universe a substance of a different nature, an active being to which movement must be attributed as it is to the first cause, a Motor that is not itself matter.[93]

---

[91] E.g., *Le déisme réfuté par lui-même* (Paris, 1765); *Certitude des preuves du christianisme* (Paris, 1767); and *Apologie de la religion chrétienne* (Paris, 1768), a refutation of d'Holbach's *Le christianisme dévoilé*.

[92] See Kors, *Coterie*, pp. 113–17, and 'The Atheism of d'Holbach and Naigeon', pp. 289–90; Buckley, *Origins*, pp. 253–5.

[93] I, p. 154. Cited in Kors, *Coterie*, p. 65, n. 68, *q.v.* Writing in his *Anti-dictionnaire philosophique*, 2 vols. (Paris, 1775), the Benedictine Louis-Mayeul Chaudon also saw the study of physics as the best antidote to atheism (and superstition): 'It proves that there is an intelligent first cause, and it

Diderot and d'Holbach were equally pleased to have the issue disputed along just these lines, being confident that the scientific evidence proved movement to be essential to matter, which is both active and self-regulating, so that there is no need in the universe for a substance of a different kind to explain motion and the organizations of matter. Each side claimed victory, but neither would yield ground to the other.

Though not the centre of public interest during the Revolution, their differences played themselves out indirectly in the political sphere. On the one hand, Jacques-André Naigeon (1738–1810) expressed his deepest desire to see a France without religion, but would settle more realistically for a Jefferson-like separation of the public affairs of state from the private interests of religion or irreligion;[94] on the other hand, Jesuit-educated Maximilien de Robespierre (1758–94) pushed to establish by decree the existence and cult of the Supreme Being as the civic religion of Republican France.[95] Both were partially successful in the shorter term. In the longer term, Robespierre's cult yielded to Napoleon's new concordat with the Vatican, the terms of which were to remain in force for a century or so. The materialism of Diderot, d'Holbach and Naigeon, however, continued to dominate French science during the next century. As a result, the 'warfare between science and religion' became entrenched on at least that side of the Channel.

The debate about God was in remission in France, but it continued in Britain – where the scientists exhibited far more positive support for God and the established religion of the land. Indeed, the argument from design was never more popular than it was in Great Britain during the first half of the nineteenth century. Why did *le Dieu de Clarke et de Newton* continue to have appeal among intellectuals in Britain long after leading French intellectuals had come to regard the word 'God' as no more than an anthropomorphic way of talking about nature?

---

makes known the particular mechanical causes of this and that effect. Physics augments admiration and diminishes astonishment.'

[94] See Naigeon's *Adresse à l'Assemblée nationale* (Paris, 1790).

[95] The first article of the *Décret* on religion declares, 'The French people recognizes the existence of the Supreme Being, and the immortality of the soul.' The entire decree, setting out the prescribed festivals of the Supreme Being, but guaranteeing also freedom of worship and forbidding any congregation of aristocrats, is printed in J. M. Thompson, *Robespierre* (Oxford, 1939), pp. 494–6.

APPENDIX[96]

Prologue: via antiqua and via moderna

The last lecture ended in the thirteenth century, with the Franciscans and Thomists locked in a rivalry of wills at the University of Paris.[97] In time, of course, the Thomistic-Aristotelian via moderna overcame the Augustinian-Platonic via antiqua, even among the Franciscans. But triumphs of modernity over tradition are ever temporary. History cunningly conspires to ensure that one generation's via moderna is a later generation's via antiqua. We see this no more clearly than by locating ourselves again just where we were at the close of the previous lecture, namely, on the *rive gauche* in Paris, but transporting ourselves forward in time some four hundred years to the dawn of Enlightenment. Over against the scholastic method of old stands now a new via moderna. Call it the Cartesian method, not because Descartes invented it, any more than Thomas Aquinas had invented the Thomistic method, but because it came to be symbolically linked to his name. In this lecture we want to see how this conflict of methods between the via antiqua and the via moderna, played out before a new kind of student audience (an audience more likely destined for the civil service than it was for clerical orders), may itself have contributed to the ironic conclusions that came to be drawn from their own skilfully crafted arguments pro and contra.

For, if the results of recent studies are to be believed, the conflict of methods within theology is itself a major cause of the rise of modern atheism. At least of its rise in France: for (as in most things) a different

---

[96] Editors' note: The material included in this Appendix to Chapter 8 was originally prepared as part of John Clayton's seventh Stanton Lecture. Clayton's outline of chapters for *Religions, Reasons and Gods*, however, specified that his work on early-modern French, German and British philosophy be treated as distinct chapters, with the seventh Stanton Lecture at the core of this volume's Chapter 10. The sections included in this Appendix augment Chapter 8 by providing a more thorough treatment of the global (political, economic and religious) context for the increasing 'thinkability' of atheism in France. They also indicate Clayton's growing interest in the institutional contexts, as well as broader social and intellectual trends and processes, which shape the formulation and reception of philosophical and theological positions. These concerns find considerable voice in Chapter 10 of this volume.

[97] Editors' note: This refers to the sixth of the Stanton Lectures. According to Clayton's initial summary of the Stanton Lectures, 'the sixth lecture "locates" Anselm's argument (*ratio anselmi*) in eleventh-century monastic life and traces the changing fortunes of that proof once it had left the Cloister and moved on to the University. An explanation is sought for the different reception given Anselm's proof by the Franciscans (Bonaventura) and by the Dominicans (Thomas) at the University of Paris in the thirteenth century.'

narrative has to be spun for Britain than that tale told by scholars to signify the French *mentalité*.

From inconceivable to irresistible: the rise of atheism in France

We have grown so used to the presence of atheists in our time that we may want reminding that atheists were not always so common. In *The Problem of Unbelief in the Sixteenth Century*, Lucien Febvre argued that atheism was at that time in some strong sense of the term 'unthinkable'. It was a time when people wanted to believe in God, and had no real alternative to belief, even though people did have a limited choice between systems of belief even in Christianity, the one Catholic and the other Protestant.

'Atheism' was in such an era an emotive term, according to Febvre, whether hurled at others in abuse or maybe even at God as a cry of pain, to be withdrawn after healing or recovery; but for the sixteenth century, 'atheism' was not as an intellectual position 'thinkable'.[98] Anyone could say in his heart 'there is no God', but not even a fool could think with his mind 'there is no God'. The thinkability of atheism required the philosophical revolution of the seventeenth century, a revolution that made heterodoxy possible by providing a discourse in which atheism could be thought. It was a revolution that replaced the Latin language of the traditional scholastics with the French language of the trendy Cartesians. The old 'via moderna', now the new 'via antiqua', was supplanted by a new 'via moderna'. And this was a necessary condition for the thinkability of atheism, judges Febvre, whose account locates the causes of atheism within the ideologically deviant heterodox culture of the day. But another possibility presents itself: namely, that the thinkability of atheism may depend at least as much on the orthodox culture of Catholic France as it did on the heterodox culture of the philosophes and those whom they admired.

Let us consider the example of Jean Meslier, an obscure and not unusually gifted *curé*. But when he died in 1729, two generations before 'atheism' came out of the closet in Enlightened France, Meslier left behind in manuscript an amazing 'testament' in which he argued with much passion and some sophistication the case for his disbelief in God's existence. And this Meslier managed to do without access to any of the heterodox sources from which he might have filched ungodly thoughts.

---

[98] Lucien Febvre, *The Problem of Unbelief in the Sixteenth Century*, trans. Beatrice Gottlieb (Cambridge, MA, 1982).

His own library consisted only of books that were religiously orthodox, books that aimed soundly to ground the self-same belief he had come to repudiate.[99] And this Jean Meslier did some forty years before the publication of d'Holbach's *System of Nature,* the first openly atheistic book to have been published during the lifetime of its author.

How did it happen that the unthinkable could come to be regarded by a Jean Meslier as irresistible? Is it possible that modern atheism is as much a product of the orthodox culture of Christianity as it is of the heterodox culture of the philosophes? One eighteenth-century freethinker quipped that it would never have occurred to anyone to doubt God's existence if theologians had not tried so hard to prove it. This gibe by Anthony Collins, of King's, in reference to the Boyle Lectures by Samuel Clarke, of nearby Caius, may contain in it rather more substance than one might have imagined, if one had been inclined to treat it as no more than the sort of bon mot that might have been found amusing in the Fellows' parlour over port.

Two recent studies, by the Jesuit Michael Buckley and by the historian Adam Charles Kors, have concluded that modern atheism is in effect a theological own goal. Both of them trace (by different routes) the first cause of it all to the way early-modern theologians used theistic arguments in defence of belief in God. They both locate the fateful moves toward modern atheism within the passionate debate about natural theology in mainly French theology and philosophy in the seventeenth century. It is the case, to be sure, that the threat of atheism exercised Christian theologians and philosophers long before there was any reliable evidence of widespread disbelief. It is also the case that Christian theologians increasingly sought to defend belief in God through ingenious philosophical proof, so that theistic arguments acquired more independence and greater prominence during the seventeenth and eighteenth centuries. And it is the case that opposing groups of theologians seemed so concerned that the theistic arguments preferred by their rivals would not stand up to the imagined wiles of fictive but still dreaded atheists that they spent seemingly more energy attacking the opposing school's proofs than they devoted to the direct fight against atheism itself. It is almost as if, by their fixation on that than which no more dreadful can be imagined, the theologians caused their own worst fear to materialize before them. Was

[99] Editors' note: See n. 56 above.

it then the theologians' dialectical construction of atheism that gave rise to its public profession? One would find it hard to imagine a greater irony.

Irony is the most subtle weapon of history's cunning craft. It is a weapon that regularly reaches its target unawares in religious realms. Intra-Christian disputes in matters doctrinal have sometimes had unexpectedly radical consequences. Early differences between Roman Catholics and self-consciously Protestant Anglicans over the nature of sacramental presence, for instance, provided welcome ammunition for David Hume's altogether more sceptical attack on traditional Christian doctrines such as the bodily Resurrection of Christ, doctrines that early Protestant and Catholic divines would most likely have been equally willing to defend to the death if the situation had required it. This particular irony was given a further twist when later generations of analytic philosophers pushed Hume's mitigated scepticism in theological matters all the way to outright atheism, a shove which Hume himself would surely have wanted to resist.[100] The history of philosophy generally and the history of philosophy of religion particularly can be told as a history of concepts and arguments being developed in a given context for a specific purpose and being used later in other contexts to serve different and frequently incompatible ends.

The distant Other: 'atheists' on the horizon

People in the seventeenth century were much exercised about atheism, even though they claimed paradoxically that the proof of God was so certain that it could not be doubted. How do we account for that

---

[100] Editors' note: J. C. A. Gaskin concurs in his *Hume's Philosophy of Religion*, 2nd edn (London, 1988). Gaskin writes: 'Again and again in private and published work Hume gives explicit or implicit assent to the proposition *that there is a god*' (p. 219). After a discussion of some of these remarks from Hume's writings, Gaskin observes:

So my contention is that Hume gives some sort of genuine assent to the proposition *that there is a god*. This assent that 'lyes in the middle' is between deism and atheism. It is fostered by the feeling of design and given a weak rational basis by recognition that the order to be found in nature *could* (not must) be explained as the work of an ordering agent. But this ordering agent – and this is the aspect of the *Dialogues* which easily deceives those in search of Hume's theism or his atheism – cannot be known to have any attributes other than those just sufficient to produce the given result; that is to say, the power of an agent together with 'some remote analogy to human intelligence'.

(p. 221)

Gaskin adds: 'I shall call the "plain, philosophical assent" to the existence of a god as indicated by the vestiges of the design argument, a god whose sole attribute is an intelligence which may bear some remote analogy to the intelligence of man, "attenuated deism". Hume would not have welcomed the appellation, but it fits' (p. 223).

paradox? Was it maybe a matter of repression, as David Berman has suggested, of the obsession with atheists in Britain at a time when none was to be found?[101] There are more straightforward explanations. For instance, atheists may not have reached one's own locality, but they loomed on the horizons of early-modern consciousness: atheists were for early moderns 'the distant Other', both in time and in space.

The 'atheist' in ancient times

Part of the recovery of classical learning was a renewed encounter with the 'atheism' and materialism of ancient times. This provided an awareness by description of an alternative metaphysic that was otherwise thought to be 'unthinkable'. Even if not in one sense 'unthinkable', however, atheism was held incapable of providing moral order for human life, social or personal.

The 'atheists' in far-away places

Reports of explorers, traders and naturally missionaries (especially Matteo Ricci, 1552–1610) to exotic far-away places like the Americas or Asia offered another vision: atheism is after all a possible basis for society, without resulting in less orderly social life or in less virtuous personal life. This remote Other was sometimes used to intra-European ends by being constructed as a foil for more proximate enemies. For instance, Leibniz composed his *Discourse on the Natural Theology of the Chinese*, based on Ricci's journals, in order to show the basic compatibility of Chinese thought with the doctrines of Christianity, but possibly also to show the compatibility of his own heterodox views with Christianity by 'christening' the Chinese.[102] Note also the Malebranche *Dialogue between a Christian Philosopher and a Chinese Philosopher on the Existence and Nature of God* in which he used his attack on neo-Confucian philosophy (knowledge of which he gained in casual conversations over port) as a foil for the real object of his ire: namely, the Jesuits (who claimed to have found in China an indigenous 'natural' knowledge of God, a claim that

---

[101] David Berman, *A History of Atheism in Britain: From Hobbes to Russell* (New York and London, 1988).

[102] Gottfried Wilhelm Leibniz, *Discourse on the Natural Theology of the Chinese*, translated with an introduction, notes and commentary by Henry Rosemont, Jr and Daniel J. Cook (Honolulu, 1977).

challenged Malebranche's view of original sin as corrupting also reason). He cleverly drew parallels between the Chinese and Spinoza, making the situation for the Jesuits as difficult as possible.[103]

But in either case, the discussion generated forced into European consciousness the thinkability of the denial of God. It was not only the Fool who could entertain the possibility that there is no God. Both the ancient wise and the remote worthy, each of whom was regularly idealized, could clearly think the unthinkable. The early-modern missionaries, who went half-way round the world to convert the heathen, ended up sometimes calling into question the absoluteness of the gospel, on the one hand, and undermining confidence in the universality of theistic belief, on the other. They unwittingly provided ammunition to atheists in Europe and contributed decisively to discrediting the venerable 'consent' argument.

The dialectical Other: 'the atheist' in debate

The otherwise remote 'distant Other' became imaginatively present to the mind in literature, but the Atheist became hypothetically possible to the mind in debate as the 'dialectical Other'. Now hypothetically possible, the once unthinkable was not far from becoming a real possibility. In the nature of the scholastic method that provided the rules of debate, there was not much scope for originality in the way the case for Christianity was made; the only scope for innovation in the scholastic debate was the case made on behalf of the hypothetical atheist. One could draw atheistic conclusions from the critique of Aristotle in recent science; or one could draw on travellers' reports from foreign lands; or one could draw on classical literature, interpreted anachronistically; and could draw on one's imagination, which was the most positively dangerous source once the Other had become invisible. The hypothetical Other is a far greater threat than any real Other, since the one responsible for writing his brief was an insider who knew all the weaknesses of the case for Christianity.

But for the hypothetical to be come real, a new audience was required for the internal debates of scholastic theologians to replace the one that had typically listened to them say *propositio, sed contra* and *responsio* for

---

[103] Nicolas Malebranche, *Dialogue between a Christian Philosopher and a Chinese Philosopher on the Existence and Nature of God*, translation and introduction by Dominick A. Iorio (Washington, DC, 1980).

over four hundred years. That audience was in fact created, but not entirely *ex nihilo*, in seventeenth-century France.

Higher education in seventeenth-century France

Thomistic theology had gone stagnant from lack of first-rate representatives; the science faculties had undermined its metaphysical foundations. Cartesian theology gained impetus from the ascendency of Cartesian 'science' (the application of Cartesian method to theology and extension to its proven use in science), but as the implications of that science began to be worked out within the science faculties, Cartesian theology went into decline. Neither 'old' scholastics nor 'modern' Cartesians were able convincingly to defend natural theology against the critiques it received from without the theological faculty. Moreover, scholastic theology was so identified with the Catholic Church in France (and the Catholic Church itself virtually equated with Christianity), that an attack on scholastic theology (and the 'natural theology' it had come to depend upon) was in effect an attack on Christianity, and that in this context meant an attack on God, so that the anti-clericalism of the French Enlightenment escalated quite naturally into anti-theism.

Creating an audience for the Enlightenment

Brockliss has studied the dissemination of ideas through the seventeenth- and eighteenth-century French classroom by examining intellectual formation in the humanities and sciences of the group he describes as 'the liberal professional élite'. The picture that emerges from a close examination of the curricula of the French higher-education system in the period shows that system playing a paradoxically dual role in French culture. On the one hand, it acted to justify the divine-right absolute monarchy of the *ancien régime*, and on the other hand, it acted as the vital agent in the transmission and popularization of new scientific and philosophical ideas which would contribute to the overthrow of that state.

The existence of a professional urban caste most of whom experienced the same institutionalized education provides the book 'with a social focus a purely intellectual history might otherwise lack'.[104] They had not merely local but national significance:

---

[104] Brockliss, *French Higher Education*, p. 5.

it was from the ranks of either prospective or established *professeurs, avocats, juges, conseillers,* urban *curés,* canons, bishops and physicians that the leading figures not simply in the provincial but also in the national cultural life of seventeenth and eighteenth century France were drawn. Molière, Racine, Diderot, Bayle, Bossuet, Montesquieu, Voltaire, and nearly all the other famous *gens de lettres* had either entered a profession that required institutionalized education in the humanities and sciences or had undergone some sort of training to do so . . . More importantly, it was from this milieu too that all the leading figures in French Government and administration in the seventeenth and eighteenth centuries emerged . . . In studying the intellectual formation of a particular urban caste in ancien-régime France, the book is ultimately tracing the education of the nation's administrative élite.[105]

Whatever their future niche, all members of the liberal professional élite initially went through the same educational mill.[106]

The most striking feature of the moral and metaphysical sciences in seventeenth- and eighteenth-century France was the way in which both their structure and content remained virtually unchanged. In the first place, the material for debate and the order in which it was presented were determined by a series of authoritative texts on which the courses were essentially commentaries, even if dressed up as independent cursus. It was the thought of Aristotle and Aquinas and others that was the real subject of analysis, not the substantive topics of philosophy. In the second place, the ways in which the texts of these authors were treated almost always followed the same standardized and highly predictable route. The teaching of the moral and metaphysical sciences, then, was 'not simply structurally conservative but more importantly intellectually stagnant'.[107]

Brockliss's book traces differences between developments in the teaching of the natural sciences on the one hand and the moral and metaphysical sciences on the other in France in the seventeenth and eighteenth centuries. He writes,

The histories of the teaching of physics and medicine in seventeenth- and eighteenth-century France betray a striking similarity. Both sciences for the greater part of the seventeenth century were ultimately founded on Aristotelian metaphysics that sought an explanation for the apparently occult movements of certain natural phenomena and the bodily parts in their substantial form. Both sciences too rejected this qualitative explanatory strategy in the 1690s and embraced thereafter a mechanist ideology, which stressed that all kinds of motion ultimately stemmed from a physical, if often invisible, pressure.[108]

---

[105] *Ibid.,* p. 8.   [106] *Ibid.,* p. 105.   [107] *Ibid.,* p. 331.   [108] *Ibid.,* p. 441.

Furthermore, Brockliss observes: 'The histories of the teaching of the moral and of the natural sciences were thus very different: the former had a history of stasis, the other of change.'[109] Novelty was willingly embraced, even when it had uncomfortable effects on existing doctrine and theory. The future liberal professional elite 'would have . . . gained their conception of the state of the natural sciences as collégiens while studying physics. Clearly, the picture they would have taken with them into the outside world would have been one of progress and promise.'[110]

The promotion of scientific revolution by institutions of higher education had a double significance. In the first place, it brought the work of experimental philosophers to a wider audience than would otherwise have been possible:

by giving future *avocats* and clerics a detailed introduction to the mechanical philosophy, the colleges guaranteed that the Scientific Revolution was the property of the professional liberal élite as a whole, not the esoteric possession of a small fringe community. Thereby Cartesian and later Newtonian science became as much a part of the dominant culture in France as Gallicanism or absolutism. Both became part of the mental set of the institutionally educated Frenchman, their principles a fecund store to be transmuted into literary metaphors and political analogies.[111]

Secondly, colleges and faculties helped ensure that the new science would not be a merely transitory movement. In this regard, the contrast with Great Britain is illuminating.

'In Revolutionary and Napoleonic France scientists were legion and their work often highly mathematical and theoretical. In Britain, on the other hand, at the same date great names were few and their work more often than not narrowly experimental.'[112] Physics was taught in some 150 *collèges de plein exercise* throughout France at a time when it was taught in England only at its two universities.

Both these points together emphasize the role of French institutions of higher learning in creating an audience for the more subversive Enlightenment ideas:

the colleges, in disseminating the new science, ensured the French philosophes an audience that could comprehend what they were trying to do, irrespective of whether or not it sympathized with their conclusions. In eighteenth-century

---

[109] *Ibid.*
[110] *Ibid.*, p. 443. Editors' note: The present paragraph has been constructed by the Editors around quotations from Brockliss that featured in Clayton's original manuscript.
[111] *Ibid.*, pp. 451–2. [112] *Ibid.*, p. 452.

France the liberal professional élite was instructed in an epistemology of natural science which was justified in terms of its simplicity and social utility and which increasingly stressed the conditionality of all conclusions and their need to be continually tested on the anvil of carefully regulated empirical enquiry. Moreover, from the mid-eighteenth century if not before, the epistemology of natural philosophy was presented in the colleges as a particular aspect of a general theory of knowledge taught as part of the study of logic. The liberal professional élite as a group, then, regardless of individual political or religious convictions, would have had no difficulty in understanding the Enlightenment enterprise. Its members could follow the philosophes' critique of Church and State without necessarily condoning it. And herein lay the philosophes' chance to corrupt. Thanks to their education the liberal professional élite was a susceptible target for the insidious idea that religious, social, cultural, and political conventions should be investigated, compared, and judged solely in terms of their mathematical symmetry or their tendency to promote human happiness. If once attracted into reading Enlightenment literature as adults (from empathy with Voltaire's wit or Rousseau's sentimentalism perhaps) they could quickly learn to embrace this utilitarian approach without having the slightest desire at the outset to change the status quo. Members of the group could thus be drawn into the philosophe camp without realizing the dangerous road down which they were travelling.[113]

I am not claiming, of course, that these institutions wanted to further the cause of the Enlightenment. However, they unwittingly helped create the possibility of the acceptance of Enlightenment ideas. As Brockliss remarks,

People cannot change their ideas in the same way as they change their clothes . . . In other words, somewhere within their cultural consciousness there must already exist a mental state or attitude that will lend a novel idea the necessary cogency to allow it adoption.

Unwittingly, therefore, and ironically a set of institutions devoted above all in the seventeenth and eighteenth centuries to maintaining the French absolute State ultimately helped to destroy it.[114]

The enfleshed Other: et in intellectu et in re

The 'distant Other' of ancient times and remote places became hypothetically possibilities in debate and, having become present as intellectual possibility in the minds of an audience prepared for Enlightenment, the once unthinkable then became almost irresistibly enfleshed *et in intellectu et in re*. And atheism had now become a cultural possibility, but not a cultural necessity. We must, I think, resist the line taken by Buckley that

[113] *Ibid.*, p. 454.   [114] *Ibid.*, pp. 456–7.

atheism was the inevitable outcome of the style of natural theology that had been adopted by the seventeenth-century theologians. I have no particular wish to absolve the theologians from complicity in their own downfall, but I also wish to avoid the kind of intellectual reductionism which sees ideas alone as the agents of intellectual history. It is finally persons who are the agents of intellectual history, and persons are not reducible to their mental acts. But neither do I wish to succumb to the reductionism of any other kind of determinism (social or cultural or psychological). And this means that mental acts might at least in principle be counted amongst the factors that can affect the course taken by intellectual history.

'Atheism' entailed by the Other's theism: Thomists versus Cartesians

Since at least the Middle Ages, philosophers and theologians of all confessions had used as a debating technique the attempt to show that the opponent's position, if followed consistently (more consistently than the opponent is in fact willing to follow it), will lead necessarily to the worst imaginable consequence. The Thomists and the Cartesians at Paris were in this respect following a time-honoured procedure when each argued that the Other's theism in fact entails atheism. Nor can they be blamed if they proved so convincing in their skills of dialectic that some of their students decided to agree with the conclusions of each party about the Other. Nor is it their fault if their students of the seventeenth and eighteenth centuries, unlike those of the thirteenth and fourteenth, were more destined for civil professions than they were for the church, so that they did not feel under the same constraints as their predecessors or, for that matter, as their current masters. Nor is it anyone's fault in particular if the modern students followed the wider debates about atheism in far-away lands that were featured in the new popular journals that had begun to spring up in France to satisfy demand for reading material.

Though no one in particular was at fault, the outcome of the prolonged philosophical and theological debates about which form of natural theology was the superior defence of God was, to say the least, ironic in that it encouraged in many the abandonment of all belief in the God that both camps had set out to defend.

'Atheism' becomes a cultural possibility: theism's worst fear realized

Atheism was, until the modern era, each generation's worst fear. Whatever was perceived to be a threat to orthodoxy or to civil order was often said to lead to atheism or to be atheism itself. In ancient times, 'atheism' was commonly identified with belief that gods are not concerned with human affairs and, therefore, do not require our worship. (In the Hebrew Bible, the 'fool' of the Psalms was likely to be one who held that God did not notice human actions.) Theistic proofs sometimes used to encourage performance of cultic acts (e.g. Socrates in Xenophon).[115] In the Middle Ages, theologians – Christian, Jewish or Muslim – held that heresy would lead to atheism and asserted the importance of uniformity in belief. Orthodoxy was seen as the only sure protection against the threat of atheism. Theistic proofs were often used to reinforce an orthodox view of deity.

In the Enlightenment, philosophers and freethinkers held that religious dogmatism would lead to atheism, and asserted the importance of tolerance and rational religion, which alone would overcome the divisions of positive religions: competing religious dogmatic claims, bloody religious intolerance and priestly corruption. On this view, natural theology is the only sure protection against the threat of atheism. Ironically, it may in fact have cultivated it. Modern atheism, as rejection of this style of natural theology, is then rejection of the generic God and the Utopian reasons which were offered as a disembedded foundation. Even if this should prove to be true of atheism in France (where Thomist and Cartesian fought fiercely and on Catholic soil), is it equally true of Britain?

First let us recapitulate how far we have come: The fear of atheists in France led to greater weight being placed on the importance of theistic arguments, but they were unable to deliver what was required of them, with the result that the case of atheism was greatly strengthened. This is nowhere more ironically realized than in the mainly intra-Christian debates in France between early-modern defendants of traditional scholastic arguments, on the one hand, and the proponents of the newer Cartesian philosophy, on the other. But these consequences were only possible in an intellectual community which had come to equate confidence in the existence of God with confidence in the provability of that

---

[115] See Xenophon's *Memorabilia*, Book I, Chapter 4. Xenophon recounts a conversation between Socrates and Aristodemus upon the former's discovery that the latter 'neither sacrificed to the gods when he was not engaged in battle, nor consulted (*chresthai*) divination, but even ridiculed those who did these things' (Xenophon, *Memorabilia*, translated and annotated by Amy L. Bonnette with an introduction by Christopher Bruell (Ithaca, 1994), p. 22). Xenophon concludes by commenting: '[i]n my opinion by saying these things he made his companions refrain from the unholy, unjust, and shameful things, not only when they were seen by human beings, but even when they were in solitude, since they believed that nothing they might do would ever escape the notice of gods' (p. 26).

existence. Through the application to religious questions of the newer conception of evidence or proof that developed within the sciences, expectations about what theistic argument could or should achieve were greatly heightened. Within Catholic culture this combined with a traditional confidence in natural theology to produce a foundationalist conception of natural theology that made the rational proof of the existence and nature of God a purely philosophical question that was beyond the competence of theologian qua theologian. Theistic proofs became not just sufficient for knowledge of God, but also necessary in a strong sense of that term.

Within Protestant cultures, theistic arguments had a more ancillary function, so that their critique had less devastating effect than within Catholic cultures. Indeed, their critique within Protestant cultures was often encouraged and supported by the church leadership. And the audience in such cultures 'heard' things differently. Bayle's audience in the Low Countries heard him with different ears than did his predominantly Catholic (or 'post-Catholic') audience in Paris, who drew consequences from his writings that his Protestant contemporaries did not draw.

CHAPTER 9

The Enlightenment project and the debate about God in early-modern German philosophy

It has become commonplace in recent philosophical discussion in Europe and America to speak, be it approvingly or disapprovingly, of something called the *Modern project* or the *project of Enlightenment* or the *Enlightenment project*. Each of these phrases has its own local appeal and creates its own conceptual problems. Each can be given a certain tone, so that in one voice it can evoke all the aspirations of the human spirit made free from self-imposed chains; in another voice each phrase can evoke a sense of cultural fragmentation and loss of community. If we try, against all the odds, to encapsulate that project in a single paragraph, we could do worse, I think, than propose something like this:

'The Enlightenment project in its most general form is an attempt to identify and to justify without recourse to outside authority or private passion but by the exercise of reason and the limits of experience alone what we can truly know, what we ought rightly to do and what we may reasonably hope. Public rationality requires us in all our deliberations to achieve neutrality by divesting ourselves of allegiance to any particular standpoint and to achieve universality by abstracting ourselves from all those communities of interest that may limit our perspective. By this means, the sovereign self sets out to lay sound foundations on which to build with reasoned confidence.'[1]

This seems near to what Descartes proposed in his *Discourse on Method* and attempted in his *Meditations*; it is reminiscent of what Bayle advocated in his monumental *Dictionary*; and it is what Mendelssohn and Kant commended in their separate essays in answer to the question, 'What is Enlightenment?'

What effect would it have on the discussion of religious issues if they were disputed according to these general principles of enquiry? In such

---

[1] J. Clayton, 'Thomas Jefferson and the Study of Religion'. Editors' note: See Chapter 2 of the present volume.

matters, the Enlightenment project can be portrayed as an attempt to establish from a tradition-free, confessionally neutral starting-point whether there are logically sound and universally compelling reasons to accept the existence of God, the immortality of the soul and the authority of the moral law. The question of God becomes an enquiry like any other in the public realm, one in which we suspend prior judgement, be it pro or con, and weigh the arguments on both sides by the scales of reason alone:

'Thus, for a certain time, that is when each party is alleging their reasons, [says Pierre Bayle,] both those who deny and those who affirm ought to lay aside their thesis and neither affirm nor deny it. It will be then a question; it will be a matter of enquiry, to proceed impartially in which we must not suffer our preconceived opinions to add any weight to the arguments that favour them nor to weaken their contrary reasons. We must examine everything as if we were a tabula rasa. It is not necessary actually to doubt, and much less to affirm, that all we have believed is false: it is sufficient to keep it in a kind of suspense; that is, not to suffer our persuasion to bias us in the judgment we are to pass on the proof of the existence of a God and the difficulties and arguments of the atheists.'[2]

Built into the framework of the Enlightenment project is a distinction between *natural religion,* on the one hand, which is supposed to be universal in embrace, rational in character, and benign in its consequences to the extent that it is presumed to contribute to the stability of the social order and to the unity of humankind into what was once called, much too restrictively by our lights, 'the brotherhood of man'. The 'positive' or *determinate religions,* on the other hand, are imagined to have no more than local appeal, to be based on irrational authority, to be sustained by priestcraft or demagoguery, and to lead to intolerance and division within and between peoples. In the Enlightenment enterprise, natural or rational religion is thought fit for public space, but more sectarian or group-formed commitments are confined to private space.

Left at this level of generalization, my brief characterization of the Enlightenment project would apply almost equally to Descartes, Spinoza, Locke, Bayle, Diderot, Voltaire, d'Holbach, Mendelssohn and Kant, not to mention Thomas Jefferson and a host of others. At this level of generalization, the Enlightenment project is by no means limited to the so-called Age of Enlightenment (i.e. that epoch in Western cultural

---

[2] 'Maldonet', §L, *Dictionnaire.*

history from about the middle of the seventeenth century to roughly the end of the eighteenth). The account also rings remarkably true to what goes on under the rubric 'Philosophy of Religion' at least in English-speaking universities, especially in philosophy departments, which are still typically dominated by analytic philosophy.

The so-called Age of Enlightenment was itself much more complex than this account suggests. One could with good reason protest that it was not dominated by a single project, that this project is itself a later construction imposed on the past as a way of establishing a canon of approved philosophers whose names can in turn be intoned in order to legitimate the authority of certain sorts of 'normal' philosophical enquiry and to exclude other sorts of 'deviant' enquiry from the academy. It can also with good reason be protested that what has been described as the 'Enlightenment project' is not peculiar to the European Enlightenment. Practitioners can be found, for instance, in early-modern or 'baroque scholasticism'. Perhaps it would be better to speak instead of, say, a 'Modern project'? That would be fine except that most features of this project were anticipated in late-mediaeval philosophy in Europe and in even older forms of philosophy elsewhere in South and East Asia – but that is another story for some other occasion!

No name for the project under review is wholly satisfactory, so I propose to stick with the 'Enlightenment project', which is quite adequate for my present needs. In doing so, however, I want to under-score that it leads to distortion to lump the likes of Descartes and Kant together, as Rorty and MacIntyre are inclined to do.

A great deal of differentiation is required if we are to make sense of the Enlightenment enterprise. No grand narrative can do justice to the individual story lines that are woven together in the European Enlighten-ment, especially in regard to the debate about God. A different tale has to be told for the debate in France and Britain and Germany, owing in part to the way their distinctive confessional cultures disposed philosophers to attach differing weight to – say – the success or failure of the proofs of God. In France, for instance, Thomists and Cartesians may have bickered about whose preferred argument could be counted on to establish the existence of God, but they were in agreement that some such proof is necessary if belief in God is to have a sound basis. Only the Jansenists and the Protestant minority doubted the claim that faith requires prior proof if it is not to be in vain. Distinctive intellectual traditions also led German philosophers to focus their attention more on the so-called 'ontological argument', while philosophers in Britain had long shown a preference for the 'argument from design'. In my contribution to this volume, I want to sketch out the main outlines of the debate about God in early-modern German thought; what I want to say about the Low Countries, France and Britain will have to wait for another occasion.

Modern German philosophy has its origins in reactions to scholasticism in the latter half of the seventeenth century. The issues that divided pietists and rationalists decisively shaped the debate about the provability of God in German lands to the end of the eighteenth century. The story begins with Leibniz and Spener, continues with Wolff and Baumgarten, Thomasius and Francke, and arrives at its paradoxical conclusion with Mendelssohn and Kant and controversies they both helped to ignite.

SCHOLASTICISM, PIETISM AND RATIONALISM

German philosophy prior to Leibniz had been locked in a debate defined by confessional rivalries stretching back to the Protestant and Catholic Reformations, a debate left untouched by the advances in science and mathematics that had revitalized philosophy elsewhere. The old divisions were perpetuated in a proliferation of confession-specific universities located in duchies and principalities all governed by the principle *cuius regio eius religio* first agreed at the Diet of Augsburg (1555) and reaffirmed in the Peace of Westphalia (1648). That principle would have long-term effects on German education. It legitimized confessional pluralism and institutionalized the divisions of the Reformation and Counter-Reformation. It also arguably reinforced the role of scholastic philosophy in the public realm as a master discourse in which competing religious groups could precisify their own positions and contest the claims of rival groups, with the result that an ever-refined sense of irreconcilable difference hardened along the boundaries that divided the established confessions: Catholic, Lutheran and Reformed or Calvinist.

Reaction against the hegemony of scholasticism over German philosophy began in the second half of the seventeenth century mainly within Protestant lands, coming from two directions: pietism and rationalism.

Although more a devotional than an intellectual movement, *pietism* had direct and indirect influence on philosophical debate by its opposition to rationalism and its insistence on the primacy of the will. Pietism, of which there were localized varieties, represented at first a popular reaction against the over-intellectualization of religion in scholastic orthodoxy and a rediscovery of spiritual disciplines, personal piety and morality. The impact of the movement on the history of philosophy arises from the suspicion it created about the capacity of reason to ground religious certainties and from the prominence it gave to inner experience and moral rectitude. Several leading German philosophers came from pietistic homes, and this may have had an effect on their stance toward the issue whether the proofs of God are foundational for knowledge of God's being. At a time when he still proffered a version of the proof *a priori*, the so-called 'pre-critical' Kant could also write, 'It is absolutely necessary that we be convinced of God's existence, but not nearly so needful that it be demonstrated.'[3]

The view expressed here by Kant was not unusual in German Protestant circles. Amongst orthodox rationalist and pietistic Protestants alike, there were lower expectations for the proofs of God than there had been in French Catholic thought. Even when theistic proofs were allowed as *sufficient* for true knowledge of God, they were not regarded as *necessary*. Among other things, this implies that the existential stakes (in both senses) were not likely to be as high in the German debate about proofs of God as they had been in the French debate.

Gottfried Wilhelm Leibniz (1646–1716) had no pietistic background, but his *rationalism* represents the second direction from which scholasticism came under attack in the second half of the seventeenth century. Leibniz was determinative for the German debate about God in the eighteenth century in at least three ways.

1. Although he cannot be said to have broken its hold altogether (and can be said to have perpetuated some of its arcane features), Leibniz did loosen the grip of traditional scholasticism on German philosophy, without sacrificing either its logical rigour or its metaphysical aspirations, by introducing into philosophical method modes of thinking originating in science and mathematics. The philosophical mimicry of serial deduction in particular gave to Leibniz's philosophical style persuasive power in an era when mathematics enjoyed high prestige. His method is, in this respect, closely connected with that of Descartes and Spinoza. But in matters religious, his mode of thinking seemed to lead to less disturbing results than did theirs, not least, one supposes, because he (like Locke) left room for the possibility that things could be beyond reason without on that ground being dismissed as contrary to reason and because he (this

---

[3] *KA* II, p. 163.

time, unlike Locke) was genuinely possessed of a religious sense that inclined him naturally to orthodoxy. He was possibly for this reason also less disposed than Locke to reserve to reason the authority to decide which of those things that lie beyond its grasp are tenable and untenable. Leibniz left natural theology subordinate to revelation and thus kept more space for orthodox Christian doctrine than did the author of *The Reasonableness of Christianity*.

2. Built into Leibniz's reflections on God and the world were elements that have periodically occasioned the charge of Spinozism or pantheism. Even if it should be allowed that Leibniz did finally manage to extricate himself from the web of Spinozism and to reaffirm something akin to an orthodox Christian belief in God, the 'Spinoza question' thereafter was never far below the surface in eighteenth-century German debates about God. Spinozism never lost its power to capture the imagination, alluring and repelling with equal force, as shown pre-eminently in the *Pantheismusstreit* that raged after the death of Lessing in 1781.

3. At every stage in his development, Leibniz was fully convinced that the existence of God as the unique subject of all perfections or *ens perfectissimum* could be proven with the certainty of a mathematical demonstration. Leibniz's preferred proofs of God became the focus of debate in German philosophy for most of the eighteenth century. Whilst offering others as well,[4] Leibniz typically favoured three arguments for God's existence: a non-demonstrative argument *from presumption* modelled on jurisprudential practice; an *a priori* proof *from possibility* intended to correct the Cartesian proof in the fifth of his *Meditations*; and an *a posteriori* proof *from contingency* based on the principle of sufficient reason. The arguments from contingency and possibility set the agenda for the ensuing German debate on the possibility of a proof of God. Physico-theology did not have the prominence in Germany that it enjoyed in Britain, possibly because German science at the time shared the French penchant for mathematical theory rather than the British enthusiasm for experimental science. Leibniz himself damned with faintest praise the proof from the order of things.[5]

---

[4] For instance, Leibniz repeats in §384 of the *Theodicy* a mathematical proof for God's existence that he had taken over from his former teacher Erhard Weigel (1625–99), one-time professor of mathematics at Jena.

[5] *New Essays on Human Understanding* (Cambridge, 1981), p. 438.

PIETISM AND RATIONALISM AT THE UNIVERSITY OF HALLE

The two main sources that fed the debate about God in eighteenth-century German philosophy came together after 1694 at the newly established University of Halle. Foremost among the rationalists were Christian Wolff (1679–1754) and Alexander Gottlieb Baumgarten (1714–62). Rationalists were at first a minority party at Halle and remained so until shortly before the accession of Frederick II to the Prussian throne in 1740. Pietists were the dominant party from the beginning, led by the founding Rector and Law Professor Christian Thomasius (1655–1728), and the Theology Professor August Hermann Francke (1663–1727).

The clash at Halle between pietists and rationalists localized tensions that were a general feature of the German Enlightenment. The extent to which the polarity was considered to be peculiarly Hallensian, however, is suggested by the popular jibe that anyone who began their studies at Halle would complete them either a fanatic or an atheist.[6] The pietists in the Faculty of Theology did their best to ensure that no one at Halle finished their studies an atheist. Just to make sure, however, theological students were forbidden to attend Wolff's lectures in the philosophy faculty.

Francke's chance to rid himself of this troublesome rationalist came in 1721 when Wolff entered the controversy about the Chinese, by arguing in a lecture that the discovery of sound moral maxims by Confucius without the benefit of revelation proved (as Thomasius also held) that unaided reason can attain to moral truth. On account of this lecture, Wolff was surprised to find himself accused of teaching atheism. As a result of skilful manoeuvring by Francke and sharp polemic by Johann Franz Budde (1667–1729) and Joachim Lange (1670–1744), Wolff was eventually dismissed from his post at Halle and banished from Mark Brandenburg. He immediately accepted a previously offered position as Professor at Marburg and there completed most of his Latin works, including the *Theologia Naturalis*. But Wolff was able to return to Halle in 1740, when the newly crowned Frederick II invited him to become Professor of Law and shortly to become Chancellor of the University. Some historians of philosophy mark Frederick's accession in Brandenburg-Prussia, Wolff's rehabilitation in Halle and the re-establishment of the Royal Prussian Academy in Berlin as the beginnings of the German Enlightenment.[7]

---

[6] F. Paulson, *German Education: Past and Present* (New York, 1908), p. 120.
[7] E.g. L. W. Beck, *Early German Philosophy: Kant and his Predecessors* (Cambridge, MA, 1969), pp. 243ff.

The Enlightenment may have arrived a little later in German lands than elsewhere, but the professionalization of philosophy within the academy began earlier there than elsewhere. The invention of professional philosophy as an independent academic discipline in which one might be a 'specialist' can be said to have taken place at the new University of Halle. Credit for its invention goes largely to Wolff, who mapped out the branches of modern philosophy, created a specialized language for philosophy in the vernacular and generated textbooks in each of its subdisciplines with the systematic thoroughness and architectonic zeal for which subsequent German philosophy has been both admired and ridiculed. To say that Wolff was not an 'original thinker', therefore, is as misleading as it is accurate.

His claim to originality lies not least in his having systematized the disparate branches of philosophy. Descartes and Leibniz had approached the topics of philosophy methodically or 'systematically', to be sure, but Wolff had set about synthesizing philosophy into a system in which all parts are connected to one another. The outlines of this system are sketched in *Discursus Praeliminaris de Philosophia in Genere* (1728), and elaborated in a series of works – some obscenely large – first in German at Halle and then in Latin mainly at Marburg on logic, ontology, cosmology, empirical and rational psychology, natural theology, practical philosophy, natural and positive law, ethics and economics. In all these writings, Wolff aimed to achieve a synthesis of human knowledge in which all its branches would be shown to be elements in a formal, deductive scheme established on putatively rational principles.

Wolff's authorship as a whole constitutes a new *summa philosophiae*, as scholastic a production as the scholastic philosophy it was intended to supplant. Operating under Cartesian and Leibnizian stimulus, Wolff not only pushed German academic philosophy boldly forward into modernity, but at the same time ensured by the elaboration of his deductive system that the hold of scholastic-rationalist thinking on the German mind would not finally be broken for another half-century.

Wolff invented no new proof of God. He did invent a new taxonomy of the branches of philosophy, however, and achieved a new clarity on the place of the existing proofs in them. Through the widespread use of his *Theologia Naturalis* as a textbook in philosophy and theology faculties alike, Wolff's account of the proofs became a template to be copied by followers and opponents alike. In this way, Wolff shaped the framework of a debate to which he had little original to contribute substantively. Moreover, his taxonomy of philosophical disciplines and designation of theology's place in them provided essential ingredients for the taxonomy Kant would later use in his critique of rational theology.

In line with Wolff's conception of philosophy as the science of possibles,[8] natural theology is declared the science of those things that are possible *per Deum,* for and through God.[9] In Wolff's scheme of things, natural theology is not a free-standing activity, capable of generating all its own principles. It depends, rather, on the other branches of metaphysics (ontology, cosmology and psychology) for its necessary principles.[10] Though theology does not depend directly on physics for its principles, the conclusions of teleology nonetheless serve to confirm what is known independently in natural theology.[11] Implicit in the account of ontology, cosmology, teleology (as a sub-branch of physics) in the *Discursus Praeliminaris* are links to the three proofs of God discussed in Wolff's writings: the *a priori* proof *from possible being,* the *a posteriori* proof *from the contingency of the world* and a 'teleological' proof *from order and purpose* in the world. Although he does not explicitly identify the three proofs with ontology, cosmology and teleology, he does in effect associate each proof with principles generated by each of those branches.[12] And he explicitly associates the proof from contingency with the principles of cosmology:

If [the existence, attributes, and operations of God] are to be treated demonstratively, then what is predicated of God must be inferred from certain and immutable principles. Such immutable principles, from which God's existence and attributes can be firmly concluded, must be derived from a contemplation of the world. For we argue conclusively to the necessary existence of God from the contingent existence of the world. And we must predicate those attributes of God which explain the unique Author of the world. Therefore, natural theology borrows principles from cosmology because general cosmology is the general

---

8   Christian Wolff, *Discursus Praeliminaris de Philosophia in Genere* (Frankfurt and Leipzig, 1728), §29.
9   Christian Wolff, *Theologia Naturalis,* 2 vols. (Frankfurt, 1736–7), I, §1ff.; *Discursus Praeliminaris,* §57.
10 *Discursus Praeliminaris,* §96; *Theologia Naturalis,* I, §11.
11 *Discursus Praeliminaris,* §101.
12 Wolff does this most clearly in the *Discursus Praeliminaris* by associating the 'teleological' argument with physics and the *a posteriori* proof with cosmology. See again §96, where he explicitly links the *a posteriori* proof to the principles of cosmology, but links theology to ontology in only a general sense. In the *Theologia Naturalis,* II, he reaffirms that natural theology borrows its principles from ontology, cosmology and psychology (Praef.). Whilst he does not link the proof *a priori* exclusively to ontology, he does carefully note each of the principles of ontology that are required to sustain the notion and existence of a Supremely Perfect Being [§§1–78]. Only when he has established the existence of the *ens perfectissimum* and wished further to prove that that *ens* is *Deus* does he begin to borrow propositions from other branches of metaphysics, and then in the spirit of negative theology; namely, to show what God is by showing what God is not: e.g. 'Deus non est ens compositum. Sed mundus ens compositum est . . . Ergo mundus Deus esse nequit.'

contemplation of the world, which reveals the dependence of the world on the divine attributes.[13]

Wolff's way of classifying the proofs of God would be taken over by other philosophers, including Mendelssohn and Kant. It would be Kant, however, who gave names to the proofs that are derived from Wolff's classification of philosophy's branches: *onto*-theology, *cosmo*-theology and *physico*-theology. And it would be Kant who first recognized and exploited the implications of Wolff's account of the necessary dependency of physics and cosmology on ontology for the proofs of God that are associated with each: physico-theology and cosmo-theology both depend finally for their success on principles secured by onto-theology. The contingency of the teleological and cosmological proofs is grounded in and subsumed by the necessity of the ontological proof. If that one proof should fail, however, the other two would necessarily fail as well.

MENDELSSOHN AND KANT

The fate of that single proof in German discussion in the latter half of the eighteenth century was closely bound up with the work of Moses Mendelssohn (1729–86) and Immanuel Kant (1724–1804). They came to philosophy by different routes and worked toward different goals, but they shared in a common philosophical tradition transmitted through Wolff, and became convinced that it required extensive reform. Both men remained irredeemably religious souls from child-hood, but the one managed to stay *frum* in a way that the other did not stay *pietistisch*.

Philosophy for Mendelssohn was an entrée into gentile society, to be sure, but it was also the discourse that allowed him to make a connection between the Jewish intellectual tradition represented by Maimoni-des (1135–1204) and the modern Western intellectual tradition represented by Locke, Leibniz, Wolff. The crucible was the Berlin of Frederick the Great, where Mendelssohn lived from 1743 until his death in 1786. When fourteen-year-old Moshe-mi-Dessau arrived in Berlin to study Talmud, he knew little German and no other European language, classical or modern. His first brush with a book of non-Jewish philosophy impressed Mendelssohn out of proportion to the

---

[13] *Discursus Praeliminaris*, §96, trans. R. J. Blackwell (Indianapolis, 1966).

merits of the book itself.[14] The first non-Jewish philosopher of substance (*sic!*) he studied was John Locke, having learned the language well enough to work his way through the *Essay concerning Human Understanding* in Latin translation. Within ten years of arriving in Berlin, Mendelssohn could speak perfect German and tolerable French, read Latin well, and had a good knowledge of modern European philosophy. In his first major philosophical piece, the *Philosophische Gespräche* of 1755, Mendelssohn showed not only that he had assimilated the Leibniz–Wolffian discourse, but that he could apply it with a lightness of touch that had eluded either Leibniz or Wolff and with an originality of mind that was lacking in most products of German academic philosophy at the time. Mendelssohn's originality is masked at times by his talmudic skill in making innovation appear as reaffirmation of tradition, and by his often subtle irony in redirecting established ideas to unexpected conclusions. Mendelssohn's having adopted the British essay style of philosophical writing in the *Gespräche* was, moreover, a step toward the *Populärphilosophie* that flourished outside the academies and universities in the third quarter of the century and was an indirect indicator of openness to foreign (notably British and French) philosophical influence that marked the Enlightenment of Frederician Berlin off from that of rationalist Halle.[15]

Philosophy for Kant was the entrée into a world of thought unrestricted by the narrow focus of the pietism of his childhood and youth, but it was also a discourse that enabled him gradually to resolve the cognitive dissonance between the increasingly naturalistic conclusions of post-Newtonian science and his own residually religious convictions about the starry skies above him and the moral law within him. Immanuel Kant entered the University in Königsberg a student of theology destined for the Lutheran pastorate, but became instead a student of philosophy destined, after anxious delay, for a chair in the subject at the same university at age forty-six. Kant had been taught philosophy by Wolffian Martin Knutzen (1720–56), who also introduced him to the writings of Leibniz's rival Newton and to those of Wolff's critic, Christian August

---

[14] Quite by accident, Mendelssohn stumbled onto the then only recently published *Betrachtungen über die Augsburgische Confession* (Berlin, 1740), by the Wolffian Lutheran philosopher Johann Gustav Reinbeck, in which twenty-seven chapters are given over to arguments for God's existence, attributes and operations.

[15] See, e.g., M. Kuehn, 'The German Aufklärung and British Philosophy', in *Routledge History of Philosophy*, vol. V: *British Philosophy and the Age of Enlightenment*, ed. S. Brown (London, 1996), pp. 309ff.

Crusius (1715–75) – all of whom added to the eclectic mix that eventually made up Kant's critical philosophy. The importance Kant attached to Crusius and Newton is evident in his first philosophical productions, especially in the *Allgemeine Naturgeschichte* (1755), *Nova Dilucidatio* (1755) and *Monadologia Physica* (1756). The two dissertations also show how tied Kant the university teacher was to the conventional academic style that had been initiated by Leibniz and developed by Wolff into a rationalist scholasticism – no hint here of philosophical revolutions, or trace of the lightness of touch that makes Mendelssohn a delight to read! Kant's philosophical model was and arguably remained throughout his life as an author the scholasticism of Wolff, Baumgarten & Co.

In their early writings, Mendelssohn and Kant were quite near to each other on many issues. Neither of them doubted the possibility of meta-physical cognition, though they each questioned some of its currently fashionable principles. Nor did they doubt the provability of God's existence, even if they queried the soundness of particular proofs. Al-though they sometimes endorsed other proofs as well, each of them was inclined toward the proof *a priori* and offered a new version, putatively free from the defects of previous versions. Mendelssohn never lost confi-dence in his version of the proof; Kant's attitude toward his own version is more complex.

Each sketched his revised proof *a priori* in his entry to the Prussian Royal Academy essay competition for 1763. The revival of the Academy, originally founded by Leibniz but under Frederick more nearly controlled by Newtonians, provided an institutional basis for encouraging the dis-semination of new ideas at a time when Wolffian philosophy was in decline. The new Prussian King famously encouraged openness to foreign ideas, as well as a new freedom for academic philosophy in the academies and universities within his realm. Essay competitions were used to en-courage fresh approaches to the problems of philosophy, and topics were occasionally chosen with the evident aim of embarrassing the Wolffians. The topic for 1763 invited entrants to consider if it were possible to attain in metaphysics, especially in natural theology and ethics, the degree and kind of evidential certainty that is attainable in geometry.

Kant's essay was more adventurous, but it was also less elegant and more obscure; Mendelssohn was awarded the prize in a close contest decided in the end by the chair's casting vote. Mendelssohn gamely argued that metaphysics could achieve the same certainty as mathematics, though it had greater difficulty achieving the same perspicuity. Such transparency eludes metaphysics because its principles have to be applied to the world of objects and cannot be restricted to abstract entities (numbers) and because metaphysics up to then had lacked the rigour that comes from formalization. Kant showed greater awareness of the differences between the methods of metaphysics and mathematics and greater sensitivity to the difficulty of attaining certainty in metaphysics. In particular, he emphasized the inappropriateness of applying to metaphysics the quasi-mathematical method of demonstration used by Wolff and his followers. Even so, Kant agreed with Mendelssohn that it is possible to achieve apodeictic certainty in the knowledge of God's being, attributes and operations. Like Mendelssohn, Kant looked to Baumgarten's theory of existence based on the principle of thorough determination to make good the deficiencies of the Cartesian proof *a priori*. But, whereas Mendelssohn had used Baumgarten to do more effectively what the Leibniz–Wolffian philosophy normally did, namely, to find a way to move from possibility as ground to God as consequence, Kant used Baumgarten to do something rather novel, namely, to reverse the Leibniz–Wolffian procedure in order to move from possibility as consequence to God as ground.

The proof of God hastily sketched by Kant in his Academy *Untersuchung* summarized thinking he had been doing for some years. In his academic dissertation that appeared as *Nova Dilucidatio* in 1755, Kant rejected as unsound the Cartesian proof *a priori* and outlined an alternative version of the proof which was original to him,[16] though he elsewhere incomprehensibly attributed it to Alexander Pope.[17] Kant elaborated his version of the proof *a priori* further in *Der einzig mögliche Beweisgrund zu einer Demonstration des Daseins Gottes*, a monograph which Mendelssohn reviewed favourably if also a little condescendingly in one of the new popular magazines, a review which helped establish Kant's reputation as a major philosopher.[18] Although it went unremarked in Mendelssohn's review, a minor landmark in the history of ideas was made in Kant's essay by his having there first given the proofs *a priori* and *a posteriori* the then novel names 'ontological proof' and 'cosmological proof'.[19] In *Der einzig mögliche Beweisgrund*, Kant refuted the Descartes–Leibniz proof *a priori* on grounds that are virtually identical to those that survive in his

---

[16] *KA* I, pp. 395ff.   [17] *KA* XVII, pp. 232–4; *KA* II, §3704.

[18] *GS/JA*, V/I: *Rezensionsartikel in Briefe, die neueste Litteratur betreffend (1759–1765)*, ed. E. J. Engel (Stuttgart, 1991), pp. 602–16.

[19] 'Man erlaube mir, daß ich den ersten Beweis den ontologische, den zweiten aber der kosmologischen nenne.' *KA* II, p. 160. He also there collects arguments from order in nature under what he calls, though not originally, 'physico-theology'. *KA* II, pp. 116f.

refutation of the 'ontological' argument in the first *Critique*.[20] That appears to be the end of the matter in the first *Critique*, but in the 1763 monograph, Kant used his new basis for a demonstration to show how the traditional proofs *a priori* and *a posteriori* could be reformulated as sound arguments. That is to say, even if 'existence' is a grammatical and not a real predicate and if the reality of something cannot be inferred from its concept, some version of the proof *a priori* may still be sound. Kant's proposed transcendental proof runs as follows:

Alle Möglichkeit setzt etwas Wirkliches voraus, worin und wodurch alles Denkliche gegeben ist. Demnach ist eine gewisse Wirklichkeit, deren Aufhebung selbst alle innere Möglichkeit überhaupt aufheben würde. Dasjenige aber, dessen Aufhebung oder Verneingung alle Möglichkeit vertilgt, ist schlechterdings nothwendig. Demnach existirt etwas absolut nothwendiger Weise.[21]

And that something is 'God', the ultimate rational ground of all possibility. This, then, is the proof reiterated in Kant's prize essay. It is a proof which he never repudiated. Not even in the *Critik der reinen Vernunft*, where his early refutation of the Cartesian proof *a priori* was repeated with little alteration. What do we make of this curious fact? Do we excuse Kant's apparent oversight by claiming that his early argument did not require special refutation since the existence of the *Critique* itself effectively constitutes its refutation? Or are we left to wonder if his earlier proof *somehow* managed to survive in the first *Critique* as a lingering presence, like a shade from the past?

Against the prevailing weight of counter-opinion, I am inclined to the latter view. But in order to clarify the issue, it is helpful to look more precisely at the transformation of Kant's thought between 1763 and 1781.

A convenient place to take soundings is the treatment of rational theology in Kant's 1773–4 lectures on metaphysics – lectures happily located mid-point between the *Beweisgrund* and the first *Critique*. They show that the explanation is to be found not in ontology or epistemology but in practical philosophy or ethics. Ethics had not figured at all in the scheme of the *Beweisgrund*, much less in the account there of possible proofs of God. It was mentioned – as required by the terms of the competition – in the *Untersuchung*, but there as philosophy's Cinderella, neglected and unappreciated, certainly not as something that might offer a proof of God's existence. How different it is in the lectures on metaphysics, where Kant

---

[20] *KA* II, pp. 72ff.; cf. A592ff./B620ff.   [21] *KA* II, p. 83.

asserts the primacy of practical reason over speculative reason in philosophy, including in rational theology:

The main thing is always morality: this is the holy and the sacred which we must guard; this is the ground and aim of all our speculations and inquiries. All metaphysical speculation begins here and goes out from here. God and the other world are the only goal of all our philosophical inquiries, but if these concepts should lose their inner connexion with morality, they would no longer benefit us.[22]

We live within the boundaries of our experience of this world, marked off *a parte ante* by God and *a parte post* by the world to come. Since these things lie beyond the limits of our experience, however, we cannot actually *know* them. Yet a belief in a Creator of this world and a hope for a future life arise in us as naturally as knowledge of possible objects of human experience. Indeed, belief in a Creator and Governor of the world is necessary for us in order to make sense of our intuitions, of our experience and of the moral law's demands on us. The *existence* of such a being can be no more than a presumption,[23] but the *concept* of God is a necessary hypothesis or presupposition of pure, empirical and practical reason. The traditional proofs of God are thereby transformed by Kant from abortive efforts to demonstrate the *existence* of such a being into viable ways to construct a *concept* of God sufficient to the needs of reason, experience and morality.

Kant's earlier proof *a priori* survives explicitly in the lectures on metaphysics, and implicitly in the first *Critique*, not as a transcendental proof of God's existence, but as a necessary presupposition of pure reason able to give practical certainty to our natural belief in what he would later term the Transcendental Ideal (A571–84/B599–612). The earlier proof's continued presence in the first *Critique* is sometimes overlooked because it does not appear in the account of rational theology, which has been simplified to make sharper the critique of any possible proof, be it transcendental or natural, that employs reason speculatively and not practically.

Paradoxically, the traditional proofs of God became necessary for Kant as *postulates* in a way they never had been for Kant as *demonstrations*. They took on the function of regulating or correcting false and impure concepts of God.[24] In tandem with his own novel moral argument, they provided the support for a rational belief in God that had been provided by revelation in the systems of Leibniz and Wolff. In their systems, natural

---

[22] *KA* v/1, p. 301.   [23] *KA* v/1, pp. 304, 322.   [24] *KA* v/1, p. 307.

theology was there to confirm what is known independently in holy scripture. Religious scriptures for Kant were less resources for true belief than reservoirs of corrupted images of God.[25] A profound suspicion of the claims to special revelation or direct knowledge of God pervades all Kant's writings on religious topics, from *Die Träume eines Geistersehers* (1766) to *Religion innerhalb der Grenzen der bloßen Vernunft* (1793). But that suspicion did not lead him either to rest all on the allegedly apodeictic certainties of speculative reason or to abandon religious belief altogether in the way that had become fashionable among materialists beyond the Rhine. Kant's critical philosophy was the first major attempt to construct a rational theology grounded neither in the truths of revelation nor in the truths of speculative reason. This proto-non-foundationalism is managed by Kant's making theoretical reason serve the needs of practical reason, so that moral certainty is all that would be required to sustain a rational belief in God.[26]

Kant made no effort to show that the God who is a natural and necessary postulate of reason is also the God of Abraham, Isaac and Jacob. Kant's purified God is the God of the philosophers *par excellence*; Mendelssohn, by contrast, asserted that the God of the philosophers is the God of Abraham, Isaac and Jacob. Mendelssohn was as suspicious of the claims of revealed religion as was Kant. The proximate cause of suspicion for Mendelssohn (as for Kant) was the extravagance of claims to knowledge of divine truths by Christian theologians. In Mendelssohn's case, however, there were additional reasons: namely, the proselytizing zeal of some Christian theologians and the curtailment of civil rights for Jews, which limited the right of access to public life even in 'Enlightened' Prussia.[27] In respect to proselytizing zeal, Mendelssohn wrote in the heat of the Spinoza controversy that he had been able to resist Jacobi's thinly disguised attempt to convert him by insisting that his knowledge of divine things was grounded in reason alone:

in respect of doctrines and eternal truths [Mendelssohn told Jacobi], I recognized no conviction that was not founded on reason. Judaism prescribes faith in historical truths, in facts on which the authority of our positive ritual law is

---

[25] An exception to prove the rule: Kant allowed that the holiness of God had somehow managed to survive in its purity in the Christian gospel! *KA* v/3, p. 306.

[26] *KA* v/1, p. 304. Though her specific interest does not lie in philosophy of religion, Onora O'Neill has explored the ramifications for the primacy of practical reason in Kant's theoretical philosophy in *Constructions of Reason: Explorations of Kant's Practical Philosophy* (Cambridge, 1989).

[27] See S. Stern, *Der preussische Staat und die Juden*, 3 vols. (Tübingen, 1971), and D. Hertz, *Jewish High Society in Old Regime Berlin* (New Haven, 1988).

based. The existence and authority of the Supreme Lawgiver, however, must be cognized by reason, and here no revelation and no faith are applicable, according to the principles of Judaism. Judaism is not a revealed religion, but a revealed law. As a Jew, I said, I had special reason to seek conviction through rational arguments.[28]

In respect to civil liberties, Mendelssohn opposed Jewish separatism and championed Jewish emancipation. A connection between sought-for political emancipation and rational religion was made in his *Jerusalem* almost as clearly as the connection between the existing social order and natural theology had been made in Paley's writings on natural theology and social philosophy. For Mendelssohn, however, 'natural theology' was not a tool to use (as Paley had used it) to legitimate the status quo; it was for him, rather, an intellectual weapon to use in the cause of Jewish emancipation. Equality in our knowledge of God stood behind the call for equality in the rights of groups within civil society. Universalizability is a criterion of public access. The particularity of religious practices (or 'revealed law') precludes them being public in the same way. Difference is privatized. *Natural* theology became for Mendelssohn *political* or civil theology. Moreover, the priority Mendelssohn gave to the proof *a priori* in natural theology harmonized with his political aims, by making knowledge of God wholly independent of the contingencies of the established (social) order, and mirrored the determination of early-modern German intellectuals to establish knowledge of God with mathematical certainty. This determination led to ironic consequences in the controversies that were ignited toward the end of the eighteenth century.

PANTHEISM, ATHEISM AND THE ONTOLOGICAL ARGUMENT

Historians of philosophy seem keen for Kant's critical philosophy to be seen as the end (in both senses) of German philosophy in the eighteenth century. Two events impinge on the triumph of Kantianism in the last decades of the eighteenth century: the *Pantheismusstreit* following Lessing's death (1781) diverted some attention from Kant's achievement and pushed Mendelssohn into the limelight, where he stayed until his death in 1786; the *Atheismusstreit* in 1798 left an elderly Kant confused by the transformations of critical philosophy at the hands of Fichte and others from the generation destined to take German philosophy into the new century.

---

[28] Cited by A. Altmann in *Moses Mendelssohn: A Biography* (London, 1973), p. 731; cf. pp. 534ff.

1. From the early part of the eighteenth century, Spinoza had had a few enthusiasts in German states, to be sure, but no one had managed to interpret his system in a way which managed to remove from it the suspicion of fatalism that denied free will to God and persons alike or the suspicion of atheism that cancelled every difference – theoretical or practical – between the pantheism of *deus sive natura* and no God at all. For most of the century, 'Spinozist' was typically an emotive ejaculation, a term of abuse hurled at real or imagined adversaries. But the term – in much the same way as the term 'sceptic' – also serves, more interestingly, as a kind of boundary to mark the point at which arguments or concepts had led to rational or practical consequences that were untenable or unwelcome. In the case of God, there was the fear that 'God' for the Spinozists was a redundant concept, a superfluous flourish in the conceptual scheme. This would seem to be what Wolff feared at the end of his detailed critique of Spinozism in his *Theologia Naturalis* when he concluded that Spinozism was not far from atheism and, for its greater plausibility, more dangerous [II, §§ 671–716]. Wolff's critique was published separately in German, with the ironic result that it generated wider interest in Spinoza's ideas. In his *Philosophische Gespräche*, Mendelssohn had made the first philosophically astute attempt in German to come to terms with Wolff's critique and to rehabilitate Spinoza, by making sufficient adjustments in his ideas to bring him more nearly into the intellectual mainstream as a precursor of Leibniz. Mendelssohn's skills at mediation were similarly applied in the controversy following Lessing's death, provoked by the accusation by Friedrich Heinrich Jacobi (1743–1819) that Lessing had confessed to being a 'Spinozist', which *for Jacobi* made Lessing an atheist.[29] The controversy began as private correspondence, but spilled out into the open after Mendelssohn's pre-emptive defence of his old friend Lessing in *Morgenstunden oder Vorlesungen über das Dasein Gottes* (1783), Mendelssohn's most sustained contribution to the German debate about God. The main issue focused in the Jacobi–Mendelssohn controversy was not the fact of God's existence, but the kind of God that might be thought to exist.

The provability of God's existence was an issue, but the adequacy of particular proofs did not receive extended attention in the correspondence

---

[29] Friedrich Heinrich Jacobi, *Werke*, ed. F. Roth, 6 vols. (Leipzig, 1812–25), IV/I, pp. XXXVI *et passim*. Note also Jacobi's counter-intuitive charge that Jews are more inclined to pagan views of God than are Christians!

between Jacobi and Mendelssohn. True to his pietistic upbringing, Jacobi grounded religious certainty in the immediacy of feeling, not rational argument. In harmony with Hume and Kant, he held it impossible for reason to take knowledge beyond sense experience. That which lies beyond our senses can be known only in so far as it is *given to us*.[30] There is no way from nature to God and the Cartesian proof he dismissed elsewhere as 'hocus pocus'.[31] The only God who might be proved by a demonstration would be a fatalistic, monistic God lacking in intelligence and feeling and will.[32] Jacobi thereby revived polemic long familiar in the anti-rationalist works of Hallensian pietists who made the God of Spinoza also the God of Leibniz–Wolff.

Mendelssohn took the point, but rejected the consequences, in his *Morgenstunden*, where he sketched the 'refined pantheism' which, were it not a bit anachronistic, might better be called *panentheism*. The defence of Lessing was not the main point of Mendelssohn's lectures on the existence of God. And, although Jacobi had become an irritant, he was not the target at whom Mendelssohn aimed his metaphysical guns. The *Morgenstunden*, which a few of his contemporaries regarded as Mendelssohn's counter-achievement to Kant's *Critik der reinen Vernunft*, constitutes the last grand attempt in German philosophy to demonstrate the existence of God in the manner of Leibniz and Wolff. In the penultimate chapter, Mendelssohn gave a novel proof for the existence of an independent and necessary being from the necessary incompleteness of my knowledge of myself and from the necessary conditions of the possibility of my existence as body and soul.[33] In the final chapter, he attempted to defend against Kantian objections a modified version of his proof *a priori*.[34] Kant was unimpressed, dismissing Mendelssohn's attempt as a masterwork of reason's self-deception.

2. Kant had watched the *Pantheismusstreit* from the sidelines, intervening most reluctantly and then mainly to save himself from the charge of Spinozism.[35] Ideas inspired by Kant, if not he himself, were more central to the *Atheismusstreit* a decade or so later. The story begins in 1791 when

[30] *Werke*, IV/2, p. 155.
[31] *Briefwechsel*, I/1 (Stuttgart, 1981), p. 160, cited by J. Rohls, *Theologie und Metaphysik. Der ontologische Gottesbeweis und seine Kritiker* (Gütersloh, 1987), p. 352.
[32] *Werke*, IV/1, p. 223, IV/2, pp. 125ff.
[33] *GS/JA*, III/2, pp. 138–47.
[34] *GS/JA*, III/2. For an account of Mendelssohn's proof *a priori* and the reactions it provoked, see Rohls, *Theologie und Metaphysik*, n. 31, pp. 337–55.
[35] 'Was heißt: Sich im Denken orientiren?' (1789), in *KA* VIII, pp. 131–47.

Kant was sent a manuscript by a young, unknown scholar from Saxony, who – under the spell of the second *Critique* – had rigorously applied Kantian principles to religious themes. Kant was so impressed with what he read that he persuaded his own publisher to bring out the book. Unfortunately, when *Versuch einer Kritik aller Offenbarung* appeared in 1792, the author's name and preface had been inexplicably left out. So Kantian was the tone of the book and given that it was published by Hartung, the volume was read as a sort of 'fourth critique' by Kant himself. To end the rumours, Kant identified the author as Johann Gottlieb Fichte (1762–1814), and the publisher brought out a second, corrected edition in which Fichte's name finally appeared[36] – all of which created greater interest in the *Versuch* and greater curiosity about its author. In the *Versuch einer Kritik aller Offenbarung*, his most parasitically Kantian production, Fichte adopted the transcendental mode in order to deduce the idea of revelation by the principles of practical reason. He thereby showed essential agreement with Kant that morality is the *Hauptsache*, that practical reason is the ground of metaphysics and of religion, too. Religion is understood not as belief in the existence of a being called 'God', but as belief in the moral law as divine, with the divine attributes of holiness, etc. adding to its authority in our lives.[37] To arrive at the idea of revelation from principles of practical reason, without recourse to revelatory claims of any particular religion, however, Fichte made unconventional use of the shadowy proofs of God, understood with Kant as necessary postulates of reason.[38]

Among those caught up in the enthusiasm for the volume in Weimar was Goethe, who became instrumental in Fichte's appointment in 1794 to the chair in philosophy at Jena left vacant by the departure of Austrian Karl Leonard Reinhold (1758–1823), who had made Jena an early centre of Kantian ideas. The brilliance of Fichte's early work as professor at Jena gained attention, especially his various productions in *Wissenschaftslehre*, in which an increasingly original effort was made to work out the implications of the Kantian primacy of practical reason for the main theoretical problems of philosophy. Fichte also became a controversial figure in Jena in virtue of his enthusiasm for French

---

[36] Cf. the publisher's embarrassed explanation in the second edition (1793) and Fichte's two prefaces. Johann Gottlieb Fichte, *Werke*, ed. F. Medicus, 6 vols. (Leipzig, 1908–12/1954), V, pp. 12–14.

[37] *Werke*, V, pp. 39ff.

[38] Fichte makes novel use to new ends of the moral proof (*Werke*, V, pp. 39ff.), the proof *a priori* (V, pp. 79ff.), the proof *a posteriori* (V, pp. 84ff.) and the 'physical' or teleological proof (V, pp. 106ff.).

Republican ideals, his championship of academic freedom and his effrontery in holding lectures on Sunday mornings at the hour appointed for worship.

Though he was reputed to have been a difficult colleague and intolerant of the excesses of the student *Verbindungen*, his lectures were popular and Fichte gathered around him a circle of keen philosophy students, whose development he oversaw. Among those he encouraged was Friedrich Forberg (1770–1848), whose essay on the 'Entwicklung des Begriffes der Religion' was published in the *Philosophisches Journal* he co-edited together with a covering essay of his own 'über den Grund unseres Glaubens an eine göttliche Weltregierung',[39] thereby unwittingly initiating the so-called *Atheismusstreit* that occasioned Fichte's unwilling and probably avoidable resignation from Jena in 1799. The decisive factor in Fichte's departure was less likely to have been his alleged 'atheism' than his stubbornness of character and his contempt for the educational authorities, a contempt that alienated even Goethe from his cause. Fichte's heterodox views on religion nonetheless still point in one direction Kant's ethics might guide philosophy of religion.

To borrow a distinction more expected in accounts of nineteenth-century German philosophy, Forberg and the early Fichte might be called *left-wing Kantians* in that they drew the radical consequences for religion of the primacy of practical reason and repudiated all efforts by (shall we say) *right-wing Kantians* such as Fichte's predecessor Reinhold to use Kant's moral argument theoretically in an effort to regain epistemically what had been lost in Kant's critique of the traditional proofs of God. And pietists, who had little concern at all for the fate of theistic proofs, still welcomed Kant's emphasis on virtue and duty and on God as Lawgiver and Judge.

Fichte and Forberg concluded that the Kantian critique of natural theology[40] and the Kantian elevation of practical reason to primacy affect not just *the way* we postulate God, but also *the God* that is postulated. The God that is a necessary postulate of pure practical reason is not a being (*ein Seyn*) who may or may not exist; the God that is necessary is pure act (*ein reines Handeln*).[41] God is the striving after the triumph of good over evil; to speak of God is to speak of the sovereignty of the moral law.[42] Whether God as an independent being exists or not

---

[39] Both of them appeared in *Philosophisches Journal* 8 (1798), 1–20, 21–46.
[40] See Fichte, *Werke*, v, pp. 267ff.   [41] *Werke*, v, pp. 261, 267.
[42] *Werke*, v, pp. 185, 186, 187f.

has no practical consequences; however, whether we work for the triumph of good or not does matter supremely.

What would it be then to be an atheist?

The 'true atheist', Fichte pleaded, is not the person who denies that God has independent existence, but the person who fails to follow the sovereign moral principle in their lives, the person who thinks that evil means can achieve the good.[43] A person believes in God, according to Fichte, in so far as striving toward the moral good is sovereign in their lives. Is this statement a *criterion* or a *definition* of belief in God? Although the texts are not unambiguous, both Forberg and Fichte seemed inclined to the latter. God *is* the moral order; to follow the moral law *is* to believe in God.

Since Kant, there has never been a time when German academic philosophy could not be divided into a pro-Kant party and an anti-Kant party, though the 'Kant' in question may have varied with the circumstance.[44] In respect to philosophy of religion, it was more nearly his 'critique of all theology' than his positive application of the proofs of God as necessary postulates of reason that has made the more lasting impact on the parties pro and con.[45] This is a pity because Kant's relatively ignored positive reflections may well suggest philosophical possibilities that could be developed in a variety of directions, one of which was advocated by Forberg and the early Fichte. This focus on Kant's negative critique is a pity also because his specific criticisms of natural theology were not very original. The most telling criticisms made by Kant had been in circulation not just for decades but for centuries, and his suspicion of reason's powers to carry us beyond the bounds of sense was already commonplace in British and French philosophy and in those parts of German philosophy formed by pietistic influence. Not even his most famous example, regarding real and imaginary Thalers, can be attributed to Kant.[46] Most damagingly, however, Kant's critique of all theology was not finally effective in what it set out to do; namely, to dispose

---

[43] *Werke*, v, pp. 188, 185.

[44] See K. Chr. Köhnke, *Entstehung und Aufstieg des Neukantianismus. Die deutsche Universitätsphilosophie zwischen Idealismus und Positivismus* (Frankfurt, 1986).

[45] By the time Hegel gave his *Lectures on the Philosophy of Religion* [I, p. 419], the Kantian critique of reason was given as the principal reason that the proofs of God (which Hegel was intent on restoring to a place of honour) had 'been discarded, consigned so to speak to the rubbish heap'.

[46] See J. Bering, *Prüfung der Beweise für das Dasein Gottes aus den Begriffen eines höchstvollkommenen und notwendigen Wesens* (Gießen, 1780), p. 80: 'Denn bei Hundert Thalern, die ich besitze, habe ich keine Realität mehr als bei Hundert Thaler, und bei Hundert, die ich nicht habe, aber doch besitzen kann, habe ich keine weniger als Hundert, nur mit dem handgreiflichen Unterschiede, daß mir für diese Niemand etwas gibt' [spelling modernized]. Cited by J. Rohls, *Theologie und Metaphysik*, p. 263, n. 31. The Thaler example in the *Critik der reinen Vernunft* is to be found on A599/B627.

of every possible proof of God by undermining confidence in the so-called 'ontological' argument. Even if we accept that every possible theistic argument rests finally on some form of 'ontological' argument, Kant's critique of what he calls the ontological argument cannot cover every type of proof *a priori*, including perhaps the one he himself formulated as a young man.

The hydra-headed argument *a priori* would not be so easily destroyed. It is with us still. And it persisted under Kant's critical nose. Even if Mendelssohn's version were not itself finally victorious, the proof *a priori* did gain new devotees in Germany in the wake of the Jacobi–Mendelssohn controversy. Take, for example, the unashamed endorsement of that proof by Kant's erstwhile but disaffected pupil Johann Gottfried Herder (1744–1803) in *Gott: Einige Gespräche* (1787), a second edition of which appeared in 1800 as *Einige Gespräche über Spinozas System*. Having been born out of the *Pantheismusstreit* (and having been reborn out of the *Atheismusstreit*), it is little wonder that the independent existence of God is a central topic of discussion. Kant's strictures on the powers of reason and his objections to the ontological argument notwithstanding, Herder has his spokesman in the dialogues confidently speak of God as the necessary condition for the possibility of rationality itself, so that if there were no God, there could be no rationality.[47]

Others internalized the controversies over Kant, Spinoza and atheism differently. From his own private study of the texts, for instance, Schleiermacher (1764–1834) had concluded that Kant and Spinoza were complementary figures.[48] In his notebooks, he generally sided with Spinoza against Jacobi, but was in the process also influenced by Jacobi.[49] In the end, he can be said to have interlaced Jacobi's emphasis on feeling as the seat of religion, 'Saint' Spinoza's pantheism and Kant's strictures on the use of reason in his *Reden über die Religion* (1799), a book which – more than Kant's book on *Religion* (1793) – pointed the direction philosophy of religion would next take. Schleiermacher, the self-styled 'pietist of a higher order', had no need for rational proofs to add certainty to what was already a matter of immediate self-consciousness, but a transformed ontological proof was soon given new life by Hegel (1770–1831) as part of a speculative project the boldness of which Kant could scarcely have imagined possible.

---

[47] *God: Some Conversations*, trans. Fredrick Burkhardt (Indianapolis, 1940), pp. 149ff.
[48] *KGA* I/1, pp. 573–7, pp. 526f.
[49] See, e.g., *KGA* I/1, pp. 513–58. On the extent of Jacobi's influence on Schleiermacher, see E. Herms, *Herkunft, Entfaltung und erste Gestalt des Systems der Wissenschaften bei Schleiermacher* (Göttingen, 1974).

CHAPTER 10

The debate about God in early-modern British philosophy*

INTRODUCTION

My thesis concerning theistic arguments in the modern period is fairly straightforward: disembedded from their traditional contexts, in which they had served mainly tradition-specific ends, they were asked more and more to serve tradition-neutral ends by carrying the full load of justifying the rationality of basic religious claims. This was a job for which they were ill equipped, and they eventually collapsed, surviving only when they did not serve the whims of this 'disembedded foundationalism'. It is less surprising that they failed to do what they were not equipped to do than that they held up for as long as they did. How do we account for that?

FROM MEDIAEVAL TO MODERN: DAWNING OF THE ENLIGHTENMENT IN EUROPE

An unclear divide: the mediaeval mentalité and the marks of modernity

Some accounts of modernity apply equally to the thirteenth century and to post-Enlightenment Europe. It is not surprising that some intellectual historians now push the origins of modernity further and further back into what we once with no sense of unease called the 'Middle Ages'.[1] This unclear divide has led some to say that there is no unique modernity. It is true that we need thoroughly to reassess the intricate links between modern and mediaeval, as well as the similarity between the modern

---

* Editors' note: This chapter has its origins in John Clayton's seventh Stanton Lecture. As indicated in the Appendix to Chapter 8 of this volume, part of the seventh lecture has been extracted and moved to that Appendix in congruence with Clayton's outline for *Religions, Reasons and Gods*. Clayton left this chapter unfinished. We have added a historical section and an Appendix, drawing on Clayton's research, in an attempt to render his arguments more accessible.
[1] See Amos Funkenstein, *Theology and the Scientific Imagination from the Middle Ages to the Seventeenth Century* (Princeton, 1986).

and what used to be called in our anthropological innocence 'primitive', but we should not allow ourselves to become blind to the fact that there remains a distinct difference.

The old secularization model will not do. As regards the theme of these lectures, the secularization comes not in the 'rationalization of belief' or in the giving of reasons for the existence and nature of God, but in the disembedding of those reasons from the particular religious projects of which they were an integral part, in the service of a generic God which is the God of everyone and of no one.

A distinct difference: Thomas versus Locke

Despite his anti-scholastic rhetoric and his attempt to deal directly with philosophical problems, John Locke took over many of the very distinctions that were basic to the scholastic tradition, not least the distinction between natural knowledge of God and revealed knowledge of God. Much of what Locke says on these topics seems sound enough by scholastic standards, but there is a subversive strand that marks his project off from theirs, so that that his is unmistakably modern and theirs unmistakably mediaeval. Locke held the following four propositions to be true:

1. There are two sources of true knowledge of God, reason and revelation. (Some things can be known either way.)
2. Revelation is capable of extending knowledge beyond what can be known by reason alone. (Revelation may be beyond reason.)
3. Revelation can never be contrary to reason.
4. Reason is the censor that judges what is to count as revelation.

Thomas could have accepted 1–3, but he may not have meant thereby precisely the same as Locke meant. But he would have blanched at 4: revelation is for him more reliable than reason. Where they appear to differ, reason has gone astray and must be corrected. Locke held reason to be the only licit censor of revelation. Thomas held revelation – and authority – as more certain than reason. The difference between their positions is the distance between mediaeval and modern.

Of course, it is not the case that no one in the Middle Ages espoused the view that Locke held. However, their views were by definition outside the mainstream. Within mediaeval Christianity such a view of the place of reason was regarded as sufficiently a threat to be condemned toward the end of the thirteenth century in a series of edicts against 'Averroism'.

Nor is it the case, of course, that no one in the modern period has continued to espouse the view that reason is subservient to the authority of tradition, but it must be allowed that this view cannot carry the degree of conviction in wider culture in the modern era that it most surely carried in Thomas's day.

A heightened expectation: proofs as sufficient and proofs as necessary for knowledge of gods

Traditionally, most Christian theologians (and in this respect they differed little from most of their Jewish and Muslim cousins in the Jerusalem family of religions)[2] have allowed that reason is sufficient to yield knowledge of the existence of God. Paul said as much in his letter to the Romans, and most Christian theologians have cited him in support of their own claim. Augustine thought so, as did Anselm and Thomas, and so likewise did Luther and Calvin.

But all these theologians, and virtually all others of their times, would have held that God is better known through revelation, because of the two revelation is by far the surer. Besides, some things about God and the divine purpose could be known only through revelation. Reason was for all these theologians ancillary to revelation and was never thought to be its censor. That's one difference between them and the modern expectation of reason in matters theological. But there is another, related, difference. In the modern period and from the purest of motives, natural theology came to be regarded as the 'preamble of faith' in a stronger sense, namely, as the foundation on which faith in God is grounded. Theistic proofs came to be seen not just as sufficient for true knowledge of God, but also as necessary.

From this point forward, the existence of God can be said to have become a purely philosophical question, one which a theologian qua theologian had no specific competence to answer.[3] Most surely the

---

[2] Editors' note: In the Stanton Lectures, Clayton used a distinction between the 'Benares' family of religions and the 'Jersusalem' family of religions in his comparative discussion of debate, commentary, law and logic.

[3] Editors' note: Funkenstein's *Theology and the Scientific Imagination from the Middle Ages to the Seventeenth Century* appeared in Clayton's notes in connection with this chapter. In relation to the present discussion it may well be that Clayton had in mind Funkenstein's work regarding the transition taking place in early-modern philosophy. Funkenstein discusses the shift from theological disputants being professional clergy to being laity in the early-modern period. He writes, 'Never before or after were science, philosophy, and theology seen as almost one and the same occupation' (p. 3). Funkenstein identifies several causes for this change. First, literacy increased significantly during the

theologian had no right to declare what would count as reasons in support of the existence or metaphysical character of God. For those reasons were now restricted to public, tradition-neutral reasons, not reasons that arise out of the peculiarities of individual religious traditions. Divine proofs (whatever their original purpose may have been) were pressed into the service of providing *religion in general* with universal or, as I would say, Utopian, reasons for the existence of a *generic* God. Henceforth, natural theology was tied to the fortunes of disembedded foundationalism and was expected to establish the rationality of basic religious claims without building on the *terra firma* of any tradition-specific grounds. If the enterprise succeeded, natural theology could be expected to show that belief in a generic God is justifiable to all rational beings by the same means that were proving to be so effective in the advancement of the natural and physical sciences of the early Enlightenment.

Such raised expectations were always in danger of deepening the disappointment if the proofs should be seen to fail to provide the foundations required for the edifice in question. Could such disappointment be averted?

From evidences to evolution: fading of design in Britain

In England, it was neither the cosmological proofs of the scholastics nor the ontological proofs of the Cartesians that held dominion. In this green and pleasant land, it was instead the design argument, as articulated by Samuel Clarke and a host of others, each struck with the wondrous order and marvellous beauty of nature, the cause of which could be no less than divine. In histories of philosophy, it is common to take as one's examples

sixteenth century, producing an educated lay public. Second, the Protestant rule of faith – *sola scriptura* – encouraged lay theology. Third, while Aristotelianism had held to the principle that each discipline has its own proper method, new ideas began to emerge about methods of enquiry. Funkenstein observes:

What was a methodological sin to Aristotle became a recommended virtue in the seventeenth century. Since then we have been urged to transport models from mathematics to physics and from physics to psychology or social theory. The ideal of a system of our entire knowledge founded on one method was born . . . The ideal of one, unified system of knowledge could hardly exclude theological matters, down to Spinoza's treatment of God *more geometrico.* These are some of the reasons why God ceased to be the monopoly of theologians even in Catholic quarters. (p. 6)

This goal of articulating a universal method of acquiring knowledge, combined with the cultural influence of Protestantism, went a long way toward constructing the tradition-neutral space within which early-modern discourse about God would take place. Moreover, the British Act of Uniformity (1662), which removed many dissenting ministers from their posts, aided in producing an educated laity concerned with theological matters (e.g. John Ray).

from the canon the writings of Clarke or Butler, on the one hand, and those of Hume, on the other, to narrate the fate of the design argument in Britain.

These are philosophically unimpeachable choices, but history cannot be relied upon to take advice from philosophers who are left to flap their wings when the day is done and Evensong has been sung. And it is one of history's ironies that the classical defence of the design argument, by the Archdeacon of Carlisle, was published over a generation after its classical refutation by Hume. Moreover, that proof continued to flourish throughout the length and breadth of Britain, despite the cleverly crafted arguments of Hume's spokesman Philo, until an event in 1859 from which it has to this day never fully recovered, despite the care lavished on it by the finest doctors of theology Britain can summon. Why was it able to survive Hume's wounds, and why did it fail at least as a justificatory argument to survive those inflicted by Darwin? To answer that question fully would take us well beyond the limits of this lecture, but a part of that answer can be given by telling a tale that centres on three old members of Cambridge University: two former students at Christ's, William Paley and Charles Darwin, and a former Master of Trinity, William Whewell, a native of Lancaster, who became Vice-Chancellor of the University and (like the current holder of that office)[4] served as a Commissioner during one of the periodic reforms that British Governments like to inflict on higher education. Whewell is reputed to have agreed to become a Commissioner in order to ensure that nothing was agreed that would have any effect whatever on Cambridge.[5]

EVIDENCES OF DESIGN: WILLIAM PALEY (1743–1805)

Paley eclipses Hume's 'classic refutation'

The classical statement of the design argument was published more than a generation after its classical refutation. Moreover, that classical statement of that argument by William Paley for a good half-century can be said to have eclipsed that earlier classical refutation by David Hume. How is that to be accounted for? There is a social explanation, which gives part of the story (and a vital part, too), but it is not in my view sufficient to explain entirely the continuing success of Paley's proof.

---

[4] Editors' note: At the time the Stanton Lectures were delivered in 1992.
[5] Today Whewell is most likely remembered for the likeness of him in Trinity College Chapel.

The social cohesion of a designer universe

(a) Place of natural theology tradition in Great Britain

Editorial addition *Clayton held that certain aspects of Paley's popular articulation of natural theology, as well as the survival of the design argument after Hume's devastating philosophical critique, are better understood when placed against the prevailing tradition of natural theology in Great Britain. That is, Clayton emphasized the intellectual as well as the social conditions of possibility for the vitality of natural theology in the eighteenth and nineteenth centuries. The next two sections, about John Ray and Joseph Addison and Hume and his critics, written primarily by Thomas D. Carroll, develops themes found in notes and research notebooks belonging to Clayton. While the voice belongs to the editors of the present volume and draws on additional research undertaken by Carroll, the ideas are substantially Clayton's.*

THE EARLY-MODERN DISCOURSE OF NATURAL THEOLOGY:
JOHN RAY AND JOSEPH ADDISON

Over one hundred years before William Paley wrote the *Natural Theology* (1802), a nonconformist botanist and naturalist, John Ray (1627–1705), argued for the existence of God on the basis of detailed observations of adaptation of species to their environments in his highly influential work *The Wisdom of God in the Works of Creation* (1691). A contemporary of John Locke, Ray embraced the new ideas about scientific methods emerging out of seventeenth-century British natural philosophy. Although many of his works were concerned primarily with plant and insect life, he considered *The Wisdom of God* to be his magnum opus. In this text, Ray makes the connections between investigation of the natural world and awareness of God's intelligence and concern for creation.

The Wisdom of God went through four editions during the remaining fourteen years of Ray's life, expanding from 249 pages in 1691 to 464 pages in the 1704 edition; the table of contents itself went through considerable amplification, from a single page in the first edition to a thoroughly detailed thirteen pages by the fourth. The changes between editions involved adding observations on various features of the natural world. Biographer Charles Raven writes, 'In 1691 the work had been an experiment. The rapid demand for new editions had given him the opportunity to develop and enrich the theme so that the book became a storehouse of data covering the whole field of contemporary science and containing many points, especially of his own observing, which are startlingly modern in character.'[6] A key area of focus, however, was design apparent in the phenomena under study: Ray lists observations on vegetables, flowers, grains, birds, fish, insects, biological processes – including pro-creation, the human body itself, and stellar objects. Raven writes of Ray's highly influential text: 'The novelty of the book consists in the fact that Ray turns from the preliminary task of identifying, describing and classi-fying to that of interpreting the significance of physical and physiological processes, studying the problems of form and function and of adaptation to environment, and observing behavior and recording the achievements of instinct.'[7] Unlike the natural theology of a Newton or a Clarke, the persuasiveness of the case presented lay not so much in rigorous abstract reasoning as in the numerous and detailed observations of adaptation of species to their respective environments.

Ray intended his text to be generally accessible to the reading public, and to this text he brought both his vigorous religious devotion[8] and broad experience as a naturalist. His appetite for knowledge is revealed through his extensive travels to nearly every county in England, Scotland and Wales to collect plant specimens and to Continental Europe, where he encountered fossilized remains of aquatic life in mountainous terrain. Also illuminating in this regard is his correspondence with other natural-ists (e.g. Sir Hans Sloane), in which observations – and sometimes local specimens – were traded.

Less than a decade after Ray's death, Joseph Addison (1672–1719), politician and literary figure, was involved in 'educating' the public via periodicals such as *The Tatler* and *The Spectator*. Addison was active in British Government, serving for a time as an official in Ireland and later as Britain's Secretary of State. However, from his student days at Oxford, he developed a love for poetry and continued writing poems in his spare time, even while a diplomat.

Peter Smithers, in *The Life of Joseph Addison*, writes that Addison 'set to work upon a book defending the fundamentals of Christianity. This

[6] Charles Raven, *John Ray, Naturalist: His Life and Works* (Cambridge, 1986), p. 476.
[7] *Ibid.*, pp. 452f.
[8] Ray's religious identity is something of a mystery to historians since he famously declined to agree to the conditions of the Act of Uniformity of 1662, the result of which was his being barred from teaching at Trinity College, Cambridge. This would seem to align Ray with the nonconformists, but his lack of any overt association with movements such as Puritanism make it difficult to write definitively about his religious views. However, it can perhaps be said that he took his Christian faith very seriously, as even a glance at *The Wisdom of God* suggests. For more on Ray's religious identity, see Susan McMahon, 'John Ray (1627–1705) and the Act of Uniformity 1662', *Notes Rec. R. Soc. Lond.* 54/2 (2000), 153–78.

was the product of a resolve to spend the years of retirement in the study of religion and, as Tickell reports, in writing divine poetry.'[9] However, Addison's health deteriorated rapidly in the last year of his life. Nevertheless, *The Evidences of the Christian Religion* (1730), though incomplete, was published posthumously. Originally intended for a popular audience, his posthumous *Evidences* offered a rather strong polemic against the evils and ignorance of atheism. Interestingly, Addison sees design of a sort – providence – in the workings of the history and development of Christianity:

It happened very providentially to the honour of the Christian religion, that it did not take its rise in the dark illiterate ages of the world, but at a time when arts and sciences were at their height, and when there were men who made it the business of their lives to search after truth, and sift the several opinions of Philosophers and wise men, concerning the duty, the end, and chief happiness of reasonable creatures.[10]

Elsewhere in Addison's life, we can see an interest in design of the natural world. In 1712, he asked William Whiston, an astronomer and mathematician, recently of Cambridge, to give a series of lectures on astronomy in London. It was during this time that Addison wrote his famous ode 'The Spacious Firmament', which was soon afterwards published in *The Spectator* and included later in the posthumous *Evidences*.

The writings of Ray and Addison display a recurrent theme worth noting in early-modern discourse of natural theology in Britain. This theme is the interweaving of design in natural history with design (i.e. providence) in human history. This connection was made in a variety of ways. We see in Addison an interest in disseminating information about order in the natural world for use in supporting the current social order. In criticizing atheists, infidels and freethinkers, Addison argued that such deviants were basing their thought upon ignorance. The original freethinkers, the ancient pagan philosophers, were neutral in debates between the Christians and Jews in antiquity. Addison writes, 'The heathen converts, after having travelled through all human learning, and fortified their minds with the knowledge of arts and sciences, were particularly qualified to examine these prophecies with great care and impartiality, and without prejudice or prepossession.'[11] Contrary to the activity of his

[9] Peter Smithers, *The Life of Joseph Addison*, 2nd edn (Oxford, 1968), pp. 436–7.
[10] Joseph Addison, *The Evidences of the Christian Religion . . . to which are Added Several Discourses against Atheism and Infidelity, and in Defence of the Christian Revelation, etc.* (London, 1730), p. 27.
[11] *Ibid.*, p. 74.

contemporary freethinkers, Addison held that genuine freethinking took place in antiquity among the pagan philosophers. The contrast with contemporary sceptics is remarkable: 'I cannot bear mentioning a monstrous species of men, who one would not think had any existence in nature, were they not to be met with in ordinary conversation, I mean the Zealots in Atheism.'[12] Emphasizing the ignorance at the heart of atheism and infidelity, Addison writes:

I would fain ask of one of these bigoted Infidels, supposing all the great points of Atheism, as the causal or eternal formation of the world, the materiality of a thinking substance, the mortality of the Soul, the fortuitous organization of the body, the motion and gravitation of matter, with the like particulars, were laid together and formed into a kind of Creed, according to the opinions of the most celebrated Atheists; I say, supposing such a Creed as this were formed, and imposed upon any one people in the world, whether it would not require an infinitely greater measure of faith, than any set of articles which they so violently oppose.[13]

Atheism is here depicted as wilful ignorance and resistance to the most reasonable doctrines of Christianity.

Addison was neither the first nor the last to articulate a connection between order in natural and human history; before him, such a connection is also found in the work of seventeenth-century theologian and naturalist John Wilkins. Biographer Barbara J. Shapiro remarks of Wilkins, 'The doctrine of Providence made men cheerful and thankful in times of mercy; in times of suffering it should make them patient and submissive. The doctrine of Providence, as propagated by Wilkins, had many affinities with Stoicism, and was a favorite of those influenced by Roman thought.'[14]

THE PLACE OF HUME AND OF HIS CRITICS IN THE HISTORY OF NATURAL THEOLOGY IN BRITAIN

As in the companion chapters on early-modern thought about God in France and Germany, Clayton argues in the present chapter that the gradual displacement of theistic arguments from their tradition-specific uses is a story that runs parallel to the eventual emergence of atheism as a live intellectual option. During the second half of the seventeenth and the first half of the eighteenth centuries, British tracts and tomes on natural

---

[12] *Ibid.*, p. 222.   [13] *Ibid.*, p. 224.
[14] Barbara J. Shapiro, *John Wilkins (1614–1672): An Intellectual Biography* (Berkeley, 1969), p. 70.

theology were a means of presenting naturalist enquiry; sometimes these texts became invectives against the feared emergence of atheism. With the publication of David Hume's *Philosophical Essays concerning Human Understanding* (1748), later receiving the title *An Enquiry concerning Human Understanding*, a relatively open debate begins to emerge on the adequacy of the evidence for belief in a God.[15] Nevertheless, while Hume is remembered as a pivotal figure in the debate over natural theology, the amount of work being written in defence of natural theology far outweighs that challenging it during this time. Hume's posthumous *Dialogues concerning Natural Religion* (1779) would one day be widely recognized for its devastating criticisms of the argument from design, but that day, as Clayton's research suggests, was yet somewhat distant.

Hume (1711–76), of course, needs little introduction, but perhaps this study will suggest some reason for reconsidering the circumstances in which Hume's work achieved the canonical role in modern philosophy it now enjoys. Clayton's research provides reason to question Hume's pre-eminent role in the philosophical discourse of *his day* with respect to natural theology, as well as in the decades immediately following his death. Hume's status as a canonical voice in the history of modern philosophy, and as the pre-eminent critic of the design argument, seems to unfold gradually. The story suggested by Clayton's research points to other reasons lying behind the resilience of natural theology, a resilience which will be explored in the following section of the present chapter.

Hume's *Dialogues concerning Natural Religion* were published posthumously in 1779 by his nephew, also named David Hume. This is a well-known part of Hume's story: approaching his death, Hume secured in his will that if Adam Smith (to whom the job of publishing the *Dialogues* had been left) had not in fact published the dialogues within two years, the duty would fall to Hume's nephew. However, what is striking is the

---

[15] It is not as if early-modern European philosophers had not previously raised concerns about the evidence for certain classes of religious beliefs. John Locke's Latitudinarian-influenced philosophy and its criticisms of extra-biblical miracle accounts come to mind here as an early forerunner in some respects of Hume's sceptical philosophy. Nevertheless, the preponderance of religious nonconformists, deists and perhaps atheists by Hume's time had *begun* to shift the intellectual terrain from one slanted toward the authority of the Church of England to one in which the evidence, whatever it might be, would be the arbiter of truth. As will be seen in the present discussion, the emergence of disembedded foundationalism was by no means universal in its progression; thinkers in different quarters recognize it at different points in the development of philosophy, theology and natural science as the venue in which knowledge-claims are to be debated.

irregularity of the publishing history of this now classic text during the first century of its public existence.[16]

In 1907, Bruce M'Ewen republished the *Dialogues*, along with an extensive introduction to the text. In this introduction, M'Ewen intriguingly observes:

In professing to call attention to this forgotten work of the great Scottish philosopher, one cannot help noticing how very similar the reception accorded to it by the outside world has been to its treatment at the hands of the author himself. During his lifetime he kept it in the safe obscurity of his study drawer, where it lay until the day of his death.[17]

It may be rash to refer to the *Dialogues* as 'forgotten', given the discussion, albeit brief, Thomas Henry Huxley offers of the text in his book on Hume (1878/1881). However, the text appears to have been neither well known nor widely respected during much of the nineteenth century.[18]

All of this seems to support the observation of Green and Grose (who reissued the *Dialogues* in conjunction with a republication of *Hume's Works* in 1874/1876) that 'Although perhaps the most finished of its author's productions, it has not excited general attention. There seems to be a deep-seated reluctance to discuss such fundamental questions.'[19]

---

[16] It is difficult to trace the circumstances of this initial publication as no publisher is listed on the title pages of the first or second editions (both 1779), although Norman Kemp Smith notes that the first edition was 'known to have been published by Robinson' and that the third edition (1804), a reissue of the second except for a modified title page, identifies Thomas Hughes as the publisher of the second edition (David Hume, *Hume's Dialogues concerning Natural Religion*, edited with an introduction by Norman Kemp Smith (Oxford, 1935), p. xii). Kemp Smith adds: 'As to the reasons for this change of printer and publisher in the very year of the appearance of the first edition, we have no information.' After that initial year of publication, the *Dialogues* were republished in 1780 (French), 1781 and 1787 (German), 1793 as part of a collection called *Essays and Treatises*, 1824/1826 included in the collection of his *Philosophical Works*, 1874/1876 in a collection *Philosophical Writings* edited by Green and Grose, and 1875 in German and also in English. Four more editions are published through the 1880s and 1890s. Very few of these sources provide any editorial commentary on the *Dialogues*, despite the fact that reissued editions of the *Enquiries* or the *Treatise* included introductory commentary. The irregularity of these editions is all the more striking when compared with the frequent reissuing of Paley's *Natural Theology* throughout the first sixty years of the nineteenth century.

[17] *Hume's Dialogues concerning Natural Religion*, with an introduction by Bruce M'Ewen (Edinburgh, 1907), p. vii.

[18] M'Ewen observes in connection with this point:

As a separate work, it has appeared once in England in 1875, when it was used as one of a series of brochures issued privately in London by a Mr. T. Scott in the interests of a Society of Freethinkers. It is not too much to say that, with the exception of this reprint, unworthy in itself, and by reason of the strongly biased remarks which introduce it 'to the reading public', it has been completely ignored by those who have undertaken to supply English libraries of the past century with ready means of access to Hume's far-reaching speculations. (p. xiii)

[19] T. H. Green and T. H. Grose, eds., *Hume's Works*, III, p. 80. Cited in M'Ewan, *Hume's Dialogues*, p. xiv.

The *Dialogues* were clearly known by many British philosophers and theologians in the eighteenth century (George III had a copy in his library), and Hume's trusted inner circle knew of and dreaded for decades the prospect of their publication. Furthermore, after their posthumous publication, the *Dialogues* attained considerable notoriety in German philosophical circles as Johann Georg Hamann translated the work in 1780.[20] Kant was preparing his first *Critique* shortly after reading the *Dialogues*, which he refers to explicitly in the conclusion to his *Prolegomena to any Future Metaphysics* (1783).

Nevertheless, the public response to Hume's *Dialogues* in Britain seems not to have been equal to their present esteem in the history of philosophy. Several features of eighteenth-century criticism of Hume on religion become evident. First, the amount of criticism devoted to the essay 'On Miracles' is considerably greater than that dealing with the *Dialogues*. Second, the interest in 'On Miracles' is not displaced by critical interest in the *Dialogues*. It seems that the *Dialogues* were perceived to be an additional example of Hume's sceptical critique of religion, but that the posthumous text was not taken to supersede 'On Miracles' in terms of its importance as a target for Christian apologists. Third, the amount of critical attention given to the *Dialogues* is at least to some extent at odds with conventional accounts of the impact of Hume and the *Dialogues*. James Fieser, who has reissued in two volumes early editions of some initial responses to Hume's writings on religion,[21] remarks on the response to the *Dialogues*:

When Hume's *Dialogues* was published . . . at least six reviews of that work appeared, the majority of which were very critical. Throughout the eighteenth and nineteenth centuries, books, pamphlets and journal articles appeared that analysed different parts of the *Dialogues*, but the most systematic studies of the work only appeared later in the twentieth century.[22]

Besides Joseph Milner, Joseph Priestley, Thomas Hayter and a few others there do not seem to have been many British philosophers who wished to engage the book directly. While polemical texts criticizing Hume's views on religion are published during this time, a greater number of such texts are concerned with his essay 'On Miracles' from

---

[20] Although Kant urged Hamann to publish his translation, Hamann demurred; another translation, by K. G. Schreiter (Leipzig, 1781), was under way to be published soon.
[21] See James Fieser, ed., *Early Responses to Hume's Writings on Religion*, 2 vols. (Bristol, 2001 and 2005).
[22] *Ibid.*, I, p. xx.

the first *Enquiry* than with his critique of the design argument in the *Dialogues*.[23] Fieser writes on this matter:

The first early response to 'Of Miracles' appeared in 1749 by Philip Skelton, and a steady stream of responses has continued to the present time. The longest of these were by William Adams (1752), John Leland (1755), and George Campbell (1762). Although Hume avoided responding to his critics as a matter of principle, he nevertheless kept track of printed criticisms as they appeared. In the last decade of his life he wrote 'I cou'd cover the Floor of a large Room with Books and Pamphlets wrote against me' . . . Hume told Richard Kirwan that 'twenty-two answers had been made [to 'Of Miracles'], hinting, that if any of them had been satisfactory any other would have been judged superfluous' . . . In addition to works devoted exclusively to 'Of Miracles', critics of Hume's other writings on religion routinely included brief attacks on that essay.[24]

A noteworthy example (mentioned above) of the wide interest in Hume's attack on the credibility of miracle reports is found in George Campbell's *A Dissertation on Miracles* (1762/1797). Campbell's *Dissertation* is concerned solely with the irreligious arguments Hume puts forward in the first *Enquiry*; however, even in the later editions, while he takes time to observe his own correspondence with Hume following the publication of the 1762 edition, there is no mention of the *Dialogues*.

Another critic of Hume's, Samuel Vince, Professor of Astronomy and Experimental Philosophy at Cambridge, wrote his text *The Credibility of Christianity Vindicated, In Answer to Mr. Hume's Objections* in 1798, just four years before Paley's *Natural Theology*. In this text, Vince explores all of the themes previously identified as pertaining to the discourse of natural theology in Britain. He connects design with providence, considers natural theology to be the last recourse to save atheists from their eternal punishment, and yet agrees that the burden of proof is upon the

---

[23] Indeed, this preoccupation with Hume's treatment of miracles continues into the nineteenth century. In *Study of the Evidences of Christianity* (1860), Baden Powell, in discussing the difficulties Mr Darwin's hypothesis spells for Christian belief, discusses at length the use of miracle reports in evidentialist arguments. Even in light of the developing evolutionary paradigm, Powell referred to Hume as a critic of the credibility of miracle reports, not as a critic of the design argument. Perhaps this strong focus on the role of miracles as evidence for the reliability of revealed theology stems in part from Locke's early influential appeal to miracles in his *The Reasonableness of Christianity*. But Locke's exploration of the epistemology of miracle reports was itself informed by disputes between Protestants and the Catholic Church over which version of revealed theology should be deemed trustworthy. It is noteworthy too that in one of the two second editions (1779) of the *Dialogues* in the collection of the British Library, Hume's text is bound with a text preceding it which, while defending the design argument, offers a criticism of Hume's arguments not against design but against the reliability of miracle reports.

[24] Fieser, ed., *Early Responses*, p. xix.

Christian in defending the faith. To this apologetic end, while Vince considers Hume's objections to the trustworthiness of miracle reports, he ultimately thinks that natural theology is the proper arena for bringing atheists back into the fold. Vince writes:

If the Christian Religion be true, that is, if it be the will of God communicated to man, and intended, from its first promulgation, to be a law for future ages, it's evidence will undoubtedly rest upon such proofs as are always sufficient to produce conviction to every sincere and impartial enquirer; for otherwise, we must suppose that God requires our belief, without reasonable evidence to command it.[25]

Once again highlighting the connection between natural theology and providence, Vince appeals to Addison's argument that the evidence in antiquity was overwhelming; that this evidence may be missing today does not impugn belief in the Christian revelation. If we honour the ancient philosophers, then we are to honour their judgment in deeming Christianity reasonable and true. Vince writes:

Christianity must therefore have been first received from a full conviction of the truth of the miracles said to have been wrought; it did not owe it's establishment to the persuasions of philosophers and oraters, or to the influence of civil or military power, but *altogether* to the force of its own evidence . . . The very extraordinary manner in which the world was converted to Christianity, stands an everlasting monument of its truth; and seems intended by Providence as an argument to future generations of it's divine authority.[26]

Among those who responded to Hume's critiques of religion, comparatively few actively engaged the thought contained in the *Dialogues*. One is left wondering why what is now commonly accepted as a philosophical classic inspired so little criticism from those who would have had such a stake in its conclusions. One might first wonder if the text was widely read during this period, and if so, whether it was considered to be as much of a threat to established religion and social order as Hume's argument against the reliability of testimony about miracle reports was taken to be. After all, the reliability of miracle reports had been used in apologetic theology to justify belief in the truths of revealed religion. For published texts criticizing Hume during the last two decades of the eighteenth century, the periodic absence of Hume's *Dialogues* from consideration in texts

---

[25] Samuel Vince, *The Credibility of Christianity Vindicated, In Answer to Mr. Hume's Objections* (Cambridge, 1798), p. 1.
[26] *Ibid.*, p. 25.

otherwise devoted to challenging Hume's criticisms of religion should be surprising to contemporary scholars who might otherwise consider the *Dialogues* to have been Hume's most important work dealing with natural theology.

Criticism of Hume's *Dialogues* during this period tends to centre around the following issues. First, Hayter, Priestley and Milner all identify the character of Philo as being Hume's true voice, despite cues Hume offers perhaps to subvert this reading. Second, all three question Hume's character in the course of or as part of their critical arguments; this will prove philosophically significant if any of them were able to connect cultivation of virtue with the quest for knowledge of divine matters. However, one does not get the sense that these early critics of Hume fully understood the impact that Hume's criticism of design would have on later generations of philosophers and theologians.

In *Gibbon's Account of Christianity Considered: Together with some Strictures on Hume's Dialogues concerning Natural Religion* (1781), Joseph Milner handles two critics of religion, but Milner seems to consider Gibbon's history of antiquity to be a greater threat to Christianity than Hume's philosophical arguments. Gibbon's history presents a considerable obstacle to the idea of there being a divinely ordered historical order. When Milner addresses Hume, he identifies part of the problem Hume has made for design arguments: 'Mr. Hume calls those who represent goodness in God of the same nature as in man, by the hard name of *Anthropomorphites*.'[27] However, Milner does not seem to see what a problem this poses to the argument from design:

A hard name weighs little with those whom reason governs rather than fancy. Scepticism should know some bounds. Justice and goodness are what they are in Spirit or in Man; and injustice and malice must be detestable in either: Our feelings tell us this; and I would no more reason with any who dispute this, than I would fight with a lion or a tiger.[28]

Rather than engaging Hume's ideas on their own rational territory, Milner dismisses Hume's manner of enquiry as impious. It is interesting to see that while some of Hume's disputants during this time will cede the territory of argument to the sceptic, Milner is unwilling to do so. Some theologians and philosophers during this period were increasingly

---

[27] Joseph Milner, *Gibbon's Account of Christianity Considered: Together with some Strictures on Hume's Dialogues concerning Natural Religion* (York, 1781), p. 208.
[28] *Ibid.*

welcoming the shift to what Clayton called in the opening chapter 'extra-religious contexts'. In other words, theologians and philosophers during the early-modern period were slowly shifting from the intra- and inter-religious contexts of the Reformation and Counter-Reformation to the extra-religious contexts of theistic argument, so commonly associated with intellectual life in secular societies.[29] And yet, in Milner, we see a figure who is unwilling to cede such territory.

Thomas Hayter, in his *Remarks on Mr. Hume's Dialogues concerning Natural Religion* (1780), focuses on a challenge to the idea of providence taken from Philo's treatment of the problem of evil. Hayter disputes the facts of suffering, arguing in defence of the idea of providence:

Without however, pressing the Philosopher either with his character or declarations, let us look abroad into the world, and see whether the want of 'ecstasy and rapture' be very generally and seriously deplored. That part of mankind, which is engaged in constant employment, and which possesses at the same time either a competence or at worst a bare sufficiency of necessities, comprehends probably near two thirds, at all events half of the human race. Now amongst this very large body it is much to be doubted if the scarcity of 'ecstasy and rapture' has, ever since the creation, been the transient occasion of a single sigh. These contented mortals dream not of raptures, but enjoy satisfaction: they have not the word ecstasy in their mouths, but solid tranquility in their hearts: they wish not to be angels, and are happy men: they have not yet schooled themselves into discontent: nor learnt the sublime science of becoming metaphysically miserable.[30]

In reinforcing the social order with the ideal of providence, natural theologians and religious apologists repeatedly suggest that those who question the goodness of the natural or social order are ignorant. This is in line with the mode of anti-atheistic polemics previously seen with Addison: that supposed atheists are ill-informed.

Priestley (1733–1804) offers a more subtle criticism of Hume,[31] but this criticism still retains the larger format of arguing that the atheist is

---

[29] See Chapter 1 above for Clayton's use of the categories intra-religious and inter-religious contexts.

[30] Thomas Hayter, *Remarks on Mr. Hume's Dialogues concerning Natural Religion* (Cambridge, 1780), pp. 17–18.

[31] By a considerable margin, Clayton took the most note of Priestley among Hume's critics; therefore, the following discussion will reflect some of the depth of Clayton's reflections. Priestley is an unusual figure, at once exemplifying the thesis of the present essay and also connecting the present discussion with that of Chapter 2: 'Thomas Jefferson and the Study of Religion'. Priestley is remembered mostly for being a dissenting minister, an early figure in the development of Unitarianism, and an influential chemist. Priestley discovered oxygen in 1774, although this is questioned by some because of his acceptance of the theory of phlogiston. He was associated with a circle of scientists called the Lunar Society, which included among others James Watt and Erasmus Darwin. Priestley's theological writings not only criticize atheism and support theistic belief, but

approaching the enquiry in an incorrect manner: Hume's criticism of design may be fine as far as it goes, but he neglects to approach the question of God's existence from the proper perspective. In his early work, including particularly the first part of his *Letters to a Philosophical Unbeliever* (1780), Priestley develops an overarching argument against atheism. Despite arguing against atheism, Priestley clearly has more intellectual respect for it than did Addison, or for that matter many of Priestley's contemporaries.

In the *Letters*, Priestley distinguishes between two varieties of atheism, practical and speculative.[32] He writes:

> [I]t is very possible that a merely *nominal believer* in a God may be a *practical atheist*, and worse than a mere speculative one, living as *without God in the world*, intirely of his being, perfections, and providence. But still nothing but *reflection* is wanting to reclaim such a person, and recover him to a proper dignity of sentiment, and a propriety of conduct; whereas an atheist thus sunk has not the same *power of recovery*. He wants both the *disposition* and the necessary *means*. His mind is destitute of the latent *seeds* of future greatness.[33]

A practical theist is one who engages the question of God's existence and nature from the standpoint of one deeply concerned with the answer; to approach the question from a disinterested standpoint would be foolish for Priestley. Priestley develops a philosophy of mind influenced by Dr Hartley – whose psychology Priestley prefers to Hume's:

> In infancy we feel nothing but what affords us for the moment; but *present feelings* bear a less and less proportion to the general mass of sensation, as it may be called, consisting of various elements, the greatest part of which are borrowed from the *past* and the *future*; so that, in our natural progress in intellectual improvement, all temporary affections, whether of a pleasurable or of a painful

---

also seek to undermine the Trinitarian Christian thought of the established Anglican Church. His sympathies with the French Revolution angered some in the town of Birmingham, where he was a minister at a local dissenting parish; in 1791 he fled the town following riots in which a mob burned both his home and laboratory. After these events, he found himself shunned by members of the Royal Society, and reluctantly, he moved to America in 1794. Despite the loss of his wife during the last decade of his life, these years in a kind of exile were not without value as it was during this time that he made contact with Thomas Jefferson. Correspondence between Priestley and the soon-to-be President show evident regard: Jefferson took particular interest in Priestley's late tract 'Socrates and Jesus Compared' (1803), a copy of which was in Jefferson's library, and Priestley again and again shows sympathy in his writings with an ideal of a public space for enquiry and debate where no religion has any unearned advantage over another.

[32] Clayton recorded this fact in his notebook with great interest.

[33] Joseph Priestley, *Letters to a Philosophical Unbeliever. Part I. Containing an Examination of the Principal Objections to the Doctrines of Natural Religion and Especially those Contained in the Writings of Mr. Hume* (Bath, 1780), pp. xii–xiii.

nature, will come at length to be wholly inconsiderable; and we shall have, in a greater degree than we can at present conceive, an equable enjoyment of the whole of what we *have been*, and *have felt*, and also of what we have a confident *expectation of being* and of feeling, in future. Our progress, however, in this intellectual improvement is capable of being accelerated, or retarded, according as we accustom ourselves to reflection, or live without it. For certainly, though, while we retain the faculties of memory and reasoning, we cannot, whether we chuse it or not, wholly exclude reflection on the past, or anticipation of the future (and, therefore, some kind of advance in intellectual improvement, is unavoidable to all beings possessed of intellect) yet it is in our power to exclude what is of great moment, viz. All that is *voluntary* in the business; so that being, in a great measure, deaf to what is behind, and blind to what is before, we may give ourselves up to mere sensual gratifications, and, consequently, no question concerning what is *past*, or future, may interest us. In this state of mind a man may think it absurd to trouble himself either about how he came into the world, or how he is to go out of it.[34]

Continuing, Priestley writes,

This, indeed, comes within the description of a proper insanity; but then it may be justly asserted, that, in a greater or less degree, all persons who do not prize every thing according to its real value, and regulate their pursuits accordingly, are insane; though, when the degree is small, it passes unnoticed and when the consequences are inconsiderable, it is far from being offensive.[35]

We are shocked at a man's insanity only when it makes him inattentive to things that immediately concern him, as to the necessary means of his subsistence or support, so that he must perish without the care of others. But when the interest, though real, is *remote*, a man's inattention to it passes unnoticed. By this means it is that, without being surprised, or shocked, we every day see thousands, who profess to believe in a future world, live and die without making any provision for it; though their conduct is much more inexcusable than that of the atheist, who, not believing in futurity, minds only what is present.[36]

What we see in these passages is the construction of an epistemology holding that in order to know certain truths, one must be existentially (to use an anachronistic term) engaged with the question. Only then will the mind be in a proper place to assess the evidence. For Priestley something like the existential orientation of the epistemic enquirer is crucially important for certain kinds of enquiry, such as that which explores the nature of divinity.

This principle is deeply significant for Priestley's natural theology. Priestley writes: 'The great Book of Nature is always open before us,

---

[34] *Ibid.*, pp. vi–vii.   [35] *Ibid.*, p. viii.   [36] *Ibid.*, p. ix.

and our eyes are always open before it, but we pass our time in a kind of *reverie*, or absence of thought, inattentive to the most obvious connections and consequences of things.'[37] It is important to note here that nature does not compel belief in God.

Priestley's approach applies equally to conclusions about design in both natural and human history, a connection that is especially important for rebuffing Gibbon's critical historical work. Priestley, while devoting some of his text to Hume, focuses primarily on confronting Gibbon's history. This seems to suggest that Gibbon's historical challenge to providence was seen by Priestley as a greater threat to religious thought and order than was Hume's philosophical critique.

This factor is further supported after examining Priestley's correspondence: in particular, that with Gibbon, whom Priestley famously 'challenged' to debate.[38] In Priestley's other correspondence of the time in which he discussed the *Letters*, he mentions them in connection with Gibbon, not Hume. When Priestley does engage Hume's ideas, in Letter IX, he is dismissive of the value of Hume's thought:

With respect to Mr. Hume's metaphysical writings in general, my opinion is, that, on the whole, the world is very little the wiser for them. For though, when the merits of any question were on his side, few men ever wrote with more perspicuity, the arrangement of this thoughts being natural, and his illustrations peculiarly happy; yet I can hardly think that we are indebted to him for the least real advance in the knowledge of the human mind.[39]

Perhaps Hume's lack of actual (i.e. personal) interest in the outcome of the question of God's existence lies behind Priestley's contention that little wisdom lies in Hume's metaphysical writings. Against Hume's ideas

---

[37] *Ibid.*, p. xv.
[38] See *Theological and Miscellaneous Works of Joseph Priestley*, ed. with notes by John Towill Rutt (Bristol, 1999), vol. XVII: *Memoirs and Correspondence, 1733–1787*, pp. 533–6. Gibbon did not respond to Priestley's challenge as the latter had hoped, and the correspondence unravelled from there. At many points in his corpus, Priestley indicates the hope he has for an intellectual space free from the bias of authority. That others did not share in this hope did not seem to impede Priestley's vision: 'I myself have no opinions that I wish to shelter behind any *authority* whatever; and should rejoice to see the time, (and that time, I doubt not, as the world improves in wisdom, will come,) when the civil powers will relieve themselves from the attention they have hitherto given to all matters of speculation, and religion amongst the rest, an attention which has proved so embarrassing to the governors, and so distressing to the governed; and when no more countenance will be given to any particular mode of *religion* than is given to particular modes of *medicine*, or of *philosophy*' (*Additional Letters to a Philosophical Unbeliever* (1782), *Theological and Miscellaneous Works of Joseph Priestley*, IV, p. 412).
[39] *Theological and Miscellaneous Works of Joseph Priestley*, XVII, p. 106.

on causation and inference, Priestley argues that we can reason back from effects to causes as far as we want,

[A]nd then, feeling that it is absurd to go on in infinitum in this manner, to conclude that, whether he can comprehend it or not, there must be some uncaused intelligent being, the original and designing cause of all other beings. It is true that we cannot conceive how this should be, but we are able to acquiesce in this ignorance, because there is no contradiction in it.[40]

The modesty of the position Priestley defends would be remarkable were it not evident from other writings that he bases much upon this slender foundation. One might be excused for agreeing with his critics (such as the anonymous theist 'A Christian'[41] and the anonymous atheist 'William Hammon'[42]) that Priestley's position amounts to a tacit deism or atheism. Priestley seems to think in his many writings, both philosophical and practically religious, that one may infer the existence of God only from such a passionately engaged epistemic position. Nevertheless, Priestley saw natural theology as an enterprise that was important for the intellectual foundations of religion and that was still viable after Hume's critiques.

Apologetic theology in Britain during the eighteenth century contained an internal tension: despite the fact that opponents of atheism as different as Addison and Priestley considered atheism to be based in ignorance (of one sort or another), these apologists nevertheless thought atheism threatening enough to merit the effort of seeking to undermine its intellectual foundations. While not all of Hume's critics agreed with Priestley's opinion that Hume's thought was worthless, (e.g. George Campbell),[43] all sought to discredit his arguments because in some manner, theologians and

---

[40] *Ibid.*, p. 112.

[41] A Christian, *An Essay of the Immateriality and Immortality of the Soul, and It's Instinctive Sense of Good and Evil; In Opposition to the Opinions Advanced in The Essays Introductory to Dr. Priestley's Abridgement of Dr. Hartley's Observations on Man* (London, 1777).

[42] Priestley suspected that the name 'William Hammon' was a pseudonym [Cf. David Berman, *A History of Atheism in Britain: From Hobbes to Russell* (London, 1990), pp. 112–16]. Interestingly, the two themes of design and providence appear in Hammon's criticism as well. Hammon's argument against the idea of providence stems from the problem of evil: 'Though the deity should not interfere unless there be a worthy cause, agreeable to the Horatian rule: "Nec Deus intersit nisi dignus vidice nodus" Yet surely from the same principles it should follow that the Deity ought to interfere where there is a worthy cause . . . A particular providence must indeed prove one of these two principles, either that God was imperfect in his design, or that inert matter is inimical to the properties of God' [William Hammon, *Answer to Dr. Priestley's Letters to a Philosophical Unbeliever* (London, 1782), pp. xxix–xxx].

[43] Indeed, in so far as 'Of Miracles' inspired criticism, often from the clergy, from the time it was originally published, clearly Hume's thought was respected enough to merit such critique.

philosophers of the day recognized that Hume's arguments undercut aspects of revealed and natural religion. However, here it may be that Hume's criticism of the reliability of miracle testimony went further than his criticism of design did in challenging one of the means by which Anglicans asserted their intellectual superiority over the Roman Catholic Church, on the one hand, and the dissenting churches, on the other.

Against this background, it may be less surprising that Paley did not engage Hume's *Dialogues* in *Natural Theology*.[44] Hume was taken seriously especially by those concerned with shoring up the rationality of revealed theology or with addressing the threat of atheism. Paley wrote about natural theology for another reason altogether. In his dedicatory letter to the Hon. and Rt Revd Shute Barrington, Lord Bishop of Durham, at the beginning of his widely read *Natural Theology* (1802), Paley writes, 'In the choice of subject I had no place left for doubt: in saying which, I do not so much refer, either to the supreme importance of the subject, or to any scepticism concerning it with which the present times are charged, as I do, to its connection with the subjects treated of in my former publications.'[45] As for those former publications, they concern largely ecclesiastical matters and advice in the development of personal faith; although that personal faith may well coincide with reinforcement of the prevailing social structure of Britain – see, for example, Clayton below on Paley's pamphlet 'Reasons for Contentment'.[46] That Paley's thought should embrace order both in natural and human history should come as no great surprise in light of the history of the discourse about design in early-modern Britain.

(b) Paley more than hints at a connection between the fixed order of the natural realm and the fixed order of the social realm. He says that his main works have to do with the evidences of revealed and natural religion 'and an account of the duties that result from both'.[47] Natural theology in particular makes us open to revelation and attentive to civic duties. The idea of retribution in the next life, an idea to which he held firmly as revealed truth, can also be said to make us mindful of our civic duties and

---

[44] While Paley mentions Hume once in the *Natural Theology*, it is not in connection with design but with the question of the origin of evil in human behaviour. Paley addresses 'Of Miracles' directly in *A View of the Evidences of Christianity, In Three Parts, etc.* (London, 1794).

[45] William Paley, *Natural Theology; or, Evidences of the Existence and Attributes of the Deity, Collected from the Appearances of Nature* (London, 1802), p. vii.

[46] William Paley, *Reasons for Contentment; Addresses to the Labouring Part of the British Public* (Carlisle, 1792). See below, pp. 266–7, 315–16.

[47] Paley, *Natural Theology*, p. vii.

quiescent in the face of unequal and 'promiscuous distribution' of power and wealth in this life, by promising future order, making 'the moral world of a piece with the natural'.[48]

In a tract entitled *Reasons for Contentment; Addresses to the Labouring Part of the British Public*, the hint is made strongly, a hint that is underscored by the tract's being published in his *Works*[49] as an appendix to his volume on *Natural Theology*:

Human life has been said to resemble the situation of spectators in a theatre, where, whilst each person is engaged by the scene which passes before them, no one thinks about the place in which he is seated. It is only when the business is interrupted, or when the spectator's attention to it grows idle and remiss, that he begins to consider at all, who is before him, or who is behind him, whether others are better accommodated than himself, or whether many be not much worse. It is thus with the various ranks and stations of society. So long as a man is intent upon the duties and concerns of his own condition, he never thinks of comparing it with any other; he is never troubled with reflections upon the different classes and orders of mankind, the advantages and disadvantages of each, the necessity or non-necessity of civil distinctions, much less does he feel within himself a disposition to covet or envy any of them. He is too much taken up with the occupations of his calling, its pursuits, cares, and business, to bestow unprofitable meditations upon the circumstances in which he sees others placed. And by this means a man of sound and active mind has, in his very constitution, a remedy against the disturbance of envy and discontent. . . The wisest advice that can be given is, never to allow our attention to dwell upon comparisons between our own condition and that of others, but to keep it fixed upon the duties and concerns of the condition itself.[50]

But in case any of the labouring population are unconvinced that they should not compare their lot with that of others, Paley goes on to reassure them that the life of labour, when compared to that of the rich, is in fact better in important ways:

The wisest advice that can be given is, never to allow our attention to dwell upon comparisons between our own condition and that of others, but to keep it fixed upon the duties and concerns of the condition itself.[51] If, in comparing the different conditions of social life, we bring religion into the account, the argument is still easier. Religion smooths all inequalities, because it unfolds a prospect which makes all earthly distinction nothing. And I do allow that there are many cases of sickness, affliction, and distress, which Christianity alone can comfort.

---

[48] Paley, *A View of the Evidences of Christianity*, Part III, p. 226.
[49] William Paley, *Paley's Works; Consisting of Evidences of Christianity, Moral and Political Philosophy, Natural Theology, and Horae Paulinae* (London, 1835).
[50] *Ibid.*, p. 391.   [51] *Ibid.*, p. 392.

But in estimating the mere diversities of station and civil condition, I have not thought it necessary to introduce religion into the inquiry at all; because I contend, that the man who murmurs and repines, when he has nothing to murmur and repine about, but the mere want of independent property, is not only irreligious, but ill founded and unreasonable in his complaint; and that he would find, did he know the truth, and consider his case fairly, that a life of labour, such, I mean, as is led by the labouring part of mankind in this country, has advantages in it which compensate all its inconveniences. When compared with the life of the rich, it is better in these important respects: It supplies employment, it promotes activity. It keeps the body in better health, the mind more engaged, and, of course, more quiet. It is more sensible of ease, more susceptible of pleasure. It is attended with greater alacrity of spirits, a more constant cheerfulness and serenity of temper. It affords easier and more certain methods of sending children into the world in situations suited to their habits and expectations. It is free from many heavy anxieties which rich men feel; it is fraught with many sources of delight which they want.[52]

And, if this were not enough, he warns that changes in our natural station can only make us unhappy. And even to consider seizing higher station by force 'is not only wickedness, but folly, as mistaken in the end as in the means'.[53] Our place in society is fixed, as our order in creation is fixed, and it is fixed by the same being, our maker and our judge, who will mete out rewards and punishments with supreme fairness. Religion, it is then thought, is the ultimate guarantor of justice, 'because it unfolds a prospect which makes all earthly distinction nothing'.

The ends of Paley's argument, it would seem, must include some reference to the political order. And it would be tempting to try to make his blatant linkage between the divinely ordained social order and the divinely ordained natural order in the decades after Revolution in France and rumours of impending revolution at home the explanation of why Paley's designer universe was preferred to Hume's uncertain universe, with its irrational overtones and possibly anarchic political implications. Not all temptations should be succumbed to so easily; and this is one that I think we ought to resist, not because it does not form part of the picture, but because it might claim to be the whole explanation.

For Paley, if read with a view to determining what job or jobs his arguments are intended to do, it becomes clear that his intended audience is more nearly fellow believers than it is real or imagined sceptics concerning the existence of God. Paley's arguments are more nearly expressive of a faith already present, a detailing of the intricacies of the designer

---

[52] *Ibid.*, pp. 402–3.   [53] *Ibid.*, p. 403.

universe for those who already believe that it exhibits at every point the work of a divine hand. I do not deny its partially apologetic intent, but I question whether this is the reason why it [*Natural Theology*] went through so many printings and was read by so many people in the first half of the nineteenth century.[54] It was more nearly its ability to express what the faithful already believed that occasioned its great success. But this in itself does not account for its having eclipsed the impact of David Hume's critique of natural theology.

The other reason for generations of the British reading public preferring Paley to Hume comes, I think, in part from Hume's failure in the *Dialogues* to offer an alternative analogy to the teleological model defended by Paley.[55] By 'failure to offer', I do not of course mean 'failure to mention', for other candidates he mentions aplenty, not least through the mouth of his spokesman, Philo, 'the careless sceptic' in the *Dialogues*. But, precisely because he is a 'careless sceptic', Philo does not commit himself to or defend any of them: their job is to show that the designer analogy has no intrinsic authority. But in the end, it is the superior analogy that wins the day, not doubts about the authority of analogical reasoning. Darwin, like Paley but unlike Hume, defends an alternative analogy, an analogy which has come to be compelling, so that we now find it difficult to see the biological world in any other way. His analogy has for our time the kind of compelling obviousness that Paley's may have had for his.

Hume's critique of the design argument was not sufficient to persuade that design is inadequate, in part because he failed to produce a compelling alternative analogy that would be seen as an alternative account. But that is precisely what Darwin in effect did, and this immediately was perceived to be what he had done because of the structural parallels between his account and Paley's own account. The result was that new

---

[54] Editors' note: Further support for Clayton's view may be found in the varieties of editions of Paley's *Natural Theology* that appeared in Britain (and also in the United States) through the first sixty years of the nineteenth century; these included editions with illustrations (William Paley, *Natural Theology; or, Evidences of the Existence and Attributes of the Deity Collected from the Appearances of Nature*, illustrated by a series of plates and explanatory notes by J. Paxton, 2 vols. (Oxford, 1826), abridged for youth as William Paley, *An Abridgement of Dr. Paley's Natural Theology: Containing Some of the most Popular Arguments of that Work, as Evidence of the Existence and Attributes of the Deity, Collected from the Works of Nature. Adapted for Youth* (London, 1820), and adapted for the blind as William Paley, *Natural Theology, etc.* (Boston, 1859)).

[55] Editors' note: George Jacob Holyoake, in his *Paley Refuted in His Own Words* (London, 1847), writes: 'Hume pointed out that all a-posteriori reasoning must fail to establish the existence of the Deity, and had he pointed out *how*, with Paley's force and fulness, there would have been little occasion for this work' (p. 10).

currency may have been given to Hume's earlier critique: so much so that if the textbooks are to be believed, there was no persuasive power left in the design argument after Hume. Not so. It was as powerful in the 1830s and 1840s as it had ever been in British public discourse. Only after Darwin, and more particularly Huxley's popularization of Darwin, did the design argument fade from public view.

EVOLUTION OF SPECIES: CHARLES DARWIN (1809–82)

As a student at Christ's, Darwin was given rooms that Paley had occupied as a student. In those days, Darwin was quite fond of Paley's writings, especially the book on *Christian Evidences*, on which Darwin was required to sit an examination. Although not examined on it, he also read and later reread the *Natural Theology*. As if there were not enough ironies already in this lecture, Darwin set out in his early researches to produce a superior version of natural theology, by removing the defects that had begun to worry him in Paley's.[56]

As a result of a scheme adopted by Senate in 1822, all Cambridge undergraduates in the fifth term of residence were required to pass an examination on one of the Gospels or the Acts in Greek, a prescribed part of a classical Greek or Latin author, and Paley's *Evidences of Christianity*.[57] In the same year, it was agreed that all candidates for a pass degree should be examined over four days on the following topics: the first two days on mathematics, the third day on Locke's *Essay concerning Human Understanding* together with Paley's *Evidences* and his *Moral Theology*, and on the final day on passages for translation from the *Iliad* and the *Aeneid*.[58]

Although he later repudiated it, Paley's style of natural theology made a deep mark on Darwin, and it is possible that he never entirely freed himself from it.[59] This is hardly surprising, given that – as my colleague John Hedley Brooke has pointed out – 'the theory of natural selection emerged through dialogue with prevailing concepts of design', with the result that 'there are certain structural continuities between the theory and natural theology which can all too easily be overlooked'.[60] For instance,

---

[56] This was an important motive in his scientific researches, one which may have delayed the discovery of what we have come to know as Darwin's theory.

[57] See Denys Arthur Winstanley, *Early Victorian Cambridge* (Cambridge, 1940), p. 68.

[58] *Ibid.*, p. 70.

[59] Editors' note: Clayton noted particularly the work of John Hedley Brooke on this matter. See Brooke's 'The Relations Between Darwin's Science and his Religion', in *Darwinism and Divinity*, ed. J. R. Durant (Oxford, 1985), pp. 40–75.

[60] *Ibid.*, p. 47.

Darwin sometimes offers solutions to questions first raised by Paley.[61] In his *Natural Theology*, Paley at one point posed the problem of species appearing and becoming extinct by chance, a view he rejects on the grounds that it would serve no conceivable purpose, and nothing happens in nature without serving some purpose. There is a sense in which one of the problems facing Darwin as he struggled toward his theory was to explain why extinction occurs, if nature is geared to the preservation of adaptation. It is also arguable that at least the rudiments of Paley's view of a harmonious and teleologically ordered universe may survive submerged in Darwin's mature theory. Even the choice of the term 'selection' introduces a certain ambiguity into Darwin's theory and makes it difficult for him in the *Origin* to avoid personifying nature as some higher intelligence that 'selects' as a human agent might select certain plants for breeding or cultivation.

None of which is to say that Darwin's thought is a form of 'natural theology' without God, so to say, but it is to suggest why a generation that found a Paley-style natural theology attractive might also find in Darwin's theory of natural selection an alternative analogy that could compete with Paley precisely where Paley is most winsome in a way that Hume could not. Darwin's theory, moreover, is seen by many as being more 'harmonious' with the new social order of industrial and urban Britain than was that more idyllic, rural order of 'happy nature' seen by Paley as exhibiting design of a divine hand that made it all. Witness, for instance, Desmond and Moore reflecting on Darwin's writing of 'The Struggle for Existence' less than two years before the *Origin* finally appeared:

A week on and he was well into 'The Struggle for Existence'. Here he would show how the variants were weeded, how endless numbers fell into the 'War of Nature'. His new theory of divergence created a chilling image. Nature became a seething slum, with everyone scrambling to get out, rushing to break from the rat-pack. Only the few survived, bettering themselves by creating new dynasties. Most remained trapped on the breadline, destined to struggle futilely, neighbours elbowing one another aside to get ahead, the weak trampled underfoot. Sacrifice and waste were endemic, indeed necessary. Nature was abortive, squandering, profligate. Her failures were discarded like the breeder's runts to rot on some domestic dump. In Victorian poor-law society, the image did not seem unduly sombre . . . Nature's depravity cried out against a noble Providence.[62]

---

[61] Editors' note: see *ibid.* for more on types of structural parallels between natural theology and Darwin's science (esp. p. 48).

[62] Adrian Desmond and James Moore, *Darwin: The Life of a Tormented Evolutionist* (New York, 1992), pp. 448–9.

The brutish quality of London's slum existence, recorded by Henry Mayhew,[63] seemed but to mimic the 'savagery beneath Nature's surface'.[64] Desmond and Moore continue:

How different from Archdeacon Paley's 'happy' nature in his *Natural Theology.* The world had been turned upside down in fifty years. Seen through Paley's rose-tinted spectacles, it was a continual summer's afternoon, with the rectory garden buzzing with contented life. But no longer. An expanding industrial society meant that more and more people were herded, hungry and angry, into factory towns. Those on the sharp end had been hammering away at Paley's image for ages. Working-class agitators had denounced Paley's pernicious justification of the status quo. George Holyoake had long ago written *Paley Refuted in His Own Words,* after his two-year-old daughter died of malnutrition . . .[65]

Darwin peered hard into nature's 'horridly cruel' face; the time had come for him too to challenge Paley, whose words he had once embraced.[66]

But the result of *The Origin of Species* was widely perceived to undermine the confidence in the design argument that had been so central in the British natural-theology tradition since at least the seventeenth century. Darwin himself, perhaps out of a sense of what it is to be a gentleman, did not choose publicly to emphasize its consequences for religious belief (but privately he was more openly agnostic, though not a fully orthodox agnostic, since he never lost the conviction that the world was designed, even if he was not sure what weight should be given to such convictions). The radical consequences of Darwin's theory were drawn and shouted publicly by Huxley, Darwin's propagandist and popularizer (who also drew parallels with Hume's earlier critique).[67]

This would seem to be the end of the story, and for someone like Richard Dawkins it is indeed the end of the story: Paley was right (as

---

[63] Editors' note: Henry Mayhew's *London Labour and the London Poor,* apparently the first study of poverty of its kind, no doubt could not be ignored because of the encyclopaedic nature of the text (three volumes published over several months in 1851). In the preface to the first volume, Mayhew writes: 'It is curious . . . as supplying information concerning a large body of persons, of whom the public had less knowledge than of the most distant tribes of the earth – the government population returns not even numbering them among the inhabitants of the kingdom; and as adducing facts so extraordinary, that the traveller in the undiscovered country of the poor must . . . until his stories are corroborated by after investigators, be content to lie under the imputation of telling such tales, as travellers are generally supposed to delight in' (p. iii).

[64] Desmond and Moore, *Darwin,* p. 449.

[65] *Ibid.,* pp. 449–50. See also Adrian Desmond's 'Artisan Resistance and Evolution in Britain, 1819–1848', *Osiris,* 2nd series, 3 (1987), 77–110.

[66] Desmond and Moore, *Darwin,* p. 450.

[67] Editors' note: This paragraph comes from Clayton's research notes, but we found it helpful to ground the current discussion.

against more sceptical critics) to think that the natural order requires an explanation, he was wrong in the explanation he offered, but Darwin provided the right and sufficient explanation for why the natural order is the way it is and not some other way. This was the moral of the story as told by Huxley, and it is the moral of the story as retold by Dawkins. But this does not explain why the natural-theology tradition has survived in these isles, so that even today – not least in this University[68] – it is strongly defended and powerfully represented.

How do we account for its persistence in this country as part of public discourse?

This is not an easy question to answer, and an impossible one to answer in the few minutes remaining: but I want to suggest the lines along which an answer might be sought.

First, one must look back at the story that has been spun and call attention to clues left lying about, but not picked up at the time. There are in fact two strands in the British tradition of natural theology that want to be distinguished, even though they are more often interlaced, double-helix-like, at any given time: I will call these strands

a. Apologetic-justificatory
b. Expressive-explanatory.

The teleological argument seems peculiarly well designed to serve these dual ends: it can be developed in detailed engagement with the prevailing scientific theory of the day,[69] and it can with appropriate evocations of awe and wonder express the believer's sense of the universe as manifesting the caring touch of the hand of God.

Sometimes the one strand dominates, sometimes the other: in the writings of most deists, the justificatory strand may predominate, whereas in the more devotional musings of a John Ray or, from the other side of the Atlantic, of a Jonathan Edwards the expressive strand is pre-eminent. It can even be sung as a hymn, as in Addison's hymn 'The Spacious Firmament', which though not, I think, much sung these days is still to be found in *Hymns Ancient and Modern* (662):

---

[68] Editors' note: This refers to Cambridge University, where Clayton delivered the Stanton Lectures.

[69] Though the teleological argument is also the most susceptible to obsolescence if scientific theory alters; but this is also one reason for its resilience: natural theology of this kind could adapt to scientific discovery in a way that the Thomistic arguments, tied as they were to Aristotle, could not easily do. So, natural theology of the teleological variety tended to become diversified, rather than destroyed by scientific advances; it survived the way natural species survive – through adaptation.

The Spacious Firmament on high,
With all the blue Ethereal Sky,
And spangled Heav'ns, a Shining Frame,
Their great Original proclaim:
Th'unwearied Sun, from day to day,
Does his Creator's Pow'r display,
And publishes to every Land
The Works of an Almighty Hand.

Soon as the Evening Shades prevail,
The Moon takes up the wondrous Tale,
And nightly to the list'ning Earth
Repeats the Story of her Birth:
Whilst all the Stars that round her burn,
And all the Planets, in their turn,
Confirm the Tidings, as they roll,
And spread the Truth from Pole to Pole.

What though, in solemn Silence all
Move round the dark terrestrial Ball?
What tho' nor real Voice nor Sound
Amid their radiant Orbs be found?
In Reason's Ear they all rejoice,
And utter forth a glorious Voice,
For ever singing, as they shine,
'The Hand that made us is Divine.'[70]

The two strands have also been interlaced in varying proportions. But what I want to suggest is that the more specifically apologetic-justificatory strand, which tries to ground belief in God in the natural order, has been more likely to suffer from the critique of a Darwin than has the expressive-explanatory strand, which begins with a prior belief in a God whose excellences are exhibited in the excellences of natural order.

What Darwin accomplished, directly or indirectly, was not so much to show that God does not exist or that the world cannot have been designed or even that the world does not display in its details the handiwork of God; what he accomplished was to undermine any confidence in the attempt to infer from the world that there must be a designer. Hume had, of course, done this by calling attention to the limits of analogical

[70] *Hymns Ancient and Modern,* revised (London, 1950), 662. See also Joseph Addison, *The Spectator,* No. 465 (23 August 1712), reprinted in *The Spectator,* edited with an introduction and notes by Donald D. Bond, IV (Oxford, 1965).

reasoning. He suggested that other analogies present themselves, though they were offered more in the sense of providing a cumulative *reductio* than in the hope that one of them might be adopted (Philo was after all a careless sceptic). But (and this is where irony enters): analogical reasoning is so firmly embedded in everyday experience (and the sheer number and detail of Paley's examples reassured those who wanted to be reassured) that it held Humean scepticism in check. Even if a necessary component in undermining confidence in design, Hume's critique did not show itself to be sufficient.

Darwin, on the other hand, was not a careless sceptic: he offered in his theory an alternative analogy which through its simplicity, its comprehensiveness and its ability to account for phenomena that were central to the Paley-argument proved in many cases compelling. Although the design argument did not simply disappear, it was able to survive only by adapting to its new environment. And the specimens that survived are much more modest life-forms than those from which they evolved: for example the name of an earlier Stanton lecturer, F. R. Tennant, comes to mind.[71]

Darwin (to use the name more as a symbol for all that came in his wake) may have closed the door on any demonstrative use of design, but it has left open the door to non-demonstrative uses, some of which are nearer to its original pre-modern impulse within religious sentiment. But there are assuredly moderns who can be cited as continuers of that

---

[71] The design argument in that older sense never recovered from Darwin. When it returned in the twentieth century by the efforts of F. R. Tennant, it came back a much more modest affair. Editors' note: Two quotations from Tennant's *Philosophical Theology* (Cambridge, 1968) are revealing in this context:

The empirically-minded theologian adopts a different procedure [from that of trying to prove the existence of a 'Real counterpart to a preconceived idea of God']. He asks how the world, inclusive of man, is to be explained. He would let the Actual world tell its own story and offer its own suggestions: not silence it while abstractive speculation, setting out with presuppositions possibly irrelevant to Actuality, weaves a system of thought which may prove to conflict with facts. (p. 78)

The forcibleness of Nature's suggestion that she is the outcome of intelligent design lies not in particular cases of adaptedness in the world, nor even in the multiplicity of them. It is conceivable that every such instance may individually admit of explanation in terms of proximate causes or, in the first instance, of explanation other than in terms of cosmic or 'external' teleology. And if it also admits of teleological interpretation, that fact will not of itself constitute a rigorous certification of external design. The forcibleness of the world's appeal consists rather in the conspiration of innumerable causes to produce, by their united and reciprocal action, and to maintain, a general order of Nature. Narrower kinds of teleological argument, based on surveys of restricted spheres of fact, are much more precarious than that for which the name of 'the wider teleology' may be appropriated in that the comprehensive design-argument is the outcome of synopsis or conspection of the knowable world. (p. 79)

tradition: Ray (1627–1705), Edwards (1703–58), and in the nineteenth century, albeit ambiguously, the Lancastrian William Whewell, who coined the term 'scientist' and invented the history and philosophy of science.

INDICATORS OF GOD: WILLIAM WHEWELL (1794–1866)

I call attention to William Whewell, the native of Lancaster who became Master of Trinity College and who was one of the most important cleric-scientists of his day, making contributions to the physical sciences, mathematics and cosmology, but also to natural theology, by means of his influential Bridgewater Treatise during the 1830s.

Both apologetic and expressive strands are interlaced in Whewell's writings, and he is often taken to be an old-style apologist of just the kind that had been made extinct by Darwin's theory. Although it is true that Paley's appeal to design is more vigorous than it had a right to be after Hume's devastating critique, Whewell's use of physico-theology may be less similar to Paley's than at first sight it appears to be. In his writings, however, it becomes clear that the justificatory or apologetic is subordinated to the expressive or devotional, almost in the older style of a Ray or an Edwards.

For instance, Whewell concluded a small volume of extracts from his massive *History and Philosophy of the Inductive Sciences* – called by him *Indications of the Creator* [1845] – with the following words, showing the way in which the justificatory use of argument is held subordinate to the expressive-devotional:

And thus, in concluding our long survey of the grounds and structure of Science, and of the lessons which the study of it teaches us, we find ourselves brought to a point of view in which we can cordially sympathize, and more than sympathize, with all the loftiest expressions of admiration and reverence and hope and trust, which have been uttered by those who in former times have spoken of the elevated thoughts to which the contemplation of the nature and progress of human knowledge gives rise . . . When we have advanced so far, there yet remains one step . . . When we are thus prepared for a higher teaching, we may be ready to listen to a greater than Bacon, when he says to those who have sought their God in the material universe, 'Whom ye ignorantly worship, Him declare I unto you.' And when we recollect how utterly inadequate all human language has been shown to be, to express the nature of that Supreme Cause of the Natural, and Rational, and Moral, and Spiritual world, to which our Philosophy points with trembling finger and shaded eyes, we may receive, with the less wonder but with the more reverence, the declaration which has been vouchsafed to us:

IN THE BEGINNING WAS THE WORD, AND THE WORD WAS WITH GOD, AND THE WORD WAS GOD.'[72]

Whewell represents the position that prior belief in God may be made stronger or more vivid by contemplating the wonders of the natural world, but not the position that a study of the natural world (or even the productions of natural theology) was sufficient – let alone necessary – to produce such belief.[73] Scientific knowledge and the sort of natural theology appropriate to it were typically spoken of by Whewell as confirmations of prior faith, not grounds for that faith. This has been borne out, too, by a recent study by my colleague John Hedley Brooke of Whewell's natural theology, a study much enriched by reference not just to Whewell's volumes large and small, but also to his sermons preached in Trinity Chapel and elsewhere, which confirm (so to speak) that for Whewell, 'propositions referring to final causes were not so much inference from facts as presuppositions of a fruitful interpretation of nature'.[74]

That is to say, our prior expectations about nature will affect what we find there, just as our prior expectations about matters religious will affect what we find there. We begin with a paradigm in terms of which we model the universe, and, though it can certainly be modified or abandoned, it is not itself an inference from observation statements.

We then ask, which God is it for Whewell that is the focus of such prior commitment? Here his philosophical works when read in the light of his sermons and *vice versa* make clear that for Whewell it is most definitely not the generic God of theism who acts as a regulative principle of his enquiry: it is in his case the God of Christianity. And the reasons that Whewell offers as reasons for thinking that the study of nature confirms such belief are in all cases reasons that are reasons for Christianity. It is not enough, he says, to say that the works of nature

impress us with wonder and admiration, and that there is in these feelings a deep religious import: – for what religion is there or what value, in any mere admiration of nature, if it in no way connects with reverence and love for a God who sees and hears us, our Redeemer and Comforter . . . the Lord *our* God.[75]

---

[72] William Whewell, *Indications of the Creator: Extracts, Bearing upon Theology, from the History and Philosophy of the Inductive Sciences* (London, 1845), pp. 169–71.

[73] Editors' note: See Appendix for some expansion on the two strands evident in Whewell's thought.

[74] John Hedley Brooke, 'Indications of a Creator: Whewell as Apologist and Priest', in *William Whewell: A Composite Portrait*, ed. Menachem Fisch and Simon Schaffer (Oxford, 1991), p. 163.

[75] William Whewell, Sermon, Sept. 1841, Whewell Papers, Trinity College Library, Cambridge University, R6 17⁴⁹, quoted in John Hedley Brooke, 'Indications of a Creator: Whewell as Apologist and Priest', p. 165.

Natural theology, I wish in conclusion to suggest, was for Whewell the public discourse in which a Christian belief in God was expressed, elucidated and explained. It was an antidote to privatization of belief in a time when theology was withdrawing into itself.[76] Ironically, there are only recently uncovered tendencies within Whewell's thought that would have allowed a different line of development, a line of development that is paradoxically both more akin to that range of uses commonly encountered in pre-modern religious thought and, at the same time, also more akin to a little-appreciated moment of Kant's thought. And I will add to this the observation of an outsider that the same can be said of the most outstanding representatives of the natural-theology tradition in Britain, past and present. The embeddedness of theistic argument within a religious tradition, to which it remains subordinate, is in my view finally what accounts for its persistence here.

The secularization comes not in the giving of reasons for the existence and nature of God but in the disembedding of those reasons from the particular religious projects of which they were an integral part in the service of a generic God which is the God of everyone in general and of no one in particular. Natural theology seems to remain healthy and vigorous in Britain well into the nineteenth century. Especially 'physico-theology' prospered under the more friendly relations between science and religion that existed in nineteenth-century Britain.

APPENDIX: EXPRESSIVIST USES OF THE DESIGN ARGUMENT IN
GREAT BRITAIN

The following appendix develops themes found in notes and research notebooks belonging to Clayton. Although the voice of the appendix belongs primarily to Thomas D. Carroll, and draws on his additional research, the ideas are substantially Clayton's.

---

[76] Editors' note: This observation by Clayton is further supported by evidence both from Whewell's sermons at Trinity College and from remarks found in texts addressed to more of a popular audience, such as his contribution to the Bridgewater Treatises, *Astronomy and General Physics Considered with Reference to Natural Theology* (1833). The privatization of religious discourse, already increasingly prevalent in French Catholic traditionalism of this period, did not emerge at this point in the British theological context. Whewell's efforts, among those of other natural theologians, were intended to illustrate natural theology for the Christian reader, not to a general, tradition-neutral public. Where his more specifically scientific and philosophical works made reference to a final cause, this seemed to reflect the intellectual endeavours of a religious man.

Clayton's use of Brooke on natural theology in Britain

In his notes for this chapter, Clayton made considerable use of the work done by John Hedley Brooke on the history of the relationship between religion and science in the context of early-modern Britain. In particular, Brooke's essay 'Why Did the English Mix their Science with their Religion?'[77] seems to have been influential.

Clayton took particular notice of the reasons Brooke thought that religion and science mixed in Great Britain. Clayton writes of Brooke's idea that the prominence and vitality of the design argument was not simply identifiable with the growth of deism: (1) some prominent naturalists used natural theology in order to defend Christianity; (2) there were resources within Protestant Christianity which allowed a prominence to be given to natural theology without making it 'the sum total of religion'. 'Protestant Christianity could be quite elastic in the scope it was prepared to give to the book of God's works.'[78] Clayton also noted the reasons Brooke provides regarding why this mixture worked in the seventeenth through early nineteenth centuries in Great Britain:

1. Natural theology was encouraged at a time when commitment to traditional religion was perceived to be weakening: 'A new form of natural theology could be a powerful resource, both for proving the rationality of Christian doctrine and for reproving those who mocked or ignored it.'[79]

2. But late-seventeenth-century scientists had another motive, in that they 'experience a sense of awe and wonder through their study of nature which could easily graduate into a religious response' (the micro-world, e.g., opened up by investigation of the microscope).[80]

3. The God of nature was approachable and could be acknowledged by all. Ray, in *Wisdom of God*, wrote that argument from created order was equally compelling, and equally accessible, to all, of whatever rank or education. 'Later naturalists who found natural theology a vehicle for promotion of science were to be less than happy with this formulation since it implied that no scientific education was necessary to decode divine wisdom. But for Ray and his generation the universality of the argument was part of its appeal.'[81]

---

[77] John Hedley Brooke, 'Why Did the English Mix their Science with their Religion?', in S. Rossi (ed.), *Science and Imagination in XVIIIth-Century British Culture* (Milan, 1987), pp. 57–78.
[78] *Ibid.*, p. 59   [79] *Ibid.*, p. 60.   [80] *Ibid.*   [81] *Ibid.*, p. 61.

4. Following a period of religious warfare, etc. natural theology 'came into prominence as a healing agent':[82] design argument survived by ambiguity, so that it could be embraced by all and sundry. This *convenience of the ambiguity of design* (Clayton's phrase) manifested itself in three ways (as articulated by Brooke in 'The Natural Theology of the Geologists: Some Theological Strata'[83]):

a. Pragmatically ambiguous: 'invoked by Christians and deists alike'.[84]
b. Philosophically ambiguous: 'had been promoted as part and parcel of philosophies of nature that were in every other respect at variance'.[85]
c. Theologically ambiguous: 'because they did not commit one to a specific doctrinal position, they could mediate between contending theologies when it was desirable to do so'.[86]

In addition to these features, Brooke discusses several other factors that may have influenced the pervasive appreciation of design in Britain. In particular, Clayton notes: 'Certain political events encouraged natural theology of a particular kind: the Revolution of 1688, removing James II from the throne, encouraged in the climate of the times a justification of the revolution in theological terms, with the result that there was a new emphasis on God's providence in history: God's will had to take priority over a doctrine of the divine right of kings.'[87]

Clayton also highlights Brooke's exploration of Roy Porter; in particular, Clayton takes interest in Porter's observation that Enlightenment goals in England 'thrive within piety'.[88] Brooke concludes from the above discussion: 'Natural theology could therefore flourish as a manifestation of that more general phenomenon of inclusiveness – especially when so many cultivators of natural history were themselves clergymen.'[89] Brooke observes that this 'does not mean there was never conflict between the interests of science and of religion', but that natural theology provided 'an acceptable vocabulary for meeting the challenge'.[90] Clayton found helpful

---

[82] *Ibid.*
[83] John Hedley Brooke, 'The Natural Theology of the Geologists: Some Theological Strata', in L. J. Jordanova and Roy S. Porter, eds., *Images of the Earth: Essays in the History of the Environmental Sciences* (Chalfont St Giles, 1979), pp. 39–64.
[84] *Ibid.*, pp. 42f.   [85] *Ibid.*, p. 43.   [86] *Ibid.*, pp. 43f.
[87] Brooke, 'Why Did the English Mix their Science with their Religion?', p. 63. Cf. Margaret Jacob, *The Newtonians and the English Revolution* (Hassocks, 1976).
[88] Roy Porter, 'The Enlightenment in England', in Roy Porter and Mikulás Teich, eds., *The Enlightenment in National Context* (Cambridge, 1981), pp. 1–18, esp. p. 6.
[89] Brooke, 'Why Did the English Mix their Science with their Religion?', p. 65.
[90] *Ibid.*, pp. 65f.

Brooke's observation that '[C]ircumstances other than scientific and philosophical fashions affected the relation, or the perceived relation, between science and religion. There was, for example, a greater pressure for men of science in England to show that their science held no terrors for religion in the decades immediately following the French Revolution than in those before.'[91] This is just the opposite of France, where Brooke draws on the work of Dorinda Outram: 'the pressure was just the opposite: "it would have been very difficult there for men of science to revive the arguments of natural theology without appearing to be supporters of the ancien régime"'.[92]

Expressivist uses of the design argument before Paley

For Paley, as for many British natural theologians in the seventeenth and eighteenth centuries, order in natural history and human history were mutually reinforcing ideas. Paley was not unusual in drawing a connection here. However, Clayton argues that this alone does not explain the prevalence of the design argument after Hume. Clayton identifies a further factor in the observation that design arguments have been used both apologetically and expressively. The purpose of this appendix is to show the recurrence of this expressivist dimension to natural theology during what has sometimes been thought of as a merely apologetic era.

We are already acquainted with John Ray from the earlier editorial addition to the present essay. However, some further examination of this early figure in British natural theology will reveal some striking expressivist dimensions to his thought, dimensions that are so striking that one would be at a loss to account for them without a thesis such as Clayton's. One biographer observes: 'A sentence from a letter to a friend is relevant: "Divinity is my Profession. The study of plants I never lookt upon as my businesse more than I doe now, but my diversion only."'[93] Yet, Ray's work was no less serious despite its diversionary nature: 'Ray's classification of plants, more than that of any other botanist of the seventeenth

---

[91] *Ibid.*, pp. 73f.

[92] *Ibid.*, p. 76. Cf. D. Outram, 'The Pure and Sensible Eye: The Man of Science and Revolutionary Culture in France', paper presented to the conference on 'New Perspectives in Nineteenth-Century Science', under the auspices of the British Society for the History of Science at the University of Kent at Canterbury, Easter, 1984.

[93] Sir Albert Charles Seward, *John Ray: A Biographical Sketch Written for the Centenary of the Cambridge Ray Club and Read, in part, at the Dinner in the Hall of Trinity College on 16 March 1937* (Cambridge, 1937), p. 21.

century, was a definite attempt to recognize and express natural affinities; he was a pioneer in the systematic treatment of animals as well as plants; he prepared the way for Linnaeus, who was born two years after Ray died.'[94] One is left with the impression that the location of Ray's naturalist work within his faith inspired him to show great care in the organization of his investigations.

The dedicatory letter for *The Wisdom of God*, to the Lady Lettice Wendy of Cambridgeshire, indicates that Ray offers the text to the family of his patron in part as a means to cope with the pain that accompanies chronic illness, a fact all the more interesting given Ray's own struggles with chronic disease (as reflected in much of his correspondence from the 1680s until his death).

Furthermore, devotion to the acquisition of knowledge permeates *The Wisdom of God*. Ray begins his text with a brief meditation on Psalm 104:24. He writes:

How Manifold are thy Works O Lord? In Wisdom hast thou made them all. In these Words are two Clauses, in the first whereof the Psalmist admires the Multitude of God's works, *How Manifold are thy Works O Lord?* In the second he celebrates his Wisdom in the creation of them; *In Wisdom hast thou made them all.*

Of the first I shall say little, only briefly run over the Works of this visible world, and give some guess at the Number of them. Whence it will appear, that upon this account they will deserve Admiration, the Number of them being uninvestigable by us; and so affording us a demonstrative Proof of the unlimited extent of the Creator's Skill, and the foecundity of his Wisdom and Power.[95]

Raven notes this dynamic in Ray's thought again and again, one imagines, in part because of Raven's own identity as an amateur naturalist who was expressing his own nonconformity to the British war effort in the 1940s. Raven writes:

There was for him nothing incongruous in seeing the objects of his study, the order of the universe, the life of plants and animals, the structure and functioning of nature, as the manifestation of the Mind of God. Indeed the wonder with which he regarded the works of creation, and the thrill which accompanied his growing insight into the processes of their growth and function, were to him, as to mankind in general, essentially religious. He found in this new approach to the physical world the awe and reverence, the release and inspiration which psalmists, poets, thinkers and explorers have always found; and though it was difficult to reconcile his discoveries with the formulae of Christian tradition it was

---

[94] *Ibid.*, pp. 23f.
[95] John Ray, *The Wisdom of God Manifested in the Works of the Creation* (London, 1691), p. 1.

impossible not to find in them a profound religious and indeed Christian significance.[96]

While Raven's biography occasionally shows signs of some enthusiasm for its subject, it is intriguing that Ray's work continued to inspire edification some 250 years after the fact. All the greater, one senses, would have been its influence in the eighteenth century.

We are already familiar with Joseph Addison's sentiments of edification evident in his ode 'The Spacious Firmament'; of course, these themes are interwoven with his apologetic moods. The two cannot be separated without distorting his thought. Addison recognized that hearing about debates over the rationality of religious faith could be unsettling. Given this reality, he recommended for the public five rules:

1. '[W]hen by reading or discourse we find ourselves thoroughly convinced of the truth of any article and of the reasonableness of our belief in it, we should never after suffer ourselves to call it into question.'[97]
2. '[L]ay up in [our] memories, and always keep by [us] in a readiness, those arguments which appear to [us] of the greatest strength, and which cannot be got over by all the doubts and cavils of infidelity.'[98]
3. Practise morality.[99]
4. Habitual adoration and worship of the Supreme Being.[100]
5. Frequent retirement from the world and meditation.[101]

It is in connection with this last rule that Addison includes 'The Spacious Firmament'. Reflecting further on the last rule, Addison writes,

The cares or pleasures of the world strike in with every thought, and a multitude of vicious examples give a kind of justification to our folly. In our retirements every thing disposes us to be serious. In courts and cities we are entertained with the works of men; in the country with those of God. One is the province of art, the other of nature. Faith and devotion naturally grow in the mind of every reasonable man, who sees the impressions of Divine Power and Wisdom in every object, on which he casts his eye. The Supreme Being has made the best arguments for his own Existence, in the formation of the heavens and the earth, and those are arguments which a man of sense cannot forbear attending to, who is out of the noise and hurry of human affairs.[102]

---

[96] Raven, *John Ray, Naturalist: His Life and Works*, p. 455.
[97] Joseph Addison, *The Evidences of the Christian Religion*, p. 232.
[98] *Ibid.*, pp. 234f.   [99] *Ibid.*, p. 235.   [100] *Ibid.*, pp. 235f.
[101] *Ibid.*, pp. 236f.   [102] *Ibid.*, p. 237.

The immediate goal of these rules is to edify faith for one whose certainty is shaken; theistic arguments, *alongside devotional and ethical practices*, serve this goal.

While Ray was associated with the nonconformists and served his God outside of official ministry (which perhaps afforded him the freedom to be the vigorous naturalist he became), Addison was an establishment figure. His writings were concerned not so much with accounting for the diversity of flora and fauna that may be encountered in the British countryside and surrounding regions. Instead, for Addison, the priority behind his work lay with instructing the public on how to behave well in the emerging modern world. His protestations against the development of atheism and his emphasis on the providential nature of history suggest divine design in the socio-political status quo in Britain, a reassuring principle with some practical benefit for people beginning to sense the coming changes associated with methodological revolutions in the natural sciences and contested sources of religious, and thus political, authority.

Hume's sceptical arguments produced a variety of responses from people of faith. While some offered yet further strident defences of the traditional design argument (e.g. Hayter, Milner), there yet were those who begin to offer counter-arguments that bring to mind fideistic apologetics. Milner writes in response to the *Dialogues*, '[T]he human mind is so totally incompetent to decide on these points, and the divine essence is so entirely removed from our comprehension, that nothing is more easy than for a man of lively imagination, unawed by the fear of God, that is to say Mr. Hume, to represent many various views of the kind; and yet as the process is carried on without any date, the whole must be, "the baseless fabric of a vision".'[103] Yet, unlike fideistic responses, which would become more popular in the late nineteenth and early twentieth centuries, Milner recognizes the need for arguments for God. First, he offers an argument from conscience: 'What renders its empire decisively great, is the little or no connection which it has with any elaborate process of reasoning. Its voice is plain and strong, not inimical to, but far superior to the voice of reason.'[104] Second, Milner argues that Hume's objections are futile. Inability to account for phenomena should not count as a reason against the reasonableness of belief in God. Being able to explain everything would lead to 'very mean and debasing conceptions of his majesty and greatness', and this would tempt one 'to think wickedly, *that God was even*

---

[103] Milner, *Gibbon's Account of Christianity Considered*, p. 220.
[104] *Ibid.*, p. 204.

such a one as himself.[105] Even here in an apologetic appropriation of scepticism, we see an emergence of the expressivist branch of natural theology: being able to explain everything could lead to pride and negatively impact one's character. Confrontation with mystery reinforces the humble epistemic position of a created being. The danger of wickedness is as much a reason against scepticism as are tradition-neutral reasons, such as the fortuitousness of the moral conscience.

The thought of Priestley also shows evidence of expressivist uses of design. The fact that he treats of both speculative and practical atheism in his *Letters to a Philosophical Unbeliever* discussed earlier suggests that he thought of Christian faith as involving far more than mere rational belief. Sources both earlier and later in his corpus also show this dimension to his thought. Central among such sources would be those he composed for the edification of the young members of his dissenting congregation such as the *Institutes of Natural and Revealed Religion* (1772/1782). In the preface to this text, Priestley writes:

> It was on your account that I composed these *Institutes of natural and revealed religion*, and to you I take the liberty to dedicate them.
>
> It is the earnest wish of my heart, that your minds may be well established in the sound principles of *religious knowledge*, because I am fully persuaded, that nothing else can be a sufficient foundation of a virtuous and truly respectable conduct in life, or of good hope in death. A mind destitute of knowledge (and, comparatively speaking, no kind of knowledge, besides that of *religion*, deserves the name) is like a field on which no culture has been bestowed, which, the richer it is, the ranker weeds it will produce. If nothing good be sown in it, it will be occupied by plants that are useless or noxious.[106]

We can see here the elements of the epistemology Priestley would work out in greater detail in his book on Hartley (1775) and in the *Letters*. Although not rationally compelling by itself, natural theology forms the foundation for religious faith according to Priestley. Also, like Addison, Priestley was drawn to write a hymn to the creator God.[107]

As discussed earlier in connection with the *Letters to a Philosophical Unbeliever Part I*, Priestley did not think that natural theology was rationally compelling; the mind had to be engaging the evidence in the right way in order to see the evidence as pointing to an intelligent

---

[105] *Ibid.*, p. 210.

[106] Joseph Priestley, *Institutes of Natural and Revealed Religion*, 3 vols. (London, 1772–4), pp. iiif.

[107] 'To God Supreme and Ever Kind', printed in *Joseph Priestley (1733–1804): Scientist, Teacher, and Theologian: A 250th Anniversary Exhibition – Bodleian Library, Oxford* (Oxford, 1983).

designer. Natural theology can then be seen as a part of religious practice, a way of confirming and strengthening a pre-existent faith. Far from seeing this as a problem, Priestley condemns Hume's putatively sopho-moric attitude that perception of order in the natural world alone should be adequate to infer the existence of a God.

Priestley, in commenting on the *Dialogues*, may offer a clue as to the influence of the *Dialogues* in the years immediately following their initial publication. He writes in connection with his assessment that despite the suggestion that Cleanthes is victorious in the *Dialogues*, in fact Philo presents the stronger case:

And though the debate seemingly closes in favor of the theist, the victory is clearly on the side of the atheist. I therefore shall not be surprised if this work should have a considerable effect in promoting the cause of atheism, with those whose *general turn of thinking*, and *habits of life*, make them no ill-wishers to that scheme.[108]

What is of particular interest here is the observation that the *Dialogues* would edify those disposed toward atheism (either speculatively or prac-tically). Recall that for Priestley, the manner in which one engages a question determines much of what one will find in the investigation (assuming that the evidence underdetermines particular conclusions). Dispassionate enquirers may find themselves agreeing with Philo, but according to Priestley, such dispassionate enquirers would have already been practical atheists; the unravelling of the design argument by Hume would merely push the practical atheist into speculative atheism. But according to Priestley, practical atheists are already very close to specula-tive atheism. So despite there being few published critiques of Hume's *Dialogues* in Britain, given the social cost involved in admitting to atheism, one can imagine atheistic readers of Hume's *Dialogues* prudently remaining silent in their sceptical edification.

Other figures during this time offer their views of the causes of atheism. It is interesting that writers had been attacking atheism for some time in Britain, but that William Hammon, in his *Answer to Dr. Priestley's Letters to a Philosophical Unbeliever* (1782), was the first to admit publicly to being an atheist. Reflecting the gradual emergence of atheism as a live option, discourse about God during this period begins to shift from an intellectual environment where theism was presumed to one in which neither theism nor atheism has such an advantage.

---

[108] Priestley, *Letters to a Philosophical Unbeliever Part I*, pp. 108f.

In 1783, John Ogilvie presented his *An Inquiry into the Causes of the Infidelity and Scepticism of the Times: With Occasional Observations on the Writings of Herbert, Shaftesbury, Bolingbroke, Hume, Gibbon, Toulmin, etc.* Ogilvie recognizes that the burden of proof is shifting from theism to the open ground of natural reason:

Let us, however, acknowledge, that disquisition of this nature, addressed to the rational, intelligent and dispassionate readers, is circumscribed as to its influence, by motives of powerful efficacy and operation. For it is not with him who examines a tenet of religion, as it is with him who investigates a proposition of philosophy. Reason, which, in the latter case, judges according to the nature and force of evidence, is obstructed in the former instance by the influence of passion, prepossession and prejudice.[109]

Despite his defence of religion, Ogilvie recognizes that religious faith can cloud one's judgment and ability to consider evidence. If anything, it looks as though Ogilvie recognizes that the burden of proof is shifting in such a way that the theist must not justify religious belief. Ogilvie identifies five sources of unbelief:

1. 'The love of singularity, or an inordinate desire to extract novelty from every subject, and in particular, from points that have been formerly canvassed'
2. 'A propensity to reject whatever bears the stamp of vulgarity, and to conform our principles, in the same manner as our dress, to the prevailing taste and fashion of the times'
3. 'A desire of imitating the manners of men whom we have been taught to esteem very highly, and of appearing to adopt their opinions'
4. 'Our natural inclination to reject those tenets as being false to which our actions are irreconcilable, and to adopt the contrary'
5. 'Certain changes of a very dangerous tendency, respecting either the general scheme of Christianity, or its peculiar doctrines; the nature of its evidence, or the character of its teachers; of which the effect is heightened in the writings of its adversaries, by all the arts of plausible reasoning, insinuation, ridicule, and abuse'.[110]

While Ogilvie does directly address Hume in this regard, his focus is on Hume's *Essays Moral and Political*, not the *Dialogues* (published just four

---

[109] John Ogilvie, *An Inquiry into the Causes of the Infidelity and Scepticism of the Times: With Occasional Observations on the Writings of Herbert, Shaftesbury, Bolingbroke, Hume, Gibbon, Toulmin, etc.* (London, 1783), pp. iiif.
[110] *Ibid.*, p. 15.

years previously). Ogilvie writes 'You ask a Christian upon what foundation he builds his faith, or his conviction of the truth of his religion. He will answer readily, that he believes this religion to be of divine authority, because its doctrines and precepts are in his opinion adapted to promote those purposes which a Being of consummate wisdom and benevolence would propose to accomplish by revelation.'[111] The confirmation of this revelation comes, for the Christian, in the confirmation of Old Testament prophesies and in the miracles of the New Testament.

As mentioned in the editorial addition to the present chapter, when George Campbell wrote his *A Dissertation on Miracles: Containing an Examination of the Principles Advanced by David Hume* (1762/1797), he concerned himself entirely with the essay 'On Miracles'. Campbell considers Hume's essay to be 'one of the most dangerous attacks that have been made on our religion'.[112] Although he added a new preface to the 1797 edition, he made no mention of the *Dialogues*, but did mention a correspondence he had with Hume following the initial publication of the *Dissertation*. In the correspondence, Hume thanks Campbell for his civility, something not at all to be taken for granted in theological and philosophical enquiry. Also in the letter Hume wrote to Campbell is added the following anecdote:

It may perhaps amuse you to learn the first hint which suggested to me that argument which you have so strenuously attacked. I was walking in the Cloysters of the Jesuit College of la Fleche, (a town in which I passed two years of my youth), and was engaged in conversation with a Jesuit of some parts and learning, who was relating to me, and urging some nonsensical miracle performed lately in the Convent; when I was tempted to dispute against him; and as my head was full of the topics of my Treatise of Human Nature, which I was at that time composing, this argument immediately occured to me, and I thought it very much gravelled my companion. But at least he observed to me that it was impossible for that argument to have any solidity; because it operated equally against the Gospel as the Catholic miracles; which observation I thought proper to admit as a sufficient answer.[113]

Interestingly, during the remainder of this text Campbell wishes to defend the reality of the New Testament miracles, but not the 'Popish' or pagan miracle accounts.

---

[111] *Ibid.*, p. 243.
[112] George Campbell, *A Dissertation on Miracles: Containing an Examination of the Principles Advanced by David Hume, Esq, in an Essay on Miracles* (Edinburgh, 1762), p. viii.
[113] This is quoted from the third edition (London, 1797), pp. 8ff.

As seen in the present chapter, expressivist moods prevail alongside apologetic uses in the work of natural theologians up to at least the early nineteenth century. These expressivist moods do not suggest a modern fideistic retreat from apologetic uses of the design argument, a retreat that would signal an awareness of the futility of justificatory argument for belief in a deity. Instead, expressivist uses of design are present throughout the history of the natural-theology tradition in Britain. Certainly, some philosophers, naturalists and theologians expressed their wonder at divine ingenuity in greater portions than others; here perhaps we can think of Ray and Addison as being emblematic of these two poles.

Expressivist uses of design after Paley: Whewell

During the nineteenth century, both design and providence came under increasing scrutiny. As Clayton notes, a greater awareness not just of the accidents of natural history (such as fossils, extinct species and evolution) but also of the accidents of human history (strife, suffering, poverty) pervades thought about nature and society during this time.

These social and intellectual changes are evident in Whewell's dedicatory letter to his Bridgewater Treatise:

The subject proposed to me was limited: my prescribed object is to lead the friends of religion to look with confidence and pleasure on the progress of the physical sciences, by showing how admirably every advance in our knowledge of the universe harmonizes with the belief of a most wise and good God. To do this effectually may be, I trust, a useful labour. Yet, I feel most deeply, what I would take this occasion to express, that this, all that the speculator concerning natural theology can do, is utterly insufficient for the great ends of Religion; namely, for the purpose of reforming men's lives, of purifying and elevating their characters, of preparing them for a more exalted state of being. It is the need of something fitted to do this, which gives to Religion its vast and incomparable importance; and this can, I well know, be achieved only by that Revealed Religion of which we are ministers, but on which the plan of the present work did not allow me to dwell.

The examination of the material world brings before us a number of things and relations of things which suggest to most minds the belief of a creating and presiding Intelligence. And this impression, which arises with the most vague and superficial consideration of the objects by which we are surrounded, is, we conceive, confirmed and expanded by a more exact and profound study of external nature.[114]

---

[114] William Whewell, *Astronomy and General Physics Considered with Reference to Natural Theology* (London, 1833), pp. vif.

Something of the idea of providence remains in Whewell's thought – in the expression of God as governor of the world – but like his use of design, it is an impression that the mind is drawn to, rather than an idea that must be preserved as the foundation of society:

The contemplation of the material universe exhibits God to us as the author of the laws of material nature; bringing before us a wonderful spectacle, in the simplicity, the comprehensiveness, the mutual adaptation of these laws, and in the vast variety of harmonious and beneficial effects produced by their mutual bearing and combined operation. But it is the consideration of the moral world, of the results of our powers of thought and action, which leads us to regard the Deity in that light in which our relation to him becomes a matter of the highest interest and importance.[115]

In this case, the inexplicable order lies in morality – in the impression that above and beyond our material nature being guided by divine laws, our moral being importantly draws our minds to the existence of a God. Whewell asks rhetorically:

Must we not suppose that He who created the soil also inspired man with those social desires and feelings which produce cities and states, laws and institutions, arts and civilization, and that thus the apparently inert mass of earth is a part of the same scheme as those faculties and powers with which man's moral and intellectual progress is most connected?[116]

Whewell's goal in this treatise is to show how the use of natural reason leads one to reflect upon the deity as well as on the insufficiency of the knowledge possible of this deity from natural reason alone. This is the elevation of revealed religion above natural religion. Rather than being a reactionary motive, of entrenching religion away from rational enquiry, Whewell's vision is progressive and confident: while he believes that natural theology must adapt to changes in the sciences, he also believes that serious reflection upon it will lead ineluctably to belief in a God, and eventually to an awareness of a need for more (i.e. revealed religion). In this vein, Whewell writes, 'We are very far from believing that our philosophy alone can give us such assurance of these important truths as is requisite for our guidance and support; but we think that even our physical philosophy will point out to us the necessity of proceeding far beyond that conception of God.'[117] A few pages later, Whewell continues in something of an expressivist mood:

---

[115] *Ibid.*, p. 251.　　[116] *Ibid.*, pp. 260f.　　[117] *Ibid.*, p. 367.

How strongly then does science represent God to us as incomprehensible! His attributes as unfathomable! His power, his wisdom, his goodness, appear in each of the provinces of nature which are thus brought before us; and in each, the more we study them, the more impressive, the more admirable do they appear. When then we find these qualities manifested in each of so many successive ways, and each manifestation rising above the preceding by unknown degrees, and though a progression of unknown extent, what other language can we use concerning such attributes than that they are *infinite*? What mode of expression can the most cautious philosophy suggest, other than that He, to whom we thus endeavor to approach, is infinitely wise, powerful, and good?"[118]

As discussed above, both Brooke and Clayton find in Whewell's sermons an interest in design that goes beyond the justificatory strand of theistic argumentation into the expressivist strand. Two examples from sermons given in 1842 illustrate the significance design and providence have for moral edification. The first example comes from a sermon Whewell preached on Proverbs 15:3 during Easter Term:

[W]hen we consider man as not merely endowed with faculties for his own amusement and gratification; – as not merely the gifted *possessor* of certain wonderfully constructed and subtle powers, – Reason and Imagination, Memory and Invention, – but as *responsible* for the use which he makes of these exquisite instruments; – as not merely enjoying and exercizing their powers, but as having a Living Soul, in which these wonderful faculties have their roots; – in which they are subject to the influence of each other and of all that in any way affects man's inner being; – in which too by their mutual influence, and by the discipline to which they are subjected, they co-operate in no small degree in shaping the soul itself and determining its character, and therefore its eternal destiny; – when we *thus* consider man, what is there then which we can justly call entirely temporal and secular? – what is there, which may not have a powerful efficacy in determining his spiritual condition, and thence, in deciding his final lot, and the place which will be assigned him by the Supreme and Everlasting Governor of the world?"[119]

The second example comes from a sermon Whewell preached on Ephesians 4:1–2 during the Michaelmas Term:

I also endeavored to bring to your minds several calls which *all* of you have received, besides those other special calls with which the peculiar Providences of God, – events in your outward history, or in the history of your spirit within you, – may have addressed different persons, each in his own appointed time.[120]

[118] *Ibid.*, pp. 372f.
[119] William Whewell, *Sermons Preached in the Chapel of Trinity College, Cambridge* (London, 1847), pp. 40f.
[120] *Ibid.*, p. 57.

The first example contains an appeal to design as a means of expressing wonder at the moral responsibility human beings have as a part of their condition and at possessing a soul which is cultivated through its influences. In the second example, Whewell links the idea of having a vocation with God's providence in the world. Of course, this providence may manifest itself in both the individual and corporate vocations to which human beings may feel called. In these two examples from Whewell's sermons, we see the invocation of design for the purpose of moral and spiritual edification, a goal that includes the expressivist use of theistic argument but that makes no obvious use of epistemological justification.

CHAPTER 11

Beyond the 'Enlightenment project'?*

PROLOGUE: PUBLIC AND PRIVATE IN THE
JEFFERSONIAN PROJECT

The American Thomas Jefferson, whom we met in the opening lecture of this series, remarked once in passing in a letter to John Adams (8 April 1816) that unbelief or infidelity in Catholic countries expressed itself as atheism, but in Protestant countries, as theism. That is in fact not far off what we found in the previous lecture, 'Of Ancients and Moderns',[1] which detailed the rise of atheism in France and the fading of design in Britain.

Jefferson himself never lost confidence in the design argument, holding that, if one viewed the universe 'in its parts general or particular . . . it is impossible . . . for the human mind not to believe that there is, in all this, design . . .'.[2] As I noted at the time, Jefferson did not seem acquainted with Hume's critique of design, although he did know some of Hume's writings; but he seems not to have known any of Kant's writings, although Immanuel Kant did know those of the author of the Declaration of Independence and the Founder of the University of Virginia.

Earlier, I used Jefferson to exemplify the European Enlightenment, not least in regard to his sharp division between natural religion's right of access to public space and sectarian religion's confinement to the private realm, a division critical to the success of the Enlightenment enterprise, ensuring both the rationality of the public and the toleration of the private. According to Jefferson's construction of the difference, the public

---

* Editors' note: This concluding chapter is adapted from the eighth and final lecture of the Stanton Lecture series.

[1] Editors' note: This refers to Lecture Seven of the Stanton Lectures, the text of which forms the basis for Chapter 10, 'The Debate about God in Early-Modern British Philosophy', and the appendix to Chapter 8, 'The Debate about God in Early-Modern French Philosophy'.

[2] Editors' note: See Chapter 2, p. 25 above.

realm was identified as rational, universal and embodying common beliefs and values, which can contribute to social unity and public order, whereas the private realm was characterized as irrational, particular and – if not contained – likely to create social divisions and confusion by disturbing public tranquillity. For a new nation, one whose identity was not yet fully formed, and one which was constituted by a plurality of peoples from a variety of ethnic backgrounds, the need to get right the balance between public access and private freedom was clearly a matter of some urgency.

In respect to religion, Jefferson believed strongly that individual religious groups should be able to organize and perpetuate themselves with neither hindrance nor support from the state. A man of many inconsistencies in private and public life, Jefferson was utterly consistent in his conviction that in matters of conscience, there is no place for government involvement: there should be, in his lasting phrase, 'a wall of separation between church and state'. But this did not mean for Jefferson that public space should be a sort of 'religion-free zone'. It should be free from particular religious interests (or what he called 'the sects'), to be sure, but access to public space was in Jefferson's view allowed to 'natural religion', that universal religious sentiment which – in his view – expressed the consensus of humankind about the existence and nature of God, the duties and obligations under the moral law, and the future state of the soul. At the University of Virginia, there may have been no provision for a professor of divinity, but there was provision that the topics of natural theology should be covered by the professors of philosophy.

There are three points to underscore about this construction of 'public' and 'private' as regards religion. First, natural religion, grounded in universal reason, binds the community together in common beliefs and values, and is fit for public space. Second, sectarian religion, grounded in particular revelations and other authorities, is irrational and likely to divide and offend the community if it is not confined to the private sphere, where it is due the protection of the state. Third, Jefferson is developing here a model of pluralism in which particularity is privatized and access to public space is gained by adopting tradition-free reasons and forgoing appeal to tradition-specific reasons, that is, reasons that might count as reasons for one group but would not count as reasons for everyone.

This is by no means the only model of public and private that emerged in the European Enlightenment, but the Jeffersonian model remains one very influential way of trying to handle problems of pluralism in a free society. For Jefferson himself, of course, this model presupposed that natural religion was consensual and uncontroversial and that it provided a common foundation for all the particular religious traditions that were represented within society at large. What would happen to the Jeffersonian strategy for coping with religious pluralism, however, if that trusted foundation itself became uncertain and itself became virtually as contentious as the idiosyncratic structures that were imagined by him to have been built upon it?

KANT'S CRITIQUE OF ALL THEOLOGY: A CONSTRUCTION

A philosopher for all seasons: 'Kantrezeptionen'

We tend to think of the last *fin de siècle* as the era of the neo-Kantian revival in philosophy, a time when a fresh attempt was made to recover Kantian insights and to put them to work in all branches of philosophy, both the pure and the applied. And so it was. But in his analysis *Entstehung und Aufstieg des Neukantianismus,* Klaus Christian Köhnke has shown convincingly that there never has been a time since his activity as an author when there was not a Kant party and an anti-Kant party. But the 'Kant' whom the opposing parties have rallied round in support or whom they have circled around in attack is different in every generation.[3]

Kant has been in turn both a rationalist and a sceptic, both an idealist and a positivist, both a Freiburg phenomenologist and an Oxford analyst, both a rather humourless foundationalist and a more playful post-modernist. It seems that in each generation the opposing sides seek to engage the philosophical enemy either by enlisting selected Kantian elements in support or by attacking specific targets inside Kant's critical philosophy. Our generation is no exception. We, too, have imagined Kant in wonderfully contradictory ways. We see him as both an archetypical Enlightenment foundationalist (à la Rorty or MacIntyre) and more recently as a prototype anti-foundationalist (à la Onora O'Neill).[4]

Without having to agree entirely with Professor O'Neill's provocative interpretation of Kant, I want to suggest a connection between some aspects of her interpretation and Kant's importance for the enterprise on which we have been embarking in these lectures. This may not seem an

---

[3] Editors' note: See Klaus Christian Köhnke, *Entstehung und Aufstieg des Neukantianismus* (Frankfurt, 1986).

[4] Editors' note: See for the former view Richard Rorty, *Philosophy and the Mirror of Nature* (Princeton, 1979), and Alasdair MacIntyre, *After Virtue: A Study in Moral Theory* (Notre Dame, IN, 1981), and *Whose Justice? Which Rationality?* (Notre Dame, IN, 1988). See Onora O'Neill, *Constructions of Reason: Explorations of Kant's Practical Philosophy* (Cambridge, 1989), for the latter view.

initially promising undertaking. For surely Kant was committed to religion in general, Utopian rationality and the generic God against which the whole thrust of this series has been directed?

This conventional reading of Kant is in large measure accurate, though recent studies have shown his motives to have been religiously more complex than was once imagined (these accounting for otherwise inexplicable tensions in his thought). Moreover, despite his apparent commitment to a more tradition-neutral approach to religious issues, not even Kant was above appealing to the gods in support of his theological constructions from pure practical reason. When the Kant of the *Vorlesungen über die philosophische Religionslehre* wanted to justify his choice of holiness, goodness and justice as the defining moral qualities of God, he showed no hesitation in seeking support from the history of religions. Such trinitarian thinking was 'very old' and could be found in virtually all religions, he confidently claimed, it having been expressed as divine powers by the Indians as Brahma, Visnu and Siva; by the Persians as Ormuzd, Mithra and Ahriman; by the Egyptians as Osiris, Isis and Horus; and by the Goths and Germans as Odin, Freya and Thor.

The Kantian construction of 'public' and 'private'

Jefferson's public space (like Descartes's?) is a realm of neutrality and consensus. However, Kant's public space, if Onora O'Neill is right, does not imply consensus, though it does require a commitment to the categorical imperative interpreted as a constraint on pure and practical reason alike: an open space fit for reasonable partisans.

In pointing to the Categorical Imperative as the supreme principle of reason, Kant is true to his insistence that we can obtain only negative instruction. The Categorical Imperative is only a strategy for avoiding principles of thinking, communicating and acting that cannot be adopted by all members of a plurality whose principles of interaction, let alone actual interaction . . . are not established by any transcendent reality. The supreme principle of reason does not fix thought or action in unique grooves; it only points to limits to the principles that can be shared.[5]

Critique of reason is possible only if we think of critique as recursive and reason as constructed rather than imposed. The constraint on possibilities of constructions is imposed by the fact that the principles are to be found for a plurality of possible voices or agents who share a world. Nothing has been established about principles of cognitive order for solitary beings. All that has

---

[5] O'Neill, *Constructions of Reason*, p. 24.

been established for beings who share a world is that they cannot base this sharing on adopting unsharable principles. Presumably many specific conformations of cognitive and moral order are possible; in each case the task of the Categorical Imperative is not to dictate, but to constrain possibilities for acting and for cognition. Theoretical rationality constrains but does not determine what can be thought or believed, just as practical rationality constrains but does not dictate what may be done.[6]

Here we see the import of treating Utopian, and not universal, rationality as opposite to local rationality. Because Kant's universalization is an extension of locality, in this case, I do this thing if by so doing it here and now I can will it to be done in all places in similar circumstances. The sense of justification here is not a transcendental justification, but a localized justification, whereby reason constitutes itself by its own application. It requires neither neutrality nor consensus; it requires contestability. If the aim of these lectures were to offer a theory of rationality, we would have to consider Kant's contribution here at greater length. As it is, our concern is with the activity of giving reasons, not the theory of rationality. Let us apply that technique to Kant by seeing how his anti-foundationalist, anti-rationalist critique of reason exhibits itself in his deconstruction of natural theology.

In his *Critique of Pure Reason*, Kant devised the classification of theistic argument that has become virtually universal in modern philosophy of religion. Kant, too, seemed pleased enough with his effort. In the *Prolegomena*, Kant said that he had nothing to add about transcendental theology to what he had already written in the *Critique of Pure Reason*, which on this issue is 'easily grasped, clear and decisive'. On the one hand, Kant gave us the taxonomy according to which the past was organized and perceived. This affects the way we see theistic arguments, so that it is very difficult to see them otherwise. But they were not nearly so neat as Kant suggests. It would be more adequate to see them as constituting a continuum, stretching from the ontological at one end to the teleological at the other. On the other hand, Kant gave us the taxonomy according to which subsequent discussion was ordered. After Kant, philosophers developed their arguments for the existence of gods in terms of his taxonomy. In effect, it shaped the future perception of the field, and philosophers nowadays have difficulty conceiving theistic arguments in any other terms.

So, Kant simultaneously rewrote the past and pre-saged the future. He also did more, and it is to this 'more' that we shall return. Kant's critical

[6] *Ibid.*, p. 27.

philosophy may have undermined confidence in foundationalist uses of theistic argument, but it does not have the same erosive effect on non-foundationalist uses of theistic argument identified in these lectures as having played so diverse a role in pre-modern (and occasionally modern) religious thought.

Kant's critique of all theology is well known, and therefore it is not necessary to go over it in detail; but it is worth reviewing its architecture, just to hold up for admiration its structure and also to emphasize its importance as a construction of the problem of natural theology. Kant defined the point of the proofs: speculative use of reason beyond its proper limits. He also limited the criterion of success to something which they could not even in principle achieve; all proofs are built on the same mistake, namely, the illicit attempt to derive the existence of God from the concept of God. Kant does not necessarily have a quarrel with the concept of God constituted by the proofs!

Now I maintain that all attempts to employ reason in theology in any merely speculative manner are altogether fruitless and by their very nature null and void, and that the principles of its employment in the study of nature do not lead to any theology whatsoever. Consequently, the only theology of reason which is possible is that which is based upon moral laws or seeks guidance from them.[7]

[A]ll merely speculative proofs in the end bring us always back to one and the same proof, namely, the ontological.[8]

The physico-theological argument can indeed lead us to the point of admiring the greatness, wisdom, power, etc, of the Author of the world, but can take us no further. Accordingly, we then abandon the argument from empirical grounds of proof, and fall back upon the contingency which, in the first steps of the argument, we had inferred from the order and purposiveness of the world. With this contingency as our sole premiss, we then advance, by means of transcendental concepts alone, to the existence of an absolutely necessary being, and [as a final step] from the concept of the absolute necessity of the first cause to the completely determinate or determinable concept of that necessary being, namely, to the concept of an all-embracing reality. Thus the physico-theological proof, failing in its undertaking, has in face of this difficulty suddenly fallen back upon the cosmological proof; and since the latter is only a disguised ontological proof, it has really achieved its purpose by pure reason alone – although at the start it disclaimed all kinship with pure reason and professed to establish its conclusions on convincing evidence derived from experience.[9]

---

7 Immanuel Kant, *Critique of Pure Reason*, trans. Norman Kemp Smith (London, 1953), A636/B664, p. 528.
8 *Ibid.*, A638/B666, p. 529. 9 *Ibid.*, A629/B657, pp. 523–4.

Kant limited the number of proofs to four, three of speculative and one of practical reason. This both rewrote the past and preset the future discussion of theistic proofs. All discussion of past proofs and all proposals of new proofs generally conform to Kant's ideal types.

But this critique would apply only to cases where an epistemic gap exists, which the proofs attempted to overcome through inference (i.e. it requires dualism and a foundationalist project). There was no shortage of those, then or more recently, either who denied that such a gap exists (e.g. Romanticists) or who argued that the gap could not be overcome through inference. So, it is mainly their foundationalist use that has been undermined by Kant. When Kant says in the *Prolegomena* that metaphysics is in disrepute, it is precisely foundationalist metaphysics that is in disrepute; that Kant himself has been read as a foundationalist shows the tenacity with which that paradigm continues to hold our minds against our wills, so to speak.

And in the *Vorlesungen*, Kant thought that the foundationalist programme was unworthy of God, since it made divine existence a hypothesis, a matter of probabilities. Moreover, there is no need for speculative proofs, which cannot yield certainty, because we have practical proof. Kant speaks of moral theology as a certain foundation for belief that cannot be undermined. It is as certain as a mathematical demonstration, though it yields *Glauben*, not *Wissen*. The existence of God is not a contingent hypothesis, as in physico-theology, but is a necessary postulate of pure practical reason. This gives greater certainty because it does not rest on contingent fact; the existence of God is not a matter of probability. We have had occasion to observe in the history of religious philosophy examples when theistic arguments were put to non-inferential uses or examples of religious thinkers who were themselves critical of inferential applications. The religious significance of theistic arguments would seem in many cases to be independent of their adequacy as inferences.

THE RELIGIOUS IMPORT OF THEISTIC ARGUMENT: A REMINDER

The ends of theistic argument in religious contexts

But the use of theistic argument in the examples taken from the period surveyed in these lectures does not readily conform to the use of proofs that is vulnerable to Kant's critique. The exploration of these examples is not intended as a complete survey; other examples might be adduced to support a foundationalist use of proofs in pre-modern times. But this is only a problem if one wants to say that proofs were never used that way, which is not what I want to claim. On the other hand, counter-examples to the foundationalist claim might damage that claim, in so far as it requires all proofs to be foundationalist.

Endorsing the use of proofs: Udayana, Ghazali, Anselm and Whewell[10]

Their functions, for those who endorsed the use of proofs, are more directly shaped by their place in the life-projects of religious traditions: they correct the heretic, give courage to the waverer, edify the faithful, guide the interpretation of texts, express awe and wonder. Their function is more to serve as tokens of belief than to provide its grounds.

Repudiating the use of proofs: Ramanuja and ha-Levi[11]

Those who repudiated the use of proofs repudiated their being conceived as necessary grounds for belief.[12] But neither of our examples used their repudiation of theistic argument so understood as a reason for abandoning philosophical language in favour of the purely idiosyncratic discourse of their own traditions. They do not abandon philosophical discourse as a means of communication, or as an instrument for clarification. In neither case do they use their opposition to a foundationalist use of theistic argument to cut off religious claims from the public realm, in which claims are publicly contestable, sometimes by standards other than those provided by their own traditions.

This is shown poignantly in ha-Levi's case by his having written the *Kuzari* in the public language of commerce and the academy, namely, Arabic, rather than in the more private language of the community, the language in which he tended to write his religious poetry. In Ramanuja's case it is shown by his having structured his arguments against the foundationalist use of proofs in terms that would be accessible to anyone competent to use terms in which knowledge claims were publicly contested. Their reasons for repudiating the foundationalist use of theistic argument were tradition-specific reasons: Vedic or biblical revelation in

---

[10] Editors' note: Clayton notes that his reference to Whewell is intended as a reminder that 'it is not just a difference of modern and pre-modern mentalities'.

[11] Editors' note: Ramanuja and ha-Levi received treatment in the Stanton Lectures, for which this chapter was originally prepared as a concluding lecture.

[12] Editors' note: Clayton notes: 'This suggests that some others were perceived to be using proofs in a foundationalist sense.'

both cases or, in ha-Levi's case, the salvific acts of God in the history of Israel. But it would be wrong to assume that theistic proofs are themselves tradition-neutral. This they most surely are not.

Historically, the choice of proofs to be used has been conditioned by what antecedently are allowed to count as reasons within the tradition of the proof's purveyor. We learned this from Udayana, but it applies equally to Thomas Aquinas: proofs are preferred which support or can be adapted to support the doctrine of gods operative within the tradition itself, though sometimes the choice of proofs used in any given circumstance is conditioned by the ends to which the proof is being used and the audience for which it is intended, whether that primary audience be fellow lawyers or fellow monks. The meanings of the substantive terms vary systematically according to the tradition of the purveyor: the gods of particular proofs are not generic gods but some God, whether it be Siva/Visnu/Brahma or Allah or the one whose name is too sacred to utter or the God and Father of our Lord Jesus Christ.

The proofs have formed part of the lived narrative of a tradition: an aspect of the tradition's textuality, which they lived with an immediacy we would find it difficult to recover. But also important for purposes of communication is the inherent ambiguity of the proofs: 'God' must be able to be heard in a sense other than the specific sense in which it is said; 'causality' must be flexible enough to become a point of contact between traditions for whom the gods act causally in very different senses.

THE FALL OF MODERNITY: NO TEXTUAL IMMEDIACY

We have spent much time in this series wandering in past times and foreign places: but we must not idealize the past and its securities or the Orient and its mysteries. We may visit past times and far-away places, but we cannot live there. We visit them not in search of a lost paradise or a golden age to which we should repair. Paradise, once lost, cannot be regained except in the imagination and in story. We can still learn from the past and I have tried to identify things we might learn from the past, but there is one thing I am most doubtful of a modern's being able to recover. And that is the immediacy with which pre-moderns related to, formed themselves through their sacred texts. We have in modern times experienced something of a fall from the possibility of that kind of immediacy.

And therein lies much of our problem with pre-modern theistic argument. If these uses of argument that we have been identifying are not uses with which we ourselves can identify, it may be because we do not identify with the kinds of activities with which those arguments were associated. 'Disembeddedness' (à la Giddens) has another twist: if theistic arguments no longer make sense to so many of us today, it may be because we can no longer participate in the forms of life in which they were embedded.[13] That, I say, rather than the reverse: it is not because they make no sense that we no longer participate, but because we do not participate, they no longer make sense. Understanding of some kinds can come more readily through doing than it does through thinking.

That is to say, and to adopt the language of Christianity (but without restricting the point to that particular religious tradition), an understanding of divine things sometimes arises more readily through liturgy than it does through theology or philosophy. Here one thinks as much of Udayana as one does of Anselm. It may be because the forms of life with which they were bound up are not our forms of life. To recover an appreciation for those uses of argument may require not just or even primarily a change of mind; it may require more importantly a change of life. For some of us that may be possible, but for many of us that way is cut off either by choice or by fate. What remains for those of us to whom this remark may apply?

THE PHILOSOPHICAL IMPORT OF THEISTIC ARGUMENT: A REVISION

The end of theistic argument in philosophy

Even if one is inclined to allow that such arguments might have a religious use, one might still wish to ask what, if anything, remains of their properly philosophical significance. For the most part their philosophical significance has been judged by their place in the foundationalist programme. If that is the case, then they must be judged failures – failures not just in detail but in principle – and that for largely Kantian reasons.

So what possibilities remain for theistic arguments? First, a few comments about some recent views:

1. Theistic arguments are of antiquarian interest only: they have a place (perhaps even a distinguished and honourable place) in the history of

---

[13] Editors' note: For more on the concept of disembeddedness, see Anthony Giddens, *The Consequences of Modernity* (Stanford, 1990), and *Modernity and Self-Identity: Self and Society in the Late Modern Age* (Stanford, 1991).

philosophy, but their time is past and they have none in contemporary philosophy. We study them then for their antiquarian interest. This seems a feeble reason for keeping theistic arguments in the syllabus of philosophical *topoi*. A reason almost as unimaginative and anachronistic as the philosophical syllabus at Paris in the eighteenth century, when students were still examined on the arguments for and against the Ptolemaic theory!

2. Theistic arguments have a perverse value, because they can be turned round to show that belief in God is without rational foundation, and is therefore not a reasonable position to adopt. An example of this would be Findlay's ontological argument for the necessary non-existence of God; or perhaps Richard Dawkins's argument in *The Blind Watchmaker*.[14] This view of theistic disproof, like the apologetic view that it mimics, rests on an 'intellectualist' misunderstanding of the place of argument in religious traditions: living religions are neither formed nor prolonged by rational argument. They live instead from more characteristically religious sources of empowerment.

3. Theistic arguments have a purely negative paedagogic role in philosophical education: theistic proofs are particularly good examples of bad arguments, showing perhaps the gullibility of people as a whole and the necessity of philosophers to make us alert to the errors of our reasoning. Understood in a modern foundationalist way, they are indeed bad arguments, but their having been understood in this way derives more from philosophical projects having been imposed on religious traditions than from the gullibility of the population as a whole: my guess is that the population as a whole invested far less in these arguments than did philosophers. So there may be a lesson to be learned from the proofs, even if not the one suggested.

I want now to explore another kind of significance they might be said to have for philosophy, and a hint of it is found a little unexpectedly within Kant's own philosophy.

THE 'PURIFICATION OF THE CONCEPT OF GOD' (KANT)

Kant shows us, perhaps unwittingly, how to move beyond the Enlightenment project and its particular way of distinguishing between public and

---

[14] Editors' note: See J. N. Findlay, 'God's Existence is Necessarily Impossible', in Antony Flew and Alasdair MacIntyre, eds., *New Essays in Philosophical Theology* (London, 1955), and Richard Dawkins, *The Blind Watchmaker* (New York, 1986).

private. Kant's distinction between public and private does not entail that public space is marked off as a realm of consensus: reason is constituted by entertainment of difference; this leads to the necessity of toleration as an active, not as a passive principle.

By distinguishing within traditional theistic proofs between their conceptual and demonstrative aspects, he called attention to a difference between what they have to contribute to an understanding of the concept of God and what they have to contribute to our knowledge of the existence of God.

Which God is a necessary postulate of pure practical reason? The God of the proofs. The proofs 'purify' the concept of God: they perform a service as conceptual analysis of God as an absolutely perfect ideal:

But although reason, in its merely speculative employment, is very far from being equal to so great an undertaking, namely, to demonstrate the existence of a supreme being, it is yet of very great utility in correcting any knowledge of this being which may be derived from other sources, in making it consistent with itself and with every point of view from which intelligible objects may be regarded, and in freeing it from everything incompatible with the concept of an original being and from all admixture of empirical limitations . . . Transcendental theology is still, therefore, in spite of all its disabilities, of great importance in its negative employment, and serves as a permanent censor of our reason, in so far as the latter deals merely with pure ideas which, as such, allow of no criterion that is not transcendental. For if, in some other relation, perhaps on practical grounds, the presupposition of a supreme and all-sufficient being, as highest intelligence, established its validity beyond all question, it would be of the greatest importance accurately to determine this concept on its transcendental side, as the concept of a necessary and supremely real being, to free it from whatever, as belonging to mere appearance . . . is out of keeping with the supreme reality, and at the same time to dispose of all counter-assertions, whether atheistic, deistic, or anthropomorphic. Such critical treatment is, indeed, far from being difficult, inasmuch as the same grounds which have enabled us to demonstrate the inability of human reason to maintain the existence of such a being must also suffice to prove the invalidity of all counter-assertions. For from what source could we, through a purely speculative employment of reason, derive the knowledge that there is no supreme being as ultimate ground of all things or that it has none of the attributes which, arguing from their consequences, we represent to ourselves as analogical with the dynamical realities of a thinking being or . . . that it must be subject to all the limitations which sensibility inevitably imposes on those intelligences which are known to us through experience . . . Thus, while for the merely speculative employment of reason the supreme being remains a mere ideal, it is yet an ideal without a flaw, a concept which completes and crowns the whole of human knowledge. Its objective reality cannot indeed be proved, but also cannot be disproved, by merely speculative reasons. If, then, there should be a moral theology that can make good this deficiency, transcendental theology, which before was problematic only, will prove itself indispensable in determining the concept of this supreme being and in constantly testing reason, which is so often deceived by sensibility, and which is frequently out of harmony with its own ideas. Necessity, infinity, unity, existence outside the world (and not as world-soul), eternity as free from conditions of time, omnipresence as free from conditions of space, omnipotence, etc. are purely transcendental predicates, and for this reason the purified concepts of them, which every theology finds so indispensable, are only to be obtained from transcendental theology.[15]

But we cannot use Kant neat: his enterprise remains tied to the fortunes of the Enlightenment project, even if he also contributed to undermining its foundations. This reinterpretation of Kant is in non-foundationalist mode and with due appreciation for the positive function allowed for theistic argument by his critical philosophy: the purification of the concept of God.

For Kant 'purification' meant above all freeing the concept of God of all limitations imposed by historical religions or 'local' conceptions of divinity. In this sense he remained committed to the Enlightenment project even whilst undermining its foundationalist pretensions. In the main, however, he meant by 'purification' the freeing of the concept of God of limitations of experience and history. For us it must be otherwise: our aim is the clarification through analysis of locally valid concepts of divinity. For us 'purification' must be taken as referring to clarity achieved through analysis. What Kant contributes to our project, however, is the recognition that theistic argument can have a philosophical significance beyond the putatively demonstrative function it has customarily been assigned in Western philosophy since the Enlightenment.

1. Purification of the concept of God: in Kant's hands, purification was made to serve the Enlightenment's project of removing from all public discourse about God the residual impurities left by historical religions. *But it contains also an important insight into the point of the proofs: they are exercises in conceptual analysis and make available to public discourse consideration of what it is for gods to be gods and what kind of beings it would be proper to identify as gods.*

2. Kant's insight can be refocused on the objects identified in the opening lecture as the proper concern of philosophy of religion: religions, reasons and gods. If so, then his point can be sharpened: *those arguments which we have traditionally called 'proofs of God' do not provide a foundation*

---

[15] Kant, *Critique of Pure Reason*, A639–42/B667–70, pp. 530–1.

which would support belief in gods, but instead provide clarity about the concept of God embedded in the historical religions.

Expressed in more self-consciously Kantian terms: gods are ideals of reason that are constituted by the traditions in which they are embedded. Theistic proofs, thus, lead less to a consensus about the existence and nature of gods than to a sharper vision of the differences in understanding of gods embedded in religious traditions and what are thought to count as reasons for such. But, such proofs are not merely tradition-constituted, but are also tradition-constituting, in the sense that clarification can also force decisions or point up incoherences or whatever. They provide then a way in which traditions shape themselves and reshape themselves. In that sense, they are part of a tradition's lived narrative, its extended textuality. This suggests a way of opening religious issues to public debate without entailing that tradition-constituted reasons must be disallowed, without requiring a Jeffersonian privatization of particular commitment. And it may even suggest a way of drawing boundaries so that the division of theology and religious studies ceases to be important, without entailing that their difference is denied.

This way of understanding theistic proofs offers a public discourse in which differences can be clarified: it preserves the otherness of the Other whilst providing a discourse for communication across boundaries of more idiosyncratic discourses. However, it does not require abandoning a tradition's own reasons, nor does it entail isolation from external critique (à la D. Z. Phillips's use of Wittgenstein). It also does not guarantee that all traditions or their reasons will hold up equally well under scrutiny, as the history of Indian debate reveals. Even if one cannot expect consensus to emerge, it does not mean that nothing changes as a result of the process of the critical clarification of differences.

PHILOSOPHICAL ANALYSIS AS COMPARATIVE GRAMMAR

If we give up notions of religion in general and with it ideas of Utopian rationality in defence of a generic God, then we are left with a diversity of religions, reasons and gods and no way in advance to say how things must go. In such circumstances, a little old-fashioned philosophical analysis may prove a boon, providing of course that its practitioners can adapt to the idea that the context of a claim or argument is itself part of its analysis. In this sense, what I am proposing is a kind of extension of the work of a familiar friend: what we ordinarily mean when we say becomes what is meant in such contexts when it is said.

Theistic arguments as forms of conceptual analysis might help us better understand the place and nature of gods in religious traditions, thereby leading to a clearer sense of the comparative grammar of religion: the rules of discourse about the gods. Such rules of discourse would show what would count as gods, the kinds of properties such beings possess and their place in different religious forms of life – for we cannot assume that the gods play the same role in all traditions any more than we can assume, e.g., that constitutions play the same role in all countries. Identification of the rules of discourse about the gods might also serve specifically philosophical ends: e.g. they could be ways of getting clear about such basic notions as causality, necessity, contingency, autonomy of morality, etc.[16] From this point of view, religious contexts would provide particularly interesting examples of some of the most difficult philosophical puzzles, and could contribute to their clarification or even solution.

PUBLIC SPACE AND LOCAL REASONS: A PROPOSAL

One goal of the Enlightenment was an attempt to establish common ground religiously in universal reason. But instead of consensus, conflict was the end result: not least conflict about the ability of reason to deliver what was being required of it. What the Enlightenment did achieve, however, was the creation of a discourse in which religious matters could be publicly discussed. It would be short-sighted to give up that gain because one was unimpressed by the use to which that discourse was put in the foundationalist pretensions of the Enlightenment project.

The privatization of the particular

One effect of the Enlightenment was to privatize particular religious commitments. Critical to this process was the perception that the positive religions are divisive, whereas natural religion is unitive. The theistic arguments were central to that strategy: they were asked to state what we all agree that we hold in common. In the process, they were asked to bear more and more weight, until they collapsed under the more wide-ranging critiques of the limits of human reason and understanding by such figures as Hume and Kant. But it was not just the additional weight: by themselves becoming the subject of debate and grounds for dispute, they could no longer provide the consensual foundation that they were expected to provide.

[16] For this suggestion, I am grateful to David Bastow.

The collapse of public consensus

In modern times, access to the public realm is gained by adopting an ostensibly tradition-neutral standpoint of Utopian rationality in defence of the generic God of religion in general. This tradition-neutral standpoint involves the privatization of specific religious commitments; only natural theology is fit for the public realm; the public realm is considered as the realm of consensus.[17] In the process, natural theology is asked increasingly to bear more and more weight; not just sufficiency, but also necessity for belief.

By progressive stages, however, natural theology collapsed under the weight. Finally the public realm itself becomes a realm where religious claims are contested, not generally consented to: in place of religiously embedded conflict, we now have philosophically disembedded conflict (ideological conflict over what count as reasons, not unlike the doctrinal conflicts of the religious past).

Contrary to the dominant post-Enlightenment emphasis upon consensus, examining the actual contexts in which theistic proofs are used leads to a greater appreciation of the differences, not the sameness of humankind's understanding of divinity. The craving for rationally achieved consensus is in part an indirect reaction to the competing claims of religious traditions and more directly a protest against the sectarian bitterness that had arisen during and in the century or so of conflict after the Reformation. A Utopian dream it may have been, but its achievement should not be underestimated.[18] In any case, in a pluralistic society such as ours is increasingly becoming, substantive consensus about means or goals is unlikely; the only consensus for which one can hope is a framework in which differences can be protected as well as commonalities identified.

PUBLIC DISCOURSE AND LOCALIZED RATIONALITIES

In one sense, what I am proposing is nothing new at all: it is an aspect of what always has gone on under the name of natural theology. What is different is that I am recommending that it become the point of natural theology, not just one of its aspects.

---

[17] Consider the religious wars and proliferation of competing sects after the Reformation, in relation to which natural theology may have appeared attractive as neutral and consensual.

[18] It was also in some ways a nostalgic hankering after a past that never was.

Stripped of their foundationalist pretensions, theistic arguments would serve to clarify, say, the character of divine agency within a given religion's understanding of God. This might be called the scandal of manifold particularities: each religious tradition is unique; each tradition lives from a unique narrative, even if the story-lines do occasionally overlap. One consequence of manifold particularity is that debate is more likely to clarify difference than to establish consensus. This was one dimension of the debate between Naiyayikas and Buddhists in mediaeval India: the nature of causality as understood by each tradition was being clarified by means of a dispute over the possibility of a divine cause of all that is. We can see this as a dimension of the mediaeval debate in European traditions about which of two main causal arguments is more appropriate to the God of Islam and of Judaism and of Christianity. Saadya[19] and Ghazali, for instance, are in effect saying that what count as reasons for Aristotle's God, if it is Aristotle's God, would not count as reasons for the God of Abraham, Isaac and Jacob, and of the Prophet.

What would come out of it all if this recommendation were adopted? One thing is certain: consensus about divine things would be most unlikely to come out of it. Rather, it would provide a public discourse in which tradition-specific reasons could be put forward in order to clarify the different understandings of divine agency operative within individual religious traditions. That is also, by the way, what emerged from the mediaeval debates: differences were clarified and thereby more precisely defined. It was not, however, just that traditional positions were in all cases affirmed. The process of debate in some cases can be seen to have modified a tradition's understanding of itself. That is to say, such arguments are not only tradition-constituted (in a deterministic sense); they are also tradition-constituting in that they become foci for future debates within a tradition about itself. Identity, in other words, is formed and reformed through an encounter of the Self with the Other and of the Self with itself.

EPILOGUE: '. . . WHAT HAVOC MUST WE MAKE?'

From attending to the differences of manifold particularities we learn something of philosophical import. We can learn that there is more to philosophy than is contained in our textbooks. We can learn that

---

[19] Editors' note: Like ha-Levi, Saadya Gaon received treatment in the Stanton Lectures.

argument has uses other than justificatory uses. We can learn that it is possible to combine public debate about matters religious without doing damage to the body politic or without having to exclude from the public realm the use of tradition-specific reasons (indeed, we can learn that there are no other kinds of reasons than reasons that are reasons for someone). We can learn that the clarification of difference, and not just the achievement of agreement, is a legitimate end of argument. And even if we learn no more than this, we will have learned enough to refocus the philosophy of religion: in place of a concern with religion in general, we will have substituted specific religious traditions; in place of a generic God, we will have substituted the gods of the specific religious traditions; and in place of the ideal of Utopian rationality, we will have learned to be content with attending to the kinds of reasons that count as reasons to specific religious (and anti-religious) traditions put forward as being reasons for (or against) the gods of those traditions.

Persuaded of these principles, if we go over to the University Library, what havoc must we make? If we take in our right hand any recent volume of Oxford philosophy of religion, say, let us ask, Does it contain more than disembedded foundationalism? No. And if we take in our left hand any recent volume of Wittgensteinian philosophy of religion, let us ask, Does it allow the public contestability of tradition-specific religious claims? No. Commit them even so not to the flames, but slip them silently back onto their shelf.

Let us be historicist enough to remain mindful that what to one generation may appear to be sophistry and illusion may to some future generation be precisely what is required as an antidote to earlier enthusiasms. For the time being, however, we have plenty of other good books to read that have been authored by representatives of the Benares and Jerusalem families of religions. And among these books are also not a few volumes of divinity and school metaphysics that escaped the flames lit by a previous dark age misguidedly seeking thereby to find enlightenment.

Appendix: The 1997 Hulsean Sermon*

Let the words of my mouth and the meditations of our hearts be acceptable in Thy sight, O Lord, our Strength and our Redeemer. Amen.

The Hulsean Sermon was established at the end of the eighteenth century by the will of John Hulse, a Johnian from Cheshire. From what I can discover about him, John Hulse was not an easily admirable man. He was irritable and difficult, seemingly unable for long to sustain good relations with family or friends – not the sort of person you would readily invite to dine at your college on Guest Night: or the sort you would without qualification select as a model to 'direct our lives after his good example', as it says in the Bidding Prayer. John Hulse was a person with faults and blemishes: a person not unlike ourselves. By his benefactions to his *alma mater*, however, his munificence has continued to advantage a long chain of students of this University for over 200 years. He is properly counted among those we gratefully remembered for their beneficence in the Bidding Prayer this morning.

Having himself enjoyed the benefit of scholarships and bursaries as a student at St John's, John Hulse provided in his will scholarships for Divinity students at his old College; established the Hulsean Prize, to be awarded to an undergraduate by the Divinity Faculty; and dedicated funds to establish the office of Christian Advocate (later translated into the Hulsean and then the Norris–Hulse chair of Divinity) and of the Hulsean Lecturer or Preacher, who was charged with delivering twenty

---

* Editors' note: Clayton intended his 1997 Hulsean Sermon, delivered at the University of Cambridge, to serve as an Appendix to *Religions, Reasons, and Gods*. Anticipating the surprise such an inclusion might cause his readers, he noted that the sermon indicates that 'it is possible to deploy the same words in different contexts with different results'. Thus, in Clayton's view, his own act of sermon-giving, as well as the historically distinctive articulations of Psalm 19 to which he draws attention, exemplifies central arguments of this volume. It seems that Clayton himself quotes from Psalm 19 as it appears in the New Revised Standard Version.

apologetic sermons in this place over two terms and at the time of appointment to be under the age of forty.

As someone fast approaching the middle of his sixth decade in this incarnation, I am profoundly flattered that the Select Preachers Syndicate could, even through a dank haze rising from the Fens and at so great a distance from Lancaster, mistake me for someone under the age of forty. And I am also relieved that the Hulsean Lectures were long ago separated from the Sermon, so that my duty as Hulsean Preacher for 1996–7 is completely fulfilled by the delivery of this one Sermon – an event which, I can assure you, by itself generates more than enough anxiety in someone such as myself, who is more accustomed to *listening* in churches and *speaking* only in lecture halls.

But today I am charged with *speaking*, indeed *preaching*, from this imposing pulpit. The choice of the nineteenth Psalm as the text around which to gather some remarks was prompted by the title of John Hulse's only publication known to me – a sermon printed in London in 1745 and originally delivered at Chester Assizes on 'The Necessity and Usefulness of Laws in the Natural and Moral World' – a title that neatly epitomizes a common eighteenth-century reading of Psalm 19 and its dual focus on the natural and moral or social order as witness to the power and righteousness of God.

The Psalms do not form part of the table of lessons to be read in public services of worship, with the result that – apart from special occasions – they are not often used as texts for sermons. The Psalms are nonetheless deeply embedded in Christian worship and piety.

And so it has always been.

The early church continued the Jewish practice of singing from the Psalms, and when Christians began composing their own hymns, a few of which are preserved in the New Testament, they based them on the Psalms of the Hebrew Bible. The Rule of St Benedict endorsed and extended the place of the Psalms in devotion and worship by requiring cloistered monks to sing the complete cycle of Psalms at least once a week, whilst encouraging the devout to chant all 150 Psalms each day. The Book of Common Prayer is in this as in other matters less demanding of those who would be guided by it, providing instead a monthly cycle for the Psalms to be said at Matins and Evensong. In Christian contexts, of course, the Psalms are read as *Christian* scripture and traditionally close with a verse in praise of God as Trinity: 'Glory be to the Father and to the Son and to the Holy Spirit, as it was in the beginning is now and ever shall be, world without end. Amen.'

The Psalms have been prominent in the public worship and private devotion of the people of God from the time of King David to the present. They were originally collected and through time preserved for use in corporate worship and individual devotion. They record, therefore, not what God has to say to His people by way of command or promise or admonition, as in the Law and the Prophets, but form instead a repository of hymns addressed to God in praise or petition or thanksgiving – hymns that show their power by continuing to point all those in search of understanding and righteousness to their source in God.

What of the nineteenth Psalm in particular?

In both Jewish and Christian liturgy, it has always been a 'morning Psalm', to be sung in praise of the glory of God as manifested in the natural world and in the revealed Law. According to the Jewish prayer book, the *Siddur*, the nineteenth Psalm should be said on the morning of each Shabbat: Benedictine monks have traditionally sung the nineteenth Psalm as the second Psalm each Saturday morning at the dawn service known as 'Prime'; the Book of Common Prayer has the nineteenth Psalm said first at Matins on the fourth day of each month; and in services where preaching occurs, the final verse is routinely adapted as a preface to the sermon. The service this morning has been in this respect no exception.

The Psalm as a whole, as it has been preserved in the scriptures of the Jewish and the Christian communities, holds one message: the God of Creation and the God of Redemption is one God, the Lord of hosts, whose glory and faithfulness are manifest in nature and in revelation.

The Psalm opens not, as many do, with a call to praise God. That is already going on, day in and day out, before the Psalm begins. The stars and the planets, the moon and the sun continuously but silently proclaim by their excellences the glory of God to all people, everywhere, all the time. But their excellences are surpassed by those of the revealed Law, the perfections and benefits of which show the God whose glory is manifest in the creation also to be the God whose steadfastness and loving kindness are manifest in the revelation to His people.

In this one Psalm of praise, then, the themes of many other Psalms are pulled together into one powerful and effective hymn to the Lord – the glories of Creation (Psalm 8, Psalm 48), the love of the Law (Psalm 119), the need for forgiveness and God's readiness to redeem people (Psalm 51, Psalm 89).

On closer inspection, however, the Psalm that has been handed down to us suggests layers of meaning by virtue of complexities of composition that may threaten the simple unity of its message. For the nineteenth Psalm is forged from two formerly independent psalms: a hymn to the glory of God as displayed in the natural order and a poem praising the excellences of revealed Law or *torah*, by means of which the Lord preserves and redeems Israel. From their different vocabularies, styles, pieties and sentiments, we know that they cannot have been composed by the same person or even produced in the same milieu.

We do not and in all likelihood will never know for sure how or why the two halves of this Psalm were brought together. Was the hymn to the Law composed specifically to complement – or possibly to correct – the hymn to God in nature? Or, as seems more likely, did the two hymns have quite separate origins, with a later editor joining them into one Psalm for liturgical purposes because they seemed together to have a balance that each alone lacked? To the editor, perhaps the first six verses on their own seemed dangerously like the nature religions of Israel's neighbours, often centred on the worship of the sun. The appeal of such religion was recurringly felt by the Israelites themselves (Ezekiel 8:16), so that it is not surprising to find sun worship being specifically prohibited in the Deuteronomic account of the giving of the Law (4:19).

There were good reasons for such concern. The verses focused on the sun, for instance, are imagined by most scholars to have begun as a hymn to the sun-god and only later to have been adapted to new ends by the Psalmist. There is a strong hint of editorial adjustment in the syntax and there is a telling change of perspective when the sun makes its proud entry – a difference glossed over (with the possible aid of Psalm 148, where the sun is kept firmly in its place, so to say, alongside the moon and the shining stars) in Addison's hymn that we sang earlier:

> The unwearied sun from day to day
> Does his Creator's power display,
> And publishes to every land
> The works of an almighty hand.

At the beginning of the Psalm, the heaven, the firmament, day and night had been proclaiming the glory of God; but once we get to the verses referring to the sun, they provide only a backdrop against which the sun can display its own glory. Whatever the origin of the verses to the sun, however, the Psalmist has subsumed them in a hymn sung to Israel's God. The possibly pagan imagery remains, but its earlier meaning has been transformed to proclaim God's dominion over the natural order, including its proudest and most ostentatious member, the sun.

In the form in which the Psalm has been preserved in scripture, however, the matter does not end there. The hymn to God in nature gives way to a hymn to the Law revealed at Sinai. The excellences of God published everywhere to everyone in the natural order are not just equalled but are much surpassed by the excellences exhibited in the moral and religious Law given by God to Israel alone.

In this Psalm, nature is not inert, nor is Law dead letter. Both the natural and the moral order are presented as agents actively proclaiming the awesome power and unfailing righteousness of God. Though speechless, nature *declares* the glory of God; though inanimate, the Law *testifies* to the faithfulness of God. Neither the heavens nor the Law is here laid out as *grounds* for belief in God: their praise is rather an expression of prior conviction by the Psalmist. This vision of the Psalmist, however, has often become blurred in subsequent reflection on the knowability of God – and this not least in modern times.

In early-modern European thought, for instance, 'natural theology' came into new prominence. From about the middle of the seventeenth century onwards, attempts were habitually made by well-meaning apologists to ground knowledge of God in rational and empirical reasoning alone, independent of any reference – in the case of Christianity – to the experience of redemption through the revelation of God in Christ. There are those who have recently argued (a bit too strongly, perhaps, but with merit nonetheless) that this shift within Christian theology set modern Western thought on a course that led inevitably to the denial of God. Earnest defenders of belief in God are themselves held responsible for sowing the seeds of doubt and unbelief. As the freethinker Anthony Collins mischievously said of Samuel Clarke, whose Boyle Lectures on the existence of God had created a stir when they appeared at the beginning of the eighteenth century, it had never occurred to anyone to doubt the existence of God until Clarke tried so hard to prove it. And it must be admitted that d'Holbach's *System of Nature*, the first explicitly atheistic treatise published in the lifetime of its author, closely parallels and through mimicry parodies Clarke's Boyle Lectures, with the result that Clarke's *proofs* of God were transposed into *disproofs* of that same God.

This, however, is a complex story more suited to the lecture hall and academic monograph than to the pulpit (even *this* pulpit on the occasion of a University Sermon). The moral of the story, however, can be simply stated. By making rational proofs of God foundational for belief, apologists had at the very least raised the stakes in the debate about God: if belief required rational foundations and if such foundations were proved unsound, then belief in God would itself be untenable.

The Psalmist would never have been backed into *that* corner!

Not only would the Psalmist not have allowed that our knowledge of God is *grounded in* the natural order, the Psalmist would have insisted that true knowledge of God as Creator of the natural order requires also acquaintance with God as Redeemer of the moral and social order. Things can go seriously awry when the doctrine of God as Creator is severed from the doctrine of God as Redeemer or *vice versa*.

On the one hand, focusing on God as Creator of nature to the neglect of God as faithful and righteous Redeemer can make God seem remote and unresponsive to human need, or it can lead us to confuse the blind force of nature with the power of God, with the result that we feel orphaned in an indifferent universe. On the other hand, focusing on God as Redeemer of those graciously chosen to the neglect of God as Creator of all humankind can make us feel possessive of God's care and intolerant of those outside our community of faith, with the result that we fail to see that humankind as a whole is the people of God. Focusing over-narrowly on the doctrine of redemption to the neglect of the doctrine of creation can also mislead us into thinking the world and its resources exist only for our consuming desire, rather than accepting our responsibility for the care and repair of that part of God's creative work that we know as our world.

The two halves of Psalm 19 belong together and support each other. Each is necessary: neither is sufficient. To pursue one further thought: it also matters which half controls our understanding of the other. By this I mean that it may be important whether we allow our understanding of God as Redeemer to shape our understanding of God as Creator or *vice versa*. I have in mind the errors that can arise when the order of things in the natural world becomes the norm for the order of things in the moral and social world.

In much of the eighteenth and nineteenth centuries, for instance, the perceived order of the universe as portrayed in the so-called 'design argument' for God's existence was thought also to legitimate a particular social order. Just as the natural order exhibited in celestial mechanics was imagined to be governed by eternal and unchanging 'laws' instituted by God, so the social order – with its rigidly defined classes – was said also to be arranged as God had intended it to be. William Paley, the natural theologian who famously likened the universe to a well-designed watch, also wrote a tract entitled *Reasons for Contentment; Addresses to the Labouring Part of the British Public*, in which he hinted with over-heavy hand that British society in his day was ordered much as God had intended, and that the working class should keep its attention 'fixed upon the duties and concerns' before it rather than comparing its condition with that of other parts of society. The fact that Paley was understood as intending the natural order – the order of creation – to govern the proper order of society is underscored by his tract's having been bound together with his *Natural Theology* in some early-nineteenth-century editions of his *Works*. A sense of social justice may suffer when the moral and social order is understood in terms of the natural order. Perhaps a proper understanding of God as Creator arises out of a prior conviction of God as Redeemer? That is the thought I wish us at least to consider.

Not all early-modern thinkers, of course, saw the connection between the natural order and the ethical order in the way that Paley may have done. Some were keenly persuaded of the primacy of the 'ethical' over the 'natural' in matters religious. I have in mind particularly Immanuel Kant, who in his sixty-fifth year wrote in words that must surely allude to the nineteenth Psalm that two things filled his mind with great admiration and reverence the more he reflected on them: namely, *the starry heavens above us and the moral law within us*. But Kant went on to say that it was the primacy of our sense of the moral law that affirms our infinite worth and counters the feeling of insignificance that naturally arises when we contemplate our place under 'the starry heavens above'. Though we would be right to see a connection *of some sort* between Kant's sentiments at the end of the *Critique of Practical Reason* and those found in the nineteenth Psalm, we would be wrong to imagine that they were sentiments *of the same sort*.

That is not to say that they are not both properly religious, but they are religious in different ways. Awe and wonder for the one makes for perplexity that provokes enquiry into causes: awe and wonder for the Psalmist, however, expresses a sense of presence. It, too, may drive to enquiry, but to enquiry of a different kind, an enquiry that has been likened to *fides quaerens intellectum* or 'faith seeking understanding'.

For Kant, the irrepressible sense of 'ought' that requires us sometimes to act contrary to received values or against our own self-interest may evoke a sense of reverence, but it also stimulates us to seek an explanation. When contemplating the revealed Law and its demands, the Psalmist by contrast requires no postulate in order to give an account of it. The Cause of right *shows itself* in the Law. The Psalmist's response is instead to ask for forgiveness and guidance that he might 'be blameless and innocent of any transgression'. The Psalmist does not believe in God *because* of a sense of ought: the sense of obligation follows from belief in God as redeemer of the moral and social order.

If one shares the belief of the Psalmist, one responds to the wonders of nature and the obligations of the moral law not in search of evidence to support belief, but in fear and trembling at being in the presence of the Lord, 'our Strength and our Redeemer'.

This sense, which seems to me near to the sensibility of the Psalmist, was kept alive also in early-modern times by those Puritans who first founded the College singled out this morning in the Bidding Prayer [namely, Emmanuel College] and who fanned out from there to several other colleges in Cambridge. From thence they set out to the New World, where they sought in more than one sense to make New England 'Emmanuel's Land', to use the happy phrase of Boston's Cotton Mather, who although descended from them, was not himself a graduate of this University but of a lesser seminary in Massachusetts named after one of Emmanuel's emigrant sons. They practised, and Cotton Mather followed them in *The Christian Philosopher* (a book that is said to have brought the Enlightenment to America), the ancient Christian tradition of the two books of divine revelation – the book of nature and the book of scripture – each of which in faith helps us rightly to understand the other. Although they – Mather included – sometimes wrote as if reading the book of nature aright were a basis for being able to understand the book of scripture, their actual practice was quite the reverse. The book of scripture provided the discourse and the interpretative code that enabled them to read the book of nature the way they did. It also motivated them to enquire deeply into the ways of nature, not to discover its Cause, but to gain an understanding of God's purposes. It was their knowledge of God as Redeemer that enabled them to come through science and piety to an understanding of God as Creator, 'father of lights' (James 1:17), maker also of the sun whose

> rising is at one end of the heavens,
> his circuit touches their farthest ends:
> and nothing is hidden from his heat.

We thank Thee for the faithfulness of Thy servant, John Hulse: may we, too, be found faithful in the tasks set before us in this life.

In the name of GOD: Father, Son and Holy Spirit. Amen.

Bibliography*

Abelard, Peter. *Dialogus inter Philosophum, Judaeum et Christianum.* Ed.
R. Thomas. Stuttgart, 1966.
Abraham, William J., and Steven W. Holtzer (eds.). *The Rationality of Religious
Belief: Essays in Honour of Basil Mitchell.* Oxford, 1987.
Abrahamov, Binyamin. *Al-Kasim b. Ibrahim on the Proof of God's Existence: Kitab
al-Dalil al-Kabir.* Leiden, 1990.
Adams, Dickinson W. *Jefferson's Extracts from the Gospels.* Princeton, 1983.
Addison, Joseph. *The Evidences of the Christian Religion . . . to which are Added
Several Discourses against Atheism and Infidelity, and in Defence of the
Christian Revelation, etc.* London, 1730, ²1733, ³1742, ⁴1753, ⁵1763. Other
editions: Glasgow, 1745; Edinburgh, 1751; Glasgow, 1753; Dublin, 1755;
Glasgow, 1756; Dublin, 1758; Glasgow, 1759; Dublin, 1761; Edinburgh,
1772; London, 1776, 1790; Edinburgh, 1792; London, 1796, 1799, 1800;
Oxford, 1801; Edinburgh, 1806; London, 1807.
The Poems of Addison. The Works of English Poets, 23. London, 1779.
The Spectator. Ed. with an introduction and notes by Donald D. Bond. 5 vols.
Oxford, 1965.
Aertsen, Jan. *Nature and Creature: Thomas Aquinas's Way of Thought.* Leiden,
1988.
Alberich, Julio Cola. 'Números simbólicos y rituales en el Asia del Indo al
Mediterráneo', *Boletin de las Associacion Española de Orientalistas* 25
(1989), 199–215.
'Números simbólicos y rituales en el Extremo Oriente', *Boletin de las
Associacion Española de Orientalistas* 23 (1987), 173–94.
'Números simbólicos y rituales en la India', *Boletin de las Associacion Española
de Orientalistas* 24 (1988), 281–301.
Alexander Nequam. *Speculum Speculationum.* Ed. Rodney Thomson. Oxford, 1988.
Alexander of Hales. *Glossa in Quatuor Libros Sententiarum Petri Lombardi.*
Quaracchi, 1951.
Alexander of Hales *et al. Summa Theologica.* 4 vols. Quaracchi, 1924–48.

---

* Editors' note: We have compiled this bibliography from a list left in Clayton's files, with additions
required to complete his references.

Almond, Philip C. *The British Discovery of Buddhism*. Cambridge, 1988.

Altmann, Alexander. *Moses Mendelssohn: A Biographical Study*. London, 1973.

Amma, Visweswari. *Udayana and his Philosophy*. Delhi, 1985.

Anawati, Georges C. 'Polémique, apologie et dialogue islamo-chrétiens', *Euntes Docete* 22 (1969), 380–92.

'Une preuve de l'existence de dieu chez Ghazzali et S. Thomas', *Mélanges de l'institut dominicain des études orientales* 3 (1956), 207–58.

Andersen, Svend. *Ideal und Singularität. Über die Funktion des Gottesbegriffes in Kants theoretischer Philosophie*. Berlin and New York, 1983.

Anselm of Canterbury. *Opera Omnia*. Ed. F. S. Schmitt. 6 vols. Rome and Edinburgh, 1938–61; repr. Stuttgart-Bad Cannstatt, 2nd edn, 1984.

The Prayers and Meditations of Saint Anselm. Trans. and ed. Sister Benedicta Ward. Harmondsworth, 1973.

Proslogion. Latin–English edition. Trans. M. J. Charlesworth. Oxford, 1965.

Proslogion. Latin–German edition. Trans. F. S. Schmitt. Stuttgart, 1962.

Truth, Freedom, and Evil: Three Philosophical Dialogues [*De Veritate, De Libertate Arbitrii, De Casu Diaboli*]. Ed. and trans. Jasper Hopkins and Herbert Richardson. New York, 1967.

Arbib, Michael A., and Mary B. Hesse. *The Construction of Reality*. Cambridge, 1986.

Aristotle. *The Metaphysics*. Trans. and ed. Hugh Tredennick. 2 vols. London and Cambridge, MA, 1980, 1977 [1933, 1935].

On the Heavens. Trans. and ed. W. K. C. Guthrie. London and Cambridge, MA, 1986 [1939].

The Physics. Trans. and ed. Philip H. Wicksteed and Francis M. Cornford. 2 vols. London and Cambridge, MA, 1980 [²1957].

Armogathe, Jean-Robert. '*An sit deus:* les preuves de dieu chez Marin Mersenne', *Les Etudes philosophiques* 1–2 (1994), 161–70.

Ashtor, Eliyahu. *The Jews of Moslem Spain*. Vol. 1. Trans. Aaron Klein and Jenny Machlowitz Klein. Philadelphia, 1973.

Averroes [Ibn Rushd]. *On the Harmony of Religion and Philosophy*. Ed. and trans. George F. Hourani. London, 1961.

Tahafut al-Tahafut. Ed. and trans. Simon van den Bergh. 2 vols. London, 1954.

Bachmann, Peter R. *Roberto Nobili, 1577–1656: Ein missionsgeschichtlicher Beitrag zum christlichen Dialog mit Hinduismus*. Rome, 1972.

Bacon, Roger. *Compendium of the Study of Theology*. Ed. and trans. Thomas S. Maloney. Leiden, 1988.

Baer, Yitzhak. *A History of the Jews in Christian Spain*. Trans. Louis Schoffman *et al.* 2 vols. Philadelphia, 1978.

Bahadur, K. P. *The Wisdom of Nyaaya*. New Delhi, 1988.

Bailyn, Bernard. *The Ideological Origins of the American Revolution*. Cambridge, MA, 1967.

Balasubramanian, R. (ed. and trans.). *The Naiskarmyasiddhi of Suresvara*. Madras, 1988.

The Taittiriyopanisad Bahsya-Vartika of Suresvara. Madras, ²1984.

Barbay, Pierre. *Commentarius in Aristotelis Metaphysicam, Authore Magistro Pietro Barbay.* Paris, ²1676.
 Compendium Theologiae D. Barbaei. Paris, ²1693.
Barth, Karl. *Fides Quaerens Intellectum. Anselms Beweis der Existenz Gottes im Zusammenhang seines theologischen Programms* [1931]. Ed. Eberhard Jüngel and Ingolf U. Dalferth. *Karl Barth. Gesamtausgabe, II. Akademische Werke.* Zurich, 1981.
 Theological Existence Today. Trans. R. Birch Hoyle. London, 1933.
Bayle, Peter. *Œuvres diverses* [The Hague, 1731]. Vol. IV. Hildesheim, 1968.
Bayle, Pierre. *Dictionary, Historical and Critical.* 5 vols. London, 1734–8 [English translation of *Dictionnaire*, Amsterdam, ²1702].
 Dictionnaire historique et critique. Amsterdam, 1697; ²1702; ³1740.
 Historical and Critical Dictionary: Selections. Trans. and ed. Richard H. Popkin. Indianapolis, 1965.
 Recueil de quelques pièces curieuses concernant la philosophie de Monsieur Descartes. Amsterdam, 1684.
Beaurecueil, S. de, and G. C. Anawati. 'Une preuve de l'existence de dieu chez Ghazzali et S. Thomas', *Mélanges de l'institut dominicain des études orientales*, 3 (1956), 207–58.
Beck, L. W. *Early German Philosophy: Kant and his Predecessors.* Cambridge, MA, 1969.
Beiser, Frederick C. *The Sovereignty of Reason: The Defense of Rationality in the Early English Enlightenment.* Princeton, 1996.
Bello, Iysa A. *The Medieval Islamic Controversy between Philosophy and Orthodoxy.* Leiden, 1989.
Belvalkar, Krishna Shripad, and R. D. Ranade. *History of Indian Philosophy: The Creative Period.* New Delhi, ²1974.
Bennett, R. F. *The Early Dominicans.* Cambridge, 1937.
Berger, David. 'Gilbert Crispin, Alan of Lille and Jacob ben Reuben', *Speculum* 49 (1974), 34–47.
 'Mission to the Jews and Jewish–Christian Contacts in the Polemical Literature of the High Middle Ages', *American Historical Review* 91 (1986), 576–91.
Bergier, Nicolas-Sylvestre. *Apologie de la religion chrétienne.* Paris, 1768.
 Certitude des preuves du christianisme. Paris, 1767.
 Le déisme réfuté par lui-même. Paris, 1765.
 Examen du matérialisme, ou Réfutation du Système de la nature. Paris, 1771.
Bering, J. *Prüfung der Beweise für das Dasein Gottes aus den Begriffen eines höchstvollkommenen und notwendigen Wesens.* Gießen, 1780.
Berkeley, George. *Three Dialogues between Hylas and Philonous.* Ed. Jonathan Dancy. Oxford, 1998.
Berman, David. *A History of Atheism in Britain: From Hobbes to Russell.* London and New York, ²1990.
Bernard, Henri. *Le Père Matthiew Ricci et la Société Chinoise de son temps (1552–1610).* 2 vols. Tientsin, 1937.

Bernstein, Richard J. *Beyond Objectivism and Relativism: Science, Hermeneutics, and Praxis.* Oxford, 1983.

Bettray, Johannes. *Die Akkommodationsmethode des P. Matteo Ricci, S. J., in China.* Rome, 1955.

Bhabha, Homi K. *The Location of Culture.* London, 1994.

Bharadwaja, V. K. 'Implication and Entailment in Navya-Nyaya Logic', *Journal of Indian Philosophy* 15 (1987), 149–54.

Bhatt, Govardhan P. *The Basic Ways of Knowing: An In-Depth Study of Kumarila's Contribution to Indian Epistemology.* Delhi, ²1989.

Bhatta, Jayanta. *Nyayamanjari: The Compendium of Indian Speculative Logic.* Trans. Janaki Vallabha Bhattacharyya. Delhi, 1978.

Bhattacharya, Dineshachandra. *History of Navya-Nyaya in Mithila.* Darbhanga, 1958.

Bhattacharya, Kamaleswar. 'A Note on the Buddhist Syllogism', in *Philosophical Essays: Professor Anantalal Thakur Felicitation Volume.* Calcutta, 1987, pp. 7–10.

Bhattacharya, Tarasankar. *The Nature of Vyapti according to the Navya-Nyaya.* Calcutta, 1970.

Bhattacharyya, Gopikamohan. *Studies in Nyaya-Vaisesika Theism.* Calcutta, 1961.

Bhattacharyya, Sibajiban. *Doubt, Belief and Knowledge.* New Delhi, 1987.

Biderman, Shlomo, and Ben-Ami Scharfstein (eds.). *Interpretation in Religion.* Leiden, 1992.

Rationality in Question: On Eastern and Western Views of Rationality. Leiden, 1989.

Biechler, James E. 'A New Face Toward Islam: Nicholas of Cusa and John of Segovia', in *Nicholas of Cusa in Search of God and Wisdom: Essays in Honor of Morimichi Watanabe by the American Cusanus Society.* Ed. Gerald Christianson and Thomas M. Izbicki. Leiden, 1991, pp. 185–202.

Bijlert, V. A. van. *Epistemology and Spiritual Authority: The Development of Epistemology and Logic in the Old Nyaya and the Buddhist School of Epistemology.* Vienna, 1989.

Blackburn, Anne M. *Buddhist Learning and Textual Practice in Eighteenth-Century Lankan Monastic Culture.* Princeton, 2001.

'Looking for the Vinaya: Monastic Discipline in the Practical Canons of the Theravada', *Journal of the International Association of Buddhist Studies* 22/2 (1999), 281–309.

Blanche, F. A. 'Le vocabulaire de l'argumentation et la structure de l'article dans les ouvrages de saint Thomas', *Revue des sciences philosophiques et theologiques* 14 (1925), 167–87.

Blumenberg, Hans. *Die Lesbarkeit der Welt.* Frankfurt, 1986.

Boethius. *The Consolation of Philosophy.* Trans. and ed. H. F. Stewart. London and New York, 1918.

The Theological Tractates. Trans. and ed. H. F. Stewart and E. K. Rand, 1936.

Bonaventura. *Bonaventure.* Ed. and trans. Ewert Cousins. New York, 1978.

Opera Omnia. Collegium S. Bonaventurae edition. 10 vols. Quaracchi, 1882–1902.

The Works of Bonaventure. Ed. and trans. José de Vinck. 5 vols. Paterson, NJ, 1960–70.

Bond, H. Lawrence. 'The Journey of the Soul to God in Nicholas of Cusa's De Ludo Globi', in *Nicholas of Cusa in Search of God and Wisdom: Essays in Honor of Morimichi Watanabe by the American Cusanus Society*. Ed. Gerald Christianson and Thomas M. Izbicki. Leiden, 1991, pp. 71–86.

Booth, Edward. *Aristotelian Aporetic Ontology in Islamic and Christian Thinkers*. Cambridge, 1983.

Borowski, L. E., R. B. Jachmann and A. Ch. Wasianski. *Immanuel Kant: Sein Leben in Darstellungen von Zeitgenossen* [Berlin, 1912]. Darmstadt, 1980.

Borstin, Daniel J. *The Lost World of Thomas Jefferson*. New York, 1948.

Bougerol, Jacques Guy. *Introduction to the Works of Bonaventure*. Trans. José de Vinck. Paterson, NJ, 1964.

Bougerol, Jacques Guy (ed.). *S. Bonaventura 1274–1974*. 5 vols. Grottaferrata, 1972–4.

Bracken, Harry M. 'Bayle's Attack on Natural Theology: The Case of Christian Pyrrhonism', in *Scepticism and Irreligion in the 17th and 18th Centuries*. Ed. Richard H. Popkin and Arjo Vanderjagt. Leiden, 1993, pp. 254–66.

Breckenridge, Carol A., *et al.* (eds.). *Cosmopolitanism. Public Culture* 12/3 (2000).

Brecher, Robert. *Anselm's Argument: The Logic of Divine Existence*. Aldershot, 1985.

Brierley, Peter. *'Christian' England: What the English Church Census Reveals*. London, 1991.

Brierley, Peter (ed.). *UK Christian Handbook 1989–90*. London, 1988.

Broadie, Alexander. 'Maimonides and Aquinas on the Names of God', *Religious Studies* 23 (1987), 157–70.

Brockington, John L. *The Sacred Thread: Hinduism in its Continuity and Diversity*. Edinburgh, 1981.

Brockliss, L. W. B. 'Aristotle, Descartes and the New Science: Natural Philosophy at the University of Paris, 1600–1740', *Annals of Science* 38 (1981), 33–69.

French Higher Education in the Seventeenth and Eighteenth Centuries: A Cultural History. Oxford, 1987.

Bronkhorst, Johannes. 'God in Samkhya', *WZKSO* 27 (1983), 149–64.

'Nagarjuna and the Naiyayikas', *Journal of Indian Philosophy* 13 (1985), 107–32.

Brooke, John Hedley. 'The Natural Theology of the Geologists: Some Theological Strata', in *Images of the Earth: Essays in the History of the Environmental Sciences*. Ed. L. J. Jordanova and Roy S. Porter. Chalfont St Giles, 1979, pp. 39–64.

'The Relations between Darwin's Science and his Religion', in *Darwinism and Divinity*. Ed. J. R. Durant. Oxford, 1985, pp. 40–75.

'Science and the Fortunes of Natural Theology: Some Historical Perspectives', *Zygon* 24 (1989), 3–22.

Science and Religion: Some Historical Perspectives. Cambridge, 1991.

Brooke, Rosalind B. *The Coming of the Friars*. London and New York, 1975.

Brown, Stuart C. (ed.). *Reason and Religion*. Ithaca, 1977.

Bruce, Steve (ed.). *Religion and Modernization*. Oxford, 1992.

Brückner, Heidrun. *Zum Beweisverfahren Samkaras*. Berlin, 1979.

Buckley, Michael J. *At the Origins of Modern Atheism*. New Haven, 1987.

Motion and Motion's God: Thematic Variations in Aristotle, Cicero, Newton, Hegel. Princeton, 1971.

Buckley, Thomas H. 'The Political Theology of Thomas Jefferson', in *The Virginia Statute for Religious Freedom: Its Evolution and Consequences in American History*. Ed. Merrill D. Peterson and Robert C. Vaughan. Cambridge, 1988.

Buffier, Claude. *Eléments de métaphysique*. Paris, 1725.

Œuvres philosophiques du Père Buffier. Notes and introduction by Francisque Bouillier. Paris, 1843.

Traité des premières vérités et de la source de nos jugements. Paris, 1724.

Buijs, Joseph A. (ed.). *Maimonides: A Collection of Critical Essays*. Notre Dame, 1988.

Bulcke, C. *The Theism of Nyaya-Vaisesika: Its Origin and Early Development*. Delhi, ²1968.

Burbach, Maur. 'Early Dominican and Franciscan Legislation regarding St. Thomas', *Mediaeval Studies* 4 (1942), 139–58.

Burnyeat, Myles (ed.). *The Skeptical Tradition*. Berkeley, 1983.

Burrell, David B. *Knowing the Unknowable God: Ibn-Sina, Maimonides, Aquinas*. Notre Dame, 1986.

'The Unknowability of God in al-Ghazali', *Religious Studies* 23 (1987), 171–82.

Butterworth, Edward J. 'Form and Significance of the Sphere in Nicholas of Cusa's De Ludo Globi', in *Nicholas of Cusa in Search of God and Wisdom: Essays in Honor of Morimichi Watanabe by the American Cusanus Society*. Ed. Gerald Christianson and Thomas M. Izbicki. Leiden, 1991, pp. 89–100.

Byrne, James. *Glory, Jest and Riddle: Religious Thought in the Enlightenment*. London, 1996.

Cabrera, Miguel A. Badía. *Hume's Reflection on Religion*. Dordrecht, 2001.

Cahn, Stephen M. 'The Irrelevance to Religion of Philosophic Proofs for the Existence of God', *American Philosophical Quarterly* 6 (1969), 170–2.

Campbell, George. *A Dissertation on Miracles: Containing an Examination of the Principles Advanced by David Hume, Esq., in an Essay on Miracles*. Edinburgh and London, 1796, ³1797.

Campbell, Richard. *From Belief to Understanding*. Canberra, 1976.

Cannadine, David. *Orientalism: How the British Saw their Empire*. New York, 2001.

Carman, John B. *The Theology of Ramanuja: An Essay in Interreligious Understanding*. New Haven, 1974.

Cassirer, Ernst. *Kants Leben und Lehre* [Berlin, ²1921]. Darmstadt, 1977.

Castillon, Johann von. *Observations sur le livre intitulé Système de la nature*. Paris, 1771.

Caton, John R. (ed.). *Aristotle: The Collected Papers of Joseph Owens*. Albany, 1981.

St Thomas Aquinas on the Existence of God: Collected Papers of Joseph Owens. Albany, 1980.

Catto, J. I. (ed.). *The History of the University of Oxford*, I: *The Early Oxford Schools*. Oxford, 1984.

Chakrabarty, Dipesh. *Provincializing Europe: Postcolonial Thought and Historical Difference*. Princeton, 2000.

Chambers, Connor J. 'Prime Movers and Prim Movers', *The Thomist* 31 (1967), 465–507.

Chari, Srinivasa. *Fundamentals of Visistadvaita Vedanta: A Study based on Vedanta Desika's Tattva-mukta-kalapa*. Delhi, 1987.

Chatillon, Jean. 'De Guillaume d'Auxerre à saint Thomas d'Aquin: l'argument de saint Anselme chez les premiers scholastiques du XIIIᵉ siècle', *Spicilegium Beccense* 1 (1959), 209–31.

Chatterjee, Satischandra. *The Nyaya Theory of Knowledge: A Critical Study of Some Problems of Logic and Metaphysics*. Calcutta, ³1965.

Chattopadhyaya, Debiprasad. *Lokayata: A Study in Ancient Indian Materialism*. New Delhi, 1959, ⁴1978.

Chattopadhyaya, Debiprasad (ed.). *Studies in the History of Indian Philosophy*. 3 vols. Calcutta, 1979.

Chaudon, Loius-Mayeul. *Anti-dictionnaire philosophique*. 2 vols. Paris, 1775.

Chazan, Robert. 'The Barcelona "Disputation" of 1263: Christian Missionizing and Jewish Response', *Speculum* 52 (1977), 824–42.

'Confrontation in the Synagogue of Narbonne: A Christian Sermon and a Jewish Reply', *Harvard Theological Review* 67 (1974), 437–57.

Daggers of Faith: Thirteenth-Century Christian Missionizing and Jewish Response. Berkeley, 1989.

European Jewry and the First Crusade. Berkeley, 1987.

Chemparathy, George. 'Aufkommen und Entwicklung der Lehre von einem höchsten Wesen in Nyaya und Vaisesika'. Diss. Phil., University of Vienna, 1963.

L'autorité du Veda selon les Nyaya-Vaisesikas. Louvain-la-Neuve, 1983.

An Indian Rational Theology: Introduction to Udayana's Nyayakusumanjali. Vienna, 1972.

'Meaning and Role of the Concept of Mahajanaparigraha in the Ascertainment of the Validity of the Veda', in *Philosophical Essays: Professor Anantalal Thakur Felicitation Volume*. Ed. Rama Ranjan Mukhopadhyaya *et al.* Calcutta, 1987, pp. 67–80.

'The Testimony of the Yuktidipika concerning the Isvara Doctrine of the Pasupatas and Vaisesikas', *WZKSO* 9 (1965), 119–46.

'Two Early Buddhist Refutations of the Existence of Isvara as the Creator of the Universe', *WZKSO* 12/13 (1968/9), 85–100.

Chenu, M.-D. 'Antiqui, Moderni', *Revue des sciences philosophiques et theologiques* 17 (1928), 82–94.

Toward Understanding Saint Thomas. Trans. and ed. A.-M. Landry and D. Hughes. Chicago, 1964.

Chinchore, Mangala R. 'Post-Udayana Nyaya Reactions to Dharmakirti's *Vadanyaya* – An Evaluation', in *Studies in the Buddhist Epistemological Tradition*. Ed. Ernst Steinkellner. Vienna, 1991, pp. 3–17.

'Some Thoughts on Significant Contributions of Buddhist Logicians', *Journal of Indian Philosophy* 15 (1987), 155–71.

Vadanyaya: A Glimpse of Nyaya-Buddhist Controversy. Delhi, 1987.

A Christian. *An Essay of the Immateriality and Immortality of the Soul, and It's Instinctive Sense of Good and Evil; In Opposition to the Opinions Advanced in The Essays Introductory to Dr. Priestley's Abridgement of Dr. Hartley's Observations on Man.* London, 1777.

Christian, William A. *Doctrines of Religious Communities: A Philosophical Study.* New Haven, 1987.

Oppositions of Religious Doctrines: A Study in the Logic of Dialogue among Religions. London, 1972.

Cicero. *De Finibus Bonorum et Malorum.* Trans. and ed. H. Rackham. London and Cambridge, MA, 1971 [²1931].

De Natura Deorum. Trans. and ed. H. Rackham. London and Cambridge, MA, 1979 [1933].

De Senectute, De Amicitia, De Divinatione. Ed. and trans. William Armistead Falconer. London and Cambridge, MA, 1979 [1923].

Clayton, John. *The Concept of Correlation.* Berlin and New York, 1980.

'Gottesbeweise', in *Theologische Realenzyklopädie,* XIII (Berlin and New York, 1984), pp. 724–84.

'Religious Diversity and Public Reason', in *Perspectives in Contemporary Philosophy of Religion.* Ed. Tommi Lehtonen and Timo Koistinen (Helsinki, 2000).

'Sprache, Sinn und Verifizierungsverfahren', *Philosophisches Jahrbuch* 85 (1978), 144–62.

'Tillich, Troeltsch and the Dialectical Theology', *Modern Theology,* 4/4 (July 1988), 323–44.

'Universal Human Rights and Traditional Religious Values', in *Human Rights and Responsibilities in a Divided World.* Ed. Jaroslav Krejci (Prague, 1997), pp. 29–46.

Cobban, A. B. *The Medieval Universities: Their Development and Organisation.* London, 1975.

'Theology and Law in the Medieval Colleges of Oxford and Cambridge', *Bulletin of the John Rylands Library* 65 (1982), 57–77.

Cohen, Jeremy. *The Friars and the Jews.* Ithaca, 1982.

Cohen, Martin A. 'Reflections on the Text and Context of the Disputation of Barcelona', *Hebrew Union College Annual* 35 (1964), 157–92.

Cohen, Ted, Paul Guyer and Hilary Putnam. *Pursuits of Reason: Essays in Honor of Stanley Cavell.* Lubbock, 1993.

Colish, Marcia L. *Peter Lombard.* 2 vols. Leiden, 1994.

Cometti, Elizabeth (ed.). *Jefferson's Ideas on a University Library: Letters from the Founder of the University of Virginia to a Boston Bookseller.* Charlottesville, 1950.

Coulson, Noel J. *Conflicts and Tensions in Islamic Jurisprudence.* Chicago, 1969.

Craig, William Lane. *The Cosmological Argument from Plato to Leibniz.* London, 1980.

The Kalam Cosmological Argument. London, 1979.
Crispin, Gilbert. *Disputatio Judei et Christiani.* Ed. B. Blumenkranz. Antwerp, 1956.
The Works of Gilbert Crispin. Ed. A. S. Abulafia and G. R. Evans. Oxford, 1986.
Cronin, Vincent. *A Pearl to India.* London, 1959.
The Wise Man from the West. London, 1984 [1955].
Cunningham, Noble E. *In Pursuit of Reason: The Life of Thomas Jefferson.* Baton Rouge, 1987.
Cutler, Allan H., and Helen E. Cutler. *The Jew as Ally of the Muslim: Medieval Roots of Anti-Semitism.* Notre Dame, 1986.
Dabney, Virginia. *Mr Jefferson's University: A History.* Charlottesville, 1981.
D'Agnostino, Fred. *Free Public Reason: Making It Up as We Go.* New York and Oxford, 1996.
Dales, Richard C. *The Intellectual Life of Western Europe in the Middle Ages.* Leiden, 1992.
Medieval Discussions of the Eternity of the World. Leiden, 1990.
Dales, Richard C., and Omar Argerami (eds.). *Medieval Latin Texts on the Eternity of the World.* Leiden, 1991.
Dalferth, Ingolf U. 'Fides Quaerens Intellectum: Theologie als Kunst der Argumentation in Anselms Proslogion', *Zeitschrift für Theologie und Kirche* 81 (1984), 54–105.
'The One Who is Worshipped: Erwängungen zu Charles Hartshornes Versuch, Gott zu denken', *Zeitschrift für Theologie und Kirche* 83 (1986), 484–506.
Daniel, E. R. *The Franciscan Concept of Mission in the Middle Ages.* Lexington, KY, 1975.
Daniel, Gabriel. *Voyage du monde de Descartes.* Paris, 1702.
Daniel, Norman. *The Arabs and Medieval Europe.* London, ^{2}1979.
Islam and the West: The Making of an Image. Edinburgh, ^{2}1980.
Daniels, Augustinus. *Quellenbeiträge Untersuchungen zum Geschichte der Gottesbeweise im dreizehnten Jahrhundert.* Beiträge zur Geschichte der Philosophie des Mittelalters, VIII/1–2. Münster, 1909.
Darling, Gregory J. *An Evaluation of the Vedantic Critique of Buddhism.* Delhi, 1987.
Dasgupta, Surendranath. *History of Indian Philosophy.* 5 vols. Cambridge, 1922–54.
Davidson, Donald. *Inquiries into Truth and Interpretation.* Oxford, 1984.
Davidson, Herbert A. *Proofs for Eternity, Creation and the Existence of God in Medieval Islamic and Jewish Philosophy.* Oxford, 1987.
Davis, Richard H. *Ritual in an Oscillating Universe: Worshipping Siva in Medieval India.* Princeton, 1991.
Dawkins, Richard. *The Blind Watchmaker.* New York, 1986.
de Lange, Nicholas. *Judaism.* Oxford, 1986.
Delaney, C. F. (ed.). *Rationality and Religious Belief.* Notre Dame, 1979.
Desmond, Adrian. 'Artisan Resistance and Evolution in Britain, 1819–1848', *Osiris,* 2nd series, 3 (1987), 77–110.

Desmond, Adrian, and James Moore. *Darwin: The Life of a Tormented Evolutionist.* New York, 1992.

Deussen, Paul. *Die nachvedische Philosophie der Inder.* Vol. 1/3 of *Allgemeine Geschichte der Philosophie.* Leipzig, ³1920.

The System of the Vedanta according to Badarayana's Brahma-sutras and Sankara's Commentary thereon Set Forth as a Compendium of the Dogmatics of Brahmanism from the Standpoint of Sankara.* Trans. Charles Johnston. Chicago, 1912; repr. New York, 1973.

Devaraja, N. K. *An Introduction to Sankara's Theory of Knowledge.* Delhi, ²1972.

Dhruva, A. B. (ed.). *Nyayapravesa of Dinnaga with the Commentaries of Haribhadra Suri and Parsavadeva.* Delhi, ²1987 [Baroda, 1930].

Diderot, Denis. *Lettres à Sophie Volland.* Vol. II. Ed. André Babelon. Paris, 1938.

Œuvres philosophiques. Ed. Paul Vernière. Paris, 1964.

Dirks, Nicholas B. *Castes of Mind: Colonialism and the Making of Modern India.* Princeton, 2001.

Dodd, Dr. *A Philosophical and Religious Dialogue in the Shades, between Mr. Hume and Dr. Dodd, with Notes by the Editor.* London, 1778.

Dodge, Bayard. *Muslim Education in Medieval Times.* Washington, DC, 1962.

Donaldson, Thomas E. *Hindu Temple Art of Orissa.* 3 vols. Leiden, 1985–7.

Doniger [O'Flaherty], Wendy (ed.). *Karma and Rebirth in Classical Indian Traditions.* Berkeley, 1980.

The Origins of Evil in Hindu Mythology. Berkeley, 1976.

Douglas, Mary. *How Institutions Think.* London, 1986.

Dragona-Monachou, Myrto. *Stoic Arguments for the Existence and the Providence of the Gods.* Athens, 1976.

Du Hamel, Jean. *Quaedam Recentiorum Philosophorum ac Praesertim Cartesii Propositiones Damnatae ac Prohibitae.* Paris, 1705.

Réflexions critiques sur le système cartésien de la philosophie de M. Régis, par M. Jean Du Hamel. Paris, 1692.

Dummett, Michael. *Truth and Other Enigmas.* London, 1978.

Dunlop, D. M. 'A Christian Mission to Muslim Spain in the 11th Century', *Al-andalus* 17 (1952), 260–310.

Duns Scotus, John. *God and Creatures: The Quodlibetal Questions.* Ed. and trans. Felix Alluntis and Allan B. Wolter. Princeton, 1975.

Philosophical Writings. Ed. and trans. Allan Wolter. London, 1962.

Eadmer. *The Life of St Anselm.* Ed. and trans. Richard W. Southern. Oxford, ²1972.

Eck, Diana L. *Banaras: City of Light.* New York, 1982.

'The City as a Sacred Center', *Journal of Developing Societies* 2 (1986), 149–59.

Edwards, Jonathan. *Scientific and Philosophical Writings.* Ed. Wallace E. Anderson [Vol. VI of *The Works of Jonathan Edwards.* Ed. John E. Smith]. New Haven, 1980.

Edwards, Paul (ed.). *Encyclopedia of Philosophy.* 8 vols. New York and London, 1967.

Eisenstadt, S. N., *et al.* (eds.). *Orthodoxy, Heterodoxy and Dissent in India.* Berlin and New York, 1984.

Eisenstadt, Shmuel N., Wolfgang Schluchter and Bjørn Wittrock (eds.). *Early Modernities. Dædalus* 127/3 (Summer 1998).

Emden, A. B. *Biographical Register of the University of Cambridge to 1500*. Cambridge, 1963.

Biographical Register of the University of Oxford to AD 1500. 3 vols. Oxford, 1957–9.

Erdmann, Carl. *The Origin of the Idea of Crusade*. Princeton, 1977.

Eschmann, Anncharlott, *et al.* (eds.). *The Cult of Jagannath and the Regional Tradition of Orissa*. New Delhi, 1978.

Evans, G. R. *Anselm and a New Generation*. Oxford, 1980.

Anselm and Talking about God. Oxford, 1978.

Old Arts and New Theology: The Beginnings of Theology as an Academic Discipline. Oxford, 1980.

Evans, G. R. (ed.). *A Concordance to the Works of St. Anselm*. 4 vols. Millwood, NY, 1984.

Fackenheim, Emil. *Encounters between Judaism and Modern Philosophy*. New York, ²1980.

Fakhry, Majid. 'The Classical Islamic Arguments for the Existence of God', *Muslim World* 47 (1957), 133–45.

A History of Islamic Philosophy. London and New York, ²1983 [1970].

Febvre, Lucien. *The Problem of Unbelief in the Sixteenth Century: The Religion of Rabelais*. Trans. Beatrice Gottlieb. Cambridge, MA, 1982.

Fénélon, François. *Démonstration de l'existence de Dieu, tirée de la connoissance de la nature, et proportionnée à la foible intelligence des plus simples*. Amsterdam, 1713.

Ferreira, M. Jamie. *Scepticism and Reasonable Doubt: The British Naturalist Tradition in Wilkins, Hume, Reid, and Newman*. Oxford, 1986.

Feuerstein, Georg. 'The Concept of God (*Isvara*) in Classical Yoga', *Journal of Indian Philosophy* 15 (1987), 385–97.

The Philosophy of Classical Yoga. Manchester, 1980.

Fichte, Johann Gottlieb. 'Über den Grund unseres Glaubens an eine göttliche Weltregierung', *Philosophisches Journal* 8 (1798), 21–46.

Werke. Ed. F. Medicus. 6 vols. Leipzig, 1908–12.

Fieser, James (ed). *Early Responses to Hume's Writings on Religion*. 2 vols. Bristol, 2001, 2005.

Findlay, J. N. *Ascent to the Absolute: Metaphysical Papers and Lectures*. London and New York, 1970.

Finke, Roger, and Rodney Stark. *The Churching of America 1776–1990: Winners and Losers in Our Religious Economy*. New Brunswick, NJ, 1992.

Fisch, Menachem, and Simon Schaffer (eds.). *William Whewell: A Composite Portrait*. Oxford, 1991.

Flew, Antony. *David Hume: Philosopher of Moral Science*. Oxford, 1986.

Hume's Philosophy of Belief: A Study of his First Inquiry. New York, 1961.

Introduction to Western Philosophy: Ideas and Arguments from Plato to Sartre. Indianapolis, 1971.

Flew, Antony, and Alasdair MacIntyre (eds.). *New Essays in Philosophical Theology*. London, 1955.

Forberg, Friedrich. 'Entwicklung des Begriffes der Religion', *Philosophisches Journal* 8 (1798), 1–20.

Foreville, Raymonde (ed.). *Les mutations socio-culturelles: au tournant des xie–xiie siècles*. Paris, 1984.

Foster, Michael N. *Hegel and Skepticism*. Cambridge, MA, 1989.

Franco, Eli. *Perception, Knowledge and Disbelief: A Study of Jayarasi's Scepticism*. Stuttgart, 1987.

Franco, Eli and Karin Preisendanz (eds.). *Beyond Orientalism: The Work of Wilhelm Halbfass and its Impact on Indian and Cross-Cultural Studies*. Amsterdam, 1997.

Frauwallner, Eric. 'Die Erkenntnislehre des klassischen Samkhya-Systems', *WZKSO* 2 (1958), 84–139.

Geschichte der indischen Philosophie. 2 vols. Salzburg, 1953, 1956 [English translation: Delhi, 1973].

'Landmarks in the History of Indian Logic', *WZKSO* 5 (1961), 125–48.

Nachgelassene Werke, I. Vienna, 1984.

'Vasubandhu's Vadavidhih', *WZKSO* 1 (1957), 104–46.

Funkenstein, Amos. *Theology and the Scientific Imagination from the Middle Ages to the Seventeenth Century*. Princeton, 1986.

Ganeri, Jonardon. *Philosophy in Classical India: The Proper Work of Reason*. London, 2001.

Gaonkar, Dilip Parameshwar (ed.). *Alternative Modernities*. Durham, NC, 2001.

Gardet, Louis. *La pensée religieuse d'Avicenne*. Paris, 1951.

Gaskin, J. C. A. *Hume's Philosophy of Religion*. London, ²1988.

Gaustad, Edwin Scott. *Historical Atlas of Religion in America*. New York, ²1976.

Gay, Peter. *The Enlightenment: An Interpretation*. 2 vols. London, 1967, 1970.

Geertz, Clifford. *Local Knowledge*. New York, 1983.

Gerson, Lloyd P. (ed.). *Graceful Reason: Essays in Ancient and Medieval Philosophy Presented to Joseph Owens*. Toronto, 1983.

al-Ghazali. *The Foundations of the Articles of Faith*. Trans. Nabih Amin Farris. Lahore, 1969.

Freedom and Fulfillment. Trans. and ed. R. J. McCarthy. Boston, 1980.

'The Jerusalem Tract', trans. and ed. A. L. Tibawi, *Islamic Quarterly* 9 (1965), 95–122.

On Divine Predicates and their Properties. Ed. and trans. ʿAbdu-r-Rahman abu Zayd. Lahore, 1970.

The Recitation and Interpretation of the Qurʾan. Trans. and ed. Muhammad Abul Quasem. Kuala Lumpur, 1979.

Tahafut al-Falasifa. Ed. and trans. S. A. Kamali. Lahore, 1958.

Ghose, Ramendranath. *The Dialectics of Nagarjuna*. Allahabad, 1987.

Giddens, Anthony. *The Consequences of Modernity*. Stanford, 1990.

Modernity and Self-Identity: Self and Society in the Late Modern Age. Stanford, 1991.

Gilson, Etienne. *The Philosophy of St. Bonaventure.* Trans. Illtyd Trethowan. London, 1940.

The Philosophy of St. Thomas Aquinas. Trans. Edward Bullough; ed. G. A. Elrington. Cambridge, ²1929.

'Saint Bonaventure et l'évidence de l'existence de Dieu', *Revue neo-scolastique de philosophie* 25 (1923), 237–62.

'Sens et nature de l'argument de saint Anselme', *Archives d'histoire litteraire et doctrinale du moyen age* 9 (1934), 5–51.

Glasenapp, Helmuth von. *Buddhismus und Gottesidee.* Mainz, 1954.

Madhva's Philosophie des Vishnu-Glaubens. Ein Beitrag zur Sektengeschichte des Hinduismus. Bonn and Leipzig, 1923.

Der Stufenweg zum Göttlichen. Shankaras Philosophie der All-Einheit. Baden-Baden, 1948.

Gonda, Jan (ed.). *A History of Indian Literature.* Wiesbaden, 1977.

Goodman, Lenn E. 'Ghazali's Argument from Creation', *International Journal of Middle Eastern Studies* 2 (1971), 67–85, 168–88.

Monotheism: A Philosophical Inquiry into the Foundations of Theology and Ethics. Towota, NJ, 1981.

Goodman, Nelson. *Ways of Worldmaking.* Brighton, 1978.

Goodwin, George L. *The Ontological Argument of Charles Hartshorne.* Missoula, 1978.

Gössmann, Elisabeth. *Metaphysik und Heilsgeschichte. Eine theologische Untersuchung der Summa Halensis.* Munich, 1964.

Grabmann, Martin. 'Der Einfluss Alberts des Grossen auf das mittelalterliche Geistesleben', *Zeitschrift für katholische Theologie* 25 (1928), 153–82.

Die Geschichte der scholastischen Methode. 2 vols. Darmstadt, 1988 [1909–11].

Graham, William A. *Beyond the Written Word: Oral Aspects of Scripture in the History of Religion.* Cambridge, 1987.

Granoff, P. E. *Philosophy and Argument in Late Vedanta: Sri Harsa's Khandanakhandakhadya.* Dordrecht, 1978.

Grayzel, Solomon. *The Church and the Jews in the XIIIth Century* [vol. I: 1198–1254]. Philadelphia, 1933; New York, 1966.

The Church and the Jews in the XIIIth Century [vol. II: 1254–1314]. New York, 1989.

Greene, Jack P. *Pursuits of Happiness: The Social Development of Early Modern British Colonies and the Formation of American Culture.* Chapel Hill, 1988.

Griswold, Charles L., Jr. 'Religion and Community: Adam Smith on the Virtues of Liberty', *Journal of the History of Philosophy* 35/3 (1997), 395–419.

Grunwald, Georg. *Geschichte der Gottesbeweise im Mittelalter bis zum Ausgang der Hochscholastik.* Beiträge zur Geschichte der Philosophie des Mittelalters, VI/3. Münster, 1907.

Gupta, Anima Sen. *A Critical Study of the Philosophy of Ramanuja.* Varanasi, 1967.

Gupta, Chitrarekha. *The Brahmanas of India: A Study Based on Inscriptions.* Delhi, 1983.

Guthrie, W. K. C. *A History of Greek Philosophy.* 6 vols. Cambridge, 1962–81.

Guttmann, Julius. *Philosophies of Judaism: The History of Jewish Philosophy from Biblical Times to Franz Rosenzweig.* Trans. David W. Silverman. London, 1964.

Hacker, Paul. 'Anviksiki', *WZKSO* 2 (1958), 54–83.

'Die Indologie zwischen Vergangenheit und Zukunft', *Hochland* 60 (1967–8).

Kleine Schriften. Ed. Lambert Schmithausen. Wiesbaden, 1978.

'Religiöse Toleranz und Intoleranz in Hinduismus', *Saeculum* 8 (1957), 167–79.

Untersuchungen über Texte des frühen Advaitavada: 1. Die Schüler Sankaras. Mainz, 1951.

Halbfass, Wilhelm. *Descartes' Frage nach der Existenz der Welt. Untersuchungen über die cartesianische Denkpraxis und Metaphysik.* Meisenheim am Glan, 1968.

India and Europe: An Essay in Understanding. Albany, 1988.

'Indian and Western Philosophy: Preliminary Remarks on a Method of Comparison', *Journal of the Bihar Research Society* 54 (1968), 359–64.

'Indian Philosophers on the Plurality of Religious Traditions', in *Identity and Division in Cults and Sects in South Asia.* Ed. Peter Gaeffke and David Utz (Philadelphia, 1984), pp. 58–64.

'Observations on Darsana', *WZKSO* 23 (1979), 195–203.

On Being and What There Is: Classical Vaisesika and the History of Indian Ontology. Albany, 1992.

Studies in Kumarila and Sankara. Studien zur Indologie und Iranistik Monographie, 9. Reinbek, 1983.

Tradition and Reflection: Explorations in Indian Thought. Albany, 1991.

Halevi, Yehuda. *The Kuzari: An Argument for the Faith of Israel.* Trans. Hartwig Hirschfeld. New York, 1964.

Poems, German and Hebrew: Selections. Ed. Franz Rosenzweig and Rafael Rosenzweig. The Hague, 1983.

Selected Poems. Trans. N. Salaman. Philadelphia, 1925.

Hall, Alfred Rupert. *Philosophers at War: The Quarrel between Newton and Leibniz.* Cambridge, 1980.

Hallaq, Wael B. *A History of Islamic Legal Theories.* Cambridge, 1997.

Law and Legal Theory in Classical and Medieval Islam. Aldershot, 1995.

Halsey, A. H. (ed.). *British Social Trends since 1900.* Basingstoke, [2]1988.

Hammon, William. *Answer to Dr. Priestley's Letters to a Philosophical Unbeliever.* London, 1782.

Hammond, Phillip (ed.). *The Sacred in a Secular Age.* Berkeley, 1985.

Hankey, W. J. *God in Himself: Aquinas' Doctrine of God as Expounded in the Summa Theologiae.* Oxford, 1987.

Hara, Minoru. 'Materials for the Study of Pasupata Saivism'. Ph.D. diss., Harvard University, 1966.

Haribhadra. *Sad-Darsana Samuccaya: A Compendium of Six Philosophies.* Trans. and ed. K. S. Murty. Delhi, [2]1986.

Harré, Rom. *One Thousand Years of Philosophy: From Ramanuja to Wittgenstein.* Oxford, 2000.

Harris, James Rendel (ed.). *The Apology of Aristides on Behalf of the Christians.* Cambridge, 1893.

Harrison, Peter. *'Religion' and the Religions in the English Enlightenment.* Cambridge, 1990.

Hartshorne, Charles. *Anselm's Discovery: A Re-examination of the Ontological Argument for God's Existence.* LaSalle, 1965.

The Logic of Perfection. LaSalle, 1962.

A Natural Theology for our Time. LaSalle, 1967.

Hayes, Richard P. *Dignaga on the Interpretation of Signs.* Dordrecht, 1988.

'Principled Atheism in the Buddhist Scholastic Tradition', *Journal of Indian Philosophy* 16 (1988), 5–28.

'The Question of Doctrinalism in the Buddhist Epistemologists', *Journal of the American Academy of Religion* 52 (1984), 645–70.

Hayter, Thomas. *Remarks on Mr. Hume's Dialogues concerning Natural Religion.* Cambridge, 1780.

Healey, Robert M. *Jefferson on Religion in Public Education.* New Haven, 1962.

Heesterman, J. C. *The Inner Conflict of Tradition.* Chicago, 1985.

'On the Origins of the Nastika', *WZKSO* 12–13 (1968/9), 171–85.

Hegel, Georg Wilhelm Friedrich. *Lectures on the Philosophy of Religion: Lectures of 1827.* Berkeley, CA, 1988.

Heidegger, Martin. *Kant and the Problem of Metaphysics.* Trans. from the fourth German edition [1973] by Richard Taft. Bloomington, 1990.

Henrich, Dieter. *Der ontologische Gottesbeweis. Sein Problem und seine Geschichte in der Neuzeit.* Tübingen, ²1967.

Henry, D. P. *The Logic of Saint Anselm.* Oxford, 1967.

Medieval Logic and Metaphysics: A Modern Introduction. London, 1972.

Herder, Johann Gottfried von. *God: Some Conversations.* Trans. Fredrick H. Burkhardt. Indianapolis, 1940.

Ideen zur Philosophie der Geschichte der Menschheit [1784–91]. Darmstadt, 1966.

Herms, E. *Herkunft, Entfaltung und erste Gestalt des Systems der Wissenschaften bei Schleiermacher.* Göttingen, 1974.

Hertz, D. *Jewish High Society in Old Regime Berlin.* New Haven, 1988.

Hesse, Mary. *Revolutions and Reconstructions in the Philosophy of Science.* Brighton, 1980.

Hick, John. *Faith and Knowledge.* London, 1957.

An Interpretation of Religion: Human Responses to the Transcendent. New Haven, 1989.

Hinnebusch, William A. *A History of the Dominican Order.* 2 vols. New York, 1966–73.

Historisches Wörterbuch der Philosophie 7 (1989).

Hobsbawm, Eric, and Terence Ranger. *The Invention of Tradition.* Cambridge, 1983.

Hohenberger, A. *Ramanuja: Ein Philosoph indischer Gottesmystik — Seine Lebensanschauung nach den wichtigsten Quellen.* Bonn, 1960.

Holbach, Paul-Henri Thiry d'. *Le bon-sens, ou Idées naturelles opposées aux idées surnaturelles.* London [Amsterdam], 1772.

Le christianisme dévoilé. London, 1761.

Système de la nature; ou, Des loix du monde physique & du monde moral, par M. Mirabaud. London, 1770.

Théologie portative ou Dictionnaire abrégé de la religion chrétienne. London, 1768.

Hollis, Martin, and Steven Lukes (eds.). *Rationality and Relativism.* Oxford, 1982.

Holyoake, George Jacob. *Paley Refuted in His Own Words.* London, 1847; ²1851; ³1866.

Hopkins, Jasper. *A Companion to the Study of St Anselm.* Minneapolis, 1972.

Hourani, George. 'The Chronology of Ghazali's Writings', *Journal of the American Oriental Society* 79 (1959), 225–33.

Houtteville, Claude-François. *La religion chrétienne prouvée par les faits, avec un discours historique et critique sur la méthode des principaux auteurs qui ont écrit pour et contre le christianisme depuis son origine.* Paris, 1722; ²1740.

La vérité de la religion chrétienne prouvée par les faits. Paris, 1722.

Huet, Pierre Daniel. *Censura Philosophiae Cartesianae* [Kampen, 1690]. Hildesheim, 1971.

Nouveaux mémoires pour servir à l'histoire du cartésianisme [Paris, 1692]. Ed. Claudine Poulouin. Rezé, 1996.

Traité philosophique de la foiblesse de l'esprit humain [Amsterdam, 1723]. Hildesheim, 1974.

Hume Studies 14/2 (November 1988) – 'Philosophy of Religion Issue'.

Hume, David. *Dialogues concerning Natural Religion.* London, 1779, ²1779.

Dialogues concerning Natural Religion. London, 1875.

Dialogues concerning Natural Religion. Introduction by Bruce M'Ewen. Edinburgh and London, 1907.

Dialogues concerning Natural Religion [²1779]. Ed. Norman Kemp Smith. Oxford, 1935; London, ²1947.

Essays Moral and Political. Edinburgh, 1741.

Essays and Treatises on Several Subjects . . . Containing Essays Moral, Political and Literary, to which are Added Dialogues concerning Natural Religion. 2 vols. Edinburgh and London, 1793.

History of England from the Invasion of Julius Caesar to the Revolution of 1688. 6 vols. Edinburgh and London, 1754–62.

The Natural History of Religion [1777]. Ed. H. E. Root. Stanford, 1957.

Philosophical Essays concerning Human Understanding. London, 1748.

The Philosophical Works of David Hume, Esq., Containing Dialogues concerning Natural Religion, Essays on the Immortality of the Soul, Suicide, Fanaticism, Deism, Liberty of the Press, etc. London, 1824.

The Philosophical Works of David Hume. 4 vols. Edinburgh and London, 1826.

The Philosophical Writings of David Hume. Ed. T. H. Green and T. H. Grose. 2 vols. London, 1874 [²1878, ³1882, ⁴1886, ⁵1890, ⁶1898].

A Treatise of Human Nature, ed. L. A. Selby-Bigge Oxford, ²1978.

Hunt, R. W. *The Schools and the Cloister: The Life and Writings of Alexander Nequam (1157–1217)*. Ed. and revised by M. T. Gibson. Oxford, 1984.

Hurlbutt, Robert H., III. *Hume, Newton, and the Design Argument*. Rev. edn. Lincoln, 1985.

Hyman, Arthur (ed.). *Essays in Medieval Jewish and Islamic Philosophy*. New York, 1977.

Hymns Ancient and Modern. London, 1950.

Idel, Moshe. *Golem: Jewish Magical and Mystical Traditions on the Artificial Anthropoid*. Albany, 1990.

   Kabbalah: New Perspectives. New Haven, 1988.

   Language, Torah and Hermeneutics in Abraham Abulafia. Albany, 1988.

   The Mystical Experience in Abraham Abulafia. Albany, 1987.

Inden, Ronald. *Imagining India*. Oxford, 1990.

   'Orientalist Constructions of India', *Modern Asian Studies* 29 (1986), 401–46.

Izbicki, Thomas M. 'The Possibility of Dialogue with Islam in the Fifteenth Century', in *Nicholas of Cusa in Search of God and Wisdom*. Ed. Gerald Christianson and Thomas M. Izbicki. Leiden, 1991, pp. 175–83.

Jabre, Farid. *La notion de certitude selon Ghazali*. Paris, 1958.

Jackson, David P. (ed.). *The Entrance Gate for the Wise: Sa-skya Pandita on Indian and Tibetan Traditions of Pramana and Philosophical Debate*. 2 vols. Vienna, 1987.

Jackson, Roger R. 'The Buddha as *Pramanabhuta*: Epithets and Arguments in the Buddhist "Logical" Tradition', *Journal of Indian Philosophy* 16 (1988), 335–65.

   'Dharmakirti's Refutation of Theism', *Philosophy East and West* 36 (1986), 315–48.

Jacob, Margaret. *The Newtonians and the English Revolution*. Hassocks, 1976.

Jacobi, Friedrich Heinrich. *Briefwechsel*, I/I. Stuttgart, 1981.

   David Hume über den Glauben. Breslau, 1787.

   Werke. Ed. F. Roth. 6 vols. Leipzig, 1812–25.

Jacobi, Hermann. *Die Entwicklung der Gottesidee bei den Indern und deren Beweise für das Dasein Gottes*. Bonn and Leipzig, 1923.

Janke, W. 'Das ontologischen Argument in der Frühzeit des Leibnizischen Denkens (1676–78)', *Kant-Studien* 54 (1963), 259–87.

Jash, Pranabananda. *History of Saivism*. Calcutta, 1974.

Jayantabhatta. *Nyayamanjari: The Compendium of Indian Speculative Logic*. Trans. Janaki Vallabha Bhattacharyya. Delhi, 1978.

Jayatilleke, K. N. *Early Buddhist Theory of Knowledge*. London, 1963.

   The Message of the Buddha. Ed. Ninian Smart. London, 1975.

Jefferson, Thomas. *Extracts from the Gospels*. Ed. Dickinson W. Adams. The Papers of Thomas Jefferson, Second Series. Princeton, 1983.

   Literary Commonplace Book. Ed. Douglas L. Wilson. The Papers of Thomas Jefferson, Second Series. Princeton, 1989.

   Writings. Ed. Merrill D. Peterson. New York, 1984.

Jha, Ganganatha (ed.). *The Tattvasangraha of Santaraksita with the Commentary of Kamalasila*. 2 vols. Baroda, 1937 [reprint, Delhi, 1986].

Jha, Ganganatha (ed. and trans.). *The Nyaya-Sutras of Gautama with Vatsyayana's Bhasya and Udyotakara's Vartika.* 4 vols. Delhi, 1984 [1912–19].

The Prabhakara School of Purva Mimamsa. Delhi, ²1978 [1911].

The Vivadachintamani of Vachaspati Mishra. Baroda, 1942.

Jolley, Nicholas. *Leibniz and Locke: A Study of the New Essays on Human Understanding.* Oxford, 1984.

Jones, Richard Foster. *Ancients and Moderns: A Study of the Rise of the Scientific Movement in Seventeenth-Century England.* New York, 1982 [1936].

Junankar, N. S. *Gautama: The Nyaya Philosophy.* Delhi, 1978.

Kalupahana, David J. *Nagarjuna: The Philosophy of the Middle Way – Mulamadhyamakakarika.* Albany, 1986.

Kangle, R. P. (ed. and trans.). *The Kautiliya Arthasastra.* Bombay, 1963.

Kant, Immanuel. *Critique of Practical Reason.* Trans. Lewis White Beck. Indianapolis and New York, 1956.

Critique of Pure Reason. Trans. Norman Kemp Smith. London, 1964 [²1933].

Foundations of the Metaphysics of Morals. Trans. and ed. Lewis White Beck. Indianapolis and New York, 1959.

Prolegomena to any Future Metaphysics that Will be Able to Present Itself as a Science. Trans. and ed. Peter G. Lucas. Manchester, 1966 [1953].

Religion within the Limits of Reason Alone. Trans. and ed. Theodore M. Greene and Hoyt H. Hudson. LaSalle, 1934; New York, 1960.

Vorlesungen über die philosophische Religionslehre. Ed. Karl Heinrich Ludwig Pölitz. Darmstadt, 1982 [Leipzig, ²1830].

Werke: Akademie-Textausgabe. 9 vols. plus 2 vols. of critical notes. Berlin and New York, 1968.

Kaplan, Lawrence S. *Jefferson and France: An Essay on Politics and Political Ideas.* New Haven, 1967.

Katz, Steven T. (ed.). *Mysticism and Religious Traditions.* Oxford, 1983.

Kedar, Benjamin. *Crusade and Mission: European Approaches to the Muslims.* Princeton, 1984.

Keith, A. Berriedale. *A History of Sanskrit Literature.* Oxford, 1928.

Kenny, Anthony. *Aquinas.* Oxford, 1980.

Aquinas: A Collection of Critical Essays. London, 1969.

The God of the Philosophers. Oxford, 1979.

Reason and Religion: Essays in Philosophical Theology. Oxford, 1987.

Kienzler, Klaus. *Glauben und Denken bei Anselm von Canterbury.* Freiburg, 1981.

King, Richard. *Indian Philosophy: An Introduction to Hindu and Buddhist Thought.* Edinburgh, 1999.

Orientalism and Religion: Postcolonial Theory, India and 'the Mystic East'. London, 1999.

Kirfel, Willibald (ed.). *Beiträge zur Literaturwissenschaft und Geistesgeschichte Indiens. Festgabe Hermann Jacobi zum 75. Geburtstag.* Bonn, 1926.

Kirk, G. S., J. E. Raven and M. Schofield. *The Presocratic Philosophers: A Critical History with a Selection of Texts.* Cambridge, ²1983.

Klostermaier, Klaus K. *Mythologies and Philosophies of Salvation in the Theistic Traditions of India.* Ontario, 1984.

Knowles, David. *The Monastic Order in England: A History of its Development from the Times of St Dunstan to the Fourth Lateran Council, 940–1216.* Cambridge, ²1963.

The Religious Orders in England. 3 vols. Cambridge, 1948–59.

Knuuttila, Simo. 'Being qua Being in Thomas Aquinas and John Duns Scotus', in *The Logic of Being.* Ed. Simo Knuuttila and Jaakko Hintikka. Dordrecht, 1986, pp. 201–22.

Köhnke, Klaus Christian. *Entstehung und Aufstieg des Neukantianismus. Die deutsche Universitätsphilosophie zwischen Idealismus und Positivismus.* Frankfurt, 1986.

Kors, Alan Charles. *Atheism in France, 1650–1729.* 2 vols. Princeton, 1990, 1997. Vol. I: *The Orthodox Sources of Disbelief.*

D'Holbach's Coterie: An Enlightenment in Paris. Princeton, 1976.

Kors, Alan Charles, and Paul J. Korshin (eds.). *Anticipations of the Enlightenment in England, France and Germany.* Philadelphia, 1987.

Kraemer, Joel L. (ed.). *Perspectives on Maimonides: Philosophical and Historical Studies.* Oxford, 1991.

Kretzman, Norman, *et al.* (eds.). *The Cambridge History of Later Medieval Philosophy.* Cambridge, 1982.

Kuehn, M. 'The German Aufklärung and British Philosophy', in *Routledge History of Philosophy*, vol. V: *British Philosophy and the Age of Enlightenment*, ed. S. Brown. London, 1996.

Kuklick, Bruce. *Philosophy in History: Essays on the Historiography of Philosophy.* Ed. Richard Rorty *et al.* Cambridge, 1984.

The Rise of American Philosophy. New Haven, 1977.

Kumar, Shiv. *Samkhya-Yoga Epistemology.* Delhi, 1984.

Kumarappa, Bharatan. *The Hindu Conception of the Deity as Culminating in Ramanuja.* London, 1934.

Labrousse, Elisabeth. *Pierre Bayle.* Vol. II: *Hétérodoxie et rigorisme.* The Hague: Martinus Nijhoff, 1964.

Lacombe, Olivier. *L'absolu selon le Védânta.* Paris, ²1966.

Lakshamma, G. *The Impact of Ramanuja's Teaching on Life and Conditions in Society.* Delhi, 1990.

Lamy, François. *L'incrédule amené à la religion par la raison.* Paris, 1710.

Le nouvel athéisme renversé, ou Réfutation du sistème de Spinosa, tirée pour la plupart de la conoissance de la nature de l'homme. Paris, 1696.

Les premiers éléments des sciences. Paris, 1706.

Réponse aux Réflexions du M. Du Hamel sur le système cartésien de la Philosophie de M. Régis. Paris, 1692.

Landsgraf, Artur M. 'Zur Technik und Überlieferung der Disputation', *Collectanea Franciscana* 20 (1950), 173–88.

Lanfranc. *The Monastic Constitutions of Lanfranc.* Ed. and trans. David Knowles. Edinburgh, 1951.

Lang, Albert. *Der Wege der Glaubensbegründung bei den Scholastikern des 14. Jahrhunderts.* Münster, 1930.

Lang, Albert, Joseph Lechner and Michael Schmaus (eds.). *Aus der Geisteswelt des Mittelalters.* Münster, 1935.

Langmuir, Gavin I. *History, Religion, and Antisemitism.* London, 1990.

Larson, Gerald James. *Classical Samkhya: An Interpretation of its History and Meaning.* Delhi, 1969.

Larson, Gerald James, and Eliot Deutsch (eds.). *Interpreting across Boundaries: New Essays in Comparative Philosophy.* Princeton, 1988.

Lasker, Daniel J. *Jewish Philosophical Polemics against Christianity in the Middle Ages.* New York, 1977.

Lauth, Reinhard. *Theorie des philosophischen Arguments: Der Ausgangspunkt und seine Bedingungen.* Berlin and New York, 1979.

Lazarus, F. K. *Ramanuja and Bowne: A Study in Comparative Philosophy.* Bombay, 1962.

Leaman, Oliver. *Averroes and his Philosophy.* Oxford, 1988.

An Introduction to Medieval Islamic Philosophy. Cambridge, 1985.

Moses Maimonides. London, 1990.

Le Festugière, R. P. *La Révélation d'Hermes Trismégiste.* 4 vols. Paris, 1949–54.

Leff, Gordon. *Paris and Oxford Universities in the Thirteenth and Fourteenth Centuries: An Institutional and Intellectual History.* New York, 1968.

Richard FitzRalph, Commentator of the Sentences: A Study in Theological Orthodoxy. Manchester, 1963.

William of Ockham: The Metamorphosis of Scholastic Discourse. Manchester, 1975.

Leibniz, G. W. *Discourse on the Natural Theology of the Chinese.* Trans. and ed. Henry Rosemont and Daniel J. Cook. Honolulu, 1978.

New Essays on Human Understanding. Trans. and ed. Peter Remnant and Jonathan Bennett. Cambridge, 1981.

Philosophical Writings. Ed. G. H. R. Parkinson. Trans. Mary Morris and G. H. R. Parkinson. London and Toronto, 1973.

Sämtliche Schriften und Briefe, Series 6: *Philosophische Schriften,* 1 (1663–72). Prussian Academy of Sciences Edition. Darmstadt, 1930.

Theodicy. Ed. Austin Farrer. Trans. E. M. Huggard. New Haven, 1952.

Leland, John. *A View of the Principal Deistical Writers that have Appeared in England in the Last and Present Century; with Observations upon them, and Some Account of the Answers that have been Published against them in Several Letters to a Friend.* 3 vols. London, [3]1754–6.

Lerche, Charles O. 'Jefferson and the Election of 1800: A Case Study in the Political Smear', *William and Mary Quarterly* 5 (1948), 467–91.

Lessius, Leonardus. *Rawleigh his Ghost: or A Feigned Apparition of Syr Walter Rawleigh, to a Friend of his, for the Translating into English, the Booke of Leonard Lessius (that Most Learned Man) Entituled, De Providentia Numinus, et Animi Imortalitate: Written against Atheists, and Polititians of these Dayes.* Trans. by A.B. *1631.* Facsimile reprint. Vol. 349 of English Recusant Literature, 1558–1640. Ed. D. M. Rogers. Ilkley, 1977.

Lester, Robert C. *Ramanuja on the Yoga.* Adyar, 1976.

Levy, Leonard W. *Jefferson and Civil Liberties: The Darker Side.* Cambridge, MA, 1963.

L'Herminier, Nicolas. *Lettre d'un docteur de Sorbonne à un jeune abbé, en forme de dissertation où l'on examine quelle sorte de distinction il faut admettre entre les attributs de Dieu.* Paris, 1704.

    Summa Theologiae ad Usum Scholae Accommodata. Paris, 1701–11 [vol. I: *De Attributis Divinis,* 1709], ²1718–19 [vol. I: *De Attributis Divinis,* 1719].

Lipner, Julius J. *The Face of Truth: A Study of Meaning and Metaphysics in the Vedantic Theology of Ramanuja.* London, 1986.

Little, A. G. 'The Friars and the Foundation of the Faculty of Theology in the University of Cambridge', in *Mélanges Mandonnet,* Bibliothèque Thomiste, 14. Paris, 1930, II, pp. 389–401.

    'The Friars vs. the University of Cambridge', *English Historical Review* 50 (1935), 686–96.

Little, A. G., and F. Pelster. *Oxford Theology and Theologians, c. AD 1282–1302.* Oxford Historical Society, 96. Oxford, 1934.

Lloyd, Genevieve. *The Man of Reason: 'Male' and 'Female' in Western Philosophy.* London, 1984.

Locke, John. *An Essay in Human Understanding.* Ed. Peter H. Nidditch. Oxford, 1975.

    The Reasonableness of Christianity: As Delivered in the Scriptures. Ed. with an introduction, notes, critical apparatus and transcriptions of related manuscripts by John C. Higgins-Biddle. Oxford and New York, 1999.

Logan, Beryl. *A Religion without Talking: Religious Belief and Natural Belief in Hume's Philosophy of Religion.* New York, 1993.

Lombard, Peter. *Sententiae in IV. Libris Distinctae.* Rome, ³1971.

Long, A. A., and D. N. Sedley (eds.). *The Hellenistic Philosophers.* 2 vols. Cambridge, 1987.

Lott, Eric C. *God and the Universe in the Vedantic Theology of Ramanuja: A Study in his Use of the Self–Body Analogy.* Madras, 1976.

    Vedantic Approaches to God. London, 1980.

Lunstead, Jeffrey. 'The Development of Logic in the Madhvite School', *Wiener Zeitschrift für die Kunde Südasiens* 22 (1978), 159–70.

Luther, Martin. *Weimarer Ausgabe.* 127 vols. Weimar, 1883.

Lynch, Michael P. *Truth in Context: An Essay in Pluralism and Objectivity.* Cambridge, MA, 1998.

Maccoby, Hyam (ed.). *Judaism on Trial: Jewish–Christian Disputations in the Middle Ages.* London, 1982.

McCann, Justin (ed.). *The Rule of St Benedict.* London, 1952.

McCarthy, Richard Joseph (ed.). *Freedom and Fulfillment.* Boston, 1980.

McEvoy, James. *The Philosophy of Robert Grosseteste.* Oxford, 1982.

MacIntyre, Alasdair. *After Virtue: A Study in Moral Theory.* London, ²1985.

    Dependent Rational Animals: Why Human Beings Need the Virtues. London, 1999.

    Whose Justice? Which Rationality? London, 1988.

MacIntyre, John. *St Anselm and his Critics.* Edinburgh, 1954.

Mackie, J. L. *The Miracle of Theism: Arguments for and against the Existence of God.* Oxford, 1982.

McMahon, Susan. 'John Ray (1627–1705) and the Act of Uniformity 1662', *Notes Rec. R. Soc. Lond.* 54/2 (2000), 153–78.

Madan, T. N. (ed.). *Religion in India.* Delhi, 1991.

Madhava. *The Sarva-Darsana-Samgraha or Review of the Different Systems of Hindu Philosophy.* Trans. E. B. Cowell and A. E. Gough. Ed. K. L. Joshi. Ahmedabad, 1981.

Mahadevan, T. M. P. (ed. and trans.). *The Sambandhavartika of Suresvaracarya.* Madras, 1958, ²1972.

Maimonides, Moses. *The Guide for the Perplexed.* Trans. and ed. Shlomo Pines. Chicago, 1963.

Makdisi, George. *The Rise of Colleges: Institutions of Learning in Islam and the West.* Edinburgh, 1981.

Malcolm, Norman. 'Anselm's Ontological Arguments', *Philosophical Review* 69 (1960), 41–62.

Malebranche, Nicholas. *Dialogue between a Christian Philosopher and a Chinese Philosopher on the Existence and Nature of God.* Trans. Dominick A. Iorio. Washington, DC, 1980.

Malherbe, Michel. 'On Hume and the Art of Dialogue', in *Hume and Hume's Connexions.* Ed. M. A. Stewart and John P. Wright. Edinburgh, 1994; University Park, PA, 1995.

Malone, Dumas. *Jefferson and his Time.* 6 vols. Boston, 1948–81.

Manier, Edward (ed.). *The Young Darwin and his Cultural Circle.* Dordrecht, 1978.

Marasinghe, M. M. J. *Gods in Early Buddhism: A Study in their Social and Mythological Milieu as Depicted in the Nikayas of the Pali Canon.* Peliyagoda, 1974.

Marshall, Peter J. (ed.). *The British Discovery of Hinduism in the Eighteenth Century.* Cambridge, 1970.

Mascall, Eric L. 'Faith and Reason: Anselm and Aquinas', *Journal of Theological Studies* 14 (1963), 67–90.

Mason, H. T. *Pierre Bayle and Voltaire.* Oxford, 1963.

Mather, Richard B. 'Chinese and Indian Perceptions of Each Other Between the First and Seventh Centuries', *JAOS* 112 (1992), 1–8.

Matilal, Bimal Krishna. 'Causality in the Nyaya-Vaisesika School', *Philosophy East and West* 25 (1975), 41–8.

   'Debate and Dialectic in Ancient India', in *Philosophical Essays: Professor Anantalal Thakur Felicitation Volume.* Calcutta, 1987, pp. 53–66.

   'Error and Truth – Classical Indian Theories', *Philosophy East and West* 31 (1981), 215–24.

   Logic, Language and Reality: An Introduction to Indian Philosophical Studies. Delhi, 1985.

   Nyaya-Vaisesika. Vol. VI/2 of *A History of Indian Literature.* Ed. Jan Gonda. Wiesbaden, 1977.

Perception: An Essay on Classical Indian Theories of Knowledge. Oxford, 1986.

'Pramana as Evidence', in *Philosophical Essays: Professor Anantalal Thakur Felicitation Volume.* Calcutta, 1987, pp. 190–8.

'Reference and Existence in Nyaya and Buddhist Logic', *Journal of Indian Philosophy* 1 (1970), 83–110.

Matilal, Bimal Krishna, and R. D. Evans (eds.). *Buddhist Logic and Epistemology.* Dordrecht, 1986.

Matilal, Bimal Krishna, and Jaysankar Lal Shaw (eds.). *Analytical Philosophy in Comparative Perspective: Exploratory Essays in Current Theories and Classical Indian Theories of Meaning and Reference.* Dordrecht, 1985.

Matthew of Aquasparta. *Questiones Disputatae Selectae.* Vol. 1: *Questiones de Fide et de Cognitione.* Quaracchi, 1903.

Matthews, Scott. *Reason, Community and Religious Tradition: Anselm's Argument and the Friars.* Aldershot, 2001.

Maurer, Armand A. *Medieval Philosophy.* Toronto, ^{2}1982.

Maurer, Armand A. (ed.). *St Thomas Aquinas 1274–1974: Commemorative Studies.* 2 vols. Toronto, 1974.

Mayhew, Henry. *London Labour and the London Poor.* 3 vols. London, 1851.

Mendelssohn, Moses. *Gesammelte Schriften. Jubiläumsausgabe.* 22 vols. bound as 29. Stuttgart, 1971ff. [1929ff.].

Jerusalem and Other Jewish Writings. Ed. Alfred Jospe. New York, 1969.

Rezensionsartikel in Briefe, die neueste Litteratur betreffend (1759–1765). Ed. E. J. Engel. Stuttgart, 1991.

Mersenne, Marin. *L'impiété des déistes, athées, et libertins de ce temps combatue et renversée de point en point par raisons tirées de la philosophie et de la théologie. Seconde partie: ensemble la réfutation du 'Poème des déistes'.* Paris, 1624.

Meslier, Jean. *Œuvres complètes.* Ed. Roland Desne *et al.* 3 vols. Paris, 1970–2.

Mesquita, Roque. 'Das Problem der Gotteserkenntnis bei Yamunamuni'. Diss. Phil., University of Vienna, 1971.

Yamanucaryas Samvitsiddhi. Vienna, 1988.

'Yamunas Philosophie der Erkenntnis. Eine Studie zu seiner Samvitsiddhi'. Habilitationsschrift, University of Vienna, 1987.

Meyer, Johann Jacob (ed. and trans). *Das Altindische Buch vom Welt- und Staatsleben. Das Arthasastra des Kautilya.* Hanover, 1925.

Miller, John C. *The Wolf by the Ears: Thomas Jefferson and Slavery.* New York, 1980.

Milner, Joseph. *Gibbon's Account of Christianity Considered: Together with some Strictures on Hume's Dialogues concerning Natural Religion.* York, 1781.

Mishra, Umesha. *History of Indian Philosophy.* 2 vols. Allahabad, 1957, 1966.

Mitchell, Basil (ed.). *Faith and Logic: Oxford Essays in Philosophical Theology.* London, 1957.

Mohanty, Jitendranath. *Gangesa's Theory of Truth.* Santiniketan, 1966.

Monk, Ray. *Ludwig Wittgenstein: The Duty of Genius.* London, 1990.

Montaigne, Michel de. *In Defense of Raymond Sebond.* Trans. and intro. by Arthur H. Beattie. New York, 1976.

Morehead, Robert. *Dialogues on Natural and Revealed Religion*. Edinburgh, 1830. *Philosophical Dialogues*. London and Edinburgh, 1845.

Morris, James McGrath and Persephone Weene (eds.). *Thomas Jefferson's European Travel Diaries*. Ithaca, 1987.

Mossner, Ernst Campbell. 'The Enigma of Hume', *Mind* 45 (1936), 334–49. *The Life of David Hume*. Oxford, ²1980.

Much, Michael Torsten. 'Dharmakirti's Definition of "Points of Defeat" (*Nigrahasthana*)', in *Buddhist Logic and Epistemology*. Ed. B. K. Matilal and R. D. Evans. Dordrecht, 1986, pp. 133–44. *Dharmakirtis Vadanyayah*. 2 vols. Vienna, 1991.

Müller, F. Max. *The Six Systems of Indian Philosophy*. London, 1899.

Mullick, Mohini. 'Implication and Entailment in Navya-Nyaya Logic', *Journal of Indian Philosophy* 4 (1976), 127–34.

Mungello, David E. *Leibniz and Confucianism: The Search for Accord*. Honolulu, 1978.

Murdoch, John Emery, and Edith Dudley Sylla (eds.). *The Cultural Context of Medieval Learning*. Dordrecht, 1975.

Murrin, John M. 'The Irrelevance and Relevance of Colonial New England', *Reviews in American History* 18 (1990), 177–84.

Murty, K. S. *Philosophy in India: Traditions, Teaching and Research*. Delhi, 1985. *Revelation and Reason in Advaita Vedanta*. Delhi, ²1974.

Naigeon, André. *Adresse à l'Assemblée nationale sur la liberté des opinions, sur celle de la press, etc*. Paris, 1790.

Nasr, Seyyed Hossein. *Knowledge and the Sacred*. Edinburgh, 1981.

Neevel, Walter G., Jr. *Yamuna's Vedanta and Pancaratra: Integrating the Classical and the Popular*. Missoula, 1977.

Nelson, John S., *et al.* (eds.). *The Rhetoric of the Human Sciences: Language and Argument in Scholarship and Public Affairs*. Madison, 1987.

Nencel, Lorraine, and Peter Pels (eds.). *Constructing Knowledge: Authority and Critique in Social Science*. Inquiries in Social Construction Series. London, 1991.

Neuman, Abraham A. *The Jews in Spain: Their Social, Political and Cultural Life during the Middle Ages*. Vol. II: *A Social-Cultural Study*. New York, 1969.

Neusner, Jacob. 'Thinking about "The Other" in Religion: It is Necessary, but is it Possible?', *Modern Theology* 6 (1990), 273–85. *The Twentieth Century Construction of 'Judaism'*. Alpharetta, GA, 1992.

Nieuwentijdt [Nieuwentijt, Nieuwentyt], Bernard. *L'Existence de Dieu démontrée par les merveilles de la nature, en trois parties, où l'on traite de la structure du Corps d l'Homme, des Elemens, des Astres, & de leurs divers effets*. Amsterdam, 1714; Paris, 1725. *The Religious Philosopher, or the Right Use of Contemplating the Works of the Creator*. Trans. J. T. Desaguliers. 3 vols. London, 1718–19.

Nobili, Roberto de. *Ajnana Nirvaranam*. Trichinopoly, 1891. *Atuma Nirunayam*. Madras, 1889. *Jnanopadesam*. Vols. I and II [1775], Madras, 1891. Vol. III, Trichinopoly, 1907.

On Indian Customs. Trans. S. Rajamanickam. Palayamkottai, 1972.

Première apologie [1610]. Ed. and trans. into French by Pierre Dahmen. Paris, 1931.

Oberhammer, Gerhard. 'Ein Beitrag zu den Vada-Traditionen Indiens', *WZKSO* 7 (1963), 63–103.

'Gedanken zur historischen Darstellung indischer Logik', *Orientalistische Literaturzeitung* 59 (1964), cols. 5–19.

'Die Gottesidee in der indischen Philosophie den ersten Nachchristlichen Jahrtausends. Zur Typologie des Isvara-Begriffe', *Zeitschrift für katholische Theologie* 89 (1967), 447–57.

Strukturen yogischer Meditation. Vienna, 1977.

'Der Svabhavika-Sambandha: Ein geschichtlicher Beitrag zur Nyaya-Logik', *WZKSO* 8 (1964), 131–81.

Wahrheit und Transzendenz. Ein Beitrag zur Spiritualität des Nyaya. Österreichische Akademie der Wissenschaften, Sb. 424. Vienna, 1984.

'Zum Problem des Gottesbeweises in der indischen Philosophie', *Numen* 12 (1965), 1–34.

Oberhammer, Gerhard (ed.) *Inklusivismus: eine indische Denkform.* Publications of the De Nobili Research Library, Occasional Papers, 2. Vienna, 1983.

Offenbarung. Geistige Realität des Menschen. Vienna, 1974.

Terminologie der frühen philosophischen Scholastik in Indien. Vienna, 1991.

Oberhammer, Gerhard, and Hans Waldenfels (eds.). *Überlieferungsstruktur und Offenbarung. Aufriß einer Reflexion des Phänomens im Hinduismus.* Vienna, 1980.

Oehler, Klaus. 'Der Beweis für den unbewegten Beweger bei Aristoteles', *Philologus* 99 (1955), 70–92.

Oetke, Claus. *'Ich' und das Ich: Analytische Untersuchungen zur buddhistisch-brahmanischen Atmankontroverse.* Stuttgart, 1988.

Zur Methode der Analyse philosophischer Sutratexte. Die Pramana Passagen der Nyayasutren. Reinbek, 1991.

Ogilvie, John. *An Inquiry into the Causes of the Infidelity and Scepticism of the Times: With Occasional Observations on the Writings of Herbert, Shaftesbury, Bolingbroke, Hume, Gibbon, Toulmin, etc.* London, 1783.

O'Neill, Onora. *Constructions of Reason: Explorations of Kant's Practical Philosophy.* Cambridge, 1989.

Origen. *Contra Celsum.* Trans. and ed. Henry Chadwick. Cambridge, 1965.

Ormsby, Eric L. *Theodicy in Islamic Thought: The Dispute over al-Ghazali's 'Best of All Possible Worlds'.* Princeton, 1984.

Outram, D. 'The Pure and Sensible Eye: The Man of Science and Revolutionary Culture in France', paper presented to the conference on 'New Perspectives in Nineteenth-Century Science', under the auspices of the British Society for the History of Science, at the University of Kent at Canterbury, Easter 1984.

Owens, Joseph. 'Actuality in the "Prima Via" of St Thomas', *Mediaeval Studies* 29 (1967), 26–46.

'Aquinas and the Five Ways', *The Monist* 58 (1974), 16–35.
'Aquinas and the Proof from the *Physics*', *Mediaeval Studies* 28 (1966), 119–50.
Aristotle: Collected Papers. Ed. John R. Catan. Albany, 1981.
'Immobility and Existence for Aquinas', *Mediaeval Studies* 30 (1968), 22–46.
St Thomas Aquinas on the Existence of God. Ed. J. R. Catan. Albany, 1980.
Pailin, David A. *Attitudes to Other Religions: Comparative Religion in Seventeenth- and Eighteenth-Century Britain*. Manchester, 1984.
Pajin, Dushan. 'The Legitimacy of the Term "Philosophy" in an Asian Context', *Journal of Indian Philosophy* 15 (1987), 349–62.
Paley, William. *Natural Theology; or, Evidences of the Existence and Attributes of the Deity Collected from the Appearances of Nature*. London, 1802. Other editions: adapted for youth, London, 1820; illustrated by a series of plates and explanatory notes by J. Paxton, 2 vols., Oxford, 1826; adapted for the blind, Boston, 1859.
Paley's Works; Consisting of Evidences of Christianity, Moral and Political Philosophy, Natural Theology, and Horae Paulinae. London, 1835.
Reasons for Contentment; Addresses to the Labouring Part of the British Public. Carlisle, 1792.
A View of the Evidences of Christianity, in Three Parts, etc. London, 1794.
The Works of William Paley. 5 vols. Ed. Robert Lynam. London, 1825.
Pascal, Blaise. *Les pensées*. Ed. Phillippe Sellier. Paris, 1991.
Pathak, V. S. *History of Saiva Cults in Northern India from Inscriptions (700 to 1200 AD)*. Allahabad, 1980.
Paton, H. J. (trans.). *The Moral Law or Kant's Groundwork of the Metaphysic of Morals*. London [1947].
Patterson, Robert Leet. *The Conception of God in the Philosophy of Aquinas*. London, 1933.
Paulson, F. *German Education: Past and Present*. New York, 1908.
Pegis, Anton C. 'The Bonaventurean Way to God', *Mediaeval Studies* 29 (1967), 206–42.
'Four Medieval Ways to God', *The Monist* 54 (1970), 317–58.
'St. Anselm and the Argument of the *Proslogion*', *Medieval Studies* 28 (1966), 228–67.
'St. Bonaventure, St. Francis and Philosophy', *Mediaeval Studies* 15 (1953), 1–13.
'Toward a New Way to God: Henry of Ghent', *Mediaeval Studies* 30 (1968), 226–47; 31 (1969), 93–116; 33 (1971), 158–79.
Perrault, Charles. *Parallèle des anciens et des modernes en ce qui regarde les arts et les sciences*. Ed. H. R. Jauss and Max Imdahl. Munich, 1964.
Peterson, Merrill D. *The Jefferson Image in the American Mind*. New York, 1960.
Peterson, Merrill D. (ed.). *Thomas Jefferson: Writings*. New York, 1984.
Peterson, Merrill D., and Robert C. Vaughan (eds.). *The Virginia Statute for Religious Freedom: Its Evolution and Consequences in American History*. Cambridge, 1988.
Phelan, John Leddy. *The Millennial Kingdom of the Franciscans in the New World*. Berkeley, 1970.

Phillips, D. Z. *Faith after Foundationalism.* London and New York, 1988.
　Faith and Philosophical Enquiry. London, 1970.
　Religion without Explanation. Oxford, 1976.
Phillips, D. Z., and Timothy Tessin (eds.). *Religion and Hume's Legacy.* London and New York, 1999.
Places, Edouard des. *La religion Greque. Dieux, cultes, rites et sentiments religieux dans la Grèce antique.* Paris, 1969.
Plantinga, Alvin. *God, Freedom, and Evil.* Grand Rapids, 1974.
　God and Other Minds: A Study of the Rational Justification of Belief in God. Ithaca, 1967.
　The Nature of Necessity. Oxford, 1974.
Plantinga, Alvin, and Nicholas Wolterstorff (eds.). *Faith and Rationality: Reason and Belief in God.* Notre Dame, 1983.
Plato. *The Dialogues of Plato.* 4 vols. Ed. and trans. Benjamin Jowett. Oxford, ⁴1953.
Popkin, Richard H., and Arjo Vanderjagt (eds.). *Scepticism and Irreligion in the Seventeenth and Eighteenth Centuries.* Leiden, 1993.
Porter, Roy, and Mikulás Teich (eds). *The Enlightenment in National Context.* Cambridge, 1981.
Potter, Karl H. *Presuppositions of India's Philosophies.* Repr. Delhi, 1991.
Potter, Karl H. (ed.). *The Encyclopedia of Indian Philosophies.* 9 vols. Princeton and Delhi, ¹1983–2003.
Powell, Baden. *Study of the Evidences of Christianity.* London, 1860.
Prasada, Rama. *Ramanuja and Hegel.* Delhi, 1983.
Prasada, Rama (trans.). *Patanjali's Yoga Sutras.* New Delhi, ³1982.
Preisendanz, Karin. 'Debate and Independent Reasoning *vs.* Tradition: On the Precarious Position of Early Nyaya', in *Festschrift Minoru Hara.* Ed. Ryutaro Tsuchida and Albrecht Wezler. Reinbek, 2000, pp. 221–51.
Priestley, Joseph. *Institutes of Natural and Revealed Religion.* 3 vols. London, 1772–4.
　Letters to a Philosophical Unbeliever. Bath, 1780 (part I); Birmingham, ²1787 (parts I and II).
　Joseph Priestley (1733–1804): Scientist, Teacher, and Theologian: A 250ᵗʰ Anniversary Exhibition – Bodleian Library, Oxford. Oxford, 1983.
　Theological and Miscellaneous Works of Joseph Priestley. Ed. with notes by John Towill Rutt with a new preface by Alan P. F. Sell and a new introduction by John Stephens. 25 vols. Bristol, 1999.
Prince, Michael. *Philosophical Dialogue in the British Enlightenment: Theology, Aesthetics and the Novel.* Cambridge, 1996.
Puthiadam, Ignatius. 'Gott, Welt und Mensch bei Madhva'. Diss. Phil., University of Münster, 1969.
The Questions of King Milinda 2.1.3. Trans. T. W. Rhys Davids. Vol I. Delhi, 1960.
Quinn, John Francis. *The Historical Constitution of St. Bonaventure's Philosophy.* Toronto, 1973.

Qur'an, sura 2. Trans. A. J. Arberry, *The Koran*. Oxford, 1983.

Qvarnström, Olle. *Hindu Philosophy in Buddhist Perspective: The Vedantatattva-viniscaya Chapter of Bhavya's Madhyamakahrdayakarika*. Lund, 1989.

Raghavachar, S. S. (trans.). *Naiskarmyasiddhi of Sri Suresvaracarya*. Mysore, 1965.

Raheja, G. G. 'India: Caste, Kingship and Dominance Reconsidered', *Annual Review of Anthropology* 17 (1988), 497–523.

Ramaiah, G. Sundara. *Brahman: A Comparative Study of the Philosophies of Sankara and Ramanuja*. Waltair, 1974.

Randle, H. N. *Indian Logic in the Early Schools*. Oxford, 1930; New Delhi, 1976.

Rangacarya, M. (ed. and trans.). *The Sarva-Siddhanta-Sangraha of Sankaracarya*. Madras, 1909.

Rangacharya, M., and M. G. Varadaraja Aiyangar (trans.). *The Vedantasutras with the Sribhasya of Ramanujacarya*. 3 vols. New Delhi, I (^{3}1988 [1899]), II (^{2}1989 [1964]), III (^{2}1991 [1965]).

Rao, K. B. Ramakrishna. *Theism of Pre-Classical Samkhya*. Mysore, 1966.

Raven, Charles E. *John Ray, Naturalist: His Life and Works*. Cambridge, ^{2}1950; repr. 1986.

Ray, John. *The Wisdom of God Manifested in the Works of the Creation*. London, 1691; London ^{2}1692, ^{3}1701, ^{4}1704, ^{7}1717; repr. New York, 1977.

Redwood, John. *Reason, Ridicule and Religion: The Age of Enlightenment in England 1660–1750*. London, 1976.

Régis, Pierre-Sylvain. *Réponse aux Réflexions de M. Du Hamel sur le système cartésien de la philosophie de M. Régis*. Paris, 1692.

Système de philosophie. 3 vols. Paris, 1690.

Reinbeck, Johann Gustav. *Betrachtungen über die Augsburische Confession*. Berlin, 1740.

Renou, Louis. *Etudes védiques et paninéennes, Volume VI: Le destin du Véda dans l'Inde*. Paris, 1960.

Rex, Walter (ed.). *Essays on Pierre Bayle and Religious Controversy*. The Hague, 1965.

Ricci, Matteo. *China in the Sixteenth Century: The Journals of M. Ricci, 1583–1610*. Trans. L. J. Gallagher. New York, 1953.

The True Meaning of the Lord of Heaven [Beijing, 1603]. Trans. Douglas Lancashire and Peter Hu Kuo-Chen. Ed. Edward J. Malatesta. Taipei and Paris, 1985.

Rice, H. C. *Thomas Jefferson's Paris*. Princeton, 1976.

Ritter, Joachim, *et al.* (eds.). *Historisches Wörterbuch der Philosophie*. Vols I–XII. Basle, 1971–2004.

Robinson, J. Armitage. *Gilbert Crispin, Abbot of Westminster: A Study of the Abbey under Norman Rule*. Cambridge, 1911.

Robinson, Richard H. *Early Madhyamika in Indian and China*. Madison, 1967.

Robson, Michael J. P. 'Saint Anselm's Influence upon Saint Bonaventure's Theology of Redemption'. Ph.D. thesis, Cambridge University, 1988.

Rohls, Jan. *Theologie und Metaphysik. Der ontologische Gottesbeweis und seine Kritiker*. Gütersloh, 1987.

Rorty, Richard. *Philosophical Papers*. 2 vols. Cambridge, 1991.

Philosophy and the Mirror of Nature. Oxford and Princeton, 1980.

Rorty, Richard, J. B. Schneewind and Quentin Skinner (eds.). *Philosophy in History: Essays on the Historiography of Philosophy.* Cambridge, 1984.

Rösel, Jakob A. 'Colonial Bureaucracy vs. the Old Agrarian Order – The Transformation of an Indian Province: A Case Study of Orissa under the Rule of the East Indian Company 1803–1858', in *Hinduismus und Buddhismus: Festschrift für Ulrich Schneider.* Freiburg, 1987.

Die Hinduismusthese Max Webers. Folgen eines kolonialen Indienbildes in einem religionssoziologische Gedankengang. Munich, 1982.

Tempelstadt Puri. Pilger und Priester am Hofe des Jagannath. Freiburg, 1988.

Rosenkranz, Karl. *Geschichte der Kant'schen Philosophie.* Ed. Steffen Dietzsch. Berlin, 1987.

Ross, George MacDonald, and Tony McWalter (eds.). *Kant and his Influence.* Bristol, 1990.

Rossi, S. (ed.). *Science and Imagination in XVIIIth-Century British Culture.* Milan, 1987.

Roth, F. *The English Austin Friars: 1249–1538.* 2 vols. New York, 1961.

Rousseau, Jean-Jacques. *Confessions.* Trans. J. M. Cohen. Baltimore, 1953.

Œuvres complètes. Ed. Bernard Gagnebin and Marcel Raymond. 5 vols. Paris, 1959–95.

Rowe, W. L. *The Cosmological Argument.* Princeton, 1975.

Ruben, Walter. 'Seit wann gibt es Philosophie in Indien?', *WZKSO* 12/13 (1968/9), 295–302.

'Über die Debatten in den alten Upanisads', *Zeitschrift für die deutsche Morganländergesellschaft* 83 (1928), 238–55.

Ruben, Walter (ed. and trans.). *Die Nyayasutras.* Leipzig, 1928.

Ryan, J. K. (ed.). *Philosophical Studies in Honor of the Very Revd. Ignatius Smith, OP.* Westminster, MD, 1952.

Ryle, Gilbert. *Philosophical Arguments.* Oxford, 1975.

Saadia ben Joseph. *The Book of Beliefs and Opinions.* Trans. and ed. Samuel Rosenblatt. New Haven, 1948.

Said, Edward W. *Orientalism: Western Conceptions of the Orient.* Harmondsworth, 1991; London, 1978.

Sandal, Mohan Lal (ed. and trans). *Mimamsa Sutras of Jaimini.* 2 vols. Delhi, 1980 [1923–5].

Sanford, Charles B. *The Religious Life of Thomas Jefferson.* Charlottesville, 1984.

Santina, Peter Della. *Madhyamaka Schools in India.* Delhi, 1986.

Sarasvati, Satchidanandendra. *The Method of the Vedanta: A Critical Account of the Advaita Tradition.* Trans. A. J. Alston. London and New York, 1989.

Saraswati, Baidyanath. *Brahman Ritual Traditions in the Crucible of Time.* Simla, 1977.

Sarkar, Sumit. *Writing Social History.* Delhi and Oxford, 1997.

Sastri, Dhundhiraja (ed.). *The Atmatattvaviveka of Sri Udayanacharaya with the (Narayani) Commentary of Sri Narayanacharya Atreya and the (Bauddhadhikara) Didhiti Commentary of Sri Ragnunatha Siromans with* the *Bauddhadhikara Vivrti of Sri Gadadhara Bhattacharya*. Sanskrit text with English introduction. Benares, 1940.

Sastri, V. A. Ramaswami (ed.). *Tattvabindu by Vacaspatimisra with Tattvaibhavana by Rsiputra Paramesvara*. Reprint: New Delhi, 1991 [1936].

Sastry, Alladi Mahadeva (trans.). *The Taittiriya Upanishad with the Commentaries of Sri Sankaracharya, Sri Suresvaracharya, and Sri Vidyaranya*. Reprint: Madras, 1980.

Schacht, Joseph. *An Introduction to Islamic Law*. Oxford, 1964.

The Origins of Muhammadan [sic] Jurisprudence. Oxford, 1950.

Schick, Frederic. *Having Reasons: An Essay on Rationality and Sociality*. Princeton, 1984.

Schleiermacher, Friedrich. *Kritische Gesamtausgabe*. Ed. Hermann Fischer *et al.* 8 vols. Berlin, 1998.

Schneider, Ulrich. *Der Holzgott und die Brahmanen*. 2 vols. Wiesbaden, 1984.

Schofield, Malcolm. 'Cicero for and against Divination', *Journal of Roman Studies* 76 (1986), 47–65.

'The Syllogisms of Zeno of Citium', *Phronesis* 28 (1983), 31–58.

Schofield, Malcolm, *et al.* (eds.). *Doubt and Dogmatism: Studies in Hellenistic Epistemology*. Oxford, 1980.

Scholem, Gershom G. 'The Name of God and the Linguistic of the Kabbala', *Diogenes* 79 (1972), 59–80; 80 (1973), 164–94.

Schwab, Raymond. *The Oriental Renaissance: Europe's Discovery of India and the East, 1680–1880*. Trans. G. Patterson-Black and V. Reinking. New York, 1984.

Sell, Alan P. F. *The Philosophy of Religion, 1875–1980*. London, 1988.

Seward, Sir Albert Charles. *John Ray: A Biographical Sketch Written for the Centenary of the Cambridge Ray Club and Read, in part, at the Dinner in the Hall of Trinity College on 16 March 1937*. Cambridge, 1937.

Shanan, Robert W., and Francis J. Kovach (eds.). *Bonaventure and Aquinas: Enduring Philosophers*. Norman, OK, 1976.

Shapiro, Barbara J. *John Wilkins (1614–1672): An Intellectual Biography*. Berkeley, 1969.

Probability and Certainty in Seventeenth-Century England: A Study of the Relationships between Natural Science, Religion, History, Law, and Literature. Princeton, 1983.

Sharfstein, Ben-Ami. *The Dilemma of Context*. New York and London, 1989.

Sharma, Arvind. *Visistadvaita Vedanta: A Study*. New Delhi, 1978.

Sharma, B. N. K. *The Brahmasutras and their Principal Commentaries: A Critical Exposition*. 3 vols. Bombay, 1971–8.

History of the Dvaita School of Vedanta and its Literature. 2 vols. Bombay, 1960–1.

Philosophy of Sri Madhvacarya. Delhi, ²1986.

Sharma, Rajendra Nath. *Brahmins through the Ages: Their Social, Religious, Cultural, Political and Economic Life*. Delhi, 1977.

Shastri, Dharmendra Nath. *Critique of Indian Realism: A Study of the Conflict between the Nyaya-Vaisesika and the Buddhist Dignaga School*. Agara, 1964.

Shehadi, Fadlou. *Ghazali's Unique Unknowable God.* Leiden, 1964.

Sherry, Patrick (ed.). *Philosophers on Religion.* London, 1987.

Shunzo, Onoda. *Monastic Debate in Tibet: A Study of the History and Structure of bsDus grwa Logic.* Vienna, 1992.

Siauve, Suzanne. *La doctrine de Madhva, Dvaite Vedânta.* Pondicherry, 1968.

La voie vers la connaissance de Dieu selon l'Anuvyâkhyâna de Madhva. Pondicherry, 1959.

Siddhantashastree, Rabindra Kumar. *Saivism through the Ages.* New Delhi, 1975.

Sillem, Edward. *George Berkeley and the Proofs for the Existence of God.* London, 1957.

Ways of Thinking about God: Thomas Aquinas and Some Recent Problems. London, 1961.

Sinha, Jadunath. *Schools of Saivism.* Calcutta, 1970.

Sinha, Nandalal (ed.). *The Nyaya Sutras of Gotama.* Delhi, ²1981.

(ed.). *The Samkhya Philosophy.* New York, 1974 [Allahabad, 1915].

Smalley, B. *The Study of the Bible in the Middle Ages.* Oxford, ²1952.

Smart, Ninian. *Doctrine and Argument in Indian Philosophy.* London and New York, 1964.

Reasons and Faiths: An Investigation of Religious Discourse, Christian and Non-Christian. London, 1958.

Smith, Preserved, and H. P. Gallinger (eds.). *Conversations with Luther.* Boston, 1915.

Smith, R. Morton. 'From Ritual to Philosophy in India', *Journal of Indian Philosophy* 4 (1976), 181–97.

Smithers, Peter. *The Life of Joseph Addison.* Oxford, ²1968.

Smithies, Bill and Peter Fiddick. *Enoch Powell on Immigration.* London, 1969.

Solé, J. 'Religion et conception du monde dans le *Dictionnaire* de Bayle', *Bulletin de la Société de l'histoire de protestantisme français* 118 (1972), 96.

Solomon, Esther A. *Indian Dialectics: Methods of Philosophical Discussion.* 2 vols. Ahmedabad, 1976–8.

Sorenson, Roy. 'Rationality as an Absolute Concept', *Philosophy* 66 (1991), 473–86.

Southern, Richard W. *Robert Grosseteste: The Growth of an English Mind in Medieval Europe.* Oxford, 1986.

Saint Anselm: A Portrait in a Landscape. Cambridge, 1990.

Western Society and the Church in the Middle Ages. Harmondsworth, 1970.

Western Views of Islam in the Middle Ages. Cambridge, MA, 1962.

Sowerby, E. Millicent (ed.). *Catalogue of the Library of Thomas Jefferson.* 5 vols. Washington, DC, 1952–9 [reprint: Charlottesville, 1983].

Spinoza, Baruch. *The Collected Writings of Spinoza.* Trans. Edwin Curley. Princeton, 1985.

Opera Posthuma, etc. Ed. J. Jellis. Amsterdam, 1677.

Spinoza Opera. Ed. Carl Gebhardt. 5 vols. Heidelberg, 1925, 1972.

Srinivasdasa. *Yatindramatadipika.* Poona, ²1934.

Stcherbatsky, Th. *The Conception of Buddhist Nirvana.* The Hague, 1965 [Leningrad, 1927].

Steinkellner, Ernst. 'Augenblicklichkeitsbeweis und Gottesbeweis bei Sankarasvamin'. Diss. Phil., University of Vienna, 1963.

Steinkellner, Ernst (ed.). *Dharmakirti's Hetubinduh.* 2 vols. Vienna, 1967.

Stephen, Leslie. *History of English Thought in the Eighteenth Century.* 2 vols. London, ³1902.

Stern, S. *Der preussische Staat und die Juden.* 3 vols. Tübingen, 1971.

Stewart, M. A. 'Hume and the "Metaphysical Argument *A Priori*"', in *Philosophy: Its History and Historiography.* Ed. A. J. Holland. Dordrecht, 1985, pp. 243–70.

Stewart, M. A., and John P. Wright. *Hume and Hume's Connexions.* Edinburgh, 1994; University Park, PA, 1995.

Sweet, L. I. 'Christopher Columbus and the Millennial Vision of the New World', *Catholic Historical Review* 72 (1986), 369–82.

Swinburne, Richard. *The Coherence of Theism.* Oxford, 1977.

The Existence of God. Oxford, 1979.

Faith and Reason. Oxford, 1981.

Taber, John A. 'Utpaladeva's Isvarasiddhi', *Adyar Library Bulletin* 50 (1986), 106–37.

Tachikawa, Musashi. *The Structure of the World in Udayana's Realism.* Dordrecht, 1981.

Tennant, F. R. *Philosophical Theology.* 2 vols. Cambridge, 1928, 1930; ²1968.

Thibaut, George (trans.). *The Vedanta-Sutras* [with *Bhasyas* by Samkara and Ramanuja]. 3 vols. Oxford, 1904.

Thomas Aquinas. *Summa Contra Gentiles.* Trans. and ed. Anton C. Pegis. Notre Dame, 1975.

Summa Theologiae. 60 vols. Latin text and English translation. London, 1963–75.

Thomas, Terence (ed.). *The British: Their Religious Beliefs and Practices 1800–1986.* London, 1988.

Thompson, J. M. *Robespierre.* Oxford, 1939.

Thorndike, Lynn. *University Records and Life in the Middle Ages.* New York, 1971.

Thottakara, Augustine. *God, Man and Nature – A Vedantic Perspective: A Study of Varadaguru's Tattvasara.* Rome, 1990.

Thrasher, Allen Wright. 'The Advaita of Mandana Misra's Brahma-Siddhi'. Diss. Harvard University, 1972.

Tibawi, A. L. 'Al-Ghazali's Tract on Dogmatic Theology', *Islamic Quarterly* 9 (1965), 65–122.

Tillich, Paul. *Hauptwerke/Main Works.* Ed. Carl Heinz Ratschow. 6 vols. Berlin and New York, 1987–99.

Systematic Theology. Three volumes bound as one. Chicago, 1967 [1951–65].

Tocqueville, Alexis de. *De la démocratie en Amérique.* 2 parts. Paris, 1835–40.

Tola, Fernando, and Carmen Dragonetti (eds.). *The Yogasutras of Patanjali.* Trans. K. D. Prithipaul. Delhi, 1987.

Torsten Much, Michael. *Dharmakirtis Vadanyayah,* vol. I: Text, Vol. II: *Übersetzung und Anmerkungen.* Österreichische Akademie der Wissenschaften, phil.-hist. Kl. Sb 581. Bd.

Tournemine, René-Joseph. *Reflexions sur l'atheisme, sur la demonstration de Monseigneur de Cambrai, et sur le sistême de Spinosa, qui ont servi de préface aux éditions précedentes de la Demonstration. Augmentées de nouveau.* 1721.

Tournéy, Honoré. *De Deo et Divinis Attributis.* 2 vols. Paris, 1725.

Tucci, Guiseppe. 'Buddhist Logic before Dinnaga (Asanga, Vasubandhu, Tarka-sastras)', *Journal of the Royal Asiatic Society* 49 (1929), 451–88.

Pre-Dinnaga Buddhist Texts on Logic from Chinese Sources. Baroda, 1929 [Madras, 1981].

Tuck, Andrew P. *Comparative Philosophy and the Philosophy of Scholarship: On the Western Interpretation of Nagarjuna.* New York and Oxford, 1990.

Tully, James (ed.). *Meaning and Context: Quentin Skinner and his Critics.* Cambridge, 1988.

Türstig, Hans-Georg. *Über Entstehungsprozesse in der Philosophie des Nyaya-Vaisesika-Systems.* Wiesbaden, 1982.

Udayana. *Atmatattvaviveka*, Part I. ed. and trans. Chitrarekha V. Kher and Shiv Kumar. Delhi, 1987.

Nyayakusumanjali. Trans. E. B. Cowell. Calcutta, 1864.

The Nyayakusumanjali of Udayanacarya, vol. I: books 1–2. Trans. Ravi Tirtha. Adyar, 1946.

Upadhyaya, K. N. 'Sankara on Reason, Scriptural Authority and Self-Knowledge', *Journal of Indian Philosophy* 19 (1991), 121–31.

van der Veer, Peter. *Imperial Encounters: Religion and Modernity in India and Britain.* Princeton, 2001.

Varadacari, V. 'Nyaya-Vaisesika Tradition', in *Philosophical Essays: Professor Anantalal Thakur Felicitation Volume.* Calcutta, 1987, pp. 142–52.

Varadachari, K. C. *Sri Ramanuja's Theory of Knowledge.* Tirupati, 1980 [1943].

Varenne, Jean. *Yoga and the Hindu Tradition.* Trans. K. D. Prithipaul. Delhi, 1987.

Vasu, Chandra. *Chhandogya Upanisad with the Commentary of Sri Madhvacharya.* Allahabad, 1910 [reprint 1974].

Vasu, Chandra (trans.). *The Brihadaranyaka Upanisad with the Commentary of Sri Madhvacharya.* Allahabad, 1916 [reprint 1974].

Vattanky, John. 'Development of Nyaya Theism', in *Philosophical Essays: Professor Anantalal Thakur Felicitation Volume.* Calcutta, 1987, pp. 36–52.

Gangesa's Philosophy of God. Madras, 1984.

Vaux, Bernard Carra de. *Les grands philosophes. Gazali.* Amsterdam, 1974 [1902].

Vedantasara. Ed. V. Krishnamacharya. Trans. M. B. Narasimka Ayyangar. Adyar, 1953; ^{2}1979.

Venkataramiah, D. (trans.). *The Pancapadika of Padmapada.* Baroda, 1948.

Ventura, Moise. *La philosophie de Saadia Gaon.* Paris, 1934.

Verpoorten, Jean-Marie. *Mimamsa Literature.* Vol. VI^5 of *A History of Indian Literature.* Ed. Jan Gonda. Wiesbaden, 1987.

Vetter, Tilmann. *Erkenntnisprobleme bei Dharmakirti.* Vienna, 1964.

Studien zur Lehre und Entwicklung Sankaras. Vienna, 1979.

Vickers, Brian. *In Defence of Rhetoric.* Oxford, 1988.

Vidyabhusana, Satis Chandra. *History of Indian Logic*. Delhi, ²1971 [1920].

Vidyabhusana, Satisa Chandra (trans.). *The Nyaya Sutras of Gotama*. Revised and ed. Nandalal Sinha. Delhi, 1990 [1930].

Vidyarthi, Lalita Prasad, *et al. The Sacred Complex of Kashi: A Microcosm of Indian Civilization*. Delhi, 1979.

Vidyarthi, P. B. *Divine Personality and Human Life in Ramanuja*. New Delhi, 1978.

Knowledge, Self and God in Ramanuja. New Delhi, 1978.

Vince, Samuel. *The Credibility of Christianity Vindicated, in Answer to Mr Hume's Objections, in Two Discourses Preached before the University of Cambridge*. Cambridge, 1798.

Voltaire, François Marie Arouet de. *Dictionnaire philosophique*. Geneva, 1764.

Wade, Ira O. *The Clandestine Organization and Diffusion of Philosophic Ideas in France from 1700 to 1750*. Princeton, 1938.

The Structure and Form of the French Enlightenment. 2 vols. Princeton, 1977.

Wardy, Robert. *The Chain of Change: A Study of Aristotle's <u>Physics</u> VII*. Cambridge, 1990.

Warrier, A. G. Krishna. *God in Advaita*. Simla, 1977.

Watanabe, Morimichi. 'Nicholas of Cusa and the Idea of Toleration', in *Niccolò Cusano agli inizi del Mondo Moderno*. Florence, 1970, pp. 409–18.

Waterlow, Sarah. *Nature, Change, and Agency in Aristotle's Physics: A Philosophical Study*. Oxford, 1981.

Watson, Richard A. *The Downfall of Cartesianism, 1673–1712: A Study of Epistemological Issues in Late 17th-Century Cartesianism*. The Hague, 1966.

Watt, W. Montgomery. *Muslim Intellectual: A Study of Al-Ghazali*. Edinburgh, 1963.

Watts, Pauline Moffitt. 'Prophecy and Discovery: On the Spiritual Origins of Christopher Columbus', *The American Historical Review* 90 (1985), 73–102.

'Talking to Spiritual Others: Ramon Llull, Nicholas of Cusa, Diego Valadés', in *Nicholas of Cusa in Search of God and Wisdom*. Ed. Gerald Christianson and Thomas M. Izbicki. Leiden, 1991, pp. 203–18.

Watts, Pauline Moffitt (trans.). *Nicholas de Cusa, <u>De Ludo Globi</u>: The Game of Spheres*. New York, 1986.

Wayman, Alex. 'The Rules of Debate according to Asanga', *Journal of the American Oriental Society* 78 (1958), 28–40.

Webb, Clement C. J. *Kant's Philosophy of Religion*. Oxford, 1926.

Studies in the History of Natural Theology. Oxford, 1915.

Weisheipl, James A. 'Classification of the Sciences in Medieval Thought', *Mediaeval Studies* 27 (1965), 54–90.

'Curriculum of the Faculty of Arts at Oxford in the Early Fourteenth Century', *Mediaeval Studies* 26 (1964), 176–85.

'The Structure of the Arts Faculty in the Medieval University', *British Journal of Educational Studies* 19 (1971), 163–71.

Wezler, Albrecht. 'Der Gott des Samkhya: zu *Nyayakusumañjali* 1.3', *Indo-Iranian Journal* 12 (1969–70), 255–62.

'Zur Proklamation religiös-weltanschaulicher Toleranz bei dem indischen Philosophen Jayantabhatta', *Saeculum* 27 (1976), 329–47.

Whewell, William. *Astronomy and General Physics Considered with Reference to Natural Theology.* London, 1833.

Indications of the Creator: Extracts, Bearing upon Theology, from the History and Philosophy of the Inductive Sciences. London, 1845.

Sermon, Sept. 1841, Whewell Papers, Trinity College Library, Cambridge University, R6 17⁴⁹.

Sermons Preached in the Chapel of Trinity College, Cambridge. London, 1847.

Whitehead, Alfred North. *Religion in the Making.* New York, 1926.

Wilson, Bryan R. (ed.). *Rationality.* Oxford, 1970.

Wilson, Douglas L. (ed.). *Jefferson's Literary Commonplace Book.* Princeton, 1989.

Winstanley, D. A. *Early Victorian Cambridge.* Cambridge, 1940.

Winternitz, M. *Geschichte der indischen Litteratur.* Vol. III. Leipzig, 1922.

Wisdom, John. *Philosophy and Psycho-Analysis.* Oxford, 1953.

Wissink, J. B. (ed.). *The Eternity of the World in the Thought of Thomas Aquinas and his Receptors.* Leiden, 1990.

Wittgenstein, Ludwig. *Culture and Value / Vermischte Bemerkungen.* Ed. G. H. von Wright. Trans. Peter Winch. Oxford, 1980.

Philosophical Investigations / Philosophische Untersuchungen. Oxford, 1967.

Witzel, Michael. 'The Case of the Shattered Head', *Studien zur Indologie und Iranistik* 13 (1987), 363–415.

Wolff, Christian. *Discursus Praeliminaris de Philosophia in Genere.* Frankfurt and Leipzig, 1728.

Gesammelte Schriften. Hildesheim, 1965ff.

Theologia Naturalis. 2 vols. Frankfurt, 1736–7.

Wolfson, Harry Austryn. *Philo: Foundations of Religious Philosophy in Judaism, Christianity, and Islam.* 2 vols. Cambridge, MA, 1968.

The Philosophy of the Church Fathers, I: *Faith, Trinity, Incarnation.* Cambridge, MA, ³1970.

The Philosophy of the Kalam. Cambridge, MA, 1976.

'The Plurality of Immovable Movers in Aristotle and Averroes', *Harvard Studies in Classical Philology* 63 (1958), 233–53.

Repercussions of the Kalam in Jewish Philosophy. Cambridge, MA, 1979.

Studies in the History of Philosophy and Religion. Vol. I. Cambridge, MA, 1973.

Wollaston, William. *The Religion of Nature Delineated.* London, 1722, ²1738.

Wood, Allen W. *Kant's Rational Theology.* Ithaca, 1979.

Yandell, Keith. *Hume's 'Inexplicable Mystery'.* Philadelphia, 1990.

Philosophy of Religion: A Contemporary Introduction. London, 1999.

Yesudhas, D. 'Indigenization or Adaptation? A Brief Study of Roberto de Nobili's Attitude to Hinduism', *Bangalore Theological Forum* 1 (1967), 39–52.

Young, M. J. L., *et al.* (eds.). *Religion, Learning and Science in the 'Abbasid Period. The Cambridge History of Arabic Literature.* Cambridge, 1990.

Young, Robert M. *Darwin's Metaphor: Nature's Place in Victorian Culture.* Cambridge, 1985.

Xenophon. *Memorabilia.* Trans. and annotated by Amy L. Bonnette with an introduction by Christopher Bruell. Ithaca, NY, 1994.

Memorabilia and Oeconomicus, trans. and ed. E. C. Marchant; *Symposium and Apology,* trans. and ed. O. J. Todd. London and Cambridge, MA, 1979 [1923].

Zaehner, R. C. (ed.). *Hindu Scriptures.* London, ²1966.

Zimmermann, Albert (ed.). *Albert der Grosse: Seine Zeit, sein Werk, seine Wirkung.* Berlin and New York, 1981.

Die Auseinandersetzungen an der Pariser Universität im XIII. Jahrhundert. Berlin and New York, 1976.

Index